INVESTMENT
SOURCEBOOK

THE COMPLETE GUIDE TO FINDING
AND
UNDERSTANDING INVESTMENT INFORMATION

Michael Constas
Jae K. Shim

Glenlake Publishing Company, Ltd.
Chicago • London• New Delhi

AMACOM
New York • Atlanta • Boston • Kansas City • San Francisco • Washington, D.C.
Brussels • Mexico City • Tokyo • Toronto

This publication is designed to provide accurate and authoritative information in regard to the subject matter covered. It is sold with the understanding that the publisher is not engaged in rendering legal, accounting, or other professional service. If legal advice or other expert assistance is required, the services of a competent professional person should be sought.

© 2001 The Glenlake Publishing Company, Ltd.
All rights reserved.
Printed in the United States of America.

ISBN: 0-8144-0515-0

AMACOM
American Management Association
1601 Broadway
New York, NY 10019

Printing number

10   9   8   7   6   5   4   3   2   1

DEDICATION

To

Bill F. Roberts and C. B. McGuire
Mentors at the University of California at Berkeley

and

Bruce Miller
Mentor at the University of California at Los Angeles

ACKNOWLEDGMENTS

We are indebted to many for ideas and assistance. Our primary obligation is to C. B. McGuire and. B. F. Roberts at the University of California at Berkeley, and B. Miller at the University of California at Los Angeles to whom this book is dedicated. For those who know them, no words are necessary; for those who do not know them, no words will suffice.

It's with gratitude that we acknowledge the many sources from which the data in this book have been compiled.

ABOUT THE AUTHORS

Michael Constas, Ph.D., J.D., M.B.A., is a professor of business at California State University, Long Beach. Before teaching, he was a partner of a major California law firm. Dr. Constas earned all degrees at U.C.L.A. He has published numerous articles on investments in academic and professional journals and is an author of *Private Real Estate Syndications.*

Jae K. Shim, Ph.D., M.B.A., is a professor of business at California State University, Long Beach and president of National Business Review Foundation, an investment consulting and training firm. He is also the chief investment officer (CIO) for a Los Angeles county agency. Dr. Shim received his M.B.A. and Ph.D. degrees from the University of California at Berkeley. He has published numerous articles in academic and professional journals. He also has over fifty books to his credit, including *Personal Finance, The Personal Financial Planning and Investment Guide, Investments: A Self-Teaching Guide, Encyclopedic Dictionary of Accounting and Finance, Financial Management, Managerial Finance* and the best-selling *Vest-Pocket MBA.* Dr. Shim received the Credit Research Foundation Award in 1982 for one of his articles on investment management.

PREFACE

Knowledge is of two kinds.
We know a subject ourselves,
or we know where we can find
information upon it.
    —Samuel Johnson (1709-1784)

Labor generates income;
Investment creates wealth.
    —Anonymous

As its title indicates, this book is an investment information source book—a reference that investors must have handy in order to make informed investment decisions. At a time when investment vehicles are expanding constantly in number and variety, having the right information when you need is a must for the successful investor.

Lack of information increases the chance of bad decisions and therefore costs money not only in terms of potential income but also in terms of the invested money itself.

The book is a working guide to sources of investment information. It's designed for students of finance and investment as well as practical investors. It shows you where to find information and advice on different investment instruments, how to find it, and how to read and interpret it. Each chapter covers the background, how to choose the right kind of security in each investment category, and how to read information for each source.

The book discusses:

- how key information elements (for example, risk-adjusted yield, discount yield, dividend yield, current yield, beta, P/E ratio, and 7-day compound yield) are calculated,

- what they mean, and

• how they can be used for investment decision making.

We envision this book as not only a complete guide to sources of investment information, but also a reference on how to use the information for investment decision making. The main chapters are classified by type of investment. Within each chapter the topic is reviewed in an easily understood format. Sources of information for that investment instrument follow.

The quality of future revisions of the guide will depend largely on constructive suggestions we receive from readers. With this in mind, we ask that you submit comments directly to the publisher. Any errors or omissions are the responsibility of the authors.

We wish to express our deep gratitude to Barbara Evans, editorial director of The Glenlake Publishing Company for her outstanding editorial assistance during the project. Her input and efforts are greatly appreciated. Special thanks to Allison Shim for library research and word processing.

Michael Constas and Jae K. Shim

NOTE: *After this book was written, the Securities and Exchange Commission ordered U.S. exchanges to quote stock prices in decimals. Decimal equivalents can be found in Chapter 7, page 231.*

TABLE OF CONTENTS

Chapter 1
INVESTMENT
INFORMATION

Almost all investments have some risk, but you can control the amount by choosing your funds and investments with care. Information and advice are crucial. The financial press and investment professionals and services have filled this role. (The first issue of the *Wall Street Journal* was published on July 8, 1889.)

The traditional information environment has changed dramatically in recent years with the increased popularity of the Internet. Consider the *Encyclopedia Britannica.* It began the 1990's as the premier paper reference resource in America; its cost was considerable. It finished the decade as a free Internet service, making its revenues from advertising.

Add to this, the change in the public's interest in the stock market. More and more members of the public now invest in the stock market either directly or through pension plans. Moreover, the dramatic increase in the stock prices in recent years has made the stock market the investment of choice. New sources of financial information have developed recently in order to meet the increasing demand for financial information. Many of these sources are now free and on the Internet.

SOURCES OF INFORMATION

Throughout this book you will find examples of information. There is usually more than one source for the same information. This book consciously tries to use examples from non-traditional sources to demonstrate the wealth of financial resources. You can learn about investment opportunities from any of the following sources:

Newspapers, Magazines, Books, CDs, and Tapes

National and regional newspapers provide a wealth of information and are often written with a beginning investor in mind. Major newspapers quote prices for stocks, bonds, mutual funds, and commodities; they are easily available in public and college libraries. Besides general information newspapers, the *Wall Street Journal* and *Investor's Business Daily* specialize in providing extensive financial information to investors.

A number of magazines specialize in business and investing *(e.g., Forbes, Business Week, Fortune,* and *Money). Business Week* and *Forbes* publish weekly changes in stock indexes and provide other weekly economic and financial information. Many magazines publish lists in which they recommend, rank, or rate investments. Dow Jones & Co., the publisher of the *Wall Street Journal*, also publishes *Barron's*, which presents more comprehensive weekly financial information than the *Wall Street Journal*, along with financial news and articles. A number of books, CD-ROMs, and tapes discuss investments in detail.

TV and Radio Programs

We live in a world of mass communication and high-tech media. They provide up-to-date consumer, business, and financial news and interviews with investment experts who provide advice on local and national newscasts. The programming of a number of cable and satellite dish networks *(e.g.,* Bloomberg Television, CNBC, and CNN/fn) is solely concerned with investments and business.

The Internet

According to the U.S. Census Bureau, in 1997, approximately 32% of the adult U.S. population had access to the Internet at home or at work, and approximately 23% had used the Internet in the last 30 days. Because information can attract users to an Internet site, more and more web sites provide financial information that used to be available only through the financial media. References to Internet sites appear throughout this book, and chapter 16 shows you how to research a corporation using free information on the Internet.

Courses on Investments and Personal Finance

Courses are available in adult education and college classes. Courses are also conducted on television .

Prospectuses

A corporation or a mutual fund selling its shares must furnish potential investors with prospectuses and similar offering documents. Prospectuses can usually be obtained from stockbrokers as well as directly from the issuing entities. They describe the investments being offered, and provide useful information about the activities of the issuing entity. The initial offering of securities is generally announced in financial newspapers *(e.g.,* the *Wall Street Journal).*

Annual Reports

Annual reports are audited annual financial statements with other information regarding the operations of a company that the SEC requires corporations to send to shareholders. Quarterly reports (containing unaudited financial statements) are also required. The SEC also requires that the corporation file other information with the SEC. This information is available free to the public through the Internet (see chapter 16).

Brokers, Financial Planners, Insurance Agents, Lawyers, and Accountants

A number of professionals offer financial and investment information and advice, generally for a fee. Make sure the advisor you select specializes in the investment area of your interest. Brokers generally base their advice on their own research data. Financial planners, especially with the CFA or CLU/ChFC designations, review your assets and financial goals, provide written investment plans, and help you implement them.

Investment Clubs and Associations

These are comprised of people who meet regularly to pick investments and pool resources. Clubs can help you learn more about the capital market, especially if they include experienced investors or brokers who can give market guidance. Associations like the **American Association of Individual Investors** (AAII) offer seminars and training materials (books and tapes). AAII is located at 625 N. Michigan Avenue, Suite 1900, Chicago, IL 60611.

Investment Advisory Services and Newsletters

Investment advisory services and newsletters track investment performance and market trends. You may subscribe for a fee, which varies widely. However, most of these services will send you a free sample issue or two.

WHAT MOVES THE MARKET?

What information do you need before making an investment? It depends on what really moves the market for a particular investment vehicle. For example, as far as the stock market is concerned, the following are considered to be major movers:

Earnings

The very, very bottom line is that if a company is doing well *(i.e.,* earnings are growing), so will the stock price. Some things do not change.

Rumors

A whole industry of people make a living out of guessing where stock prices will go. Many make their trades based on rumors gleaned from other traders, corporate sources, bankers, lawyers, or whomever. In particular, takeover gossip can send a stock flying and rumors of a bankruptcy filing can make a stock nosedive. Internet Message Boards are one of the newer, non-traditional sources of financial information. Hosted by a number of different financial Internet sites *(e.g.,* Yahoo *[finance.yahoo.com]* and Motley Fool *[www.motleyfool.com]),* they consist of messages that different investors post to each other.

An example of how rapidly a rumor can move through the stock market and affect the price of a company's stock is presented in Figure 1-1. Within three hours after news of lower sales figures were leaked, the stock price of Abercrombie & Fitch had dropped approximately 20%. This was approximately 61% of the total market adjustment that occurred once the information was publicly acknowledged.

FIGURE 1-1: MARKET RESPONSE TO UNFAVORABLE NEWS

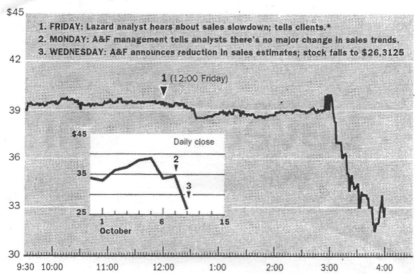

Bad News at Abercrombie & Fitch

Class A shares, at one-minute intervals Friday (main chart) and daily in October (inset chart)

1. FRIDAY: Lazard analyst hears about sales slowdown; tells clients.*
2. MONDAY: A&F management tells analysts there's no major change in sales trends.
3. WEDNESDAY: A&F announces reduction in sales estimates; stock falls to $26.3125

Source: NYSE, Tradeline, 10/14/99

Caution: *No matter how woeful or wonderful the rumors, never buy or sell solely on the basis of a story. More important, by the time you read about or hear about a company, many professional investors have already acted on the information and bought or sold the stock. As a result, the news is already discounted in the price.*

Announcements

Because traders usually know what is going on with a company, announcements of contracts, new products, or promotions don't always affect stock prices. But when an important announcement is a surprise, watch out. This is especially true when corporate earnings announcements differ from what the public expects of earnings.

Other Stocks

The prices of the stock companies in the same industry or sector often move together. Financial markets often consider the change in the economic performance of one company within an industry to indicate industry-wide-wide change. As a result, the market often assumes that other companies in the same industry or sector will experience a similar change. For example, when one computer manufacturer announces unexpected sales results, the price of the shares in other computer manufacturers often moves in the same direction because the announcement is deemed to indicate how the market for computers is changing.

Interest Rates

Stocks and interest-bearing instruments often compete for investment dollars. When interest rates change, the relative attractiveness of interest-bearing instruments changes. For example, if interest rates are falling, investors are likely to do better by shifting from bonds into stocks. As the economy ebbs and flows each day, so does cash ebb into and out of the stock market. In this way, stock prices can jump even if there is nothing unusual going on at a company.

Cycles

Many traders buy stock not because of the strength of the underlying company but on the basis of market cycles. This art is called technical analysis. There are a host of theories on how the patterns of stock trading work.

Earnings Forecasts and Broker Recommendations

Earnings forecasts made by analysts or brokerage houses often shake up traders. For example, a lower earnings estimate or expectation of a loss may knock a stock down. Buy or sell recommendations made by investment newsletters sometime make a difference.

Who Knows?

The market can take on a life of its own. A trader may sell merely because the trader next to him is selling, and the first trader believes the second has inside information. Analysts may read profound meanings into minor announcements. An opinion of a respected securities columnist or commentator on a particular stock can affect the price of that stock. In all of these examples, there is no new underlying information about a company.

Club Member

If your stock is part of a stock index, like one of the Dow Jones averages or the Standard and Poor's 500, professional traders will buy or sell the stock based on complicated formulas that also involve futures and options. Program trading, which allows the rapid buying and selling of baskets of stocks and futures, is often blamed for sharp price movements. Such trading is independent of the fundamental strengths or weaknesses of the underlying stocks.

Unexpected World Events

Sudden news of unrest anywhere in the world *(e.g.,* the Middle East, the Persian Gulf, Somalia, Chechnya, or Kosovo) can affect the market. The stock market reflects consumer psychology. Also, we now live in a integrated world economy, and unrest can disrupt it.. Financial markets are all linked. A disruption in one market can affect all financial markets.

Precious metals are investments that compete with the stock market. In times of international unrest, the legal rights of foreign investors in metals can change *(e.g.,* assets can be frozen or expropriated by governments). Many investors (especially foreign investors) view precious metals as the safest investment; in times of unrest, they move out of the stock market into precious metals. The stock market knows this and tends to anticipate it by moving stock prices lower on any news of international unrest.

NOTE: Gold (as well as other precious metals) is both liquid and mobile, and its value is intrinsic. You would have measurable wealth if you had an ounce of gold in ancient Greece. On the other hand, a thousand dollar bill probably would not get you a cup of coffee in ancient Greece.

BASIC ANALYSIS FOR INVESTMENT DECISIONS

Depending on the investment, you should be aware of economic conditions, political environment, market status, industry surroundings, and company performance. Ideally the intelligent investor should get answers to at least four basic questions:

1. **What Is the State of the Economy?** Is it a good time to invest? Where are we in the business cycle? Is the boom likely to top out shortly? Is a recession near at hand? Questions in this area will vary with the stage of the business cycle. How will likely future economic conditions affect the performance of an investment?

2. **What Is the State of the Market?** Are we in the early stages of a bull market? Has the low point of a bear market been reached? Is the bull market about to top out? The questions will vary with the state of the market. Often, financial commentators will compare the current price/earnings ratios (P/E ratios) to historical P/E ratio levels in describing whether the stock market should continue to grow or may face a price correction.

3. **What Is the State of the Industry?** If answers to the preceding two questions seem favorable, what industries are likely to grow most rapidly? Are any special factors favoring a particular industry in the current economic environment?

4. **What Company Is Desirable?** Once you have selected an industry, which company or companies within it are likely to be best? Which companies are to be avoided because of poor prospects? Often, this analysis takes the form of a comparison of: products or services, investments in research or other assets, control of expenses, and strategic planning.

Figure 1-2 summarizes factors that will go into your investment decision making, ranging from economics and the external environment surrounding the investment vehicle to the company's own performance measures.

BENEFITS AND COSTS OF INVESTMENT INFORMATION

Investment information:

- Allows you to develop expectations of the risk-return behavior of potential investments. With better estimates of risk and return, you should be able to select instruments consistent with your invest-

FIGURE 1-2: OVERVIEW OF THE INVESTMENT DECISION-MAKING PROCESS

ECONOMIC ANALYSIS

Factors considered: business cycles, monetary fiscal policy, economic indicators, government policy, world events and foreign trade, public attitudes of optimism or pessimism, domestic legislation, inflation, GNP growth, unemployment, productivity, capacity utilization, interest rates, and more.

INDUSTRY ANALYSIS

Factors considered: industry structure, growth of the industry, competition, product quality, cost elements, government regulations, labor position, business cycle exposure, financial norms and standards.

COMPANY ANALYSIS

Factors considered: growth of sales, earnings, dividends, quality of earnings, position in the industry, discount rates, fundamental analysis (balance sheet analysis, income statement analysis, cash flow analysis), analysis of accounting policy and footnotes, management, research and development, return and risk, brands, patents, goodwill, and diversification.

ment goals. It should help you make more informed and intelligent judgments.

- Helps you to avoid the undesirable consequences of a misrepresentation of facts by the issuer and/or underwriter of an investment. It is often beneficial to evaluate information from by an independent source before making a decision.

The problem with investment information is that it can cost money. Yes, there is an ever increasing amount of quality investment information from almost free sources (newspapers, magazines, and the Internet), but you still have to pay for information from a financial advisory service publication such as Value Line, Moody's, and Standard & Poor's. Luckily, public and college libraries often have these publications. Before investing in a premium financial service, make sure the information is not available for free somewhere. Market data and indexes, economic and current events, and industry and company data often can be obtained from local newspapers and magazines as well as the Internet.

TYPES OF INFORMATION

Investment information is either *descriptive* or analytical. Descriptive information tells you about the prior behavior of the economy, politics, the market, and the particular investment. *Analytical* information is based on current data and includes forecasts and recommendations as to specific securities. Both kinds of information help you assess the risk and return of a particular choice and enable you to see whether the investment conforms to your objectives.

Investment information can be broadly assigned to size categories:

Economic and Current Event Information

Provides background and forecasts on economic, political, and social trends, both on a domestic and international. Such information is useful to all investors, since it provides a basis for assessing the environment in which decisions are made.

Industry and Company Information

Provides background as well as forecast data on specific industries and companies. Investors use this type of information to assess the outlook for a given industry or company. Because of its company orientation, it is most relevant to stock, bond, or option investments.

Information on Other Investment Alternatives

Provides background and predictive data for securities other than stocks, bonds, and options, as well as for various forms of tangible investment such as real estate.

Price Quotations

On certain investment vehicles, such as stocks, bonds, and tangible investments, are commonly accompanied by statistics on the recent price behavior of the vehicle.

Investment Strategies

Provides recommendations on investment strategies and/or specific purchase or sale actions. This information tends to be advisory.

Economic and Current Events

By studying and analyzing current economic events, you can learn to predict national and international economic trends. Make a habit of reading publications like *USA Today, Wall Street Journal, Investor's Business Daily, Barron's National Business,* and *Financial Weekly,* or the business section of your local newspaper, and business magazines like *Money, Forbes, Fortune, Smart Money, Worth, Business Week, Individual Investor, U.S. News* and *World Report, Dun's Review,* and *Financial World.* A number of Internet sites contain financial news.

To learn how the national economy is doing, you might also read the *Federal Reserve Bulletin.* It contains a summary of business conditions; statistics on employment, retail prices, and other relevant trends; and the Federal Reserve Board Index of industrial production. It also gives information about gross national product and national income as well as interest rates and yields. The *Federal Reserve Bulletin* is available free on the Internet *(www.bog.frb.fed.us).*

Every month the U.S. Department of Commerce issues the *Survey of Current Business* and Business Conditions Digest. The *Survey* includes a monthly update by industry of business information about exports, inventories, personal consumption, and labor market statistics. *Business Conditions Digest* publishes cyclical indicators of economic activity including leading indicators. These publications are also available free on the Internet *(www.bea.doc.gov).* Every month the Conference Board issues economic information regarding inflation rates. These are also available on the Internet *(www.conference-board.org).*

Subscription services provide data on economic and corporate developments. They also publish forecasts of business trends and detailed economic data and analysis. Examples of such service are the *Blue Chip Consensus,* and the *Kiplinger Washington Letter.*

Market Information and Indexes

You can get quotations directly from your broker or from a ticker—an automated quotation device with a screen on which stock transactions on the exchange floor are immediately reported. Moreover, a number of web sites provide free current stock price quotations (either immediate or with a 15- or 20-minute delay). Most of these sites will allow you to construct your own portfolio and provide you with your portfolio's performance at any given time. Price quotations also appear in newspapers, electronic databases, and TV and radio networks.

Stock market indexes that show how the market is doing help you in pick the right stocks at the proper time. The behavior of the market is important: if the market is down, a particular company—even though it is financially sound—may not do well.

Stock market averages are the average prices of a group of stocks for a specified time period. These indexes measure the present price behavior of a group of stocks relative to a base value established earlier. To evaluate the strength of the market you must compare the averages and indexes at various times. A bull market exists when prices are rising. A bear market exists when prices are falling. Stock market indexes are discussed in chapter 2.

Indicators of bond performance also exist. Bond prices are stated as a percent of par. Bond yields show the return to the bondholder who holds the bond to maturity. Bond yields are generally quoted for a group of bonds of similar type and quality. You'll find yield information in various sources including the Federal Reserve, the *Wall Street Journal,* and *Barron's.* They are also available free on the Internet *(www.bondsonline.com).*

INDUSTRY AND COMPANY INFORMATION

Investment or security advisers furnish recommendations to clients for a fee. Some also manage their clients' investment portfolios and give tax advice. Investment advisers include stockbrokers, trust department bank officers (who invest funds held in trust for clients), employees of subscription services, and investment advisory firms. Most advisory firms employ specialists in certain industries or types of portfolios. Investment analysts usually select an industry that looks good before they pick a particular company. You can get industry data yourself from trade publications on a particular industry such as *Public Utilities Fortnightly.*

Financial services provide information and analysis, but most do not make recommendations. Financial advisory reports usually present one company's financial history, current financial position, and future expectations. Up-to-date supplements are issued. These services will be fully discussed later.

- Standard and Poor's publishes *Corporate Records, Stock Reports, Stock Guide, Bond Guide, Analysts Handbook, Industry Survey, The Outlook,* and *Opportunities in Convertible Bonds.*

- Mergent publishes *Moody's Manuals, Handbook of Common Stocks, Dividend Record, Stock Survey, Bond Record,* and *Bond Survey.*

- Arnold Bernhard & Co., Inc. publishes the *Value Line Investment Survey.*

- Dun and Bradstreet issues *Key Business Ratios, Million Dollar Directory, Billion Dollar Directory.* and *Business Starts.*

- Dow Jones-Irwin publishes the *Business Almanac.*

- A number of subscription services cover mutual funds. Standard and Poor's Corporation, Lipper, Inc., Morningstar, Inc., Value Line, and Wiesenberger Investment Companies are widely used. In addition, mutual fund newsletters provide financial information to subscribers, for a substantial fee.

- *Hulbert's Digest* tracks the performance of many investment newsletters.

Brokerage reports analyze companies and make recommendations to buy, hold, or sell their stocks. They also offer investment strategies and analyze specific industries and companies.

PC AND ELECTRONIC DATABASES

A personal computer can give you immediate access to business data. It will also enable you to analyze that data quickly and to compute a rating for all of your funds or stocks. Programs are available for record keeping, plotting prices, portfolio management, identifying securities meeting criteria standards, and improving the timing of buys and sells.

- Some programs allow you to perform sophisticated fundamental and technical analyses.

- Investment maintenance software lets you keep track of your investments in terms of shares, cost, and revenue.

- Some programs are equipped with the price and dividend history of certain securities; they can handle stock splits, dividends, distributions, and fractional shares.

- Investment monitoring software helps you decide whether to buy or sell a stock. It lets you keep track of your portfolio by using investment information in databases. You can add new prices to the files, modify old ones, and add in dividend information.

- Some brokers like Max Ule are on-line so that you can buy and sell securities through telecommunication from the comfort of your home.

- Tax investment software can record transactions and assist in matching sell transactions with existing positions to minimize any tax liability from to capital gains and losses. The software also helps you prepare tax schedules and reports such as Schedule D of IRS Form 1040.

Dow Jones News/Retrieval contains many databases including current and historical Dow Jones Quotes, Corporate Earnings Estimator (earnings per share estimates), Disclosure (corporate financial statements and footnote data), Media General Financial Services (stock-performance-related ratios; comparisons-to-market indicators; bond, mutual fund, and money market information), Merrill Lynch Research Service, Weekly Economic Survey and Update (economic data, trends, and analysis), and Wall Street Highlights.

CompuServe's Executive Information Service, published by Investors Management Science Company, a subsidiary of Standard & Poor's, provides financial data on companies, economic information and projections, money market trends, and price, dividend and earnings results and forecasts based on Value Line and Standard and Poor's information. CompuServe's MicroQuote provides a record of market prices, dividends, and interest paid on securities. CompuServe's mainframe will figure the worth of a portfolio for transfer to your terminal. To take advantage of these sources you will need a modem—a device that lets you communicate with other computers.

Some programs analyze and create charts of the technical behavior of price movements as well as support and resistance lines, and others evaluate the financial statements. These computerized investment programs can accommodate and track stocks, bonds, treasury securities, options, warrants, mutual funds, commodities. Some of the popular programs include the Dow-Jones Market Analyzer, the Dow-Jones Microscope, the Dow-Jones Investment Evaluator, S&P's Stockpak II, and Value Line's Value/Screen and ValuePak.

CompuStat provides 20 years of annual financial data for over 3,000 companies. Most balance sheet and income statement items are available. CompuStat tapes are compiled by Standard and Poor's. Interactive Data Corporation provides the same information. Tapes maintained by the University of Chicago in the Center for Research in Security Prices (CRSP) provide information on earnings, dividends, stock prices, dates of mergers, stock splits, stock dividends and the like. Value Line also has made available computer tapes of its 1,700 company reports.

Datext, Inc. offers corporate financial information on compact disks including financial statements, SEC documents, and investment analysts' reports.

Howard Soft's Real Estate Analyzer can make property projections considering changes in interest rates, inflation, and rental payments. There is an after-tax analysis of cash flow and profitability.

The Federal Trade Commission (FTC) has aggregate industry data, and the Federal Reserve Bank of St. Louis has made tapes of monetary data available for analysts and investors.

A detailed listing of investment software can be found in chapter 14 of this book and appear in the *Individual Investor's Guide to Computerized Investing,* published by the American Association of Individual Investors.

Nearly all on-line home services provide stock quotes, investor bulletin boards where members can exchange information, and general market updates such as the DJIA. These include America Online, CompuServe, MSN, and Prodigy.

In addition to contacting brokerages firms the traditional way, by phone, many investors now trade with dedicated software using their personal computer. For example, Fidelity Investments offers FOX for its customers to obtain quotes, place orders, and update their accounts as often as they choose. Charles Schwab offers E-Schwab, which does essentially the same thing.

In 1992, E*Trade became the first brokerage service to offer on-line trading, and by 1996 this company's rates were as low as $14.95. Discount brokerages, deep-discount brokerages, and even full-service brokerages are now offering their services on the Internet. They all provide market updates, and company financial data, and link on-line traders to other valuable investment Web sites.

NONTRADITIONAL MARKETS

We define nontraditional here as being markets other than of stocks, bonds, and government securities. A major area that has received increased attention during the last decade has been commodities and financial futures. The following is a list of typical information sources on nontraditional investments.

Commodity Yearbook

This yearly publication is a key source of information on commodity futures. The *Commodity Yearbook* runs feature articles covering commodities or situations currently in the forefront of commodity trading. It also covers each traded commodity from alcohol to zinc. For example, corn is covered in six pages. The first page describes the corn crop and occurrences for the current year. The next five pages offer tables covering the last 13 years. The tables show world production of corn, acreage, and supply of corn in the United States, and of course, the weekly high-low-close of the nearest month's futures price. The yearbook is supplemented three times a year by the *Commodity Yearbook Statistical Abstract.*

Other Publications about Futures

Main-line brokerage houses and specialty commodity brokers, and the commodities exchanges publish informative booklets and newsletters. The International Monetary Market publishes the *I.M.M. Weekly Report,* which discusses the interest rate markets, the foreign exchange markets, and gold. It also presents weekly prices for all interest rate futures, foreign exchange markets, and gold, and selected cash market information, such as the federal funds rate and the prime rate. The Chicago Board of Trade publishes the *Interest Rate Futures Newsletter.*

Stamp Market Catalog

The Scott Publishing Company has long been involved in the philatelic (stamp) market. They publish an annual catalogs with price data and pictures with descriptions. It also publishes *Stamp Market Update,* a quarterly report on current trends and prices featuring prices of major U.S. stamps and popular foreign stamps, information for specialized collectors, investment opportunities and strategies as stated by recognized experts, and special articles, statistical tables, and graphs.

APPENDIX I-A: REPRESENTATIVE INVESTMENT INFORMATION SOURCES

The *Wall Street Journal* **(200 Burnett Road, Chicopee, MA 01020)**
Published by Dow Jones, it is read by millions of investors. Virtually all "market movers," discussed earlier, are covered in the *Journal,* which regularly publishes

- Feature articles on labor, business, economics, personal investing, technology, world events, and taxes

- Corporate announcements of all kinds

- Advertisements for new offerings of stock and bonds

- Prices of actively traded securities

- Common and preferred stock prices, organized by exchange and over-the-counter markets

- Many other prices such as prices of government Treasury bills, notes, and bonds, mutual funds, put and call prices from the option exchanges, government agency securities, foreign exchange prices, and commodities future prices. The prices are listed by category and exchange

- The *Journal* publishes an educational edition that explains how to read the *Wall Street Journal* and interprets some of the data presented

Investor's Business Daily **(P.O. Box 25970, Los Angeles, CA 90025)**
Published by William O'Neil & Co., Inc., *Investor's Business Daily* reports

- **The Top Story**—The most important news event of the day

- **The Economy**—Sophisticated analysis of current economic topics and government economic reports

- **National Issue/Business**—A major national and business issue of our time

- **Leaders & Success**—Profiles of successful people and companies

- **Investor's Corner**—Coverage of a wide variety of personal finance topics

- **Today's News Digest**—35 to 40 brief but important news items

Among other things, *Investor's Business Daily* provide what it calls Smarter Stock Tables, which feature three key rankings on all 6,000 publicly traded issues. They are:

- **Earnings per Share Rank** compares a company's 5-year earnings growth record to all other publicly-traded corporations.

- **Relative Strength Rank** measures a stock's price performance over the past year compared to all other stocks.

- **Volume % Change** measures a stock's trading volume yesterday against that stock's normal trading volume over the last 50 days to alert an investor to any unusual trading activity.

Barron's

Published by Dow Jones every Monday, it contains regular features on dividends, put and call options, international stock markets, commodities, a review of the stock market, and many pages of prices and financial statistics. *Barron's* summarizes the previous week's market behavior. It also has analyses of several companies in its Investment News and Views section. The common stock section of *Barron's* not only provides weekly high-low-close prices and volume, but also gives the latest earnings per share, dividends declared, dividend record, and payable dates. The Market Laboratory section, the last pages of each issue, presents data on major stock and bond markets with the week's market statistics.

Forbes **(Subscriber Service, 60 Fifth Avenue, New York, NY 10011)**

A biweekly magazine featuring several company-management interviews. The *Forbes* management-oriented approach points up management styles and provides a look into the qualitative factors of security analysis. Several regular columnists discuss investment topics from a variety of perspectives.

Business Week (1221 Avenue of the Americas, New York, NY 10020)

This popular weekly magazine is more general than *Forbes. Business Week,* published by McGraw-Hill, Inc., includes a weekly economic update on such variables as interest rates, electricity consumption, and market prices while also featuring articles on industries and companies. The Corporate Strategy section that projects a company's future direction is first-rate.

Fortune (Time & Life Building, Rockefeller Center, New York, NY 10020-1393)

This biweekly is known for its coverage of industry problems and for specific company analyses. The Business Roundup section usually deals with a major business concern such as the federal budget, inflation, or productivity. Personal Investing is always thought-provoking, presenting ideas and analysis for the average investor.

Money (Time & Life Building, Rockefeller Center, New York, NY 10020-1393)

This is a weekly magazine about the broad areas of personal finance, covering investments, credit management, money management, insurance, taxes, college education, and retirement planning.

Other prominent periodicals are:

Bottom Line/Personal
Box 1027
Millburn, NJ 07041

Consumer Digest
5705 North Lincoln Avenue
Chicago, IL 60659

Consumer Reports
Consumers Union
101 Truman Avenue
Yonkers, NY 10703-1057

Kiplinger's Personal Finance Magazine
1729 H Street NW
Washington, DC 20006

Smart Money
224 West 57th Street
New York, NY 10019

U.S. News & World Report
Subscription Department 2400 N Street, NW
Washington, DC 20037-1196

Worth
575 Lexington Avenue
New York, NY 10022

APPENDIX I-B:
SOME USEFUL WEB SITES

The following Internet sites are a few general information sources that can be used to learn the basics of investing:

Web site Address	Primary Focus
moneycentral.msn.com	Price, Volume, and other financial information on companies
finance.yahoo.com	Price, volume, and other financial information on companies
www.aaii.com	Educational material on stocks, bonds, mutual funds, and portfolios
www.betterinvesting.org	General information about investing and its benefits
www.bog.frb.fed.us	Macroeconomic information from the Federal Reserve
www.bondsonline.com	Information on the bond market
www.conference-board.org	Offers macroeconomic information
www.investors-club.com	General information about investment clubs
www.kiplinger.com	Articles about investing and investments
www.motleyfool.com	The Motley Fool about investing
www.personalwealth.com	General information about investing and its benefits
www.quicken.com	General information about investing and its benefits
www.roadtosuccess.com	Money radio regarding investment basics

Chapter 2
GENERAL MARKET INFORMATION/ BENCHMARKS

Market price information on different investments is available from a number of sources. This chapter will emphasize stock price information, but will also include information on other investments. Data on current and recent price behavior of stocks available from the following sources:

The Internet. The Internet offers a number of advantages as a source of stock price quotations:

- It's free. Although there are premium or pay sites that offer quotation services, a number offer free stock price quotations.

- It's current. While some free quotation services are delayed 15 to 20 minutes, other sites offer real time price quotations.

- It's interactive. You select the information to be viewed. For example, you can enter the company name or the ticker symbol for which you desire a stock price quotation.

See chapter 16 for more information about Internet sources.

- **Newspapers**. Local and regional newspapers, national newspapers *(e.g., New York Times, U.S.A. Today,* and *Washington Post)*, and financial and investment dailies *(e.g., Wall Street Journal* and *Investor's Business Daily)*.

- **Television**. Check out the Bloomberg Network, CNBC (Consumer News and Business Channel), CNN/fn, Business Channel, PBS's Nightly Business Report (NBR), and Wall Street Week.

- **Stockbrokers**. Stockbrokers offer a great deal of information to their clients, in person, over the phone, and via the Internet.

- **Tickers**. A ticker is an automated quotation device with a screen on which stock transactions on the exchange floor are immediately reported

MARKET INDEXES AND AVERAGES

General Comments

Market indexes and averages are gauges used to track the general performance of the market for stocks (Figure 2-1), mutual funds, bonds, and other investments. Many indexes and averages track the performance of groups of securities. All the national and regional stock exchanges have their own indexes; major reporting companies like Dow Jones, Standard & Poor's and Value Line have long-established indexes; and there are indexes for specific industry sectors such as utilities, health care, transportation, and financial services. Indexes and averages are also used in calculating the value of index futures and index options.

Indexes have traditionally been useful to investors for two reasons:

1. Investors watch indexes to quickly gauge how their investments are performing without checking individual investments. This use has declined in recent years. As noted in chapter 16, a number of Web sites now provide free portfolio tracking services that allow investors to immediately see how their personal investments are performing. Thus, indexes have been relegated to providing market information until investors can reach their personal computers.

2. Investors examine indexes to see how potential investments are performing. For example, if you are considering investments in Internet stock, a number of indexes report on how different companies engaged in different aspects of the Internet are performing.

There are three types of stock market indexes presently in use:

- **Equal-Weighted Price Index.** The Dow Jones Industrial Average is an example of an equal-weighted *price* index. With this type of index, each component is weighted equally, and a dollar change in the price of one stock is treated the same as a dollar change in another component. These indexes reflect raw changes in the prices of their components.

FIGURE 2-1: U.S. STOCK INDEXES

Index	High	Low	Close	Net Chg.
Dow Jones Industrials	10719.10	10634.88	10648.18	-1.58
Dow Jones Transportation	3082.13	3019.42	3026.02	-55.69
Dow Jones Utilities	299.13	195.72	295.72	-3.95
Dow Jones Composite	3111.97	3067.09	3089.07	-18.81
NYSE Composite	615.11	612.27	613.33	-.18
NYSE Industrials	776.62	772.26	774.93	+1.74
NYSE Transportation	464.28	457.94	459.27	-4.80
NYSE Utilities	490.27	488.57	489.60	+.04
NYSE Finance	500.09	495.04	495.33	-4.76
AMEX Composite	790.02	781.49	790.02	+8.53
Nasdaq 100	2585.03	2555.18	2578.88	+23.52
Nasdaq Composite	2920.73	2890.54	2915.95	+29.38
Nasdaq Industrials	1684.53	1664.89	1684.51	+22.32
Nasdaq Banks	1739.72	1732.02	1733.61	-6.36
Nasdaq Insurance	2019.30	2002.55	2007.81	-8.96
Nasdaq Financials	2902.26	2865.47	2901.99	-37.11
Nasdaq Transportation	961.29	950.15	953.87	-6.16
Nasdaq Telecom	707.12	693.70	706.91	+14.73
Nasdaq NMS Comp	1328.36	1314.50	1326.17	+13.48
Nasdaq NMS Indust	694.33	686.08	694.31	+9.38
Nasdaq Computer	1588.34	1572.01	1581.33	+12.19
Nasdaq Biotech	635.47	625.67	635.47	+6.63
S&P 100	709.94	687.58	697.76	-.69
S&P 500	1344.26	1324.40	1335.21	-.81
S&P Midcap	391.56	385.07	391.56	+6.49
S&P Industrials	1660.18	1643.80	1648.96	+3.46
S&P Transportation	622.47	610.96	612.80	-9.48
S&P Utilities	240.82	238.26	238.26	-2.56
S&P Smallcap	176.78	175.71	176.78	+1.07
S&P Financial	129.88	128.15	128.15	-1.73
Major Market Index	1120.63	1111.20	1113.53	-.73
Value Line Arith	972.02	967.95	972.01	+4.06
Russell 2000	430.19	427.71	430.19	+2.48
Wilshire Smallcap	664.55	656.03	664.55	+8.32
Value Line Geometric	420.65	420.65	420.65	+1.57
Wilshire 5000	12197.10	12197.10	12197.10	+26.70

Source: Orange County Register, Monday, Oct. 11, 1999

- **Value-Weighted Price Index.** The Standard & Poor's 500 is an example of a *value-weighted* price index. With this type of index, each component is weighted by its market value. Thus, a dollar change in the price of a higher-priced stock will affect the index more than a dollar change in the price of a lower-priced stock.

- **Equal-Weighted Return Index.** The Value Line indexes are examples of an *equal-weighted return* index. These indexes report the average return of investments made in their components, with all returns weighted equally.

Availability of Index Information

Information on changes in stock and mutual fund indexes can be obtained from the same sources as stock price quotations, though with the great proliferation in indexes, not all sources will offer information on all stock indexes. Our discussion of indexes will be accompanied by sample index listings from different sources.

The Internet offers a huge array of sources for indexes. Once you've identified a source of information on the performance of a particular index, you can bookmark it. StockMaster *(www.stockmaster.com)* has an extensive list of indexes that can be easily accessed.

CBS MarketWatch (cbs.marketwatch.com) and Yahoo!Finance *(finance.yahoo.com)* both offer stock price quotation services, which carry information on selected indexes. They both offer a ticker symbol search feature. These two services treat stock indexes just like stocks. Ticker symbols can be found on the web sites to help you find the stock or index you want.

MAJOR STOCK INDEXES

- **Dow Jones Averages**

  Dow Jones & Co., publisher of the *Wall Street Journal*, also publishes three well-know stock market indexes: the *Dow Jones Industrial Average* (30 corporations), the *Dow Jones Transportation Average* (20 corporations), and the *Dow Jones Utilities Average* (15 corporations). The stocks of the 65 corporations that make up these three indexes comprise the *Dow Jones Composite Average*. These four indexes are the ones most often cited in the U.S. Dow Jones also produces indexes for other sectors *(e.g.,* the U.S. real estate investment trust (REIT) industry) and international stock indexes for global regions.

FIGURE 2-2: COMPONENTS OF THE DOW JONES INDUSTRIAL AVERAGE

Ticker Symbol	Name
AA	ALCOA, INC.
ALD	ALLIED SIGNAL INC.
AXP	AMERICAN EXPRESS
T	AT&T CORP.
BA	BOEING CO.
CAT	CATERPILLAR INC.
C	CITIGROUP
KO	COCA-COLA CO.
DIS	DISNEY (WALT) CO.
DD	DU PONT (EI)
EK	EASTMAN KODAK
XON	EXXON CORP.
GE	GENERAL ELECTRIC
GM	GENERAL MOTORS
HWP	HEWLETT-PACKARD
HD	HOME DEPOT
INTC	INTEL
IBM	INTL. BUS. MACHINE
IP	INTL. PAPER CO.
JNJ	JOHNSON & JOHNSON
MCD	MCDONALDS CORP.
MRK	MERCK & CO.
MSFT	MICROSOFT
MMM	MINN. MINING (3M)
JPM	MORGAN (J.P.)
MO	PHILIP MORRIS CO.
PG	PROCTER & GAMBLE
SBC	SBC COMMUNICATIONS
UTX	UNITED TECH CORP.
WMT	WAL-MART STORES

The Dow Jones Industrial Average (Figure 2-2) is the oldest U.S. stock market index. It was first released in 1896 as a 12-stock index and increased to 30 stocks in 1928. It is considered a "Blue Chip" index (stocks of very high quality). These 30 stocks represent about a fifth of the market value of all U.S. stocks. Until 1999, they included only stocks listed on the New York Stock Exchange. It now includes Microsoft, which is listed on the American Stock Exchange.

FIGURE 2-3: COMPONENTS OF THE DOW JONES
TRANSPORTATION AVERAGE

Ticker Symbol	Name
ABF	AIRBORNE FREIGHT
ALK	ALASKA AIRGROUP
AMR	AMR CORP.
APL	APL LTD.
BNI	BURLINGTON/SANTA FE
CBB	CALIBER SYSTEM
CRR	CONRAIL INC .
CNF	CONS. FREIGHTWAYS
CSX	CSX CORP.
DAL	DELTA AIR LINES
FDX	FED. EXPRESS
IC	ITTTNOIS CENT. CP
NSC	NORFOLK SOUTHERN
R	RYDER SYSTEM INC.
LW	SOUTHWEST AIR
UAL	UAL CORP.
UNP	UNION PAC CORP.
U	US AIRWAYS GROUP
XTR	XTRA CORP.
YELL	YELLOW CORP.

The Dow Jones Transportation Average (Figure 2-3) is also a widely watched benchmark. Transportation stocks are viewed by many analysts as highly cyclical; thus, their performance can be seen as an indicator of future economic activity. The average covers stocks of comprises 20 major companies from the airline, railroad, trucking, and shipping industries.

The Dow Jones Utilities Average (Figure 2-4) is closely watched because U.S. utility stocks are a popular investment for conservative, income-oriented investors, who are concerned about both price movement and yield. The index comprises shares in 15 large publicly owned utilities that provide consumers with everything from gas to water to electricity.

FIGURE 2-4: COMPONENTS OF THE DOW JONES UTILITIES AVERAGE

Ticker Symbol	Name
AEP	AMER. ELEC. PWR.
CX	CENTERIOR ENERGY
ED	CONS. EDISON
CNG	CONS. NATURAL GAS
DTE	DTE ENERGY CO.
EIX	EDISON INTL.
HOU	HOUSTON INDS. INC.
NM	NIAGARA MOHAWK
NAE	NORAM ENERGY
PEL	PANENERGY CORP.
PE	PECO ENERGY CO.
PGL	PEOPLES ENERGY
PGC	PG&E CORP.
PEG	PUB. SERV. ENTERP.
UCM	UNICOM CORP.

The *Wall Street Journal* also publishes the Dow Jones Industry Groups, weekly averages covering a number of industry groups and subgroups. These averages are useful to the investor following the performance of a specific industry relative to the general market.

Barron's, which is also a Dow Jones publication, compiles a 50-Stock Average (Figure 2-5) made up of leading NYSE-listed issues. These stocks are used to compute price and earnings indexes. Moreover, their prices, earnings, bond rates, and dividends are used to compute average

financial ratios. Each stock is given equal weight. These averages and
indexes can be used as a yardstick in evauating stock investments.

FIGURE 2-5: *BARRON'S* 50-STOCK AVERAGE

This 50-stock index ia an unweighted average of 50
leading issues with each stock given equal weight in determining the average. It offers comparisons to the projected
quarterly and annual earnings which appear in the table.
The earnings yield, which is the reciprocal of the
Price/Earnings Ratio (1 divided by the P/E), can be compared to bond yeilds in the table. The dividend yield equals
the dividend divided by the price of the average.

	Oct. 7 1999	Sept. 30 1999	Oct. 1998
Average price index	41.43	4098	3581
Projected quarterly earn	57.01	56.77	40.51
Annualized projected earn	228.04	227.08	162.10
Annualized projected P/E	18.2	18.0	22.2
Five-year average earn	177.42	173.49	163.11
Five-year average P/E	23.4	23.6	21.9
Year-end earn	198.68	177.89	166.50
Year-end P/E	20.9	23.0	21.5
Year-end earns yield, %	4.8	4.3	4.7
Best grade bond yields, %	7.43	7.31	6.09
Bond yields/stock yleds, %	1.55	1.70	1.31
Actual year-end divs	75.95	75.60	74.69
Actual yr-end divs yld, %	1.83	1.84	2.09

Source: Barron's, July 26, 1999

The Dow Jones & Co. indexes are available on the Yahoo! Finance
Web site *(finance.yahoo.com)* (Ticker Symbol: @^DJINDEX).

- **Standard & Poor's (S&P) Indexes**

—Standard & Poor's Corporation publishes a number of major U.S.
stock price indexes, including the *S&P 500*, the *S&P 100*, the
S&P MidCap 400, the *S&P SmallCap 600,* and a 1500-stock
Super Composite index. Standard & Poor's also publishes a number of sector indexes (*e.g.,* Utilities, Transportation, Financials,
and Industrials), and an REIT index. Unlike the Dow Jones
Averages, the components of the various S&P indexes are
weighted by market value.

—The S&P 500 is the best known index of produced by Standard & Poor's; its composite stocks are chosen for market size, liquidity, and industry group representation. Covering large, blue chip companies in leading industries, it represents approximately 80 percent of the market value of all issues traded on the NYSE.

—Considered to be very representative of the stock market as a whole, the S&P 500 is widely used to measure institutional performance. It indicates total returns on major U.S. equities. For example, the S&P 500 Index is one of the U.S. Commerce Department's 11 leading economic indicators. In addition, approximately 97 percent of U.S. money managers and pension plan sponsors use the S& P 500 as a benchmark in evaluating their own performance. Mutual funds that mimic its performance became extremely popular investments in the late 1990s. You can use the S&P indexes to gauge market direction and strength. An upward increase in the S&P index is a sign of a bull market, a downward trend of a bear market. If the overall market is improving, it's probably time to buy.

The S&P 100 Index of major blue-chip stocks across diverse industry groups is a condensed version of the S&P 500 used largely as a way to play options listed on the Chicago Board of Trade: With just 100 members it's cheaper to trade a basket of shares representing this index rather than the whole S&P 500 roster.

The S&P MidCap 400 Index tracks the performance of medium-sized companies, which some say should over time produce returns superior to larger companies because they're perceived to be more nimble managerially. Only 75 percent of Mid-Cap 400 stocks come from the NYSE, and while the median market value of an S&P 500 stock was $7 billion as of October 1998, the median market value of a Mid-Cap 400 stock was $2 billion. The first index for middle capitalization firms, it's quickly becoming a popular benchmark. Approximately 95 percent of U.S. money mangers and pension plan sponsors use it.

The S&P SmallCap 600 Index is a barometer for the nation's smaller companies. Unlike its larger brethren, the S&P Small Cap 600 Index is made up of stocks only about half of which come from the NYSE and half from the NASDAQ and Amex markets. The median market value of an S&P Small Cap 600 Index stock was $22 million as of October 30, 1998.

S&P also has numerous other indexes that track segments of the market, such as the *S&P Industrials Index* (400 corporations); *S&P Transportation Index* (20 corporations); *S&P Financials Index* (40 corporations); *S&P Utility Index* (40 corporations); *S&P REIT Index* that tracks real estate trusts; and global indexes.

S&P also issues indexes in conjunction with BARRA, Inc., an investment and money management firm. These indexes separate the S&P 500, S&P MidCap 400, and S&P Small Cap 600 indexes into growth and value sub-indexes based on various financial criteria. The S&P 500 is divided into the S&P 500/BARRA Growth Index and the S&P 500/BARRA Value Index.

FIGURE 2-6: THE S&P 500 INDEX

Industry Group Representation (as of October 30, 1998):

Industry	Number of Cos.	Number of Cos. as % of S&P 500
Industrials	378	75.6%
Utilities	38	7.6%
Financials	74	14.8%
Transportation	10	2.0%

Exchange Representation:

Exchange	Number of Cos.	Number of Cos. as % of S&P 500
NYSE	457	91.4%
NASDAQ	41	8.2%
AMEX	2	0.4%

Other Statistics:

Total market value	$8.85 trillion
Mean market value	$17.7 billion
Median market value	$7.15 billion
Largest company's market value	$284 billion
Smallest company's market value	$451 million

Source: Standard & Poor's

The S&P indexes are available on the Internet at *www.spglobal.com,* and the S&P/BARRA indexes are available at *www.barra.com.*

•Value Line Indexes

There are two major Value Line indexes, both broad-based measures of prices of NYSE, AMEX, and NASDAQ blue chip and second-tier stocks (1,700 companies). They represent approximately 95 percent of the market value of all U.S. securities. They are both popular because their components closely correspond to the variety of stocks that small investors may have in their portfolio.

To be included in either Value Line Index, a stock must (1) have a reasonable market value, or capitalization, (2) have a strong trading volume, which is a measure of investor interest, and (3) have a high degree of investor interest, as represented by the number of requests for information on a specific stock from subscribers to the Value Line

FIGURE 2-7: STOCK MARKET FIGURES

U.S. MARKETS	June 2	% change Week	Year
Dow Jones Industrials	10,577.9	-1.2	19.0
NASDAQ Composite	2432.4	0.2	38.1
NASDAQ 100	2074.5	1.0	74.8
S&P MidCap 400	396.5	0.7	11.6
S&P SmallCap 600	176.3	0.5	-6.4
S&P SuperComposite 1500	272.5	-0.6	16.9

GLOBAL MARKETS	June 2	% change Week	Year
S&P Euro Plus	1267.4	-0.8	-2.0
London (FT-SE 100)	6302.2	1.0	7.9
Frankfurt (DAX)	5040.3	-2.8	-9.7
Tokyo (NIKKEI 225)	16,418.0	1.2	5.6
Hong Kong (Hang Seng)	12,458.6	0.4	44.9
Toronto (TSE 300)	6850.8	1.0	-9.1
Mexico City (IPC)	5400.2	-3.9	20.5

SECTORS	June 2	% change Week	Year
S&P BARRA Growth	715.3	-0.1	25.9
S&P BARRA Value	59.9	-1.5	10.2
S&P Basic Materials	132.2	-0.4	-0.7
S&P Capital Goods	966.5	0.0	14.4
S&P Energy	838.6	-2.0	10.5
S&P Financials	136.8	-2.5	2.9
S&P REIT	87.6	-0.2	-15.9
S&P Transportation	745.2	-0.3	10.9
S&P Utilities	263.7	-2.1	8.1
GSTI Internet	457.1	-6.2	252.5
Morgan Stanley Cyclical	579.9	0.2	9.6
PSE Technology	531.5	1.6	62.9

FUNDAMENTALS	June 1	Week ago	Year ago
S&P 500 Divident Yield	1.25%	1.26%	1.42%
S&P 500 P/E Ratio			
(Trailing 12 mos.)	32.6	32.7	26.0
S&P 500 P/E Ratio			
(Next 12 mos.)*	23.5	23.6	21.1
First Call Earnings Revison*	-0.06%	0.40%	-0.60%
*first Call Corp.			

TECHNICAL INDICATORS	June 1	Week ago	Reading
S&P 500 200-day average	1194.4	1190.1	Positive
Stocks above 200-day avg/	57.0%	57.0%	Neutral
Options: Put/call ratio	0.50	0.52	Negative
Insiders: Vickers Sell/buy ratio	1.02	1.00	Positive

Source: Business Week, June 14, 1999

Investment Survey. Component stocks are dropped from either index only if the company has (1) gone bankrupt with little hope of revitalization and continued investor interest, (2) merged with another company, or (3) gone private.

From 1961 until 1988, there was only one Value Line Index, which was computed as an equally weighted geometric average or mean of the returns received on the component stocks. A geometric mean is calculated by multiplying N number of returns together and then taking the Nth root of that product (for example, the geometric mean of 1 and 3 is 1.732 [the square root of 1x3]). The use of the geometric mean reduces the volatility in the Value Line Index.

In March 1988, Value Line began publishing a second index based upon the arithmetic average or mean. (An arithmetic average or mean is calculated by adding N number of returns together and dividing by N. For example, the arithmetic mean of 1 and 3 is 1.5 ([1+3]/2). The only difference between the Geometric and the Arithmetic Index is the method used in calculating the average.

Value Line also maintains three lesser-known price averages representing industrial, railroad, and utility issues.

- **NASDAQ Indexes**

The NASDAQ indexes (Figure 2-8) follow the price performance of over-the-counter securities:

FIGURE 2-8: INDEXES

S&P	High	Low	Close	Change
S&P 100	722.32	704.21	717.03	+12.82
S&P 500	1371.17	1342.44	1362.93	+20.49
S&P MidCap	401.07	391.20	399.62	+8.42

Dow Jones	High	Low	Close	Change
30 Industrial	10883.1	10580.1	10729.9	+107.33
20 Transportation	3127.4	3004.8	3059.0	+45.87
15 Utilities	309.5	303.9	306.6	+.35
65 Composite	3177.4	3087.1	3130.2	+29.58

NYSE	High	Low	Close	Change
Composite	629.49	618.15	625.47	+7.32
Industrial	780.90	764.72	776.12	+11.40
Transportation	484.80	467.99	481.68	+13.34
Utility	498.31	491.30	494.02	+2.72
Financial	548.97	539.76	542.49	+1.90

Amex	High	Low	Close	Change
Major Market	802.21	793.33	800.80	+7.25

Nasdaq	High	Low	Close	Change
Nasdaq 100	2651.12	2539.93	2637.44	+97.51
Composite	2978.63	2919.37	2966.43	+91.21
Industrial	1682.35	1656.45	1674.72	+30.66
Banks	1806.91	1790.19	1801.03	+11.51
Financial	2899.03	2848.68	2855.87	+20.32
Transportation	959.16	951.893	955.33	+6.94
Utility	745.68	731.88	741.54	+17.60

Source: Los Angeles Daily News

- The NASDAQ 100 Index represents the largest non-financial domestic and international companies listed on the NASDAQ Composite. Its components are taken from major industry groups, including computer hardware and software, telecommunications, retail/wholesale trade, and biotechnology.

- The widely quoted NASDAQ Composite Index measures all NAS-DAQ domestic and non-U.S.-based common stocks listed on the NASDAQ. It includes over 5,000 companies, more than most other stock market indexes. Because NASDAQ today trades such major issues as Microsoft, Intel, and Cisco Systems, this index is no longer considered the barometer of small stocks as it once was.

- The NASDAQ National Market Composite Index consists of all companies included in the NASDAQ Composite Index that are also listed on the top tier of the NASDAQ Stock Market.

- The NASDAQ National Market Industrial Index includes over 2,000 agricultural, mining, construction, manufacturing (electronic components), services, and public administration enterprises.

- The NASDAQ Financial 100 Index consists of large financial organizations listed on the top tier of the NASDAQ Stock Market.

- The NASDAQ Bank Index includes more than 350 banks, savings and loans, and related holding companies. It also includes firms closely related to banking, such as check cashing agencies, currency exchanges, safe deposit companies, trust companies, and corporations that conduct banking overseas.

- The NASDAQ Biotechnology Index includes over 100 companies engaged in research to develop new treatments and cures for disease.

- The NASDAQ Computer Index is composed of more than 600 computer hardware and software companies, data processing services, and firms that produce office equipment and electronic components and accessories.

- The NASDAQ Insurance Index includes about 100 insurance companies including life, health, property, casualty, brokers, agents, and related services.

- The NASDAQ Transportation Index includes about 100 railroads, trucking companies, airlines, pipelines (except natural gas), services such as warehousing, and travel arrangers.

- The NASDAQ Telecommunications Index includes over 170 companies.

- The NASDAQ Industrial Index includes about 3,000 agricultural, mining, construction, manufacturing (electronic components), services, and public administration enterprises.

The NASDAQ indexes are value-weighted so that each company's stock affects the index in proportion to its market value. In 1999, the weights were adjusted to enhance diversification. Moves in NASDAQ stocks are seen as an indication of how second-tier issues are doing. The NASDAQ Composite, laden with numerous leaders in technology fields, is seen as a harbinger of how technology stocks are faring.

The NASDAQ web site *(www.nasdaq.com)* has up-to-the-minute quotes on the NASDAQ indexes throughout the trading day. They are also available at *finance.yahoo.com* (Symbol Search: NASDAQ).

- **AMEX Indexes** (Figure 2-9)

The American Stock Exchange (AMEX) compiles two major indexes: the *AMEX Composite Index* and the *AMEX Major Market Index*. The value-weighted Composite Index includes all stocks listed on the AMEX.

The Major Market Index is designed to measure the performance of the blue-chip sector of the market, based on 20 well known, highly capitalized stocks representing a broad range of industries. It's composed of 15 of the 30 Dow Jones industrials and five other large NYSE-listed stocks. Each component is weighted equally.

The AMEX also issues other indexes *(e.g.,* two AMEX/Inter@ctive Internet Indexes, the AMEX Networking Index, the AMEX Oil and Gas Index, and the AMEX Biotechnology Index). These are available on the Internet at *cbs.marketwatch.com.*

FIGURE 2-9: AMEX INDEXES

Major U.S. Indices				
	Sat Oct 30 5:04pm ET – U.S. Markets Closed			
Name	**Symbol**	**Last Trade**		**Change**
Dow Jones Averages				
30 Industrials	^DJI	Oct 29	10729.86	+107.33 +1.01%
20 Transportation	^DJT	Oct 29	3058.98	+45.87 +1.52%
15 Utilities	^DJU	Oct 29	306.61	+0.35 +0.11%
65 Composite	^DJA	Oct 29	3130.23	+29.58 +0.95%
New York Stock Exchange				
Volume in 000's	^TV.N	Oct 29	1143380	0 0.00%
Composite	^NYA	Oct 29	625.47	+7.32 +1.18%
Tick	^TIC.N	Oct 29	-207	-841 -132.65%
ARMS	^STI.N	Oct 29	0.93	+0.50 +116.14%
Nasdaq				
Composite	^IXIC	Oct 29	2966.43	+91.21 +3.17%
Volume in 000's	^TV.O	Oct 29	1441370	0 0.00%
National Market Composite	^IXQ	Oct 29	1349.50	+41.72 +3.19%
Nasdaq 100	^NDX	Oct 29	2637.44	+97.51 +3.84%
Standard and Poor's				
500 Index	^SPC	Oct 29	1362.93	+20.49 +1.53%
100 Index	^OEX	Oct 29	717.03	+12.82 +1.82%
400 MidCap	^MID	Oct 29	399.62	+8.42 +2.15%
600 SmallCap	^SML	Oct 29	175.67	+1.56 +0.90%
Other U.S. Indices				
AMEX Composite	^XAX	Oct 29	800.80	+7.25 +0.91%
AMEX Internet	^IIX	Oct 29	356.14	+11.55 +3.35%
AMEX Networking	^NWX	Oct 29	640.97	+19.23 +3.09%
Indi 500	^NDI	Oct 29	204.59	+5.78 +2.91%
ISDEX	^IXY2	Oct 29	562.72	+13.15 +2.39%
Major Market	^XMI	Oct 29	1127.82	+8.10 +0.72%
Pacific Exchange Technology	^PSE	Oct 29	664.55	+28.00 +4.40%
Philadelphia Semiconductor	^SOXX	Oct 29	555.83	+33.16 +6.34%
Russell 1000	^RUI	Oct 29	707.19	+11.74 +1.69%
Russell 2000	^RUT	Oct 29	428.64	+5.83 +1.38%
Russell 3000	^RUA	Oct 29	726.50	+11.91 +1.67%
TSC Internet	^DOT	Oct 29	750.79	+30.97 +4.30%
Value Line	^VLIC	Oct 29	414.64	+4.70 +1.15%
Wilshi 5000 TOT	^TMW	Oct 29	12449.45	+220.22 +1.80%

Source: Yahoo!Finance

- **The NYSE Composite Index**

  The NYSE Composite Index, established in 1966, provides a comprehensive measure of market trends on the New York Stock exchange. Value-weighted, it covers the prices of all the companies listed on the NYSE, over 2,000, and is made up of four subindexes: industrial, transportation, utility, and finance. Besides being a general pulse of the market, the index also provides the base for index options and for futures contracts. The index and its subindexes are available on the Internet at *finance.yahoo.com* (Symbol Search: NYSE).

- **Wilshire Equity Indexes**

  Wilshire Associates (Santa Monica, California) publishes, among others, the *Wilshire 5,000 Total Market Index* includes all common stock issues on the NYSE and AMEX, and the most active issues on the NASDAQ. Its value is in billions of dollars. It includes over 7,000 U.S.-headquartered equity securities (it included 5,000 firms when it was started) with readily available price data. Companies on the NYSE account for about 85 percent of the market value of the index, NASDAQ 13 percent, and AMEX 2 percent. The Canadian stocks are excluded. Because of the diversity of its components, the Wilshire 5000 Total Market Index is considered representative of the overall market. Its stocks are weighted by market value.

The Wilshire Large Cap 750 Index represents the largest 750 stocks in the Wilshire 5000 determined by market value of outstanding shares. The value-weighted Wilshire Small Cap 1750 Index (Figure 2-10) includes the next 1,750 largest companies from the Wilshire 5000. Companies are ranked by market value.

FIGURE 2-10: MAJOR MARKET INDEXES, WILSHIRE SMALL CAP

CBS MarketWatch — Search · Site Map
Front Page · Market Data · Portfolios · Mutual Funds · Personal Finance · Dis
Major Market Indexes
Updated as of: Oct 12, 1999 @ 3:52 pm ET

Sym.	Company Name	Last	Change	%Chg	High
$INDU	Dow Jones Industrial Average™	10437.95	-210.23	-2.0	10648.81
$TRAN	Dow Jones Transportation Average™	2961.07	-64.95	-2.1	3026.58
$UTIL	Dow Jones Utilities Average™	295.66	-0.06	-0.0	297.36
$NDX	NASDAQ 100 Index	2527.97	-50.91	-2.0	2586.33
$COMPQ	NASDAQ Composite Index	2874.02	-41.93	-1.4	2923.32
$NYA	NYSE Composite Index	603.67	-9.66	-1.6	613.33
$SPX	S&P 500 Stock Index	1313.81	-21.40	-1.6	1335.77
$MID	S&P 400 MidCap Stock Index	384.78	-6.78	-1.7	391.87
$OEX	S&P 100 Stock Index	686.88	-10.88	-1.6	698.30
$IXCO	NASDAQ High Technology Index	1561.92	-19.41	-1.2	1589.75
$PSE	PSE High Technology Index	642.69	-11.47	-1.8	656.82
$MSH	Morgan Stanley High Tech Index	1271.33	-22.55	-1.7	1297.51
$SOX	Semiconductor Index	523.94	-4.61	-0.9	546.85
$XMI	AMEX Major Market Index	1096.08	-17.45	-1.6	1113.53
$XAX	AMEX Composite Index	791.27	+1.25	+0.2	792.37
$WSX	Wilshire Small Cap Index	653.92	-10.63	-1.6	664.55
$TSE-TC	Toronto 35 Index	409.92	-0.73	-0.2	413.51
$TOP-TC	TSE 100 Index	base y	+base y	+4.4	base y
$TT-TC	TSE 300 Composite Index	7121.90	+5.86	+0.1	7164.13
$MEX	Mexico Index	85.51	-1.21	-1.4	86.72
$TNX	10 Year T-Note Interest Rate (x .10)	6.058	+0.034	+0.6	6.075
$TYX	30 Year T-Bond Interest Rate (x .10)	6.226	+0.037	+0.6	6.238
$XAU	PHLX Gold and Silver Index	77.69	-2.48	-3.1	80.70
$XOI	AMEX Oil & Gas	491.60	+1.12	+0.2	493.99
$XVG	Value Line Index (Geometric)	415.09	-5.56	-1.3	420.80
$RUI	Russell 1000	679.86	-11.60	-1.7	691.83
$RUT	Russell 2000	425.45	-4.74	-1.1	430.46
$RUA	Russell 3000	699.94	-11.65	-1.6	711.96

Wilshire releases a number of other indexes based on company size and growth potential, as well as sector indexes.

- **Russell Indexes**

   The value-weighted Russell indexes (Figure 2-11), developed by Frank Russell Co., consist of the securities of 1,000, 2,000, or 3,000 companies based on their market value. Frank Russell Co. prepared the comparison of some of its indexes with other major market indexes that appears as Figure 2-11.

   The *Russell 3000* Index tracks the broad U.S. stock market. It measures the performance of the 3,000 largest US companies based on total market capitalization; these represent approximately 98 percent of the US equity market. Average market capitalization is approximately $4.4 billion; median market capitalization is approximately $701.7 million. The index has a total market capitalization range of approximately $407.2 billion.

   The *Russell 1000* Index is made up of the largest 1,000 firms within the Russell 3,000 Index. The Russell 1000 Index represents approximately 92 percent of the total market capitalization of the Russell 3000 Index. The average market capitalization is approximately $12.1 billion; the median market capitalization is approximately $3.8 billion. The smallest company in the index has an approximate capitalization of $1.35 billion.

   The Russell 2000 Index measures the performance of the 2,000 smallest companies in the 3000 Index; it represents approximately 8% of the total market capitalization of the Russell 3000 Index. Average market capitalization is approximately $526.4 million; median market capitalization was approximately $428.0 million. The largest company in the index had an approximate market capitalization of just under $1.35 billion. The Russell 2000 Index is seen as the top barometer of performance for small company stocks in the U.S. (Many studies have shown that over time small company stocks have performed better than large.) The Russell 2000 represents approximately 10 percent of the total market capitalization of all U.S. shares.

   Russell also issues other indexes based on varying market capitalization rankings *(e.g.,* Russell 200 Index, Russell MidCap Index, and Russell 2500 Index). Russell also divides its indexes into subindexes. For example, each index has a growth and a value component. Growth shares are typically firms with higher price-to-book value ratios; value components are typically firms with lower price-to-book value ratios.

FIGURE 2-11: U.S. EQUITY INDEXES

US Equity Indexes

A Comparison of US Equity Indexes
As of June 30, 1999

Index	Russell 1000 +	Russell 2000 =	Russell 3000	Dow Jones Industrial Average	Nasdaq	S&P 500	Wilshire 5000
Representation	Large Cap	Small Cap	Broad Market	Large Cap	Nasdaq exchange	Broad Market	Broad Market
Characteristics							
Approximate number of companies in index	1,000	2,000	3,000	30	4,895	500	7000+
Distribution by Market Cap							
NYSE	83.0	51.4	80.7	100%	—	86.3	77.9
AMEX	0.3	2.4	0.4			0.0	0.9
NASDAQ/OTC	16.8	46.2	18.9		100%	13.7	21.2
Methodology							
Criteria for inclusion	Top 1,000 securities in the Russell 3000	Bottom 2,000 securities in the Russell 3000	Top 3,000 Nasdaq, NYSE & AMEX US domiciled stocks as ranked by Market Cap	Representative of US Industry	All domestic common shares traded on Nasdaq-NMS, Nasdaq Small Cap	S&P selection committee, liquidity factor	All US equities for which prices were available on that day
Weighting	Market Cap, - adjusted for large private holdings, corporate cross ownership	Market Cap, - adjusted for large private holdings, corporate cross ownership	Market Cap, - adjusted for large private holdings, corporate cross ownership	Price	Market Cap	Market Cap	Market Cap
Reconstituted	Annually	Annually	Annually	No	No	No	As needed
Objective methodology publicly available	Yes	Yes	Yes	No	Yes	No	Yes
Style indexes available	Yes	Yes	Yes	No	No	Yes	Yes

Source: Frank Russell & Co.

- **The Bloomberg IPO Index**

  Bloomberg, L.P., produces a number of indexes. One that is widely followed tracks the market movement of stocks in their first year of public trading. Bloomberg also produces international and regional indexes. The regional indexes report the stock price movement of companies headquartered in the specified region. These indexes can be accessed free at *www.bloomberg.com.*

- **Internet Indexes**

  AMEX and Inter@Active Week magazine developed the AMEX Internet Index (also called the Inter@Active Week Internet Index). It tracks a cross-section of 50 leading companies providing Internet infrastructure and access, developing and marketing Internet content and software, and conducting business over the Internet. The original index (IIO) is a value-weighted index. In March, 1999, a new index (IIX) was introduced using the same components but with a modified weighting system designed to reduce the impact of larger stocks on the index. Both indexes are reported.

  TheStreet.com *(www.thestreet.com)* produces the TSC Internet Sector Index, an equal-weighted measure of the performance of 20 prominent Internet companies. Each component is weighted equally. *TheStreet.com* also produces the TSC E-commerce Index; the component companies generate a significant portion of their revenues from commerce conducted over the Internet or have plans to develop a commercial presence on the Internet. Each component is weighted equally.

  The Dow Jones Internet Commerce Index is a modified capitalization-weighted index of 15 of the largest and most actively traded companies providing goods and services through an open network such as the Internet. The Dow Jones & Co. indexes are available at *finance.yahoo.com* (Ticker Symbol: @^DJINDEX).

  The CBOE Internet Index is an equal-dollar weighted index composed of 12 companies providing Internet access services, as well as designing and manufacturing software and hardware that facilitates Internet access.

The Goldman Sachs Internet Index is made up of 13 service and hardware corporations involved with the Internet. It's value-weighted.

USA Today publishes the *USA Today* Internet 100 Index that reports the stock market movement of companies in different Internet sectors. Market movement is reported for the entire index along with subindexes (*e.g.,* e-Business 50, e-Consumer 50, e-Infrastructure, e-Services/Solutions, e-Advertising/Marketing/ Media, e-Retail, e-Financial, e-New Media, and e-Service Providers).

OTHER INDEXES

Bond Market Indexes (Figure 2-12)

Dow Jones publishes three indexes that track movement in the bond market. The *Dow Utilities Bond Index* consists of 10 bonds. The *Dow Industrial Bond Index* is made up of 10 bonds. The *Dow 20 Bond Index* is combines first two indexes. The indexes are available at *finance.yahoo.com* (Ticker Symbol: @^DJINDEX) and at *cbs.market-watch.com* (Dow 20 Bond Index—Ticker Symbol: 26099901; Dow Industrial Bond Index—Ticker Symbol: 26099903; and Dow Utilities Bond Index—Ticker Symbol: 26099902). The Dow 20 Bond Index is also available at the Salomon Smith Barney site *(www.salomonsmithbarney.com)*.

FIGURE 2-12: BOND MARKET INDEXES

Index	Close	Chg.	YTD
Lehman Treas.	6.53%	-.01	+1.22
BonBuy Muni	5.35%		+.19
Morgan US$	105.60	-.40	-.30
CRB Index	201.35	+1.41	+10.13
DJ AIG Fut.	87.80	+.69	
Moodys Bond	7.31	-.18	+1.05
Dow Indust	102.26	+.03	-5.98
Dow Utils	96.63	-.14	-7.96
Dow 20	99.45	-.03	-6.97

Source: Orange County Register

Barron's publishes a *Best Grade Bond Index* that tracks 10 high-grade corporate bonds, and an *Interim-Grade Bond Index* that tracks 10 medium-grade corporate bonds.

Merrill Lynch publishes a number of national and global bond indexes. Monthly performance reports are posted on the Merrill Lynch Web site *(www.ml.com)*.

Lehman Brothers publishes a number of bond indexes. The *Lehman Brothers Aggregate Bond Index* includes more than 5,000 taxable government, investment-grade corporate, and mortgage-backed securities. The *Lehman Brothers Long Treasury Bond Index* is a weighted average of all U.S. Treasury securities with maturities of 10 years and longer. Both are available at the Salomon Smith Barney Web site *(www.salomonsmithbarney.com)*. The *Lehman Brothers Corporate Bond Index* includes all publicly issued, fixed-rate, non-convertible, investment-grade, and SEC-registered corporate debts with at least one year left until maturity and a par value of at least $100. Lehman bond indexes are posted at *cbs.marketwatch.com*.

The Bond Buyer issues two indexes that chart the yield levels of municipal bonds. Its *Municipal Bond Index* covers yields on AA-rated and A-rated general obligation bonds with 20-year maturities, and *The Bond Buyer Revenue Bond Index* covers revenue bonds with 30-year maturities. Both are available on the U.S. Bancorp Piper Jaffray Web site *(www.pjc.com)*, and the municipal index is also available at *www.salomonsmithbarney.com*.

J.P. Morgan issues international indexes. The *J.P. Morgan Currency Index* measures one country's currency strength relative to 18 other industrial-country currencies. The *J.P. Morgan Government Bond Index* measures the performance of leading government bond markets based on total return in U.S. currency. The *Emerging Markets Bond Index Plus* tracks total returns for traded external debt instruments in the emerging markets. These indexes are available at *www.jpmorgan.com*.

Salomon Smith Barney also produces a number of bond indexes: the *Broad Investment-Grade Index*, the *Treasury Index*, the *Government Sponsored Index*, the *Mortgage Index*, the *Corporate Index*, the *High Yield Index*, the *World Government Bond Index*, and the *Brady Bond Index*. The Salomon World Government Bond Index is available at *cbs.marketwatch.com* (Ticker Symbol: XX:1810305).

The *Value Line Convertible Index* measures the performance of convertible bonds and preferred stocks. (Convertible securities can be converted [exchanged] into common stock at an assigned date.) This equally weighted index tracks the price performance of 575 securities, including preferred, bonds, and Euro-convertibles. The *Value Line Total Returns Index* includes the income on these issues. The *Value Line Warrant Index,* also equally weighted, measures price performance of 85 warrants.

MUTUAL FUND INDEXES

Lipper, Inc. reports on the performance of mutual funds by categories. The company also compiles indexes made up of 10 or 30 mutual funds for each category (Figure 2-13).

FIGURE 2-13: LIPPER MUTUAL FUND INDEXES

Type of Lipper index	Thurs.	Total return[1] 4 weeks	1999
Balanced	0.1%	2.95	7.0%
Capital appreciation	-0.1%	5.7%	16.6%
Emerging market	-0.5%	9.3%	39.9%
Equity income	0.2%	3.2%	10.4%
European region	-0.6%	1.4%	2.8%
Financial services	-0.1%	4.5%	7.3%
Gold	-2.2%	3.5%	-5.3%
Growth	0.1%	5.7%	13.5%
Growth & income	0.2%	4.0%	13.0%
Health/biotechnology	-0.1%	4.3%	2.1%
International	-0.6%	3.6%	9.7%
Pacific region	-0.7%	10.0%	37.1%
Science & technology	-0.5%	10.5%	30.5%
Small Cap	-0.9%	5.0%	9.8%
Utilities	0.2%	0.8%	7.8%\

[1] Cap. gains and dividends reinvested through July 1

Source: USA Today

The *Norwood Index* is the most respected measure of performance of commodity mutual funds.

Moody's Equity Mutual Fund Indexes track the daily average total return of 1,857 equity-oriented mutual funds classified into 29 clusters, or peer groups. Moody's also calculates three composite indexes. The mutual fund indexes include funds with a three-year performance history that have at least 67 percent of their assets invested in stock and hybrid investment companies. Press releases detailing changes for the 29 mutual fund indexes can be located on the Moody's web site (www.moodys.com) by using the site search engine and asking for "indexes."

International Stock Averages

A number of newspapers and magazines provide information on foreign stock indexes (Figure 2-14). U.S. organizations also issue such indexes. Dow Jones global indexes are available at *finance.yahoo.com* (Ticker Symbol: @^DJINDEX). In conjunction with three European partners, Dow Jones issues 216 size and sector European stock indexes.

Morgan Stanley international indexes are available on the Morgan Stanley Capital International Web site *(www.mscidata.com)*. S&P's global indexes can be found at *www.spglobal.com*. *Forbes* provides the *AMEX International Market Index,* a value-weighted index comprising 50 largest American Deposit Receipts (ADRs). These indexes can be accessed free at *cbs.marketwatch.com.*

FIGURE 2-14: FOREIGN STOCK EXCHANGES

Index	52 wk. High	52 wk. Low	Close	Net Chg.
Amsterdam (AEX)	595.94	375.58	559.77	+4.93
Bombay	4981.74	2764.16	5031.78	+50.05
Brussels (BEL 20)	3681.92	2723.92	3026.55	-23.17
Frankfurt (DAX)	5652.02	3896.08	5429.47	+11.05
London (FT 100)	6620.60	4648.70	6234.80	+35.40
Hong Kong (IDX)	14372.51	7564.54	12992.72	-119.70
Paris (CAC 40)	4745.48	2511.40	4722.35	+.42
Mexico (IPC)	6080.47	3300.42	5331.02	+48.06
Tokyo (NIKKEI 225)	18532.58	12879.97	1806.18	-74.37
Singapore (Straits Times)				
Sao Paulo (Ibovespa)	12477.10	5057.19	11478.17	+18.67
Sydney (All Ordinaries)	3145.20	2459.30	2926.40	+29.30
Taipei (TSM)	8408.91	5474.79	7607.11	+54.13
Toronto (TSE 300)	7292.69	5397/24	7116.04	+52.58
Zurich (SMI)	7668.80	5293.70	7110.00	+13.50
Milan (MIB)	25426.00	16761.00	23854.00	-49.00
Johannesburg (Acturar)	7365.90	4997.40	7413.20	+47.30

Source: Orange County Register

Commodity Indexes

The *J.P. Morgan Commodity Index* tracks the total return of a basket of industrial commodities (55% energy, 23% precious metals, 22% base metals). The subindexes represent four main commodity groups: energy, base metals, precious metals, and agricultural products. This index is available at *www.jpmorgan.com.*

Bridge/CRB, formerly the Commodity Research Bureau (CRB), has two widely watched benchmarks for commodity prices: the *CRB/Bridge Spot Price Index* and the *CRB/Bridge Futures Price Index.* The Spot Price Index is based on prices of 23 different commodities, representing livestock and products, fats and oils, metals, and textiles and fibers; it serves as an inflation indicator.

The Futures Price Index tracks the volatile behavior of commodity prices. As the best-known commodity index, it was designed to monitor broad changes in the markets. It consists of 21 commodities; nine subindexes are maintained for baskets representing currencies, energy, interest rates, imported commodities, industrial commodities, grains, oilseeds, livestock and meats, and precious metals. All indexes have a base level of 100 as of 1967, except the currencies, energy, and interest rates indexes, which were set at 100 as of 1977. These indexes are available on the Bridge/CRB Web site *(www.crbindex.com).*

The *Economist Commodities Index* gauges spot prices and their movements. The index is a geometric weighted-average based on the significance in international trade of spot prices of major commodities. It's designed to measure inflation pressure in the world's industrial powers. It includes only commodities that freely trade in open markets, eliminating items like iron and rice, precious metals or oil. The commodities tracked are weighted by the volume of their exports to developed economies. The index may be obtained from Reuters News Services or in *The Economist* magazine. The indicators serve as barometers of global inflation and global interest rates.

Stamp Indexes

Scott Philatelic Corporation, an affiliate of Scott Publishing, computes the *Scott Index* values. These values for "fine" stamps are used in the study of quality-adjusted rates of return in stamp auctions. Linn's Stamp News publishes the *U.S. Stamp Market Index,* a weighted average of prices for U.S. 19th- and 20th-century stamps and airmails. This index also tracks prices in the stamp market. The Linn Stamp Market Index is available at *www.linns.com.*

Real Estate Performance Averages

The *S&P REIT Composite Index* tracks the market performance of U.S. REITs. The index consists of 100 REITs chosen for their liquidity and importance in representing a diversified real estate portfolio. The Index covers 80% of the securitized U.S. real estate market. S&P makes it available at *www.spglobal.com.*

The value-weighted *Wilshire Real Estate Securities Index* is a broad measure of the performance of publicly traded real estate securities, such as Real Estate Investment Trusts (REITs) and Real Estate Operating Companies (REOCs). It covers approximately 119 companies, with a total market cap of $116.97 billion. It's a value-weighted index.

The *Wilshire REIT Index* measures U.S. publicly traded REITs; it's a sub-set of the Real Estate Securities Index. Approximately 110 cap-weighted securities were included; they have a total market cap of $104.92 billion.

Both Dow Jones and the Chicago Board of Exchange (CBOE) also produce REIT indexes. These can be accessed free from *cbs.marketwatch.com.*

In addition to the REIT indexes, an index to record changes in real estate values, including leverage and equity properties, was developed in 1982 by the Frank Russell Company and the National Conference of Real Estate Investment Fiduciaries (NCREIF), which took over full responsibility for the *NCREIF Index* in 1995. NCREIF also issues a *Timberland Index* and a *Farmland Index.*

APPENDIX 2-A:
USEFUL WEB SITES

Web Address	Primary Focus
cbs.marketwatch.com	General market information
finance.yahoo.com	General market information
www.amex.com	Price quotes and other information about companies listed on the American Stock Exchange (AMEX)
www.barra.com	Information on S&P Barra indexes
www.businessweek.com	Market indexes and charts
www.cboe.com	Educational information about the Chicago Board OptionsExchange (CBOE), including products andprices
www.crbindex.com	Information on CRB indexes
www.jpmorgan.com	Information on J.P. Morgan products
www.linns.com	Linn Stamp Market Index
www.ml.com	Information on Merrill Lynch products
www.mscidata.com	Information on Morgan Stanley Capital international indexes
www.nasdaq.com	Information about the NASDAQ System and price quotations
www.nyse.com	Historical, regulatory, and listing information about The New York Stock Exchange
www.pjc.com	Information on bonds
www.salomonsmithbarney.com	Information on Salomon Smith Barney products
www.spglobal.com	Information on S&P's products and indexes
www.stockmaster.com	General market information
www.timely.com	Quotes and technical charts on indexes and companies
www.viwes.com/invest/shorts/top20/index.html	Tables of short interest in common stocks

Chapter 3
GENERAL ECONOMIC INFORMATION

The investor analyzes the economy primarily to determine investment strategy, not to formulate economic forecasts. Investors can rely on published forecasts to identify trends in the economy and adjust their investment positions accordingly. Unfortunately, there are too many economic indicators and variables to analyze all of them. Each has significance. But these variables could can also give mixed signals about the future of the economy and therefore mislead the investor.

Government agencies and private firms tabulate economic data and calculate indexes. Subscriptions for these are affordable; they can also be found in public and college libraries. They include daily local newspapers and national newspapers such as *USA Today, Wall Street Journal, Investor's Business Daily, Los Angeles Times,* and *New York Times* and periodicals such as *Business Week, Forbes, Fortune, Money, Kiplinger's Personal Finance Magazine, Worth, Barron's, Smart Money, Nation's Business,* and *U.S. News* and *World Report.* Internet users can look at the White House Economic Statistics Briefing Room *(www.whitehouse. gov/fsbr/esbr.html)* that provides easy access to current federal economic indicators. They can also check out the semiannual Livingston Survey, started in 1946 by economist Joseph A. Livingston, which is the oldest continuous survey of economists' expectations. The Federal Reserve Bank of Philadelphia took responsibility for the survey in 1990; you can find it at the bank's Web site: *www.phil.frb.org/econ/liv/welcome.html* .

ECONOMIC VARIABLES AND INVESTMENT DECISIONS

Economic indicators apply to the outlook for business. A growing economy will lead to improved profitability and dividends; thus it's bullish for stocks. A decline in real GNP will result in lower profits and dividends, causing a decline in stock prices.

Economic indicators can be used to confirm market direction. For example, if the economy is contracting at an unsustainable rate, stock prices will shortly do better, to reflect the better business environment that will emerge. Once the stock market does not react to bad news any more, the market has already discounted the bad news and stock prices should start to move upward.

A low *inflation rate* is better for equity securities. During the bull market of 1984, the yearly percent increases in the Consumer Price Index (CPI) were 4.0%, 3.8%, and 1.1%.

Monetary indicators apply to Federal Reserve actions and the demand for credit. *Long-term interest rates* are important because bond yields compete with stock yields. Monetary and credit indicators are often the first signs of market direction. If monetary indicators are favorable, any decline in stock prices may be over. But a stock market top may be ready for a contraction if the Federal Reserve tightens credit, making consumer buying and corporate expansion more costly and difficult.

Popular monetary indicators are:

- The Dow Jones 20-Bond Index

- The Dow Jones utility average

- The NYSE utility average

- The yield on Treasury bills

- The 30-year T-bond yield

Because bonds and utilities are yield instruments, they are money-sensitive. Changing interest rates affect them. If the popular monetary indicators are active and pointing higher, it's a sign the stock market will start to take off. In other words, these indicators move upward in advance of a stock market increase.

The Impact of Variables

Figure 3-1 summarizes the types of economic variables and the effect they are believed to have on the securities market and the economy in general.

FIGURE 3-1:   EFFECTS OF ECONOMIC VARIABLES ON THE ECONOMY AND STOCKS

Economic Variables	Impact on Security Market
Real growth In GNP	Positive (without inflation) forstocks
Industrial production	Consecutive drops are a sign of recession; bad for stocks
Inflation	Detrimental to stocks
Capacity utilization	A high percentage is positive, but full capacity is inflationary
Durable goods orders	Consecutive drops Signal recession; very bad for stocks in cyclical industries
Increase in business investment, consumer confidence personal income,etc.	Positive for most stocks, especially retailing; worrisome for utility shares
Leading indicators	Rise is bullish for the economy and stocks; drops are a sign of bad times ahead
Housing starts	Rise is positive for housing stocks
Corporate profits	Strong corporate earnings are positive for stocks; corporate bonds also fare well
Unemployment	Upward trend unfavorable for stocks and economy
Increase in business inventories	Positive for those fearful of inflation; negative for those looking for growing economy
Lower federal deficit	Lowers interest rates, good for many stocks; potential negative for depressed economy
Deficit in trade and balance of payments	Negative for economy and stocks of companies facing stiff import competition
Weak dollar	Negative for economy; good for companies with stiff foreign competition
Interest rates	Rising rates can choke off investment in new plants and lure skittish investors from stocks

Figure 3-1, though a handy guide, should not be construed as an accurate predictor in all cases. The anticipation of good or bad news is often built into the market and when the news come out, the reverse move happens because traders are unwinding the positions they took to profit from the news.

INDICATORS AND BOND YIELDS

Figure 3-2 shows how significant economic indicators affect bond yields. Remember, bond yields and bond prices act conversely, so a rise in yields means a fall in prices and vice versa. Figure 3-2 should not be construed as an absolutely accurate predictor. As with stocks, because the anticipation of good or bad news is built into the market, when the news come out, the reverse move happens because traders are unwinding the positions they took to profit from that news.

FIGURE 3-2: PROBABLE EFFECTS OF ECONOMIC VARIABLES ON BOND YIELDS*

Indicators**	Effects On Bond Yields***	Reasons
Business Activity		
GNP and industrial production falls	Fall	As economy slows, the Federal Reserve Bank may ease credit by allowing rates to fall
Unemployment rises	Fall	Indicates lack of economic expansion; Federal Reserve Bank may loosen credit
Inventories rise	Fall	Inventory levels are good indicators of duration of economic slowdown
Trade deficit rises	Fall	Dollar weakens; that's inflationary
Leading indicators rise	Rise	Advance signals about economic rise or continued health; Federal Reserve may tighten credit
Housing starts rise	Rise	Growing economy, increased new housing demand; Federal Reserve Bank may tighten credit
Personal income rises	Rise	Means higher consumer spending, thus inflationary; Federal Reserve may tighten credit
Inflation		
Consumer Price Index rises	Rise	Inflation is increasing
Producer Price Index rises	Rise	Early signal for inflation increase
Monetary Policy		
Money supply rises	Rise	Excess growth in money supply is inflationary; Federal Reserve may tighten credit
Fed Funds Rate rises	Rise	Increase in business and consumer loan rates; used by Federal Reserve to slow economic growth and inflation
Fed buys bills	Rise	Removes money from the economy; interest rates move up
Required reserve rises	Rise	Depresses bank lending by requiring them to hold more reserves

*This table is simply a handy guide and should not be construed as perfectly accurate.**When these indicators fall, bond yields rise.***NOTE: Because the effects are based on yield, they are the opposite of how bond prices will be affected.

KEEPING TRACK OF THE ECONOMY WITH INDICATORS

To sort out the confusing mix of statistics that flow almost daily from the government and to help you keep track of what's going on in the economy, we'll examine the indicators you should watch. Economic and monetary indicators attempt to size up where the economy seems to be headed and where it's been. Each month government agencies, including the Federal Reserve, and economic institutions publish various indicators.

Purchasing Manager's Index

The Factory Order Series presents new orders received by manufacturers of durable goods other than military equipment. Durable goods are defined as those having a useful life of more than three years. (Military equipment is excluded because new orders for such items do not respond directly to the business cycle.)

Non-defense equipment represents one-fifth to one-third of all durable goods production. The series includes engines; construction, mining, and materials handling equipment; office and store machinery; electrical transmission and distribution equipment; and other electrical machinery (excluding household appliances and electronic equipment); and railroad, marine, and aircraft transportation equipment. The monthly *Purchasing Index* from the National Association of Purchasing Management tells about buying intentions of corporate purchasing agents.

The Factory Order Series is released by the Department of Commerce. Each month, more than 2,000 companies are asked to file a report covering orders, inventories and shipments. The results can be found at *www.census.gov/econ/* on the Internet.

Economists typically count on factory production, particularly of big-ticket durable goods ranging from airplanes to home appliances, to help lift the economy. A decline in this series suggests that factories are unlikely to hire new workers. A drop in the backlog of unfilled orders also indicates possible production cutbacks and layoffs. On the other hand, the wider dispersal of gains in many types of goods is looked upon as a favorable sign for the economic recovery. The broader the dispersal of order increases, the broader the rehiring.

Purchasing managers are responsible for buying the raw materials that feed the nation's factories. Their buying patterns are considered a good indication of the direction of the economy. A reading of 50 or more percent indicates that the manufacturing economy is generally expanding. A continuing reading above 44.5% indicates that the overall economy is augmenting.

Gross Domestic Product (GDP)

Gross Domestic Product (GDP), which measures the value of all goods and services produced by the economy within its boundaries, is the broadest gauge of national economic health. The Department of Commerce compiles GDP, which is reported as a "real" figure, that is, economic growth minus the impact of inflation.

GDP is normally stated in annual terms, though data are compiled and released quarterly in the month after a quarter has ended. It's then revised at least twice, with those revisions being reported in the second and third months after the original release. GDP reports appears in most daily newspapers and online at services like America Online and the federal government statistics Web site at *www.fedstats.gov/.*

GDP is often a measure of the state of the economy. For example, many economists speak of recession when there has been a decline in GDP for two consecutive quarters. An expected GDP growth rate of 3 percent in real terms would be very attractive for long-term investment and would affect the stock market positively. Since inflation and price increases are detrimental to equity prices, a real growth of GDP without inflation is favorable and desirable.

Figure 3-3 charts a series of events leading from a rising GDP to higher security prices.

FIGURE 3-3: EFFECT OF CHANGE IN GDP ON STOCK PRICES

GDP Up ====> Corporate Profits Up ====> Dividends Up ====> Stock Prices Up.

Generally, too much growth is inflationary and thus negative for the stock and bond markets. Growing companies need workers desperately and are willing to pay big wages to attract and keep new workers. But because these wage increases raise business costs, they lead firms to raise prices and must be avoided. Too little production is undesirable as well. Low production mean layoffs, unemployment, low incomes for workers, and a depressed stock market.

Investors watching for signs of inflation should check the "deflator" portion of the GDP report. That contains what some experts feel is the most detailed government tracking of price pressures.

Housing Starts and Construction Spending

Housing is a key interest-sensitive sector that usually leads the rest of the economy out of recession. Also, housing is vital to broader economic revival not only because of its benefits for other industries but also because it signals consumer confidence about making long-term financial commitments.

The housing starts indicator (see Figure 3-4) estimates the number of dwelling units, both new homes and apartments, on which construction has begun during a stated period. This indicates the future strength of the housing sector of the economy. At the same time, it's closely related to interest rates and other basic economic factors. When the economy is about to take a downturn, the housing sector is the first to decline.

The statistics for construction spending covers homes, office buildings, and other construction projects.

Both housing starts and construction spending are issued monthly by the Department of Commerce; look for them on the Federal Government Statistics Web site *(www.fedstats.gov)*. National business daily newspapers and many local newspaper report on these property-related figures, as does any reliable Internet-based financial news service.

Index of Leading Indicators

The Index of Leading Indicators consists of indicators that tend to predict future economic activity. It was designed to reveal the direction of the economy in the next six to nine months. The meld of 10 economic yardsticks has shown a tendency to change before the economy makes a major turn; hence the term "leading indicators."

This index is calculated and published monthly by the Conference Board. It covers:

- *Average weekly hours for U.S. manufacturing workers.* Employers find it a lot easier to increase the number of hours employees work in a week than to hire more employees.

FIGURE 3-4: NEW HOUSING UNITS STARTED IN THE UNITED STATES

(Seasonally Adjusted Annual Rate)

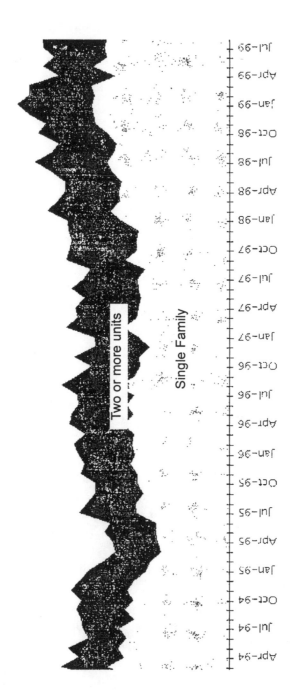

Source: U.S. Census Bureau

- *Average weekly initial claims for unemployment insurance.* The number of people who sign up for unemployment benefits tells you how much employers need workers.

- *Manufacturers' new orders, consumer goods and materials.* New orders mean more workers hired, more materials and supplies purchased, and increased output. Gains in this series usually lead recoveries by as much as four months.

FIGURE 3-5: INDEX OF LEADING INDICATORS

Leading Index Slips Slightly in August

Topic:	Economic Research and Analysis
Description:	The leading index decreased 0.1 percent, the coincident index increased 0.2 percent, and the lagging index increased 0.2 percent in August. Taken together, the three composite indexes and their components show a healthy economy
Press Release Date:	05 Oct 99

THE CONFERENCE BOARD NEWS LEADING ECONOMIC INDICATORS FOR WIRE TRANSMISSION: 10:00 A.M. ET, TUESDAY, OCTOBER 5, 1999

Composite Indexes Of Leading, Coincident, and Lagging Indicators: August 1999

The leading index decreased 0.1 percent, the coincident index increased 0.2 percent, and the lagging index increased 0.2 percent in August. Taken together, the three composite indexes and their components show a healthy economy:

--The coincident indicators point to GDP rising at a pace of 3.0 percent (annualized) in the 3rd quarter of 1999.

--The leading indicators point to a continuation of the expansion through early 2000.

--Cyclical imbalances and related economic instability problems do not seem to be a problem yet.

LEADING INDICATORS. Five of the ten indicators that make up the leading index rose in August. The most significant positive contributor to the composite leading index in August is average weekly claims for unemployment insurance. The most significant decreases-in order from the largest negative contributor to the smallest-are vendor performance (slower deliveries), stock prices, and average weekly hours in manufacturing.

With the decrease of 0.1 percent in August, the leading index stands at 107.9 (1992 equals 100). This index increased 0.3 percent in July and June (the same values as reported last month). During the six-month span through August, the leading index rose 0.7 percent, and eight of the ten components advanced (diffusion index, six-month span equals 80 percent).

Source: The Conferece Board

- *Vendor performance, slower deliveries diffusion index.* As the economy grows, firms have more trouble filling orders.

- *Manufacturers' new orders, non-defense capital goods.* Factories will employ more people as demand for big-ticket items increases, especially those not bought by the government, stays strong.

- *Building permits, new private housing units.* Optimistic builders are often a good sign for the economy.

- *Stock prices, 500 common stocks.* Stock market advances usually precede business upturns by three to eight months.

- *Money supply, M2.* A rising money supply means easy money, which sparks brisk economic activity. This usually leads recoveries by as much as 14 months.

- *Interest rate spread, 10-year Treasury bonds minus federal funds rate.* A steep yield curve, when long-term interest rates are much higher than short-term ones, is a sign of healthy economic outlook.

- *Consumer expectations index.* Consumers spend buys two-thirds of GNP (all goods and services produced in the economy), so any sharp change in their expectations could be an important factor in the economic outlook.

The monthly report is well covered by daily business publications, major newspapers, business TV shows, and financial Web sites (see especially the Conference Board's Web site, *www.conference-board.com*). If the index is consistently rising, even only slightly, the economy is chugging along and a setback is unlikely. If the indicator drops for three or more consecutive months, look for an economic slowdown and possibly a recession in the next year or so.

A rising indicator (consecutive percentage increases) is bullish for the economy and the stock market, and vice versa. Falling index results could be good news for bondholders looking to make capital gains from falling interest rates.

The press often states that three consecutive downward movements in the leading indicators signal a recession, but the Conference Board doesn't endorse such a simple, inflexible rule. Conference Board studies show that a 1% decline (2% when annualized) in the leading index, coupled with declines in a majority of the 10 components, provides a reliable, but not perfect, recession signal.

Industrial Production, Capacity, and Utilization (Figure 3-6)

The Federal Reserve Board Index of Industrial Production measures changes in the output of the mining, manufacturing, and gas and electric utilities sectors of the economy. Detailed breakdowns provide a reading on how individual industries are faring. Industrial production is narrower than GDP because it omits agriculture, construction, wholesale and retail trade, transportation, communications, services, finance, and government.

Another way to view the performance of the real economy is to look at industrial production relative to the production capacity of the industrial sector. The actual production level as a percent of the full capacity level is called the rate of capacity utilization.

Data for the monthly production index is drawn from 250 data series obtained from private trade associations and internal estimates and is released only two weeks into the next month. The rate of capacity utilization is announced every month by the Fed, one day after the Index of Industrial Production. Both are published in the *Federal Reserve Bulletin* and appear in major daily newspapers and on online computer news services such as America Online. They can be obtained free from the Federal Reserve Web site *(www.bog.frb.fed.us)*.

A rising index is a sign that the economy will strengthen and that the stock market should turn up. Falling industrial production should be a concern, for both the economy and the investor. Regardless of the state of the economy, however, detailed breakdowns of the index provide a reading on how individual industries are faring and on what industries investors should pay attention to.

Rising capacity utilization is positive for the economy and the stock market; a falling rate indicating a sinking economy is negative for the stock market.

Inflation

Inflation is the general rise in prices of consumer goods and services. The federal government measures inflation with four key indexes: Consumer

FIGURE 3-6: INDUSTRIAL PRODUCTION, CAPACITY, AND UTILIZATION

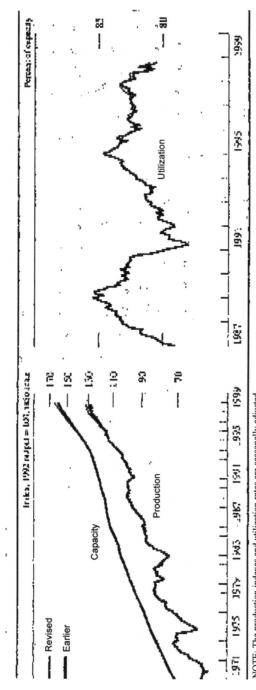

NOTE: The production indexes and utilization rates are seasonally adjusted. All the revised measures extend through November 1998; the earlier measures extend through October 1998.

Source: Federal Reserve Bulletin

Price Index (CPI), Producer Price Index (PPI), Gross Domestic Product (GDP), and the Deflator and Employment Cost Index (ECI).

Various price indexes are used to measure living costs, price level changes, and inflation. They are:

- *The Consumer Price Index* (CPI) (see Figure 3-7), the best-known inflation gauge, is used as the cost-of-living index, to which labor contracts and Social Security payments are tied. The CPI measures the cost of buying a fixed bundle of goods (some 400 consumer goods and services), representative of the purchases of the typical working-class urban family. The fixed basket categories are: food and beverages, housing, apparel, transportation, medical care, entertainment, and other. Generally referred to as the cost-of-living index, the CPI is published by the U.S. Bureau of Labor Statistics (BLS). The CPI is widely used for escalation clauses. The base year for the CPI index was 1982-84, at which time the base was set at 100. This index can be obtained free from the BLS Web site *(stats.bls.gov)*.

FIGURE 3-7: ECONOMY AT A GLANCE

A text version of this page is also available.

		Sept 1998	Oct 1998	Nov 1998	Dec 1998	Jan 1999	Feb 1999	Mar 1999	Apr 1999	May 1999	June 1999	July 1999	Aug 1999	Sept 1999
Labor Market														
Civilian Labor Force (1)		138,081	138,116	138,193	138,547	139,347	139,271	138,816	139,091	139,019	139,408	139,254	139,264	139,386
Unemployment (1)		6,263	6,258	6,080	6,021	5,950	6,127	5,783	6,022	5,795	5,975	5,947	5,853	5,836
Unemployment Rate (2)		4.5	4.5	4.4	4.3	4.3	4.4	4.2	4.3	4.2	4.3	4.3	4.2	4.2
Employees on Nonfarm Payrolls (1)		126,361	126,567	126,841	127,186	127,378	127,730	127,813	128,134	128,162	128,443	128,816	128,919(p)	128,911(p)
Hours, Earnings and Productivity														
Average Weekly Hours (3)		34.5	34.6	34.6	34.6	34.6	34.6	34.5	34.4	34.4	34.5	34.5	34.5(p)	34.4(p)
Average Hourly Earnings (3)		12.88	12.91	12.94	12.98	13.04	13.06	13.11	13.14	13.18	13.24	13.28	13.30(p)	13.37(p)
Employment Cost Index (4)		0.9		0.7			0.4			1.1			0.8	
Productivity (5)		2.7		4.1			3.6			0.6				
Prices														
Consumer Price Index (6)		0.1	0.2	0.2	0.1	0.1	0.1	0.2	0.7	0.0	0.0	0.3	0.3	0.4
Producer Price Index (7)		0.2	0.3	-0.2	0.5	0.3	-0.5	0.3	0.5	0.2	-0.1	0.2	0.5	1.1

Source: Bureau of Labor Statistics

- *Producer Price Index:* Like the CPI (see Figure 3-7), the PPI is a measure of the cost of a given basket of goods, but these are priced in wholesale markets; they include raw materials, semi-finished goods, and finished goods at the early stage of the distribution system. The PPI is also published monthly by the BLS. The PPI signals changes in the general price level or the CPI some time before they actually materialize. (Since the PPI doesn't include services, caution should be exercised when the principal cause of inflation is service prices). For this reason, the PPI and especially some of its subindexes, such as the index of sensitive materials, are closely watched by policy makers. This index can be obtained free from the BLS Web site *(stats.bls.gov).*

- *GDP Deflator* (Figure 3-8): This is used to separate price changes in GDP calculations from real changes in economic activity. The deflator is a weighted average of the price indexes used to deflate GDP so true economic growth can be separated from inflationary growth. Thus, it reflects price changes for goods and services bought by consumers, businesses, and governments. Because it covers a broader group of goods and services than the CPI and PPI, the GDP deflator is a widely used to measure inflation. The deflator, unlike the CPI and PPI, is available only quarterly. It can be obtained free from the U.S. Bureau of Economic Analysis' Web site *(www.bea.doc.gov).*

The *Employment Cost Index* is the most comprehensive and refined measure of underlying trends in employee compensation as a cost of production. It measures the cost of labor, including changes in wages and salaries and employer costs for employee benefits. ECI tracks wages and bonuses, sick and vacation pay, and benefits like insurance, pension and Social Security and unemployment taxes from a survey of 18,300 occupations at 4,500 sample establishments in private industry and 4,200 occupations within about 800 state and local governments. Federal Reserve Chairman Alan Greenspan is a big fan of the ECI as a good measure of whether wage pressures are sparking inflation. You can find this index on the BLS Web site *(stats.bls.gov).*

Price indexes get major coverage in daily newspapers and business dailies, on business television programs, cable and satellite channels *(e.g.,* CNN/fn and CNBC), and on Internet financial news services. Other gov-

FIGURE 3-8: GDP DEFLATOR

Table 4.—Chain-Type Price Indexes for Gross Domestic Product and Related Measures: Percent Change From Preceding Period
[Percent; quarters seasonally adjusted at annual rates]

	1996	1997	III 95	IV 95	I 96	II 96	III 96	IV 96	I 97	II 97	III 97	IV 97	I 98	II 98	III 98	IV 98	I 99	II 99r
Gross domestic product (GDP)	1.9	1.9	1.0	1.9	2.2	1.4	1.8	1.6	2.8	1.7	1.2	1.1	.9	.9	1.0	.8	1.6	1.3
Personal consumption expenditures	2.0	1.9	.8	1.8	2.2	2.5	1.5	2.5	2.5	1.1	1.3	1.1	-1.0	-1.8	-1.9	-1.1	-1.2	-.7
Durable goods	-.9	-2.0	-2.3	-1.3	.6	-2.1	-1.5	-1.8	-2.9	-2.5	-2.8	-2.4	-1.4	-2.2	-2.5	-2.5	-3.3	-2.1
Nondurable goods	.0	1.5	.0	-.8	3.0	-.1	.3	3.6	2.0	.9	.9	.9	-2.2	1.9	.9	.9	1.4	5.3
Services	2.7	2.9	1.9	2.9	2.1	3.0	2.7	2.9	3.5	2.8	2.5	1.9	1.4	1.9	1.7	1.9	2.2	1.7
Gross private domestic investment	-.3	-.3	-1.3	-.1	-1.0	-.8	.7	.1	-.7	.5	-.5	-.5	-2.3	-1.8	-1.9	-.6	-.8	-.4
Fixed investment	-.1	-.2	-1.3	-.1	-1.5	-.6	.7	-.6	-.5	-.5	-.5	-.5	-2.1	-1.8	-1.6	-1.6	-.8	-.4
Nonresidential	-.9	-1.9	-2.4	-.7	-1.5	-1.5	-.5	-1.1	-1.7	-1.1	-1.0	-1.6	-3.0	-3.1	-2.6	-2.5	-2.0	-1.4
Structures	2.6	3.4	-2.8	2.8	2.1	2.2	4.1	3.1	1.7	-.9	-.9	3.3	2.7	3.1	1.8	1.8	.9	2.8
Producers' durable equipment	-2.2	-3.0	-4.3	-2.0	-2.9	-2.9	-2.2	-2.6	-3.6	-3.2	-2.9	-2.2	-5.0	-5.2	-4.0	-4.0	-3.0	-2.9
Residential	1.9	2.6	2.1	1.5	1.1	1.6	4.3	1.9	2.3	1.9	1.9	2.4	.0	1.7	3.7	4.2	2.2	3.3
Change in business inventories (CBI)	...	...	...	...	...	...	...	...	...	...	...	...	...	...	...	...	...	...
Net exports of goods and services	...	...	...	...	...	...	...	...	...	...	...	...	...	...	...	...	...	...
Exports	-1.7	-2.0	-2.2	-1.8	-1.2	-1.7	-3.2	-4.2	-1.0	-1.8	-1.0	-1.6	-3.4	-1.8	-.9	-2.4	-1.6	-.2
Goods	-3.5	-3.5	-3.2	-3.1	-3.4	-2.6	-5.6	-7.2	-2.5	-.9	-2.5	-2.7	-4.7	-3.0	-2.4	-2.6	-1.9	-1.5
Services	2.7	1.8	.6	1.3	4.6	-.6	3.1	3.5	.9	-4.4	2.7	1.5	-10.4	1.1	2.6	-4.8	2.6	-1.0
Imports	-2.2	-3.7	-5.3	-3.9	-1.8	-1.5	-5.2	-3.3	-4.4	-7.1	-1.3	-2.3	-11.3	-4.5	-4.8	-5.8	-3.4	4.5
Goods	-2.9	-4.2	-6.0	-4.2	-2.4	-2.1	-6.4	-1.8	-3.0	-4.6	-8.5	-2.2	-11.3	-5.9	-6.7	-5.8	-3.4	4.5
Services	1.6	-.6	-1.4	2.0	1.5	1.4	1.9	2.0	-3.0	-3.0	.3	-2.6	1.8	2.7	-.4	-.7	9.1	1.0
Government consumption expenditures and gross investment	2.5	2.2	1.3	2.2	4.3	-1.2	2.4	2.7	3.8	1.2	.8	2.2	1.1	.8	1.5	1.5	3.1	3.0
Federal	2.9	2.0	1.1	2.5	4.2	-2.1	1.8	2.7	4.8	.3	-.2	1.4	2.7	.0	-.4	1.5	6.6	.8
National defense	3.3	1.8	1.1	2.7	6.7	-5.9	1.9	2.7	4.0	.9	-.7	1.2	2.2	-.3	.4	1.8	6.0	1.0
Nondefense	2.2	2.4	.6	2.1	-7.3	-.6	1.5	2.8	3.3	1.7	.4	1.4	.2	-.6	-.6	2.1	1.3	4.2
State and local	2.2	2.2	1.4	1.9	2.3	1.4	2.7	2.8	3.3	1.1	1.4	2.7	1.4	1.2	2.1	1.5	1.3	4.2
Addenda:																		
Final sales of domestic product	1.9	1.9	1.1	1.9	2.3	1.4	1.9	1.7	2.8	1.8	1.8	1.2	.9	.9	1.0	.8	1.6	1.4
(GDP less CBI)	1.8	1.6	.6	1.6	1.8	1.4	1.5	2.1	2.2	.9	1.1	1.0	-.2	.4	.7	.9	1.2	1.9
Gross domestic purchases	1.8	1.6	.6	1.6	2.2	1.4	1.5	2.1	2.3	2.1	1.1	1.0	-.1	.5	.7	.9	1.1	2.0
Final sales to domestic purchasers	1.9	1.8	1.0	1.9	2.2	1.4	1.8	1.6	2.7	1.6	1.2	1.1	.9	.8	1.0	.9	1.2	1.3
Gross national product (GNP)	1.9	1.8	1.0	1.9	2.2	1.4	1.8	1.6	2.8	1.7	1.2	1.2	.9	.9	1.0	.8	1.6	1.3
Implicit price deflators:																		
GDP	1.9	1.9	1.0	1.9	2.3	1.2	1.8	1.8	2.8	1.6	1.2	1.2	.8	.9	1.0	.8	1.6	1.3
Gross domestic purchases	1.8	1.6	.6	1.6	2.1	1.2	1.6	2.2	2.2	.8	1.1	1.1	.2	.9	.9	.9	1.6	1.9
GNP	1.9	1.8	1.0	1.9	2.3	1.2	1.8	1.8	2.8	1.5	1.2	1.2	.8	.8	1.0	.8	1.6	1.3

r revised

See "Explanatory Note" at the end of the tables.

Source: U.S. Department of Commerce—Bureau of Economic Analysis

ernment Web sites, like the Census Bureau's *(www.census. gov/econ/www)* also provide this data.

Check to see whether the inflation rate has been rising—a negative, or bearish, sign for stock and bond investors—or falling, which is bullish.

Rising prices are Public Enemy No.1 for stocks and bonds. Inflation usually hurts stock prices, since higher consumer prices lessen the value of future corporate earnings, which make shares of those companies less appealing to investors. When prices rocket ahead, investors often flock to long-term inflation hedges such as real estate. Figure 3-9 displays the chain of events leading from lower rates of inflation to increased consumer spending, and possibly an up stock market:

When demand for goods is so weak that merchants have to brutally slash prices just to stay in business, that's deflation. It leads to layoffs and recession. That's bad for stock investors as profits shrink, but it's good for bond holders—as long as they own a bond backed by an issuer who can pay it back.

Money Supply

Money supply is the level of funds available at a given time for conducting transactions, as reported by the Federal Reserve (Figure 3-10).

There are several categories of money supply: M1 (currency in circulation, demand deposits, traveler's checks, and money in interest-bearing accounts), M2 (the most widely followed measure, equals M1 plus savings deposits, money market deposit accounts, and money market funds), M3 (M2 plus large certificates of deposit), MZM (Money Zero Maturity, includes immediately available components of M3), and L (M3 plus Treasury bills, commercial paper, banker's acceptances and savings bonds).

The Federal Reserve System computes these measures. The weekly money supply figures are released on Thursday afternoons and reported in daily newspapers, including the *Wall Street Journal*.

Rapid growth in money supply is viewed as inflationary; a sharp drop is considered recessionary. Moderate growth is thought to have a positive impact on the economy. Economists attempt to compare money supply figures with targets proposed by the Fed.

The Federal Reserve Bank affects money supply through its monetary policy such as open market operations:

- *Easy money policy:* The Fed buys securities *so* bank reserves rise *so* bank lending is up *so* money supply is up *so* interest rates are down as bond prices rise *so* loan demand goes up *so* the stock market rises.

- *Tight money policy:* The Fed sells securities *so* bank reserves fall *so* bank lending is down *so* money supply is down *so* interest rates are up as bond prices fall *so* loan demand is down *so* the stock market falls.

FIGURE 3-9: RELATIONSHIP BETWEEN INFLATION AND THE STOCK MARKET

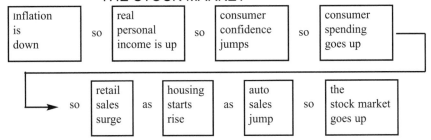

FIGURE 3-10: MONEY SUPPLY

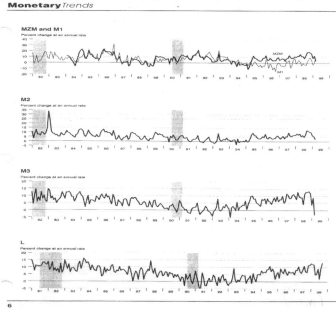

Source: Monetary Trends

Interest Rates

Interest rates represent the costs of borrowing and the value of fixed-income investments such as bonds. Rising interest rates depress values of fixed-income securities, while falling rates boost their prices. High interest rates tend to adversely affect the equity market as well.

NOTE: The basic rule to remember for investing in fixed-income securities such as a bond is this: Prices move inversely to movement in rates.

Rising interest rates send stock prices down for two reasons:

1. Higher rates mean bigger borrowing expenses for companies, which erode corporate profits and in turn depress stock prices.

2. Share values fall because high interest rates lure investors away from stocks into interest-paying investments such as money market funds.

Interest rates are controlled by the Federal Reserve Board's monetary policy. Among the Fed's monetary policy tools are: (1) changes in the required reserve ratio; (2) changes in the discount rate; and (3) open market operations—that is, purchase and sale of government securities.

The reserve requirement is that for every $100 cash in a savings account, the bank must keep $10 in cash; it can loan out $90. If the Fed raises the reserve requirement, the bank can make fewer loans, business activity will slow, and there will be a brake on economic growth.

The *discount rate* is the interest rate the Fed charges its member banks to cover their requirement. If the bank's reserves fall below the required level, the bank can borrow reserves from the Fed—for a price. Raise the discount rate, and banks will be loathe to loan up to their limit, just as when the reserve requirement is raised. More important, most institutional lenders index their loan rates to the Fed's discount rate. Therefore, an increase in the discount rate will send all interest rates up.

Cuts in the discount rate are aimed at stimulating the economy—a positive development for stocks. Figure 3-11 summarizes the effect on the economy of cutting the discount rate.

These are some of the more important interest rates (see also Figure 3-12):

FIGURE 3-11: THE EFFECTS OF LOWERING THE DISCOUNT RATE

The Players	The Federal Reserve is Nation's Bank. It regulates the flow of money through the economy.
The Action	Discount rate is what The Federal Reserve charges on short-term loans to member banks. When The Fed cuts the discount rate, it means banks can get cash cheaper and thus charge less on loans.
The First Effect	Within a few days, banks start passing on the discounts by cutting their prime rate, which is what bans charge on loans to their best corporate customers.
Impact	Businesses are more likely to borrow. Second, adjustable consumer loans are tied to the prime, such as credit card rates. These become cheaper, stimulating spending.
The Second Effect	Within a few weeks, rate on Mortgage, auto, and construction loans drop.
The Third Effect	The lower rates go, the more investors move their cash to stocks, creating new wealth.
The Goal	To kick start the economy. If lower interest rates cause businesses to start growing gain, laid-off workers get jobs, retailers start selling, and the economy starts to roll again.

FIGURE 3-12: INTEREST RATES

	Last	Wk. ago
Prime Rate	8.25	8.25
Discount Rate	4.75	4.75
Fed Funds close	5.1875	5.3125
T-Bills:		
3-month	4.79	4.70
6-month	5.08	4.82
T-Bill, annualized, adjusted for constant maturity:		
1-year	5.24	5.23
T-Notes:		
1-year	n-a	5.37
2-year	n-a	5.67
5-year	n-a	5.82
10-year	n-a	5.93
T-Bond		
30-year	6.19	6.08
Libor:		
3-month	6.17	6.12
6-month	6.08	6.00
FHLB Const of Funds, 11th District:		
Eff. Sept. 30	4.562	4.562
FNMA 30-year mortgage commitment:		
30-days	7.83	7.83
Money market fund:		
Merrill Lynch Ready Assets:		
30-day avg. yld.	4.79	4.76

Source: Orange County Register

- **Prime Rate**—the rate banks charge their best customers for short-term loans. This is a bellwether rate: It's construed as a sign of rising or falling loan demand and economic activity.

- **Federal Funds Rate**—the rate on short-term loans among commercial banks for overnight use. The Fed influences this rate by open market operations and by changing the required reserve for banks.

- **Discount Rate**—what the Fed charges depository institutions on loans. A change in the discount rate is considered a major economic event; it's expected to have an impact on security prices, especially bonds. A change in the prime rate usually follows the change in the discount rate.

- **90-Day Treasury Bills**—This yield signals the direction of short-term rates, a closely watched indicator.

- **5-Year and 10-Year Treasury Notes**—The yields on these notes give you an idea of the prevailing interest rates for intermediate-term fixed-income securities.

- **30-Year Treasury Bonds**—This yield, also called the long bond yield, is a closely watched indicator of long-term interest rates, since the entire bond market (and sometimes the stock market as well) often moves in line with this rate.

The Federal Reserve Bank of St. Louis charts these key rates and others (Figure 3-13). National, regional, and financial newspapers regularly report them.

You can discern broad trends by focusing on two rates:

1. *The prime rate* is what banks charge their best customers for short-term loans. When the prime rate is climbing, it means companies are borrowing heavily and the economy is still on an upward swing.

2. *The yield on 90-day* Treasury Bills: Sharp rises in yields on 90-day bills may signal a resurgence of inflation; the economy could be slowing down.

FIGURE 3-13: SELECTED INTEREST RATES

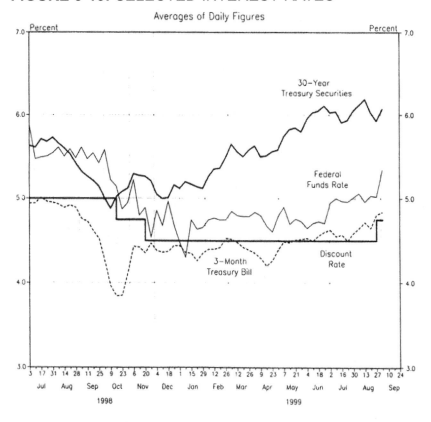

1999	Federal Funds **	3-Month Treasury Bill	1-Year Treasury Bill	5-Year Treasury Securities	10-Year Treasury Securities	30-Year Treasury Securities
Jun 11	4.71	4.50	4.84	5.81	5.89	6.03
18	4.73	4.56	4.77	5.80	5.91	6.05
25	4.71	4.61	4.85	5.88	5.98	6.11
Jul 2	4.95	4.63	4.84	5.76	5.87	6.03
9	5.00	4.55	4.78	5.75	5.87	6.04
16	4.97	4.57	4.72	5.61	5.72	5.91
23	4.96	4.50	4.71	5.61	5.72	5.94
30	5.01	4.59	4.80	5.75	5.86	6.05
Aug 6	5.06	4.65	4.85	5.86	5.95	6.12
13	4.96	4.72	4.94	5.97	6.08	6.19
20	5.03	4.65	4.91	5.81	5.91	6.03
27	5.02	4.81	4.91	5.71	5.81	5.93
Sep 3 •	5.34	4.84	5.01	5.87	5.97	6.07

Source: The Federal Reserve Bank of St. Louis, U.S. Financial Data

Personal Income and Confidence Indexes

Personal income shows the before-tax income received by individuals and unincorporated businesses, such as wages and salaries, rents, interest and dividends, and other payments such as unemployment and Social Security. Personal income data are released monthly by the Commerce Department.

Two popular indexes track consumer confidence: one is compiled by the Conference Board, an industry-sponsored, non-profit economic research institute, and the other by the University of Michigan's Survey Research Center. The Conference Board's Consumer Confidence Index (see Figures 3-14 and 3-15) measures consumer optimism and pessimism about general business conditions, jobs, and total family income. The University of Michigan's Index of Consumer Sentiment measures consumers' personal financial circumstances and their outlook for the future.

FIGURE 3-14: PERSONAL INCOME DATA

Press Release

Consumer Confidence Dips For Third Straight Month

Topic:	Economic Research and Analysis
Description:	The Consumer Confidence Index, which declined in both July and August, dipped again in September.
Press Release Date:	28 Sep 99

For Release 10 AM ET Tuesday, September 28, 1999 Release #4512

CONSUMER CONFIDENCE DIPS FOR THIRD STRAIGHT MONTH,

THE CONFERENCE BOARD REPORTS TODAY

BUT CONSUMER SPENDING PROJECTED TO REMAIN STRONG

September 28…The Consumer Confidence Index, which declined in both July and August, dipped again in September, The Conference Board reports today. The Consumer Confidence Index now reads 134.2 (1985=100), down from 136.0 in August.

The Expectations Index dropped to 105.7 in September, falling from 109.2 in August. The Present Situation Index improved moderately, rising to 177 in September, up from 176.3 last month.

The Consumer Confidence survey is based on a representative sample of 5,000 U.S. households. The monthly poll is conducted for The Conference Board by NFO Research, Inc., an NFO Worldwide Company (NYSE: NFO), of Greenwich, Connecticut.

NO LET-UP IN CONSUMER SPENDING

"Despite the September dip, confidence levels are still at historically high levels," says Lynn Franco, Director of The Conference Board's Consumer Research Center. "The latest figure is only five points off the June reading, with consumers generally optimistic about both the economy and job prospects. We anticipate no dramatic shifts soon in consumer spending patterns."

Source: The Conference Board

FIGURE 3-15: CONSUMER SENTIMENT

Consumer Sentiment (U. of Michigan)

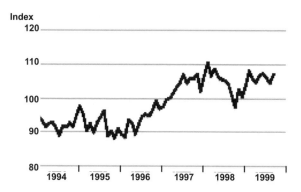

Source: National Economic Trends

The Conference Board index is derived from a survey of 5,000 households nationwide, with questions that range from home-buying plans to the outlook for jobs, both presently and during the next six months.

The University of Michigan index is compiled through a telephone survey of 500 households. Daily newspapers, financial television and online business news services such as America Online cover both surveys.

When personal income rises, it usually means that consumers will increase their purchases, which will in turn affect favorably the investment climate. The Conference Board index provides insight into consumer spending, which is critical to any sustainable economic upswing. Many economists pay close attention to it. Consumers account for two-thirds of the nation's economic activity (*i.e.,* GDP) and thus drive recovery and expansion.

Low or decreased consumer confidence indicates concern about employment prospects and earnings in the months ahead. Uncertainty requires cautions in investing. On the other hand, increased consumer confidence spells economic recovery and expansion, thus presenting an investment opportunity. In summary, an increase in personal income, coupled with substantial consumer confidence, is bullish for the economy and the stock market.

Productivity

Productivity measures the relationship between real output and the labor time required for its production, or output per hour of work. The Labor Department compiles productivity figures from the surveys that produce unemployment reports and the Commerce Department figures on GDP. Only business sector output—GDP minus government and not-for-profit organizations—is used in the productivity calculation.

Productivity measures reflect the effects of many influences, including changes in technology; capital investment; level of output; utilization of capacity, energy, and materials; the organization of production; managerial skill; and the characteristics and effort of the work force.

Daily newspapers, financial television, and online business news services cover these releases. The data are published in press releases, in BLS journals, and free on the BLS Web site *(stats.bls.gov)*.

Economists consider productivity the key to prosperity. Sizable gains mean companies can pay workers more, hold the line on prices, and still earn the kind of profits that keep stock prices rising. Increased productivity, getting more worker output per hour on the job, is considered vital to increasing the nation's standard of living without inflation.

Recession

Recession means a sinking economy. Unfortunately, there is no consensus definition and measure of recession. In general, it means that the economy is shrinking in size and that jobs lost outnumber jobs being created. Here are three primary signals of recession economists look for:

- Three or more straight monthly drops in the Index of Leading Economic Indicators

- Two consecutive quarterly drops in GDP

- Consecutive monthly drops of durable goods orders (which usually results in less production and increasing layoffs in the factory sector)

Newspapers, TV shows, and online services all try to guess when recessions start—and end.

Recession tends to dampen the spirits of consumers and investors and thus further depress prices of investment vehicles, including securities and real estate.

Retail Sales

This figure is the estimate of total sales at the retail level. Covering everything from bags of groceries to durable goods like automobiles (Figure 3-16), it's used as a measure of future economic conditions: A long slowdown in sales could spell cuts in production. Reports are issued monthly by the Commerce Department, which conducts a mail survey of about 4,100 merchants. The previous month's sales figure is an estimate of sales activity based on percentage changes by industry aggregates from older, revised, and more reliable data derived from larger samplings. The median revision is a change of two-tenths of a percentage point in sales.

Daily newspapers, financial television, and online business news services cover these releases. Commerce Department statistics can be found free at *www.census.gov/econ/www.*

Retail sales are a major concern of analysts because they represent about half of overall consumer spending. Consumer spending, in turn, accounts for about two-thirds of GDP. The amount of retail sales depends heavily on consumer confidence about the economy.

Unemployment Rate, Initial Jobless Claims, and Help-Wanted Index

Unemployment means that there are no jobs for people able and willing to work at the prevailing wage rate. The *unemployment rate* is the number of unemployed workers divided by total employed and unemployed who constitute the labor force. It's an important measure of economic health, since full employment is generally construed as a desired goal. When the economic indicators are mixed, many analysts consider the unemployment rate the most important.

Weekly *initial claims for unemployment* benefits are another closely watched indicator, along with the unemployment rate, to judge the jobless situation in the economy.

The *help wanted advertising index* tracks employers' advertisements of openings in the classified section of newspapers in 50 or so labor markets. The index represents job vacancies resulting from turnover, as work-

FIGURE 3.16: MONTHLY TRADE SURVEY

U.S. Census Bureau

MONTHLY RETAIL TRADE SURVEY

1999 Retail Sales

In millions of dollars

SIC	KIND OF BUSINESS	JAN	FEB	MAR	APR	MAY	JUN	JUL	AUG P/	TOTAL
	UNADJUSTED									
	RETAIL SALES, TOTAL	209,407	212,492	244,435	242,695	254,372	252,188	254,556	256,882	1,927,027
	TOTAL (EXCL. AUTOMOTIVE DEALERS)	158,474	157,085	178,427	179,531	188,266	184,583	187,795	188,865	1,423,026
	DURABLE GOODS, TOTAL	84,709	89,961	105,523	104,015	109,416	110,911	109,530	110,934	824,999
52	BUILDING MATERIALS GROUP STORES	10,879	11,665	14,526	16,799	17,916	17,538	16,840	16,039	122,202
521,3,5	BUILDING MATERIALS, SUPPLY, HARDWARE STORES	9,510	9,919	12,356	13,821	14,347	14,444	14,248	13,775	102,420
521,3	BUILDING MATERIALS, SUPPLY STORES	8,419	8,919	11,150	12,408	12,853	12,997	12,861	12,484	92,091
525	HARDWARE STORES	1,091	1,000	1,206	1,413	1,494	1,447	1,387	1,291	10,329
55 EX 554	AUTOMOTIVE DEALERS	50,933	55,407	66,008	63,164	66,106	67,605	66,761	68,017	504,001
551,2,5,6,7,9	MOTOR VEHICLE AND MISC. AUTOMOTIVE DEALERS	48,182	52,707	62,759	59,842	62,798	64,185	63,274	64,515	478,262
551,2	MOTOR VEHICLE DEALERS	46,229	49,937	58,911	55,708	58,370	59,823	59,230	60,838	449,046

Source: U.SCensus Bureau

ers change jobs or retire and as new jobs are created. The help-wanted figures are seasonally adjusted.

These indexes are often reported in daily newspapers, business dailies, and business TV shows, and through online services. Labor Department releases can be accessed free at stats.bls.gov.

An increase in employment, a decrease in initial jobless claims, and a decrease in unemployment are favorable for the economy and the stock market; the opposite situation is unfavorable. The help-wanted index is inversely related to unemployment. When help-wanted advertisements increase, unemployment declines, while a decline in help-wanted advertisements is accompanied by a rise in unemployment. The effect of unemployment on the economy is summarized in Figure 3-17.

FIGURE 3-17: UNEMPLOYMENT EFFECTS

- **Less Tax Revenue:** Fewer jobs means less income tax to the state and nation, which means a bigger U.S. government deficit. This forces states to cut programs to balance their budgets.

- **Higher Government Costs:** When people lose jobs, they often must turn to government benefits.

- **Less Consumer Spending:** Without a job, individuals can not afford to buy cars, computers, houses, or vacations.

- **Empty Stores:** Retailers and homebuilders can not absorb lower sales for long. Soon they have to lay off workers and, in more serious shortfalls, file for bankruptcy.

- **Manufacturing Cuts:** The companies that make consumer products or housing materials are forced to cut jobs, too, as sales of their goods fall.

- **Real Estate Pain:** As companies fail and as individuals struggle, mortgages and other bank loans go unpaid. That causes real estate values to go down and pummels lenders. One reason for the S&L crisis was the high number of defaulted loans from the recession of the early 1990s.

U.S. Balance Of Payments and the Value of the Dollar

The balance of payments is a systematic record of a country's receipts from, or payments to, other countries. In a way, it's like the balance sheets for a business but on a national level. The references you see in the media to the balance of trade usually refer to goods but not services. It's also known as merchandise or "visible" trade because it consists of tangibles like foodstuffs, manufactured goods, and raw materials. *Services,* the other part of the category, is known as "invisible" trade; it consists of intangibles like interest or dividends, technology transfers, services like insurance, transportation, or financial, and so forth.

When both the current account and the capital account yield more credits than debits, the country is said to have a surplus in its balance of payments. When there are more debits than credits, the country has a deficit in the balance of payments.

Persisting balance of payments deficits generally depress the value of the dollar and can boost inflation because a weak dollar makes foreign goods relatively expensive, often allowing U.S. makers of similar products to raise prices as well.

The U.S. Customs Service collects trade data. Figures are reported in seasonally adjusted volumes and dollar amounts. This is the only non-survey, non-judgmental report produced by the Department of Commerce. Foreign exchange rates are compiled from trading activity both in bulk transactions among dealers and in commodity markets trading forward contracts.

Trade figures and foreign exchange rates are quoted daily in business dailies as well as major newspapers, on computer services, and on financial TV networks and specialty shows.

It's necessary for an investor to know the condition of the country's balance of payments because resulting inflation will affect the market.

What is better, a strong dollar or a weak dollar? The answer, unfortunately, is "it depends." A strong dollar makes Americans' cash go further overseas and reduces import prices—generally good for U.S. consumers and for foreign manufacturers. If the dollar is overvalued, U.S. products are harder to sell abroad and at home, where they compete with low-cost imports. This helps give the U.S. its huge trade deficit.

A weak dollar can restore competitiveness to American products by making foreign goods comparatively more expensive. But too weak a dollar can spawn inflation, first through higher import prices and then through spiraling prices for all goods. Even worse, a falling dollar can drive foreign investors away from U.S. securities, which lose value along with the dollar. A strong dollar can be induced by interest rates. Relatively higher interest rates abroad will attract dollar-denominated investments that will raise the value of the dollar.

Those Americans owning foreign investments must watch the dollar carefully. A weak dollar makes overseas investments more valuable because assets sold in the foreign currency will yield more dollars. Conversely, a strong dollar will hurt the values of an American's overseas holdings. Assets priced overseas in the strong dollar scenario would cost fewer dollars due to the depressed local currency.

Figure 3-18 summarizes the impacts of changes in foreign exchange rates on various aspects of the economy.

FIGURE 3-18: THE IMPACTS OF CHANGES IN FOREIGN EXCHANGE RATES

	Weak Currency (Depreciation)	Strong Currency (Appreciation)
Imports	More expensive	Cheaper
Exports	Cheaper	More expensive
Payables	More expensive	Cheapter
Receivables	Cheaper	More expensive
Inflation	Fuels inflation by making imports more costly	Low inflation
Foreign investment	Discourages foreign investment Lower return on investments	High interest rates could attract foregin investors.
The Effect	Raising interests could slow down the economy.	Reduced exports could trigger a trade deficit.

Federal Deficit

When the government spends more than it collects in taxes, it borrows the difference. That drains the nation's savings, which should be used to finance investments—the source of economic growth. Heavy federal borrowing, on top of heavy borrowing by households and businesses, drives up interest rates. High interest rates will:

• Discourage business investment

• Make businesses seek short-term profits

• Discourage forward-looking business planning

• Make businesses less competitive internationally

Declining U.S. competitiveness keeps U.S. trade deficits high. That gives foreigners more dollars with which to buy U.S. property. Rising foreign ownership of U.S. assets means the profits from them go abroad increasingly. That drains funds needed for investment to raise future U.S. living standards.

OTHER USEFUL ECONOMIC INDEXES

Forbes publishes The Forbes Index (1976=100), a measure of U.S. economic activity composed of 8 equally weighted elements: Total industrial production, new claims for unemployment compensation, the cost of services relative to all consumer prices, new housing starts, total retail sales, the level of new orders for durable goods compared with manufacturers' inventories, personal income, and total consumer installment credit.

The Conference Board publishes the Help-Wanted Advertising Index as well as the Consumer Confidence Index. The Help-Wanted Index (Figure 3-19) measures the amount of help-wanted advertising in 51 newspapers and tells you about the change in labor market conditions.

The Dodge Index prepared by the F.W. Dodge Division of McGraw-Hill is a monthly market index that assesses the building industry in terms of the value of new construction projects.

Besides the Index of Consumer Sentiment, the University of Michigan Survey Research Center also releases the Investor Sentiment Index, which is constructed based on a survey conducted for Fidelity Investments. The index measures how consumers are planning to use their investment dollars and their overall confidence level.

The National Federation of Independent Business, a Washington-based advocacy group, publishes the Optimism Index (Figure 3-20) based on small-business owners' expectations for the economy. The benchmark year is 1978. It can be accessed free at *www.nfibonline.com.*

FIGURE 3-20: OPTIMISM INDEX

Small business optimism surges in September

Small business optimism spiked in September, according to the latest Small Business Economic Trends report from the NFIB Education Foundation. The Optimism Index rose to 102.4, the largest one-month jump since April 1998 and nearly three points higher than one year ago.

Source: National Federation of Independent Business

FIGURE 3-19: HELP WANTED INDEX

Press Release

Help-Wanted Index Edges Up One Point In August

Topic: Economic Research and Analysis

Description: The Conference Board's Help-Wanted Advertising Index rose slightly to 86 in August, up one point from July. It was 90 one year ago.

Press Release Date: 30 Sep 99

For Release 10 AM ET, Thursday, September 30, 1999 **Release #4511**

Help-Wanted Index Edges Up One Point

Unemployment Rate Could Drop Below 4 Percent

For First Time Since 1970

September 30...The Conference Board's Help-Wanted Advertising Index rose slightly to 86 in August, up one point from July. It was 90 one year ago.

In the last three months, help-wanted advertising declined in seven regions and rose in two. The biggest declines occurred in the West North Central (-10.1%), West South Central (-7.0%) and South Atlantic (-4.3%) regions. Increases were registered in the Mountain (4.9%) and East South Central (2.4%) regions.

"The pace of economic activity at the start of autumn is remarkably similar to the economic environment of last spring," says Conference Board Economist Ken Goldstein. "There are very few signs that hiring will slow as companies scramble to rebuild inventory. After another quarter of at least 3.5% GDP growth, there will be at least that much GDP growth again in the fourth quarter. This will boost hiring across America, generating about 250,000 jobs a month. That would drive down the unemployment rate to below 4 percent for the first time since January, 1970."

The Conference Board surveys help-wanted advertising volume in 51 U.S. major newspapers every month. Because ad volume has proven to be sensitive to labor market conditions, this measure provides a gauge of change in the local, regional and national supply of jobs.

Source: The Conference Board

Other Forecasting Indexes

The following are proprietary indexes that many investors also find useful.

- **Composite Forecasting Index** by Safian Investment Research of White Plains, NY

- **Macro-Economic Index** by The Jesup, Josephal & Co.

- **NBER Experimental Recession Probability Index** by National Bureau of Economic Research (NBER).

OTHER SOURCES OF ECONOMIC INFORMATION

Economic Forecasting Services

It's possible to subscribe to services that will help you interpret the future direction of the economy and the security market. Publications like *Blue Chip Consensus* (Figures 3-21 and 3-22) and *Kiplinger Washington Letter* can help you formulate a sound investment policy.

FIGURE 3-21: WHAT SOME LARGE ECONOMETRIC
SERVICES FORECASTED FOR 1999

	Percent Change 1999 From 1998 (Year-Over-Year)			Average For 1999
Forecast For 1999 (June 1999	Real GDP (Chained) (1992$)	GDP Price Index	Consumer Price Index	Unemployment Rate (Civ.)
WEFA Group	4.1	1.4	1.7	4.2
Eggert Economic Enterprises, Inc.	4.0	1.5	2.0	4.4
Michael Evans, Kellogg School	4.0	1.3	2.7	4.2
Conference Board	4.0	1.3	1.9	4.1
Merrill Lynch	4.0	1.2	2.2	4.2
UCLA Business Forecasting Project	3.9	1.4	2.1	4.3
Standard & Poor's Corp.	3.9	1.1	2.0	4.2
Bank of America Corp.	3.8	1.7	2.4	4.3
Blue Chip 1999 Consensus	3.9	1.4	2.1	4.3

Additional Blue Chip 1999 Consensus Forecasts:
Industrial Production 2.6%   Housing Starts   1.65 mil. Auto Sales 15.9 mil.

Source: Blue Chip Economic Indicators, published by Panel Publishers, a division of Aspen Publishers, Inc., 1101 King Street, Suite 444, Alexandria, VA 22314, Vol. 24, No. 6, June 10, 1999. (800-783-4903).

The Blue Chip Economic Indicators are constructed from a poll of 50 business economists working for investment houses, banks, and businesses. The National Association of Business Economists (NABE) conducts a similar survey.

There is a thriving industry of private consulting firms like DRI/McGraw-Hill, Inc. and Evans Economics that provide economic forecasts based on their own econometric models.

FIGURE 3-22: WHAT THEY FORECASTED FOR 2000

Forecast For 2000 (June 1999)	Percent Change 2000 From 1999 (Year-Over-Year)			Average For 2000
	Real GDP (Chained) (1992 $)	GDP Price Index	Consumer Price Index	Unemployment Rate (Civ.)
WEFA Gro	2.0	1.3	1.8	5.1
Eggert Economic Enterprises, Inc.	2.9	2.1	2.5	4.5
Michael Evans, Kellogg School	2.3	1.6	2.6	4.2
Conference Board	2.7	0.9	2.1	4.3
Merrill Lynch	3.1	1.1	2.0	4.1
UCLA Business Forecasting Project	2.4	1.6	2.7	4.8
Standard & Poor's Corp	2.0	1.4	2.3	5.1
Bank of America Corp.	3.1	2.3	2.5	4.2
Blue Chip 2000 Consensus	2.5	1.7	2.3	4.4

Additional Blue Chip 2000 Consensus Forecasts: Industrial Production, 2.5%; Housing Starts,.52 mil.; Auto Sales,15.4mil.

Source: Blue Chip Economic Indicators, published by Panel Publishers, a division of Aspen Publishers, Inc., 1101 King Street, Suite 444, Alexandria, VA 22314, Vol. 24, No. 6, June 10, 1999. (800-783-4903)

OTHER INFORMATION SOURCES

There are numerous sources of general economic information. They provide the investor with a convenient overview of the current state of the economy, showing many of these economic statistics and indices. They also provide economic commentary, raw statistics, and even forecasts.

These sources are either affordable or easily available at local public and college libraries. They include:

- Daily local newspapers and national newspapers such as *USA Today,* the *Wall Street Journal, Investor's Business Daily,* and the *New York Times.*

- Many periodicals, such as *Forbes, Fortune, Money, Worth, Smart Money, Barron's, Nation's Business,* and *U.S. News* and *World Report.* In each issue, for instance, Business Week reports any fluctuations in the B.W. Production Index, which measures changes in the output of steel, automobiles, trucks, electric power, crude oil, and rail freight.

Aggregate Economic Data

Economic data are necessary for analyzing the past and forecasting future directions of the economy. The present economic environment and the one expected in the future will bear heavily on the types of investments you will select in managing your investment portfolio. Information on economic growth, inflation, employment, personal income, interest rate, money supply, and the like are important to your investment decisions. Some of the major sources of economic data include:

* *Economic Report of the President:* This is a summary of the state of the economy that the president sends to the Congress every year. The report includes over 200 pages covering such issues as monetary policy, inflation, tax policy, the international economy, and review and outlook. In addition, it contains over 100 pages of tables showing historical data for GDP, price indexes, savings, employment, production and business activity, corporate profits, agriculture, international statistics, and the like.

The *Federal Reserve Bulletin* is published monthly by the Board of Governors of the Federal Reserve System. It contains:

* Monetary data, such as money supply figures, interest rates, and bank reserves

* Various statistics on commercial banks

* Fiscal variables, such as U.S. budget receipts and outlays and federal debt figures

* Data on international exchange rates and U.S. dealings with foreigners and overseas banks

Below is a sample of the table of contents. Each heading usually has more detailed sections that provide information for the previous month, the current year on a monthly basis, and several years of historical annual data.

- Domestic Financial Statistics

- Federal Reserve Banks

- Monetary and Credit Aggregates

- Commercial Banks

- Financial Markets

- Federal Finance

- Securities Markets and Corporate Finance

- Real Estate

- Consumer Installment Credit

- Domestic Non-Financial Statistics

- International Statistics

- Securities Holdings and Transactions

- Interest and Exchange Rates

Articles from the *Federal Reserve Bulletin* are available free from the Fed's Web site *(www.bog.frb.fed.us)*.

Quarterly Chart Book and Annual Chart Book: These two books are also published by the Federal Reserve Board; they present the data in the *Federal Reserve Bulletin* in graphic form.

Report on Current Economic Conditions ("The Beige Book"): This report is released about every six weeks by the Federal Reserve Board. Giving the most recent assessment of the nation's economy, with a regional emphasis, it's used to help the Fed decide on monetary policy, like changes in interest rates. It can be accessed free at *www.bog.frb.fed.us,* as well as at the Web sites of the individual Federal Reserve Banks.

Monthly Newsletters and Reviews from Regional Federal Reserve Banks: Each of the 12 Federal Reserve banks publishes its own monthly letter or review, which includes economic data about its region and sometimes commentary on national issues or monetary policy. These can be

FIGURE 3-23: NATIONAL ECONOMIC TRENDS

Table *of Contents*

Source: National Economic Trends

accessed through the Web sites of the individual banks. Their addresses and Web sites are given at the end of this chapter.

U.S. Financial Data, Monetary Trends and *National Economic Trends* (Figure 3-23): The Federal Reserve Bank of St. Louis regularly publishes some of the most comprehensive economic statistics. They include: *U.S. Financial Data, Monetary Trends,* and *National Economic Trends.*

The weekly *U.S. Financial Data* covers the monetary base, bank reserves, money supply, time deposits and demand deposits, borrowing from the Federal Reserve Banks, and business loans from the large commercial banks. The publication also includes current yields and interest rates on selected short-term and long-term securities. Examples of the charts appearing in *U.S Financial Data* appear in Figure 3-13.

Monetary Trends, published monthly, includes tables that provide compound annual rates of change and graphs of raw data with trend changes over time as well as data on federal government debt and its composition by type of holder and on the receipts and expenditures of the government. Figure 3-10 contains examples of the charts appearing in *Monetary Trends.*

National Economic Trends (Figure 3-23) presents monthly economic data on employment, unemployment rates, consumer and producer prices, industrial production, personal income, retail sales, productivity, compensation and labor costs, the GNP implicit price deflator, GNP and its components, disposable personal income, corporate profits, and inventories. This information is presented in graphs and in tables showing the compounded annual rate of change on a monthly basis.

Economic Indicators: A monthly publication of the Council of Economic Advisors, this contains data on income, spending, employment, prices, money and credit, and other factors on both a monthly and an annual basis.

Department of Commerce Periodicals: The Bureau of Economic Analysis of the U.S. Department of Commerce publishes three major economic sources: *Survey of Current Business, Weekly Business Statistics,* and *Business Conditions Digest.*

The monthly *Survey of Current Business* contains monthly and quarterly raw data. It can be accessed free on the Internet at *www.bea.doc.gov.* The Survey presents a monthly update and evaluation of the business situation, analyzing such data as GNP, business inventories, personal consumption, fixed investment, exports, labor market statistics, financial data, and much more. For example, in the personal consumption expenditure subcategories, one would find expenditures on durable goods such as motor vehicles and parts and furniture and equipment; non-durables such as food, energy, clothing, and shoes; and services.

NOTE: The Survey *can be extremely helpful for industry analysis. For example, data on inventory, new plant and equipment, production, and more can be found on such specific industries as coal, tobacco, chemicals, leather products, furniture, and paper. Even within industries such as lumber, production statistics can be found on hardwoods and softwoods right down to Douglas fir trees, southern pine, and western pine.*

Weekly Business Statistics keeps the *Survey* current. It updates the major series found in the *Survey of Current Business* and includes 27 weekly series and charts of selected series. To provide a more comprehensive view of what's available in the *Survey of Current Business* and *Weekly Business Statistics,* here's a list of the major series updates:

- GNP

- National Income

- Personal Income

- Industrial Production

- Manufacturers' Shipments, Inventories, and Orders

- Consumer Price Index

- Producer Price Index

- Construction Put in Place

- Housing Starts and Permits

- Retail Trade

- Labor Force, Employment, and Earnings

- Banking

- Consumer Installment Credit

- Stock Prices

- Value of Exports and Imports

- Motor Vehicles

The primary emphasis of the Business Conditions Digest, published monthly, is on cyclical indicators of economic activity. The National Bureau of Economic Research (NBER) analyzes and selects the time series data based on each series' ability to be identified as a leading, coincident, or lagging indicator over several decades of aggregate economic activity. Over the years, the NBER has identified the approximate dates when aggregate economic activity reached its cyclical high or low point. Each time series is related to the business cycle. Leading indicators move before the business cycle, coincident indicators move with the cycle, and lagging indicators move after the business cycle.

NOTE: Business Conditions Digest *can be very helpful in under-standing past economic behavior and in forecasting future economic activity with a higher degree of success.*

Monthly Business Starts: Dun & Bradstreet publishes *Monthly Business Starts* (Figure 3-24), which reports by industry and location the number of businesses on which Dun & Bradstreet opened files in a given month.

FIGURE 3-24: THE DUN & BRADSTREET CORPORATION— ECONOMIC ANALYSIS DEPARTMENT

U.S. BUSINESS STARTS IN 25 LARGEST CITIES

	JULY 1998		JULY 1999	
	Number	Employment	Number	Employment
NEW YORK, NY..............	342	1,870	338	2,068
CHICAGO, IL...............	122	986	111	590
LOS ANGELES, CA...........	146	824	181	1,165
PHILADELPHIA, PA..........	35	112	53	424
HOUSTON, TX...............	177	1,777	175	2,032
DETROIT, MI...............	29	277	28	97
DALLAS, TX................	118	1,596	106	1,302
SAN DIEGO, CA.............	80	453	72	378
PHOENIX, AZ...............	75	596	84	544
BALTIMORE, MD.............	67	834	41	135
SAN ANTONIO, TX...........	59	562	51	356
INDIANAPOLIS, IN..........	50	878	35	215
SAN FRANCISCO, CA.........	89	411	72	567
MEMPHIS, TN...............	35	240	34	432
WASHINGTON, DC............	59	379	40	263
MILWAUKEE, WI.............	22	268	32	336
SAN JOSE, CA..............	57	381	55	220
CLEVELAND, OH.............	63	435	45	359
COLUMBUS, OH..............	35	206	29	89
BOSTON, MA................	46	320	31	265
NEW ORLEANS, LA...........	23	98	19	103
JACKSONVILLE, FL..........	52	285	46	180
SEATTLE, WA...............	48	250	46	379
DENVER, CO................	62	370	40	267
l IVILLE, TN.............	30	215	16	471
TOTAL 25 CITIES...........	1,921	14,623	1,780	13,237
BALANCE OF COUNTRY........	11,842	67,129	11,034	64,434
TOTAL UNITED STATES.......	13,763	81,752	12,814	77,671

Source: Monthly Business Starts

Other Sources of Economic Data

In addition to what we've covered so far, much other data is available. For instance:

- Many universities have bureaus of business research that provide statistical data on a statewide or regional basis.

- Major banks, such as Bank of America, Citicorp, Morgan Guaranty, and Manufacturer's Hanover, publish monthly or weekly letters or economic reviews, including both raw data and analysis.

- The Moody's, Value Line, and Standard & Poor's investment services all publish economic data along with much other market-related information.

APPENDIX 3-A: USEFUL WEB SITES

The following Web sites offer critical information about economic analysis:

Web Address	Primary Focus
stats.bls.gov	Macroeconomic data
woodrow.mpls.frb.fed.us	Minneapolis Federal Reserve Bank
www.bea.doc.gov	Macroeconomic economic data
www.bls.gov	Most economic statistics and data
www.bog.frb.fed.us	Federal Reserve Board—Data and statistics
www.bos.frb.org	Boston Federal Reserve Bank
www.census.gov/econ/www	Census data
www.conferenceboard.com	Macroeconomic data
www.clev.frb.org	Cleveland Federal Reserve Bank
www.dallasfed.org	Dallas Federal Reserve Bank
www.fedstats.gov	Government economic data and statistics
www.frbatlanta.org	Atlanta Federal Reserve Bank
www.frbchi.org	Chicago Federal Reserve Bank
www.frbsf.org	San Francisco Federal Reserve Bank
www.kc.frb.org	Kansas City Federal Reserve Bank
www.moodys.com	Economic commentary
www.ny.frb.org	New York Federal Reserve Bank
www.phil.frb.org	Philadelphia Federal Reserve Bank
www.rich.frb.org	Richmond Federal Reserve Bank
www.stls.frb.org	St. Louis Federal Reserve Bank
www.whitehouse.gov/fsbr/esbr.html	Economic Statistics Briefing Room

Chapter 4
INDUSTRY INFORMATION

In search of a promising security, investors with a fundamentalist orientation begin by estimating the prospects for the industrial sector of which the firm is part. They consider such factors as average operating costs, competition within the industry, import competition, future tax regulations, and deregulation. Then they assess specifics for the firm: future sales, strengths of the company's present products, market share, and profit growth potential. This chapter shows you:

- How to find out how well an industry is faring in its business cycle

- Sources of industry information

INDUSTRY GROUP PERFORMANCE

Some industries do better than others, depending on the business cycle. For example, some industry groupings typically (but not always) attain earnings gains in periods when overall corporate profits decline. Historically, soft drinks, utilities, tobacco, and office equipment stocks are the Standard & Poor's groups that have done this.

Typically, recession years and the beginning stages of an economic recovery have been good periods for stock market performance. Merrill Lynch has attempted to identify industry groups that are likely to outperform the broad market averages during the early stages of a new bull market (see Figure 4-1).

FIGURE 4-1: GROUP PERFORMANCE IN THE BUSINESS CYCLE

Master Group	Dominant Investment	Best Realative Characteristics	Worst Relative Performance
Cyclical Stocks			
Credit cyclicals	Interest-rate sensitive. Perform best when rates low; most building-related	Early and middle bull markets	Early and middle bear markets—forest products excepted
Consumer cyclicals	Consumer durables and non-durables; profits vary with economic cycle	Early and middle bull markets	Early and middle bear markets—hotel/motel excepted
Capital goods (cyclical only)	Many groups depend on capacity utilization	Middle and late bull markets	Late bear markets
Energy (cyclical only)	Closely tied to the economic cycle	Early bull markets	Early bear markets
Basic industries	Profits depend on industry capacity utilization; prices may benefit from short supplies at economic peaks	Early and middle bear markets; economic peaks	Early or middle bull markets, depending on source of demand for products
Financial	Banks, insurance, and gold mining	Late bull and bear; economic troughs	Early bull markets
Transportation	Surface transportation	Late bull and bear; economic troughs	Early bear markets
Defensive Stocks			
Defensive consumer staples	Nonvolatile consumer goods	Late bear markets	Early bull markets
Energy (defensive only)	Major international and domestic oil; volatility introduced by OPEC power	Late bear markets	Early bull markets
Utilities	Large liquidity and operating stability	Late bear markets	Early bull markets
Consumer growth	Combination of growth and defensive; several subgroups offer high yields	Cosmetics, soft drinks, drugs: late bearOther subgroups: early bull	First groups have no variance in regular cyclical patternOthers: late bear markets
Capital goods-technology capital goods (growth only)	Linked to capital investment spending cycle, which tends to lag behind the economic cycle	Early and middle bull markets	Late bear markets
Energy (growth only)	Linked to economic cycle and to OPEC	Early bull markets, but varies	Varies

Source: Merrill Lynch

SOURCES OF INDUSTRY INFORMATION

Industry information can be obtained from:

- Government publications

- Private sources and advisory sources

- Industry statistics and trade journals

- Reports of compilations

- Industry studies

Government Publications

The federal government provides data on industries through the Census Bureau. The data includes employment figures, number of companies, and sales. Investors who choose to do their own detailed security analysis may find such information of real value. A number of Census Bureau publications are available on the Web at *www.census.gov.* The *Statistical Abstract of the United States* is a handy reference for this type of information.

The *Federal Reserve Quarterly Chart Book,* published by the Federal Reserve System (Publications Dept., MS 138, Washington, DC 20551; 202-452-3000). The *Chart Book* shows industry performance graphically, demonstrating how each industry may be affected differently by the business cycle. For example, the auto and housing industries are more sensitive to short-term swings in the business cycle, whereas food and pharmaceuticals find a market no matter what the stage of the cycle.

The *Quarterly Financial Report for Manufacturing, Mining, and Trade Corporations,* published jointly by the Federal Trade Commission and the SEC, provides timely information on individual industries, including sales and net profit. Individual industries can be compared to industry groups or to all manufacturing corporations. The information is organized by industry and by size of assets.

Robert Morris Associates publishes *Annual Studies* and Dun & Bradstreet publishes *Key Business Ratios.* Both provide ratios for a number of industries.

Private and Advisory Sources

The *Outlook,* published by Standard & Poor's, highlights seven industries in each week's issue. It also carries analytical articles providing investment advice about the market and about specific securities.

The *Analyst's Handbook,* also published by S&P, shows industry group trends. It presents key statistics for companies in some industries.

Industry Surveys, another S&P product, is perhaps the most comprehensive resource. It analyzes in detail operating statistics for major industries. Updated quarterly and completely revised every one to three years, it covers 22 industries.

United Business & Investment Report, published every two weeks by United Business Service, analyzes current business trends and specific industry factors.

Value Line Investment Survey, published by Arnold Bernhard & Co., Inc., analyzes the current situation and future prospects of four to six industries in each weekly issue. Company reports are organized by industry; a write-up of industry developments, financial data, and trends introduces each group of companies. *Value Line* gives you data on such variables as industry sales, operating margin, profit margin, tax rate, and capital structure. It estimates industry statistics for both the current and the coming year and also ranks all industries in terms of probable performance over the next 12 months, providing a unique and readily available short-term forecast.

McGraw-Hill's *Business Week* summarizes recent performance data on major industries on a recurring business. Early in January, it carries an Industry Outlook for the new year, a good source of information. Excerpts can be viewed free at the *Business Week* Web site, *www.businessweek.com.*

Forbes also publishes an Annual Report on American Industry at the beginning of each calendar year. It encompasses each major industry, and within each industry rates firms based on two measures of performance: growth (five-year compounded rate for both sales and earnings) and profitability (five-year average return on total assets and on equity). It analyzes the past and prospective performance of major industries. Excerpts can be viewed free at *www.forbes.com.*

Other useful publications are the *Wall Street Transcript,* which prints panel discussions of industry outlooks; *Dun & Bradstreet,* which provides key business ratios and industry norms, and *Predicast,* which summarizes industry data, employment, capital expenditures, and other useful benchmarks.

Other services you may find useful are:

- *Technical Analyses of Industry,* published by the Merrill Lynch Capital Markets Equity Research Department, gives an overview of the apparel industry, its market performance, and vital industry statistics.

- *Crandall's Business Index,* published by Crandall, Pierce & Company, provides useful industry analyses.

- *Institutional Investment Guides,* published by Brown Brothers Harriman & Co., also gives useful industry analyses and guides, primarily for institutional investors.

Private consulting firms like Chase Econometrics, Evans & Associates, and Data Resources, Inc., provide industry as well as economic forecasts based on their own econometric models.

Industry Statistics and Trade Association Periodicals

Journals published by trade associations typically discuss current developments and topics that affect their industries. You can find out which associations cover an industry you're interested in by looking at the *Directory of National Trade Associations.* Following is a list of representative trade journals; many are available in college and public libraries:

Airline Executive
American Banker
American Gas Association Monthly
American Machinist
American Petroleum Institute Statistical Bulletin
Automotive Industries
Automotive News
Aviation News Weekly
Best's Insurance Report
Brewres Digest
Broadcasting-Telecasting

Business Executive of America
Chemical Week
Coal Age
Coal Mining
Computer
Dodge Reports
Drug and Cosmetics Industry
Electrical Merchandising
Electrical World
Electronics
Engineering and Mining Journal
Engineering News-Record
Fibre Container and Paperboard Mills
Food Management
Implement & Tractor and Farm Implement News
Industry & Engineering Chemistry
Iron Age
Leather and Shoes
Modern Plastics
Oil & Gas Journal
Paper Trade Journal
Petroleum Times
Polk's National New Car Service
Printer's Ink
Public Utilities Fortnightly
Pulp, Paper, Board Packaging
Railway Age
Rock products
Television Digest
Textile Organization
Textile World
Ward's Auto World

NOTE: *The Business Periodicals Index and the Applied Science and Technology Index list articles in all trade journals.*

Industry and Other Studies

The *Encyclopedia of Associations,* published by The Gale Group, Farmington Hills, MI, and Washington Researchers (918 16th St., Washington, DC), lists trade associations, many of which issue annual reports.

Harvard Business School *(www.hbs.edu)* publishes useful information sources, including:

* Basic U.S. Statistical Sources

* Basic Investment Services

* Lists of Largest Companies

* Information on specific industries and business

* Where to find information about companies

* Business handbooks

* Sources of information for industry analysis

* Business dictionaries

Studies of individual industries are also available from private consulting firms, among them:

* Business Trend Analysts, Commack, NY *(www.businesstrendanalysts.com)*

* Arthur D. Little, Inc., Cambridge, MA *(www.adlittle.com)*

* Stanford Research Institute, Menlo Park, CA *(www.SRI.com)*

* The Gale Detroit Group, Farmington Hills, MI, which also publishes:

  —*Statistical Sources* (revised every third year, with an annual supplement)

  —*Trade Names Dictionary* (revised every other year)

—*Dictionary of Directories* (revised every other year)

• Merrill Lynch Capital Markets Equity Research Dept., New York, NY

Most notably, DRI/McGraw-Hill, Inc. (Lexington, MA), publishes the *DRI Economic Information System,* designed to facilitate industry analysis by providing macroeconomic estimates and forecasts for some 789 industries; its databank includes nearly 7,000 economic and industry time series.

Computer-Readable Data Sources

Dialog *(www.dialog.com)* provides the following resources:

• *Predicast:* Sales growth rates

• *Trade & Industry Index:* Abstracts of trade journal articles

• *Inestext:* Abstracts of market and industry studies

• *Arthur D. Little/On-Line:* A.D. Little industry reports

• *Encyclopedia of Associations:* Industry associations

Nexis/Lexis *(www.lexis–nexis.com):* Nexis/Lexis provides news and information.

Dow Jones *(www.dowjones.com):* Dow Jones provides stock quotes, financial news, and financial statement information.

APPENDIX 4-A: USEFUL WEB SITES

Web Address	Primary Focus
www. businessweek.com	*Business Week* articles and features
www. census.gov	Macroeconomic economic data
www.dialog.com	Business database service
www.dowjones.com	Financial information service
www. forbes.com	*Forbes* articles and features
www.lexis–nexis.com	General information service

Chapter 5
UNDERSTANDING
COMPANIES

As we said in the previous chapter, investors tend to look first to an industry to assess its prospects and then look for specifics on a company. This chapter discusses:

- Sources of company information

- How to read and analyze a company's annual and quarterly reports

- What you need to know about financial statements

- Securities and Exchange Commission (SEC) filings

- How to read a prospectus

SOURCES OF COMPANY INFORMATION

A number of publications and newsletters give information about companies. Figure 5-1 is a list of selected journals that provide data on individual corporations. Most of these sources, which are available by subscription, can be found in public and college libraries.

FIGURE 5-1: SOURCES OF INFORMATION ON INDIVIDUAL COMPANIES

Title	Publisher	Type of Publication
Business Week	McGraw-Hill, Inc.	Summarizes current performance and future prospects of several major firms each week.
Corporation Records	Standard & Poor's	In-depth history and recent operating data on major firms; updated frequently.
Forbes	Forbes, Inc.	The industry analysis issue early each year covers the major firms within each industry; each issue also discusses a number of firms.
Hoover's Handbook of American Business	Hoover's, Inc.	Profiles of corporations including history, business operations, financial data, competitors, and officers.
Moody's Manuals	Moody's Investor Service	In-depth history and current data on all major firms; updated frequently.
Stock Reports	Standard & Poor's	Detailed data on common and preferred stocks traded on the NYSE, Amex, and OTC markets; updated regularly.
The Outlook	Standard & Poor's	Reviews major current events affecting a specific stock; also has comparative analysis of a major industry and its firms.
United Business & Investment Report	United Business Service	Typically reviews individual firms within a selected industry. Published every 2 weeks.
Value Line Investment Survey	Arnold Bernhard & Co., Inc.	Comparative analysis of major firms within industries; each industry review is updated every 13 weeks.

THE IMPORTANCE OF READING ANNUAL (OR 10-K) AND QUARTERLY (OR 10-Q) REPORTS

A Securities and Exchange Commission study revealed that only 17% of individual investors relied on their broker's advice in reaching decisions;

86% found corporate financial statement data extremely useful or moderately useful. Investors making their own investment decisions relied on four major sources of data: (1) company-produced financial statements, (2) forecast information, (3) facts about management, and (4) market-based information.

The authors of a *Financial Executive* article discussing this survey noted that the failure of 40 to 50% of investors to read the financial statement footnotes or the auditor's report "could easily lead to an erroneous overall appraisal."

NOTE: Footnotes may describe the firm's accounting—that's essential for international companies. Those who did not read the footnotes or said they were uninterested also said the footnotes lacked clarity and understandability.

How did investors use annual reports? Well, 52% read the income statement; 40%, the balance sheet; 23%, the statement of cash flows; 26%, the statement footnotes; and 19%, the auditor's report. The latter tools may be more popular with sophisticated individual investors, institutional investors, and security analysts.

Research by the Center for the Study of Professional Accountancy found that the most important objective of both individual and institutional investors is either long-term capital gains or a combination of dividend income and long-term capital gains. Corporate annual reports were rated the most important sources of information for both groups. Individual investors rated newspapers and magazines next, but institutional investors placed advisory services second. Financial analysts rated prospectuses second and communication with management third.

HOW TO READ AN ANNUAL REPORT

If you're considering investing in a company, read and analyze its annual report. (If you already own stock in a company, you'll get it automatically.) The basic purpose of the annual report is to allow readers to assess the company's financial health. Comparative balance sheets for the last two years and comparative income statements for the last three years are provided to make it possible to identify trends.

A publicly held company must publish an annual report within 90 days of the end of its fiscal year. Since most companies are on a calendar year basis (December 31), their annual reports appear in March. The company must also file form 10-K within 90 days with the SEC; this is often more financially detailed than the annual report. A company will send you its 10-K on request.

The financial position depicted in the annual report is historical. It does not present prospective financial information. The firm will try to present its financial position in a favorable light, subject to regulatory constraints.

Many sections in the annual report must be evaluated if you are to make an informed judgment about the company's financial health: highlights, letter to stockholders, review of operations, management's discussion and analysis, the financial statements (balance sheet, income statement, and statement of cash flows including related footnotes), supplementary schedules, and the auditor's report.

Charts and graphs—perhaps charts showing dividends, earnings per share, and market price history, or percentage of revenue derived by product line—may be used to highlight or clarify information.

Photographs may project a desired corporate image. For example, there may be photographs of executives and products. Photographs can be misleading.

A typical annual report contains:

- Highlights

- Letter to Shareholders

- Review of Operations

- Financial Statements

- Report of Independent Public Accountant

- Report by Management

- Financial Statements

- Balance Sheet

- Income Statement

- Statement of Cash Flows

- Footnotes

- Supplementary Schedules

- Management's Discussion and Analysis of the Financial Condition and Results of Operations

- Investors' Information

- Directors and Officers List

Highlights

The highlights present an overview of the company and its financial standing, giving comparative information (see Figure 5-2). At a minimum, the company discusses the last two years' sales, net income, and earnings per share, using charts and diagrams for clarification. The explanations are minimal.

FIGURE 5-2: COMPANY HIGHLIGHTS

Tandy Corporation Financial Highlights

(In millions, except per share amounts and ratios)	1998	1997	1996
Net sales and operating revenues			
As reported	$ 4,787.9	$ 5,372.2	$ 6,285.5
For ongoing operations[1]	$ 3,591.2[2]	$ 3,303.9[3]	$ 3,160.5[4]
Net income (loss)			
As reported	$ 61.3	$ 186.9	$ (91.6)
For ongoing operations[1]	$ 245.2[2]	$ 214.6[3]	$ 223.6[4]
Net income (loss) available per common share:			
Basic:			
As reported	$ 0.55	$ 1.69	$ (0.82)
For ongoing operations[1]	$ 2.38[2]	$ 1.94[3]	$ 1.82[4]
Diluted:			
As reported	$ 0.54	$ 1.63	$ (0.82)
For ongoing operations[1]	$ 2.28[2]	$ 1.88[3]	$ 1.77[4]
Cash flow from operations	$ 414.8	$ 320.3	$ 307.5
Total assets	$ 1,993.6	$ 2,317.5	$ 2,583.4
Total debt	$ 468.3	$ 535.6	$ 362.3
Stockholders' equity	$ 848.2	$ 1,058.6	$ 1,264.8
Common shares outstanding at year end	97.4	102.3	114.4
Total debt as a percentage of total capitalization	35.6%	33.6%	22.3%
Return on average stockholders' equity for ongoing operations[1]	23.6%[2]	16.1%[3]	13.9%[4]

Source: Tandy Corporation 1998 Annual Report

Management attempts to provide this information in an upbeat, positive manner. To be credible, however, not only should upturns be discussed but downturns as well.

The company will of course emphasize the positive aspects to give a favorable impression. For example, an upward trend in dividends would be emphasized. If dividends were cut back, the discussion might turn on a rise in research and development activity.

Letter to Shareholders

The Letter to Shareholders is typically signed by the CEO and the President. Often, there is a picture of both. This is not a formal part of the annual report. *NOTE: Be wary when reading the president's letter; the president has a vested interest in making the company look good, in portraying the company in a favorable light so as to create a positive image. Be cautious when the president sounds too optimistic. Read the letter in light of the company's track record.*

While the letter itself is not subject to audit, it does comment on the financial results for the past year and their implications. The letter will explain the company's performance whether that be improving or deteriorating. It will also talk about future plans, directions, and goals, which are typically not found elsewhere in the annual report. Future possibilities may include mergers and acquisitions and product introductions. A comment may be made on social issues. As you read the letter, skepticism is in order. *NOTE: Evaluate future plans in light of the conditions in the industry, the economy, and the political environment.*

The president may state, "We had a difficult year because . . . ." This statement is designed to create trust. Problems are stated in the context of corrective actions. Any negative financial results are downplayed; statements about the future are optimistic. Sometimes there is a useful perspective about the company, perhaps a reference to an industry problem or a foreign risk exposure.

Be ware of euphemisms. A "challenging" year for the president was most likely a bad year for the stockholders. "The company is positioned for growth in its product line" perhaps because expected growth hasn't happened so far. Qualified statements must be read between the lines.

You can evaluate the reliability of the president's letter in the context of past experience. The firm's attorneys will prevent the company from making any outright wrong or misleading statements. But optimism, couched with the appropriate disclaimers, is always acceptable. *NOTE: A company president who has been honest in the past is likely to be so again. However, if in exaggerations in the past are likely to be repeated.*

If the company is a penny stock firm, there is high risk and probability of failure. Small companies often have no track record, so you should significantly discount the president's comments.

Review of Operations

This section typically takes the most space. Often public relations-oriented, with nice pictures, the section gives key information about the company's products, services, facilities, and future directions. The review may try to the reader away from negative realities. For example, if the review emphasizes the future rather than the present, it may be because the current situation is not good. Emphasis on employee loyalty or the company's attempt to help build America may be used to direct attention away from disappointing earnings.

Failure to discuss key areas may mean that they're negative. What's the company trying to hide and why?

If the company mentioned something last year but not this year, suspicion may be in order. For example, if last year management stated that rapid growth and expansion is expected in a particular product line or business segment but nothing is said about that prediction this year, ask yourself what happened.

Report of Independent Public Accountant

The independent auditor's report may be placed before or after the financial statement section. The auditor certifies to the accuracy and validity of the numbers in the financial statement. Four types of audit opinions that may be rendered: an unqualified opinion, a qualified opinion, a disclaimer of opinion, and an adverse opinion. The opinion is heavily relied on because the auditor is considered to be knowledgeable, objective, and independent.

Unqualified Opinion

An unqualified opinion means that the CPA is satisfied that the financial statements present the company's financial position fairly. This opinion gives the reader confidence that the financial statements accurately portray the company's financial health and operating performance.

Figure 5-3 shows the report of independent auditors that appeared in the 1998 annual report of Maytag Corporation.

FIGURE 5-3: INDEPENDENT AUDITOR'S REPORT

Report of Independent Auditors

Shareowners and Board of Directors

Maytag Corporation

We have audited the accompanying consolidated balance sheets of Maytag Corporation and subsidiaries as of December 31, 1998 and 1997, and the related consolidated statements of income, comprehensive income, shareowners' equity, and cash flows for each of three years in the period ended December 31, 1998. These financial statements are the responsibility of the Company's management. Our responsibility is to express an opinion on these financial statements based on our audits.

We conducted our audits in accordance with generally accepted auditing standards. Those standards require that we plan and perform the audit to obtain reasonable assurance about whether the financial statements are free of material misstatement. An audit includes examining, on a test basis, evidence supporting the amounts and disclosures in the financial statements. An audit also includes assessing the accounting principles used and significant estimates made by management, as well as evaluating the overall financial statement presentation. We believe that our audits provide a reasonable basis for our opinion.

In our opinion, the financial statements referred to above present fairly, in all material respects, the consolidated financial position of Maytag Corporation and subsidiaries at December 31, 1998 and 1997, and the consolidated results of their operations and their cash flows for each of the three years in the period ended December 31, 1998, in conformity with generally accepted accounting principles.

Ernst & Young LLP

Chicago, Illinois
February 2, 1999

Source: Maytag Corporation 1998 Annual Report

Even if there is an uncertainty, such as a lawsuit, an unqualified opinion may still be given—but there should be an explanation of the material uncertainty. Note any contingency and its possible adverse financial effects on the company. For example, loss of a lawsuit may result in significant damages; loss of a tax case may result in additional taxes.

Qualified Opinion

A qualified opinion may be issued when the auditor is unable to do one or more of the following: (1) gather enough evidential matter to support an unqualified opinion; (2) apply a required auditing procedure; and (3) apply one or more auditing procedures considered necessary under the circumstances. An "except for" qualified opinion may be issued, for instance, when the auditor is unable to confirm accounts receivable or observe inventory. Typical modifications to the report include:

- The phase "except as discussed in the following paragraph" at the beginning or end of the second sentence of the scope paragraph.

- A paragraph before the opinion paragraph that explains the nature of the scope limitations.

- A modified opinion paragraph explaining the possible effects of the scope limitation on the financial statements.

A qualified opinion is a "red flag" that more detailed evaluation is needed.

Disclaimer of Opinion

When the scope limitation is so severe that the auditor does not wish to simply qualify the opinion, a disclaimer of opinion is given. If the auditor cannot come up with an opinion, what is the reader to think about the accuracy of the company's financial statements?

Adverse Opinion

An adverse opinion is expressed when the financial statements don't present fairly, in conformity with generally accepted accounting principles, an entity's financial position, results of operations, retained earnings, and cash flows. The financial statements should not be relied on. *NOTE: Firing the independent CPA over a disagreement in accounting policies raises another red flag. Any CPA is reluctant to lose a client; failure to agree on an accounting policy probably means the company wants an unrealistic policy, possibly to overstate earnings. Hence, the financial statement figures may be erroneous and misleading.*

Report by Management

A Report by Management typically accompanies the CPA's report. In it management certifies its own responsibility for the financial information under audit. This section states that the information is objective and reliable, and estimates have been properly made. It assures that proper internal controls were in place. Management notes that the Board of Directors has oversight responsibility for the financial statements. It indicates that there is an audit committee including corporate directors. The report is usually signed by the chief financial officer and/or the chief executive officer.

Figure 5-4 illustrates the report by management appearing in the 1998 annual report on the Proctor and Gamble Company.

FIGURE 5-4: REPORT BY MANAGEMENT

RESPONSIBILITY FOR THE FINANCIAL STATEMENTS   The Procter & Gamble Company and Subsidiaries

Consolidated financial statements and financial information included in this report are the responsibility of Company management. This includes preparing the statements in accordance with generally accepted accounting principles and necessarily includes estimates based on management's best judgments.

To help insure the accuracy and integrity of Company financial data, management maintains internal controls designed to provide reasonable assurance that transactions are executed as authorized and accurately recorded and that assets are properly safeguarded. These controls are monitored by an ongoing program of internal audits. These audits are supplemented by a self-assessment program that enables individual organizations to evaluate the effectiveness of their controls. Careful selection of employees and appropriate divisions of responsibility are designed to achieve control objectives. The Company's "Worldwide Business Conduct Manual" sets forth management's commitment to conduct its business affairs with the highest ethical standards.

Deloitte & Touche LLP, independent public accountants, have audited and reported on the Company's consolidated financial statements. Their audits were performed in accordance with generally accepted auditing standards.

The Board of Directors, acting through its Audit Committee composed entirely of outside directors, oversees the adequacy of internal controls. The Audit Committee meets periodically with representatives of Deloitte & Touche LLP and internal financial management to review internal control, auditing and financial reporting matters. The independent auditors and the internal auditors also have full and free access to meet privately with the Audit Committee.

John E. Pepper
Chairman and Chief Executive

Erik G. Nelson
Chief Financial Officer

Source: Proctor & Gamble Company 1998 Annual Report

What You Need to Know About Financial Statements

You only want to invest in a company that has good financial health and future prospects. Is the company growing or declining? Will it be around for a long time? How profitable is it? What are its financial resources and obligations? These questions and others can be answered if you understand the financial statements in the annual report. If you don't know how the company is doing financially, how can you invest in it?

The three financial statements that are required are the balance sheet, income statement, and statement of cash flows. Although the form of these financial statements may vary among different businesses or other economic units, the basic purpose remains the same.

Financial Statement Overview

The balance sheet shows the financial position of the company at a particular point in time. It shows what's owned (assets), how much is owed (liabilities), and what's left (assets minus liabilities—known as stockholders' equity or net worth). With the balance sheet, you freeze the action of the company as of a certain date (the end of the reporting year). It's a snapshot.

The income statement, on the other hand, measures operating performance for a specified time period (for the entire fiscal year). It's a motion picture. As can be seen in Figure 5-5, the income statement serves as a bridge between the two consecutive balance sheets.

FIGURE 5-5: BALANCE SHEET/INCOME STATEMENT RELATIONSHIP

NOTE: *With the balance sheet you're asking, "How wealthy or poor is the company?" With the income statement you're asking, "How did the company do last year?" "Did it make money?" "How much?" Neither statement alone is good enough to tell you about the financial health of the company. For example, the fact that the company made a big profit doesn't necessarily mean it's wealthy, and vice versa. In order to get the total picture, you need both statements.*

Even with these, you as an investor still have problems. You'd like to know more about the company before making buy or sell decisions, such as whether the cash position of the company has changed. The statement of cash flows provides this information. It basically shows the sources and uses of cash, which external investors use for cash flow analysis. The statement aids you in answering vital questions like "Where did money come from?" and "Where was money put, and for what purpose?" Figure 5-6 lists more specific questions that can be answered by the statement of cash flows and by cash flow analysis.

FIGURE 5-6: QUESTIONS ANSWERED BY CASH FLOW ANALYSIS·

- Is the company growing or just maintaining its competitive position?
- Will the company be able to meet its financial obligations?
- Where did the company obtain funds?
- What use was made of net income?
- How much of the required capital has been generated internally?
- How was the expansion in plant and equipment financed?
- Is the business expanding faster than it can generate funds?
- Is the company's dividend policy in balance with its operating policy?
- Is the company's cash position sound?
- What effect will it have on the market price of the stock?

NOTE: You might be interested to know the cash flow per share, which is net cash flow divided by the number of shares outstanding. A high ratio indicates a liquid position.

Footnotes

The annual report often states: "The accompanying footnotes are an integral part of the financial statements." The financial statements themselves are concise and condensed; hence, any explanatory information that cannot be readily be abbreviated is provided in greater detail in footnotes.

Footnotes expand on financial statement figures and accounting policies, explain about mergers and stock options, and furnish any necessary disclosure. Examples of footnote disclosures are accounting methods used and the basis for estimates such as inventory pricing, pension fund and profit sharing arrangements, terms of long-term debt, lease agreements, contingencies, and tax matters.

NOTE: Footnote information may be quantitative or qualitative. An example of quantitative information is the fair market value of pension plan assets. An example of qualitative information is disclosure of a lawsuit against the company.

Supplementary Schedules

Supplementary schedules are provided to enhance reader comprehension of the company's financial health. Some of the more common schedules are (1) five-year summary of operations, (2) two-year quarterly data, and (3) segmental information.

Five-Year Summary of Operations
Information for five years, including dividends on preferred stock and common stock, also reveals operating trends. Some companies provide ten-year comparative data. Figure 5-7 illustrates a five-year summary of operations and year-end position for General Instrument.

FIGURE 5-7: FIVE YEAR SUMMARY

FIVE YEAR SUMMARY

			Year Ended December 31.		
(In millions, except per share data)	1998ᵈ	1997ᵇ	1996ᵃ	1995ᵉ	1994ᵈ
Consolidated Statements of Operations Data:					
Net sales	$1,988	$1,764	$1,756	$1,533	$1,275
Cost of sales	1,431	1,336	1,350	1,080	878
Gross profit	557	428	406	453	397
Selling, general and administrative	194	215	174	138	103
Research and development	244	208	198	138	105
Purchased in-process technology	—	—	—	140	—
Amortization of excess of cost over fair value of net assets acquired	14	15	14	14	15
NLC litigation costs	—	—	141	—	—
Operating income (loss)	104	(10)	(122)	22	175
Interest income (expense), net	1	(5)	(26)	(23)	(27)
Income (loss) before income taxes and cumulative effect of changes in accounting principles	94	(10)	(149)	(2)	149
Net income (loss)	$ 55	$ (16)	$ (96)	$ 4	$ 121
Earnings per share – basic	$ 0.35				
Earnings per share – diluted	$ 0.33				
Pro forma loss per share – basic and diluted (f)		$ (0.11)	$ (0.65)		

			December 31.		
	1998	1997	1996	1995	1994
Consolidated Balance Sheet Data:					
Total assets	$2,188	$1,675	$1,630	$1,354	$1,199
Other non-current liabilities	68	66	188	75	78
Stockholders' equity	1,650	1,215	1,051	926	764

Source: General Instrument 1998 Annual Report

Two-Year Quarterly Data
This schedule furnishes a quarterly breakdown of sales, profit, the high and low stock price, and common stock dividend. It's particularly useful for a seasonal business. The quarterly market price reveals fluctuations in the market price of stock; the dividend quarterly information shows how regularly the company is paying its dividends. Figure 5-8 illustrates quarterly data for Maytag Corporation.

FIGURE 5-8: QUARTERLY RESULTS

Quarterly Results of Operations

In thousands except per share data	December 31	September 30	June 30	March 31
1998				
Net sales	$ 972,003	$ 1,035,202	$ 1,021,899	$ 1,040,386
Gross profit	291,791	298,817	287,118	303,901
Income before extraordinary item	68,816	77,440	67,987	72,267
Basic earnings per share	0.77	0.85	0.73	0.77
Diluted earnings per share	0.75	0.84	0.71	0.75
Net income	66,416	73,940	67,987	72,267
Basic earnings per share	0.74	0.82	0.73	0.77
Diluted earnings per share	0.72	0.80	0.71	0.75
1997				
Net sales	$ 945,097	$ 855,804	$ 814,541	$ 792,469
Gross profit	262,827	239,534	224,445	209,482
Income before extraordinary item	51,930	49,277	43,783	38,500
Basic earnings per share	0.55	0.51	0.46	0.39
Diluted earnings per share	0.54	0.50	0.44	0.39
Net income	48,730	49,277	43,783	38,500
Basic earnings per share	0.52	0.51	0.46	0.39
Diluted earnings per share	0.50	0.50	0.44	0.39

Source: Maytag Corporation 1998 Annual Report

Segmental Disclosure

Segmental reporting provides investors with useful information to evaluate the potential profit and risk of particular aspects of a company's operation. Segmental data may be by industry, foreign area, major customer, and government contract.

A segment is reportable if any one of the following exists:

- Revenue is 10% or more of combined revenue.

- Operating profit's 10% or more of total operating profit.

- Identifiable assets are 10% or more of total assets.

A company must also disclose if foreign operations, sales to a major customer, or domestic contract revenue is 10% or more of the total, giving the percentage and the source. Figure 5-9 illustrates segmental disclosure for General Instrument.

FIGURE 5-9: SEGMENTAL DISCLOSURE

	Broadband Networks Systems	Satellite and Broadcast Network Systems	Next Level Communications[a]	Corporate Unallocated and Other	Total Company
1998					
Net sales	$1,569,483	$418,342	$ —	$ —	$1,987,825
Operating income (loss)	234,884	35,201	—	(165,838)[c]	104,247
Other income (expense) – net (including equity interest in Partnership losses of $25,089)	—	—	—	(11,815)	(11,815)
Interest income (expense) – net	—	—	—	1,217	1,217
Income (loss) before income taxes	—	—	—	93,649	93,649
Segment assets[d]	649,183	203,119	—	6,319 [c]	858,621
Capital expenditures	78,869	12,891	—	—	91,760
Depreciation and intangible amortization expense	41,215	23,975	—	18,374 [e]	83,564
Warrant costs related to customer purchases	21,834	—	—	—	21,834
1997					
Net sales	$1,292,930	$462,068	$ 9,090	$ —	$1,764,088
Operating income (loss)	218,942	(7,449)	(58,462)	(163,226)[c]	(10,195)
Other income (expense) – net	—	—	—	5,766	5,766
Interest income (expense) – net	—	—	—	(5,210)	(5,210)
Income (loss) before income taxes	—	—	—	(9,639)	(9,639)
Segment assets[d]	512,241	338,250	37,970	(19,937)[c]	868,524
Capital expenditures	42,064	26,740	10,702	322	79,828
Depreciation and intangible amortization expense	33,962	33,225	4,133	18,537 [e]	89,857
1996					
Net sales	$1,180,424	$575,161	$ —	$ —	$1,755,585
Operating income (loss)	153,388	22,229	(29,781)	(267,847)[c]	(122,011)
Other income (expense) – net	—	—	—	(1,427)	(1,427)
Interest income (expense) – net	—	—	—	(25,970)	(25,970)
Income (loss) before income taxes	—	—	—	(149,408)	(149,408)
Segment assets[d]	588,284	321,138	12,214	(13,075)[c]	908,561
Capital expenditures	99,172	27,040	8,048	93	134,353
Depreciation and intangible amortization expense	32,344	31,553	2,063	18,540 [e]	84,500

Source: General Instrument 1998 Annual Report

NOTE: *Useful segment information for investors includes sales, operating profit, total assets, fixed assets, intangible assets, inventory, cost of sales, depreciation, and amortization.*

Management's Discussion and Analysis

This section gives management's comments on operations, capital resources, and liquidity, interpreting and analyzing past and prospective financial developments. Any significant developments, favorable or unfavorable, must be discussed. Companies provide both normal operating details and unusual events, discussing uncertainties and trends and their potential effects.

With regard to capital resources, management discusses acquisitions of property, plant, and equipment and whether they were financed by equity or debt or were leased.

Liquidity is discussed in terms of working capital and liquidity ratios, including the current ratio, quick (acid-test) ratio, inventory turnover, and accounts receivable turnover.

Investor's Information

This section provides useful information about exchanges on which the stock is traded, date and place of the annual meeting, when proxy materials will be mailed, names and addresses of the registrar and transfer agent, and the names of the trustees. It also gives the number of common and preferred shareholders, and the terms of any dividend reinvestment plan.

NOTE: SEC Form 10-K contains additional information, such as historical background, experience, and compensation of senior executives, management holdings of securities, names of principal security holders, detailed financial schedules, properties held, product and service information, markets, distribution channels, employment history, number of employees, competition, backlogs, patents and licenses, franchises, backlog, and governmental regulations (e.g., environmental safety).

Directors and Officers

This section lists the names of the Board of Directors and their affiliations, the names and titles of senior executives, and the membership of various board committees such as the finance and audit committees.

NOTE: Ask questions like "How many members of the board are from outside the company?" "Are they more concerned with outside interests such as banks and suppliers than with stockholders of the company?"

History of Market Price

While it's optional for a company to provide a brief history of the market prices of its stock, many companies provide this information, often in terms of the highs and lows of the stock for each quarter. This information reveals the variability and direction in market price of stock (see Figure 5-10).

FIGURE 5-10: ABC COMMON STOCK HIGH AND LOW BID PRICES

	20x1	
	High	**Low**
First quarter	$30	$26
Second quarter	28	25
Third quarter	34	31
Fourth quarter	32	27

HOW TO READ A QUARTERLY REPORT

Besides the annual report, publicly held companies issue quarterly reports that provide updated information about sales and earnings and about any material changes in the business or operations. These quarterly reports may provide unaudited financial statements, updates on operating highlights, changes in outstanding shares, compliance with debt restrictions, and other matters affecting stockholders.

The minimum financial information that must be reported quarterly are sales, net income, taxes, nonrecurring revenue and expenses, accounting changes, contingencies such as lawsuits, additions or deletions of business segments, and material changes in financial position.

A company may provide financial figures for the quarter itself (*e.g.,* third quarter, comprising July 1-September 30) or cumulatively from the beginning of the year (January 1-September 30). However, prior year data must be provided on a comparative basis. *NOTE: Read quarterly reports in conjunction with the annual report.*

SECURITIES AND EXCHANGE COMMISSION FILINGS

The SEC, established by the Securities Exchange Act of 1934, has the power to regulate trading on the exchanges and to require corporate disclosure of information relevant to the stockholders of publicly traded companies. The SEC even has the power to dictate accounting conventions.

Information available through the SEC consists of corporate income statements, balance sheets, detailed support of accounting information, and internal data not always found in a company's annual report. The specific reports that companies are required to file with the SEC are:

- **Annual 10-K Report:** Perhaps the best-known SEC filing, the 10-K can usually be obtained free directly from the company rather than paying the SEC a copying charge. This report should be read in combination with the firm's annual report; it contains the same type of information but in greater detail.

- **8-K Report:** This report must be filed when any corporation undergoes some important event that stockholders would be interested in knowing about, such as changes in control, bankruptcy, resignation of officers or directors, and other material events.

- **Quarterly 10-Q Report:** The quarterly update to the 10-K report is filed no later than 45 days after the end of each quarter. It provides information about outstanding securities, debt compliance arrangements, changes in stockholdings, legal proceedings, and stockholder voting matters such as electing the Board of Directors. It also contains quarterly financial statements.

There are many other SEC filings. For example, companies must file proxy statement materials disclosing information relevant to stockholders' votes.

HOW TO READ A PROSPECTUS

Buying Stock as a Company Goes Public

There are few more alluring investments than a new stock in a promising growth company. For example, in 1999, numerous Internet stocks went public; many soared over 100% in the first day of trading. But the risks can be tremendous, and many suffered big losses later.

How do you separate the winners from the losers among companies making their initial public offerings? The Securities Act of 1933 offers assistance in this matter. It requires most new corporate issues to have a registration statement on file at the SEC before the offering. In it the issuer must make *full disclosure* of relevant financial statements. These documents are summarized in a booklet called a *prospectus*.

A prospectus, which is available from the company or stockbroker, is a lengthy, boring document, but few pieces of paper can help investors better understand a company, stock market professionals say. The key is knowing how to decipher the clues in a prospectus.

There are 10 key questions to ask yourself before jumping into a new issue.

1. *Who's Selling What?*

Experts say they can often tell a book by its cover. Basically, there are two key facts on the first sheet of the prospectus: what's being sold and who's doing the selling.

Investment pros like their offerings straight. Warrants, units, or bundles of preferred shares are a dead giveaway that something's amiss, they say. Another signal to the pros is the underwriters—the stock brokerages who have been hired to market these newly minted shares. If they haven't heard of the underwriter, they're not buying.

2. *Is This a Real Business?*

You don't want to invest in someone's long-term dream of success or in a slow-starting industrial giant of the future. You want to see results now.

Look for fundamentals, starting right there on page 3 of the prospectus. Here, the company's business lines and need for the new funds are quickly outlined. The summary also gives a financial snapshot of the company.

This is where you start your calculator, hoping to find a company with rapidly expanding sales figures supported by a corresponding growth in profits.

3. *Who's the Competition?*

Some businesses just lend themselves to profit—like selling the cure for cancer or AIDS or owning half the US market in something. In others, it can be success today, bankruptcy tomorrow.

A key to assessing where a company might fit's determining how much competition it has. This information is often contained in the "Company" or "Management's Discussion of Business" sections of a prospectus. Ask: Has the firm patented any products? Can it control pricing? Or is it just another name in an already crowded field?

4. *Will the Business Grow?*

You should be hung up on growth. Bigger sales means bigger profits, which means higher stock prices. But numbers don't tell the whole story. Scour the prospectus for hints about the company's growth prospects. You want to know who buys the products and who distributes them. You also want to know where the raw materials come from and how likely the future supply of those cherished goods will be.

Key information can be found in the "Risks" section as well as "Company" or "Management's Discussion of Business."

5. *Will Profits Continue?*

Anyone reviewing a prospectus should be aware that businesses planning to go public have a nasty habit of having very good financial results just before the stock sale. That's why an important question is: Will the good fortune continue once the public has been brought in as partners?

"Management's Discussion of Operations" is a fertile hunting ground for profit information. What makes the company profitable? How does gross profit margin shrink down to net income? Are the margins consistent, or do they vary seasonally or after sales promotions?

6. *What's the Real Price?*

One way to figure what newly issued shares of a company are worth on paper is to look at the "Dilution" section. Dilution, as its name implies, means how much less a share is actually worth after accounting for expenses, proceeds from the sale that don't go to the company, and readjustment of the books after the offering.

Another measure of value is the P/E ratio, but there's a catch: Do you use the last complete year's earnings figures? Or do you extrapolate a current-year number from other figures provided?

7. *What Are the Risks?*

Everyone checks out the "Risk" section. By definition, this part of a prospectus should scare off some investors. It's there to warn the public about past, present, or potential problems with the company. Some of the risks listed are boiler-plate stuff, such as "this is a relatively new company and can give no promise that its results will be good in the future," or the company is heavily dependent on managers who could leave tomorrow or no market has ever existed for the shares.

8. *Who's Running the Place?*

Review the "Management" and "Principal and Selling Shareholders" sections for the background check on top executives and major shareholders. While the one-paragraph summaries of key players' business backgrounds is by no means a definite test of management skills, the list often highlights specialties or experience gained at other firms.

9. *What Are They Getting out of It?*

Prospectuses contain some of the most intimate details about a company, especially when it comes to rewards reaped by top managers and large stockholders. Parts of "Management," "Certain Transactions," and "Principal and Selling Stockholders" can say a lot about a firm.

10. *Any Surprises Left?*

You don't want surprises. That's why you shouldn't forget to read things like footnotes, small type, and "Notes to Financial Statements."

ANALYZING FINANCIAL STATEMENTS

An investor must be interested in the present and future level of return (earnings) and risk (liquidity, debt, and activity). You, as an investor, evaluate a firm's stock based on an examination of its financial statements. This evaluation considers overall financial health, economic and political conditions, industry factors, and future outlook of the company. The analysis attempts to ascertain whether the stock is overpriced, under priced, or properly priced in proportion to its market value. A stock is valuable to you only if you can predict the future financial performance of the business. Financial statement analysis gives you much of the data you will need to forecast earnings and dividends.

Financial statement analysis attempts to answer the following basic questions:

- How well is the business doing?

- What are its strengths?

- What are its weaknesses?

- How does it fare in the industry?

- Is the business improving or deteriorating?

A complete set of financial statements, as we said, will include the balance sheet, income statement, and statement of cash flows. The first two are vital in financial statement analysis. The analysis tools that you will use in evaluating the firm's present and future financial condition include horizontal, vertical, and ratio analysis, which give relative measures of the performance and financial condition of the company.

Horizontal and Vertical Analysis

Comparison of two or more years' financial data is known as horizontal analysis. Horizontal analysis looks at trends in the accounts in dollar and percentage terms over the years. It's typically presented in comparative financial statements for five years (see the TLC, Inc. financial data in Figures 5-11, 5-12, and 5-13).

Through horizontal analysis, you can pinpoint areas of wide divergence requiring investigation. For example, in the income statement shown in Figure 5-12, the significant rise in sales returns taken with the reduction in sales for 20X1-20X2 should cause concern. You might compare these results with those of competitors.

It's essential to present both the dollar amount of change and the percentage of change since the use of one without the other may result in erroneous conclusions. The interest expense from 20X0-20X1 went up by 100%, but this represented only $1,000 and may not need further investigation. Similarly, a large number change that cause only a small percentage change may not be of great importance.

Key changes and trends can also be highlighted by the use of common-size statements. A common-size statement is one that shows the separate items appearing on it in percentage terms. Preparation of common-size statements is known as vertical analysis. In vertical analysis, a material financial statement item is used as a base value, to which all other accounts on the financial statement are compared. In the balance sheet, for example, total assets equal 100%. Each asset is stated as a percentage of total assets. Similarly, total liabilities and stockholders' equity is assigned 100%, with a given liability or equity account stated as a percentage of total liabilities and stockholders' equity. Figure 5-13 shows a common-size income statement based on the data provided in Figure 5-12.

FIGURE 5-11: TLC, INC. COMPARATIVE BALANCE SHEET
(in thousands of dollars)
December 31, 20X2, 20X1, 20X0

	20X2	20X1	20X0	Increase or Decrease 20X2-20X1	Increase or Decrease 20X1-20X0	% Increase or Decrease 20X2-20X1	% Increase or Decrease 20X1-20X0
ASSETS							
Current assets:							
Cash	$28	$36	$36	-8	0	-22.2%	0.0%
Marketable securities	22	15	7	7	8	46.7%	114.3%
Accounts receivable	21	16	10	5	6	31.3%	60.0%
Inventory	53	46	49	7	-3	15.2%	-6.1%
Total current assets	124	113	102	11	11	9.7%	10.8%
Plant and equip.	103	91	83	12	8	13.2%	9.6%
Total assets	227	204	185	23	19	11.3%	10.3%
LIABILITIES							
Current liabilities	56	50	51	6	-1	12.0%	-2.0%
Long-term debt	83	74	69	9	5	12.2%	7.2%
Total liabilities	139	124	120	15	4	12.1%	3.3%
STOCKHOLDERS' EQUITY							
Common Stock ($10 par, 4,600 shares)	46	46	46	0	0	0.0%	0.0%
Retained Earnings	42	34	19	8	15	23.5%	78.9%
Total Stockholders' Equity	88	80	65	8	15	10.0%	23.1%
Total Liabilities and Stockholders' Equity	$227	$204	$185	23	19	11.3%	10.3%

Placing all assets in common-size form clearly shows the relative importance of current as compared to non-current assets. It also shows when significant changes have taken place in the composition of the cur-

FIGURE 5-12: TLC, INC. COMPARATIVE INCOME
STATEMENT (in thousands of dollars)
December 31, 20X2, 20X1, 20X0

	20X2	20X1	20X0	Increase or Decrease 20X2-20X1	Increase or Decrease 20X1-20X0	% Increase or Decrease 20X2-20X1	% Increase or Decrease 20X1-20X0
Sales	$98.3	$120.0	$56.6	($21.7)	$63.4	-18.1%	112.0%
Sales ret & allow	$18.0	$10.0	$4.0	$8.0	$6.0	80.0%	150.0%
Net Sales	$80.3	$110.0	$52.6	($29.7)	$57.4	-27.0%	109.1%
Cost of goods sold	$52.0	$63.0	$28.0	($11.0)	$35.0	-17.5%	125.0%
Gross profit	**$28.3**	**$47.0**	**$24.6**	**($18.7)**	**$22.4**	**-39.8%**	**91.1%**
Operating expenses							
Selling expenses	$12.0	$13.0	$11.0	($1.0)	$2.0	-7.7%	18.2%
General expenses	$5.0	$8.0	$3.0	($3.0)	$5.0	-37.5%	166.7%
Total operating exp	**$17.0**	**$21.0**	**$14.0**	**($4.0)**	**$7.0**	**-19.0%**	**50.0%**
Inc from operations	$11.3	$26.0	$10.6	($14.7)	$15.4	-56.5%	145.3%
Non-operating income	$4.0	$1.0	$2.0	$3.0	($1.0)	300.0%	-50.0%
Inc before int & taxes	**$15.3**	**$27.0**	**$12.6**	**($11.7)**	**$14.4**	**-43.3%**	**114.3%**
Interest expense	$2.0	$2.0	$1.0	$0.0	$1.0	0.0%	100.0%
Income before taxes	**$13.3**	**$25.0**	**$11.6**	**($11.7)**	**$13.4**	**-46.8%**	**115.5%**
Income Taxes (40%)	$5.3	$10.0	$4.6	($4.7)	$5.4	-46.8%	115.5%
Net Income	**$8.0**	**$15.0**	**$7.0**	**($7.0)**	**$8.0**	**-46.8%**	**115.5%**

rent assets over the last year. Notice, for example, that receivables have increased in relative importance and that cash has declined. The deterioration in the cash position may be a result of inability to collect from customers.

For the income statement, 100% is assigned to net sales with all other revenue and expense accounts related to it. It's possible to see at a glance how each dollar of sales is distributed among the various costs, expenses, and profits. For example, notice from Figure 5-13 that 64.8 cents of every dollar of sales was needed to cover cost of goods sold in 20X2, as compared to only 57.3 cents in the prior year; also notice that only 9.9 cents out of every dollar of sales remained for profits in 20X2—down from 13.6 cents in the prior year.

By comparing the vertical percentages of the business with those of the competition and with industry norms, you can determine how the company fares in the industry (see Figure 5-14).

FIGURE 5-13: TLC, INC. INCOME STATEMENT AND
COMMON SIZE ANALYSIS (in thousands of
dollars)
December 31, 20X2 and 20X1

	20X2 Amount	%	20X1 Amount	%
Sales	$98.30	122.40%	$120.00	109.10%
Sales return &allowances	$18.00	22.40%	$10.00	9.10%
Net sales	$80.30	100.00%	$110.00	100.00%
Cost of goods sold	$52.00	64.80%	$63.00	57.30%
Gross profit	$28.30	35.20%	$47.00	42.70%
Operating expenses				
Selling expenses	$12.00	14.90%	$13.00	11.80%
General expenses	$5.00	6.20%	$8.00	7.30%
Total operating expenses	$17.00	21.20%	$21.00	19.10%
Income from operations	$11.30	14.10%	$26.00	23.60%
Non-operating income	$4.00	5.00%	$1.00	0.90%
Income Before Interest & Taxes	$15.30	19.10%	$27.00	24.50%
Interest Expense	$2.00	2.50%	$2.00	1.80%
Income Before Taxes	$13.30	16.60%	$25.00	22.70%
Income Taxes (40%)	$5.30	6.60%	$10.00	9.10%
Net Income	$8.00	9.90%	$15.00	13.60%

Working with Financial Ratios

Horizontal and vertical analysis compares one figure to another within the same category. It's also vital to compare figures in different categories. This is accomplished by ratio analysis. In this section, you will learn how to calculate the various financial ratios and how to interpret them. The results of the ratio analysis will allow you to:

- Appraise the position of a business,

- Identify trouble spots that need attention, and

- Provide the basis for making projections about the course of future operations.

Think of ratios as measures of the relative health or sickness of a business. Just as a doctor takes readings of a patient's temperature, blood pressure, heart rate, etc., you'll take readings of a business's liquidity, profitability, leverage, efficiency in using assets, and market value.

FIGURE 5-14: SUMMARY OF FINANCIAL RATIOS—TREND AND INDUSTRY COMPARISONS

Ratios	Definitions	20X1	20X2	Industry	Ind.	Trend	Overall
LIQUIDITY							
Net Working Capital	Current Assets - Current Liabilities	63	68	56	Good	Good	Good
Current Ratio	Current Assets/Current Liabilities	2.26	2.21	2.05	OK	Ok	Ok
Quick (Acid-Test) Ratio	(Cash + Marketable Securities + Accounts Receivable)/Current Liabilities	1.34	1.27	1.11	OK	Ok	Ok
ASSET UTILIZATION							
Accounts Receivable Turnover	Net Credit Sales/Average Accounts Receivable	8.46	4.34	5.5	OK	Poor	Poor
Average Collection Period	365 Days/Accounts Receivable Turnover	43.1 Days	84.1 Days	66.4 Days	OK	Poor	Poor
Inventory Turnover	Cost Of Goods Sold/Average Inventory	1.33	1.05	1.2	OK	Poor	Poor
Average AgeOf Inventory	365 Days/Inventory Turnover	274.4 Days	347.6 Days	N/A	N/A	Poor	Poor
Operating Cycle	Average Collection Period + Average Age Of Inventory	317.5 Days	317.5 Days	N/A	N/A	Poor	Poor
Total Asset Turnover	Net Sales/Average Total Assets	0.57	0.37	0.44	OK	Poor	Poor
SOLVENCY							
Debt Ratio	Total Liabilities/Total Assets	0.61	0.61	N/A	N/A	Ok	Ok
Debt-Equity Ratio	Total Liabilities/Stockholders' Equity	1.55	1.58	1.3	poor	Poor	Poor
Times Interest Earned	Income Before Interest and Taxes/Interest Expense	13.5 Times	7.65 Times	10 Times	OK	Poor	Poor
PROFITABILITY							
Gross Profit Margin	Gross Profit/Net Sales	0.43	0.35	0.48	Poor	Poor	Poor
Profit Margin	Net Income/Net Sales	0.14	0.1	0.15	Poor	Poor	Poor
Return On Total Assets	Net Income/Average Total Assets	0.077	0.037	0.1	Poor	Poor	Poor
Return On Equity (ROE)	Earnings Available To Common Stockholders/Average Stockholders' Equity	0.207	0.095	0.27	Poor	Poor	Poor
MARKET VALUE							
Earnings Per Share (EPS)	(Net Income - Preferred Dividend)/Common Shares Outstanding	3.26	1.74	4.51	Poor	Poor	Poor
Price/Earnings (P/E) Ratio	Market Price Per Share/EPS	7.98	6.9	7.12	OK	Poor	Poor
Book Value Per Share	(Total Stockholders' Equity - Preferred Stock)/Common Shares Outstanding	17.39	19.13	N/A	N/A	Good	Good
Price/Book Value Ratio	Market Price Per Share/Book Value Per Share	1.5	0.63	N/A	N/A	Poor	Poor
Dividend Yield	Dividends Per Share/Market Price Per Share						
Dividend Payout	Dividends Per Share/EPS						

Where the doctor compares the readings to generally accepted guidelines, such as a temperature of 98.6 degrees as normal, you, too, make comparisons to the norms.

To obtain useful conclusions from the ratios, you must make two comparisons:

- *Industry comparison.* This will allow you to answer the question, "How does this business fare in the industry?" You must compare the company's ratios to those of competing companies in the industry or with industry averages. You can obtain industry norms from financial services such as Value Line, Dun and Bradstreet, and Standard & Poor's.

- *Trend analysis.* To see how the business is doing over time, look at a given ratio for one company over several years to see the direction of financial health or operational performance.

Financial ratios can be grouped into the following types: liquidity, asset utilization (activity), solvency (leverage and debt service), profitability, and market value.

Liquidity is the firm's ability to satisfy maturing short-term debt. Liquidity is crucial to carrying out the business, especially during periods of adversity. It typically relates to the short term, typically a period of one year or less. Poor liquidity might lead to higher cost of financing and inability to pay bills and dividends. The three basic measures of liquidity are (a) net working capital, (b) the current ratio, and (c) the quick (acidtest) ratio.

Throughout our discussion, keep referring to Figures 5-11 and 5-12 to make sure you understand where the numbers come from.

- *Net Working Capital* equals current assets minus current liabilities. Net working capital for 20X2 is:

  Net working capital = Current assets - Current liabilities

  = $124 - $56
  = $68

In 20X1, net working capital was $63. The rise over the year is favorable.

• *The Current Ratio* equals current assets divided by current liabilities. The ratio reflects the company's ability to satisfy current debt from current assets.

$$\text{Current ratio} = \left(\frac{Current\ assets}{Current\ liabilities} \right)$$

For 20X2, the current ratio is:

$$\left(\frac{\$124}{\$56} \right) = 2.21$$

In 20X1, the current ratio was 2.26. The ratio's decline over the year points to a slight reduction in liquidity.

• *The Quick Ratio (Acid-Test Ratio)* is a more stringent liquidity test. Inventory and prepaid expenses are excluded from the total of current assets, leaving only the more liquid (or quick) assets to be divided by current liabilities.

$$\text{Acid - test ratio} = \frac{\text{Cash} + \text{Marketable Securities}}{\text{Current Liabilities}}$$

The quick ratio for 20X2 is:

$$\left(\frac{\$28 + \$21 + \$22}{\$56} \right) = 1.27$$

In 20X1, the ratio was 1.34. The small reduction in the ratio over the period points to less liquidity.

The overall liquidity trend shows a slight deterioration, as reflected in the lower current and quick ratios, although it's better than the industry norms (see Figure 5-14 for industry averages), but a mitigating factor is the increase in net working capital.

Asset Utilization (activity, turnover) ratios reflect how a company uses its assets to obtain revenue and profit. One example is how well receivables are turning into cash. The higher the ratio, the more efficiently the business manages its assets.

Accounts receivable ratios comprise the accounts receivable turnover and the average collection period.

- *The Accounts Receivable Turnover* is the number of times accounts receivable are collected in the year. It's derived by dividing net credit sales by average accounts receivable.

$$\text{Accounts receivable turnover} = \frac{\text{Net credit sales}}{\text{Average accounts receivable}}$$

For 20X2, the average accounts receivable is:

$$\frac{\$21 + \$16}{2} = \$18.5$$

The accounts receivable turnover for 20X2 is:

$$\frac{\$80.3}{\$18.5} = 4.34$$

In 20X1, the turnover was 8.46. The sharp reduction in the turnover rate points to a collection problem.

- *The Average Collection Period* is the length of time it takes to collect receivables, the number of days receivables are held.

$$\text{Average collection period} = \frac{365 \text{ days}}{\text{Accounts receivable turnover}}$$

In 20X2, the collection period is:

$$\frac{365}{4.34} = 84.1 \text{ days}$$

It takes this firm over 84 days to convert receivables to cash. In 20X1, the collection period was 43.1 days. The significant lengthening of the collection period may be a cause for concern. It may be a result of many doubtful accounts, or it may be a result of poor credit management.

- *Inventory Turnover Ratio and Age of Inventory:* Inventory ratios are useful especially when there is buildup in inventory. Inventory ties up cash. It can result in lost opportunities for profit as well as increased storage costs. Before you extend credit or lend money, examine the firm's inventory turnover and average age of inventory.

$$\text{Inventory turnover} = \frac{\text{Cost of goods sold}}{\text{Average inventory}}$$

The inventory turnover for 20X2 is:

$$\frac{\$52}{\$49.5} = 1.05$$

For 20X1, the turnover was 1.33.

$$\text{Average age of inventory} = \frac{365}{\text{Inventory turnover}}$$

In 20X2, the average age is:

$$\frac{365}{1.05} = 347.6 \text{ days}$$

In the previous year, the average age was 274.4 days.

Inventory is being held longer. Ask why the inventory is not selling as quickly.

- *The Operating Cycle* is the number of days it takes to convert inventory and receivables to cash.

Operating cycle = Average collection period + Average age of inventory

In 20X2, the operating cycle is:

84.1 days + 347.6 days = 431.7 days

In the previous year, the operating cycle was 317.5 days. The direction is unfavorable. Funds are tied up in non-cash assets. Cash is being collected more slowly.

- *Total Asset Turnover:* Here's how you can find out whether the company is efficiently employing its total assets to obtain sales revenue. A low ratio may indicate too high an investment in assets in comparison to the revenue generated.

$$\text{Total asset turnover} = \frac{\text{Net sales}}{\text{Average total assets}}$$

In 20X2, the ratio is:

$$\frac{\$80.3}{(\$104 + \$227)/2} = \frac{\$80.3}{\$215.5} = 0.37$$

In 20X1, the ratio was 0.57 ($110/$194.5). There has been a sharp reduction in asset utilization.

TLC, Inc. has suffered a sharp deterioration in activity ratios, pointing to a need for improved credit and inventory management—although the 20X2 ratios are not far out of line with the industry averages (see Figure 5-14). The problems appear to be inefficient collection and obsolescent inventory.

Solvency (Leverage and Debt Service) You should be concerned about the long-term financial and operating structure of any firm in which you might be interested. Solvency is the company's ability to satisfy long-term debt as it becomes due. Another important consideration is the proportion of debt in the firm's capital structure, which is referred to as "financial leverage." Capital structure is the mix of long-term sources of funds used by the firm.

Solvency also depends on earning power; in the long run a company cannot satisfy its debts unless it earns a profit. A leveraged capital structure subjects the company to fixed interest charges, which contributes to earnings instability. Excessive debt may also make it difficult for the firm to borrow funds at reasonable rates during tight money markets.

- *The Debt Ratio* reveals the amount of money a company owes to its creditors. Excessive debt means greater risk to the investor. (Note that equity holders come after creditors in bankruptcy.) The debt ratio is:

$$\text{Debt ratio} = \frac{\text{Total liabilities}}{\text{Total assets}}$$

In 20X2, the ratio is:

$$\frac{\$139}{\$227} = 0.61$$

- *The Debt-Equity Ratio* will show you how much debt the firm has in its capital structure. Large debts mean that the borrower has to pay significant periodic interest and principal. Also, a heavily indebted firm takes a greater risk of running out of cash in difficult times. The interpretation of this ratio depends on several variables, including the ratios of other firms in the industry, the degree of access to additional debt financing, and stability of operations.

$$\text{Debt - equity ratio} = \frac{\text{Total liabilities}}{\text{Stockholders' equity}}$$

In 20X2, the ratio is:

$$\frac{\$139}{\$88} = 1.58$$

In the previous year, the ratio was 1.55. The trend is relatively static.

- *Times Interest Earned:* This is the interest coverage ratio, which tells you how many times the firm's before-tax earnings would cover interest. It's a safety margin indicator in that it reflects how much of a reduction in earnings a company can tolerate.

$$\text{Times interest earned} = \frac{\text{Income before interest and taxes}}{\text{Interest expense}}$$

For 20X2, the ratio is:

$$\frac{\$15.3}{\$2.0} = 7.65$$

In 20X1, interest was covered 13.5 times. The reduction in coverage during the period is a bad sign. It means that less earnings are available to satisfy interest charges.

Also note liabilities that have not yet been reported in the balance sheet by closely examining the footnotes. Find out about lawsuits, noncapitalized leases, and future guarantees.

Profitability: A company's ability to earn a good profit and return on investment is an indicator of its financial well-being and the efficiency with which it's managed. Poor earnings have detrimental effects on market price of stock and dividends. Total dollar net income has little meaning unless it's compared to what goes into getting that profit.

- *Gross Profit Margin* shows the percentage of each dollar remaining once the company has paid for goods acquired. A high margin reflects good earning potential.

$$\text{Gross profit margin} = \frac{\text{Gross profit}}{\text{Net sales}}$$

In 20X2, the ratio is:

$$\frac{\$28.3}{\$80.3} = 0.35$$

The ratio was 0.43 in 20X1. The reduction shows that the company now receives less profit on each dollar of sales. Perhaps a higher relative cost of the merchandise sold is at fault.

- *Profit Margin,* which shows the earnings generated from revenue, is a key indicator of operating performance. It gives you an idea of the firm's pricing, cost structure, and production efficiency.

$$\text{Profit margin} = \frac{\text{Net income}}{\text{Net sales}}$$

The ratio in 20X2 is:

$$\frac{\$8}{\$80.3} = 0.10$$

The profit margin for the previous year was 0.14. The decline in the ratio shows a downward trend in earning power.

NOTE: These percentages are available in the common-size income statement as given in Figure 5-13.

Return on investment is a prime indicator because it allows you to evaluate the profit you will earn if you invest in the business. Two key ratios are the return on total assets and the return on equity.

- *Return on Total Assets* shows whether management is efficient in using its resources to make a profit.

$$\text{Return on total assets} = \frac{\text{Net income}}{\text{Average total assets}}$$

In 20X2, the return is:

$$\frac{\$8}{(\$227 + \$204)/2} = 0.038$$

In 20X1, the return was 0.077. There has been deterioration in the productivity of assets.

- *Return on Equity (ROE)* reflects the rate of return earned on the stockholders' investment.

$$\text{Return on common equity} = \frac{\text{Net income available to stockholders}}{\text{Average stockholders' equity}}$$

The return in 20X2 is:

$$\frac{\$8}{(\$88 + \$80)/2} = 0.095$$

In 20X1, the return was 0.207. There has been a significant drop in return to the owners.

The overall profitability of the company has decreased considerably, causing a decline in both return on assets and return on equity. Lower earnings may have been due in part to higher costs of short-term financing arising from the decline in liquidity and activity ratios. Moreover, as turnover rates in assets go down, profit will also decline because of a lack of sales and higher costs of carrying higher current asset balances. Industry comparisons reveal that the company is faring very poorly in the industry. Figure 5-15 shows industries with high return on equity (above 20%).

FIGURE 5-15: INDUSTRIES WITH HIGH RETURN ON EQUITY (ROE) RATES (in excess of 20%) 1998

Cars and trucks	62.4%
Personal care	31.0
Eating places	22.9
Food processing	24.8
Beverages	32.0
Business machines and services	20.6
Telephone	28.6

Source: Corporate Scorecard, by Business Week, McGraw-Hill, March 1999, pp. 75-91.

Market Value ratios relate the company's stock price to its earnings (or book value) per share. Also included are dividend-related ratios.

- *Earnings Per Share (EPS)* is the ratio most widely watched by investors. EPS shows net income per common share owned. You must reduce net income by the preferred dividends to obtain the net income available to common stockholders. Where there is no preferred stock in the capital structure, you determine EPS by dividing net income by the weighted average of the number of common shares outstanding throughout the period. EPS is a gauge of corporate operating performance and of expected future dividends.

$$EPS = \frac{\text{Net income - Preferred dividend}}{\text{Common shares outstanding}}$$

EPS in 20X2 is:

$$\frac{\$8,000}{4,600 \text{ shares}} = \$1.74$$

For 20X1, EPS was $3.26. The sharp reduction over the year should cause alarm among investors. As you can see in Figure 5-14, the industry average EPS in 20X2 is much higher than that of TLC, Inc. ($4.51 per share vs. $1.74 per share).

FIGURE 5-16: 1998 HIGHLY PROFITABLE COMPANIES
(in terms of EPS)

Ford	$17.76
U.S. Home	4.68
Alcoa	4.84
CIGNA	6.05
IBM	6.57
Washington Post	41.10

Source: Corporate Scorecard, by Business Week, McGraw-Hill, March 1999, pp. 75-91.

Figure 5-16 provides a list of highly profitable companies in terms of EPS.

- *The Price/Earnings Ratio (P/E),* also called the earnings multiple, reflects the company's relationship to its stockholders. The P/E ratio represents the amount investors are willing to pay for each dollar of the firm's earnings. A high multiple (cost per dollar of earnings) is favored since it shows that investors view the firm positively. On the other hand, investors looking for value would prefer a relatively lower multiple (cost per dollar of earnings) as compared with companies of similar risk and return.

$$\text{Price/earnings ratio} = \frac{\text{Market price per share}}{\text{Earnings per share}}$$

Assume a market price per share of $12 on December 31, 20X2, and $26 on December 31, 20X1. The P/E ratios are:

$$20X2 : \frac{\$12}{\$1.74} = 6.9$$

$$20X1 : \frac{\$26}{\$3.26} = 7.98$$

From the lower P/E multiple, you can infer that the stock market now has a lower opinion of the business. Some investors do argue that a low P/E ratio can mean that the stock is undervalued. Nevertheless, the decline over the year in stock price was 54% ($14/$26), which should cause deep investor concern.

NOTE: What does it mean when a firm's stock sells on a high or low P/E ratio? To answer this question, the Gordon's dividend growth model can be helpful. (The model will be taken up again in Chapter 6.) If a company's dividends are expected to grow at a constant rate, then

$$P_0 = \frac{D_1}{r-g}$$

where P_0 = the current price of stock, D_1 = the expected dividend next year, r = the return required by investors from similar investments, and g = the expected growth in dividends. In order to find the P/E ratio, divide through by expected EPS.

$$\frac{P_0}{EPS} = \frac{D_1}{EPS} x \frac{1}{r-g}$$

Thus, a high P/E ratio may indicate that

- *Investors expect high dividend growth (g), or*

- *The stock has low risk; therefore investors are content with a low prospective return (r), or*

- *The company is expected to achieve average growth while paying out a high proportion of earnings (D1/EPS).*

Figure 5-17 shows P/E ratios of certain companies.

- *Book Value per Share* equals the net assets available to common stockholders divided by shares outstanding. By comparing it to market price per share you can get another view of how investors feel about the business.

The book value per share in 20X2 is:

$$\text{Book value per share} = \frac{\text{Total stockholders' equity - Preferred stock liquidation value}}{\text{Common shares outstanding}}$$

$$= \frac{\$88,000 - 0}{4,600} = \$19.13$$

FIGURE 5-17: P/E RATIOS

Company	Industry	1998
Boeing	Aerospace	32
General Motors	Cars and trucks	21
Goodyear	Tire and rubber	13
Gap	Retailing	52
Intel	Semiconductor	37
Pfizer	Drugs and research	88

Source: Corporate Scorecard, by Business Week, McGraw-Hill, March 1999, pp. 75-91.

In 20X1, book value per share was $17.39.

The increased book value per share is a favorable sign, because it indicates that more assets to back each share. However, in 20X2, market price is much less than book value, which means that the stock market does not value the security highly. In 20X1, market price did exceed book value, but stockholders now have some doubt about the company. However, some analysts may argue that the stock is under priced.

- *The Price/Book Value Ratio* shows the market value of the company in comparison to its historical accounting value. A company with old assets may have a high ratio compared to one with new assets. Note the changes in the ratio as you appraise the corporate assets.

The ratio equals:

$$\text{Price/book value} = \frac{\text{Market price per share}}{\text{Book value per share}}$$

In 20X2, the ratio is:

$$\frac{\$12}{\$19.13} = 0.63$$

In 20X1, the ratio was 1.5. The significant drop in the ratio may indicate that investors have a lower opinion of the company. The market price of the stock may have dropped because of deterioration in the liquidity, activity, and profitability ratios. The major indicators of a company's performance are intertwined (one affects the other) so that problems in one area may spill over into another. This appears to have happened to the company in our example.

- *Dividend Yield and Dividend Pay-Out:* Dividend ratios help you determine the current income from an investment. Two relevant ratios are:

$$\text{Dividend yield} = \frac{\text{Dividends per share}}{\text{Market price per share}}$$

$$\text{Dividend pay-out} = \frac{\text{Dividends per share}}{\text{Earnings per share}}$$

Figure 5-18 shows the dividend pay-out ratios of some companies.

FIGURE 5-18: DIVIDENT YIELD RATIOS 1998

General Electric	1.2%
General Motors	2.3
Intel	0.1
Wal-Mart	0.4
Pfizer	0.5
Hewlett Packard	0.9

Source: MSN Money Central, April 11, 1999.

There is no such thing as the "right" pay-out ratio. Stockholders look unfavorably on reduced dividends as a sign of possibly deteriorating financial health. However, companies with ample opportunities for growth at high rates of return on assets tend to have low pay-out ratios.

SUMMARY OF FINANCIAL RATIOS

A single ratio or group of ratios is not adequate for assessing all aspects of the firm's financial condition. Figure 5-14 summarizes the 20X1 and 20X2 ratios calculated in the previous sections, along with the industry average ratios for 20X2. The figure also shows the formula used to calculate each ratio. The last three columns of the figure contains subjective assessments of TLC's financial condition, based on trend analysis and

20X2 comparisons to the industry norms (though five-year ratios are generally needed for trend analysis to be more meaningful).

Appraising the trend in the company's ratios from 20X1 to 20X2, we see from the drop in the current and quick ratios that there has been a slight detraction in short-term liquidity, although both ratios have been above the industry averages. But working capital has improved. A material deterioration in the activity ratios calls for improved credit and inventory policies. These ratios are not terribly alarming, however, because they are not far out of line with industry averages. But total utilization of assets, as indicated by total asset turnover, also shows a deteriorating trend.

Though leverage (amount of debt) has been constant, there is less profit available to satisfy interest charges. In 20X2, TLC's profitability is consistently below the industry average in every measure. In consequence, the return on owner's investment and the return on total assets have gone down. The earnings decrease may be partly due to the firm's high cost of short-term financing and partly due to operating inefficiency. The higher costs may be due to receivable and inventory difficulties that forced a decline in the liquidity and activity ratios. Furthermore, as receivables and inventory turn over less, profit will fall off from a lack of sales and the costs of carrying more in current asset balances.

The firm's market value, as measured by the P/E ratio, is respectable compared with the industry, but it shows a declining trend.

The company is doing satisfactorily by industry norms in many categories, but the 20X1-20X2 period suggests that the company is heading for financial trouble in terms of earnings, activity, and short-term liquidity. The business needs to concentrate on increasing operating efficiency and asset utilization.

Is Ratio Analysis A Panacea?

While ratio analysis is an effective tool for assessing a business's financial condition, you must also recognize its limitations:

- Because accounting policies vary among companies, they can inhibit useful comparisons. For example, the use of different depreciation methods (straight-line vs. double declining balance) will affect profitability and return ratios. Depreciation methods are discussed in detail in Chapter 9.

- Management may "window-dress" the figures. For example, it can reduce research expense just to bolster net income. Practices like these will almost always hurt the company in the long run.

- A ratio is static; it does not reveal future flows. For example, it will not answer questions like: "How much cash do you have in your pocket now?" or "Is that sufficient, considering your expenses and income over the next month?"

- A ratio does not indicate the quality of its components. For example, a high quick ratio may contain receivables that may not be collected.

- Reported liabilities may be undervalued. An example is a lawsuit on which the company is contingently liable.

- The company may have multiple lines of business, making it difficult to identify the industry group the company should be compared to.

- Industry averages cited by financial advisory services are only approximations. Hence, you may have to compare a company's ratios to those of competing companies in the industry.

SOURCES OF INDUSTRY FINANCIAL RATIOS

There are six major sources of industry financial ratios that you can use as comparisons with the ones of the company you are analyzing.

1. *Key Business Ratios* (published annually): This Dun & Bradstreet publication contains 14 significant ratios on each of 800 different lines of business listed by SIC (standard industrial classification) code. Examples of ratios included are current assets to current debt, net profits on net sales, and total debt to tangible net worth.

2. ***Annual Statement Studies*** (published annually): Robert Morris Associates, a banking industry group, provides common-size statements and financial ratios on over 150 industry classifications.

3. ***Leo Troy's Almanac of Business and Industrial Financial Ratios*** (published annually): This is an exhaustive source, published by Prentice-Hall, Inc., that contains common-size income statements and financial ratios by industry and by size of companies within each industry.

4. ***Dow Jones-Irwin Business and Investment Almanac*** (published annually): This comprehensive source, published by Dow Jones-Irwin, contains mostly industry financial ratios and common-size income statements. Some information is given on very large companies.

5. ***Standard & Poor's Industry Survey*** (published annually): The Survey contains various statistics, including some financial ratios, by industry and on leading companies within each industry grouping.

6. ***Business Week, "The Top 1,000."*** (published annually in March or April): Business Week has a special issue every year that provides numerous financial ratios on the 1,000 largest companies in the U.S.

APPENDIX 5-A:
USEFUL WEB SITES

Web Address	Primary Focus
reality.sgi.com/rchiang_esd/invest-research.html	Links to other web sites that offer historical information and projections
www.bankofny.com/adr	Educational material on the definition and trading of ADRs, along with a listing of all ADRs in the U.S. markets
www.bloomberg.com	Information on companies and markets
www.bridge.com	Information on companies and markets
www.firstcall.com	Earnings estimates on companies
www.hoovers.com	Selected financial and descriptive information on companies
www.ibbotson.com	Historical information on companies and markets
www.ipocentral.com	Information about recent and upcoming initial public offerings
www.ipo-fund.com	Information about recent and upcoming initial public offerings
www.ipomaven.com	Information about recent and upcoming initial public offerings
www.marketguide.com	Company ratios and industry links
www.marketguide.com/mgi/products	Company profiles, some ratios, and market quotes
www.pathfinder.com	Access to summaries of feature articles published by Money, Fortune, Time, and several other magazines
www.reportgallery.com	A library of annual reports
www.valueline.com	Selected financial and descriptive information on companies
www.zacks.com	Selected financial and descriptive information on companies

Chapter 6
COMMON AND PREFERRED STOCK

Securities cover a broad range of investment instruments, including common stocks, preferred stocks, bonds, and options. The two broad categories of securities available to investors are equity securities, which represent ownership of a company, and debt securities, which represent a loan from the investor to a company or government. Each type of security has not only distinct characteristics, but also unique advantages and disadvantages that vary by investor.

WHAT IS COMMON STOCK?

Common stock is a security that represents an ownership interest in a corporation. For example, if you hold 5,000 shares of ABC Corporation, which has 100,000 shares outstanding, your ownership interest is 5%. You acquire an equity interest in the corporation by buying its stock. The interest is evidenced by a transferable stock certificate. As a stockholder, you can vote for the board of directors of the corporation. An equity investment has no maturity date. Common stock return comes in the form of dividend income and appreciation in the market price of stock.

The characteristics that make common stock an attractive investment alternative (see Figure 6.1) are that:

- Common stocks represent ownership; fixed income securities like bonds, do not.

- Common stocks provide income potential not only in terms of current income (dividends) but also future appreciation.

- Common shareholders can participate in the firm's earnings, laying claim to all residual profits.

- Common stock can be a good inflation hedge when the total return (dividends plus appreciation in price) exceeds the rate of inflation.

- The variety of stocks available allows the investor to choose from a broad spectrum of risk-return combinations.

FIGURE 6-1: CHARACTERISTICS OF COMMON STOCK

Voting Rights	One vote per share
Income	Dividends; not fixed
Capital Gain/Loss Potential	Yes
Price Stability	No
Inflation Hedge	Yes
Preemptive Right	Yes
Priority of Claim	Residual after all other claims paid
Unit of Purchase	Usually in units of 100 shares

Some key common stock terms are:

- *Par value*—the value assigned to each share of stock in the company's charter; traditionally set at a low price partly for tax purposes; a corporation may also issue no?par stock.

- *Book value*—the net worth (assets minus liabilities) of the corporation divided by the number of shares outstanding.

$$\text{Book value} = \frac{\text{Assets - Liabilities (less liquidation payments to preferred shareholders)}}{\text{Number of shares outstanding}}$$

- *Market price*—the price of a share of stock currently quoted in the market The market value or capitalization of a firm is its stock price times the number of shares outstanding. The ratio of a stock's market price to its book value (price/book ratio) indicates how investors regard the company. Dividing the share price by the book value gives a market/book ratio; the higher the ratio, the more expensive the stock (compared with its book value).

ROLE OF STOCKHOLDERS

A corporation's stockholders have certain rights and privileges including:

- **Control of the Firm.** The stockholders elect the firm's directors who in turn select officers to manage the business.

- **Preemptive Rights.** This is the right to purchase new stock. This allows a common stockholder to keep the same proportional ownership when any new stock is being offered or any securities are convertible into common stock.

  (a) Value of right *"cum rights"*

  If a stock is selling for $60 and 2 rights are required to purchase a single share at the subscription price of $51, the value of a single right would be ($60-$51)/ (2 + 1) = $3. If the stock is now "ex-rights" its market value should reflect that and be $60-$3 or $57. Thus, we have ($57-$51)/ 2 = $3.

  $$\text{Value of a right} = \frac{\text{Market price (M) - Subscription price (S)}}{\text{Number of rights required (N)} + 1}$$

  (b) Value of right "ex-rights"

  $$\text{Value of a right} = \frac{\text{Adjusted M - S}}{N}$$

EXAMPLE 1

- **Voting Rights.** Shareholders can vote on all important matters affecting them:

  –Alterations to the corporate charter: mergers and acquisitions

  –Recapitalization (*e.g.,* an exchange of bonds for stock)

  –Financial reorganization

  –Election of the Board of Directors

- **Cash Dividends.** Cash dividends are paid to investors if declared by the Board of Directors. Important dates to remember:

  –Declared date: The date on which the board declares the dividend.

  –Record date: The date (set by the board) by which investors must buy stock in order to receive the dividend.

  –Ex-dividend date: The date that a stock will begin trading without the value of the pending dividend factored into its market value; The ex-dividend date is four business days before the record date.

EXAMPLE 2

Sunday	Monday	Tuesday	Wednesday	Thursday	Friday	Saturday
	1	2	3	4	5	6
7	8	9	10	11	12	13

Suppose you buy the stock on the 3rd day of the month (trade date). You are entitled to the dividend.

- **Payable date.** The date on which investors on record will receive dividends.

- **Stock Dividends.** A dividend payable in additional stock rather than cash. For example, if XYZ Corp. declares a 5% stock dividend, a holder of 200 shares would receive a stock certificate for 10 additional shares. If a stock dividend results in a fraction--an investor has 205 shares and is owed 10.25—the fractional is usually paid in cash.

- **Stock Splits.** Each old share is equal to some number of new shares. Because stock splits don't change the underlying value of the corporation, the other values are changed proportionately.

- **Reverse Splits.** Each old share is equal to some fraction of a new share.

EXAMPLE 3

A stock with a par value of $1 and a market price of $20 that had a 2-for-1 *stock split* would now have twice as many authorized shares. But both the par and market values would be halved. In a 1-for-2 *reverse split,* 200 shares of old stock would be 100 shares of the new stock, and both the par and market values would be doubled.

TYPES OF STOCKS

The stock you buy should be best for your particular circumstances and goals. The types of stock include:

- **Income Stocks**. These pay high dividends that provide a fairly stable stream of earnings. They're desirable if you want high current income instead of capital growth, and less risk. An example is utility companies. Income stocks give you the highest stable income to satisfy your present living needs.

- **Cyclical Stocks** are stocks whose price movements follow the business cycle. Prices increase in expansion and decline in recession. These stocks are thus somewhat risky. Examples include construction and airlines.

- **Defensive Stocks,** often called counter-cyclical stocks, remain stable during periods of contraction. They are safe and consistent the return earned is lower. An example is consumer goods stocks.

- **Growth Stocks** are those of companies evidencing higher rates of growth in operations and earnings than other firms. An example is high-technology firms. These stocks normally pay little or no dividend. Growth stocks usually increase in price faster than others, but they may fluctuate more. They appeal to investors seeking capital appreciation rather than dividend income.

- **Blue Chips** are common stocks that provide uninterrupted streams of dividends and strong long-term growth prospects, such as General Electric. These stocks have low risk and are less susceptible to cyclical market changes than other stocks. They are unlikely to surprise you.

- **Penny Stocks.** These stocks are stocks that usually have market prices below $1 a share. They are issued by financially weak and risky companies.

- **Speculative Stocks** are ones for which there is an opportunity for large profits, but there are no guarantees and earning are uncertain. You buy a speculative stock if you are willing to take a high risk for a prospect of very high return. Speculative stocks have high price fluctuations and price-earnings ratios. Examples include mining and biotechnology company stocks.

YIELD ON COMMON STOCK

The term "yield" is used in two stock contexts. The dividend yield is the periodic payment to stockholders of a share of the earnings of a corporation expressed as a percentage of the value of common stock at its initial cost or present market value. This creates a statistic that is roughly equivalent to interest.

$$\text{Yield} = \frac{\text{Dividend per share}}{\text{Price per share}}$$

EXAMPLE 4

You paid $80 for a stock currently worth $100. The dividend per share is $4. The yield on your investment is:

Based on initial cost:

$$\frac{\$4}{\$80} = 0.05 = 5\%$$

Based on market value:

$$\frac{\$4}{\$100} = 0.04 = 4\%$$

You can use dividend yield to assess the reasonableness of the price of the stock, particularly when dividends are stable (*e.g.,* utilities). Dividend yield is also helpful to an income?oriented investor who wants to compare equity dividend returns with the return on fixed income securities.

Second, the term "yield" can be used to describe the total return to an investor from an investment for a particular period. This return combines price movement (the capital gain yield) and dividend payments (the dividend yield), is deflated by the price of the stock at the beginning of the period. This calculation creates a percentage return (like interest) based upon the investment (market price) at the beginning of the period. More exactly, the yield on your stock investment for a single period can be calculated using the formula:

$$\text{Return} = \frac{\text{What you get from owning a stock for a given period}}{\text{What you had when the period started}}$$

$$\text{Return} = \frac{\text{Change in price of the stock during period} + \text{Dividend payment during period}}{\text{Price of the stock at the beginning of the period}}$$

$$\frac{(P_1 - P_0) + D_1}{P_0}$$

where,

D_1=Dividend at the end of the period

P_1=Price per share at the end of the period

P_0=Price per share at the beginning of the period

Investor return or yield can also be thought of as follows:

Return = Dividend yield + Capital gain yield

$$\text{Return} = \frac{\text{Dividends}}{\text{Beginning price}} + \frac{\text{Capital gain}}{\text{Beginning Price}}$$

$$\text{Return} = \frac{D_1}{P_0} + \frac{(P_1 - P_0)}{P_0}$$

EXAMPLE 5

Consider a stock selling for $50. The company is expected to pay a $3 cash dividend at the end of the year, and the stock's market price at the end of the year is expected to be $55 a share. Thus, the expected return would be:

$$\text{Return} = \frac{D_1 + (P_1 - P_0)}{P_0} = \frac{\$3 + (\$55 - \$50)}{\$50} = \frac{\$3 + \$5}{\$50} = \frac{\$8}{\$50} = 16\%$$

Or,

Dividend yield	=	$3/$50 6%
Capital gain yield	=	$5/$50 10%
Total yield	=	16%

Forecasting Stock Price—A Pragmatic Approach

To project stock price at some future date, analysts use the simple formula:

Forecasted price = Estimated future EPS x estimated P/E ratio

Of course, for this method to work, you have to (a) correctly projected earnings and (b) apply the appropriate P/E multiple. Forecasting EPS is not an easy task. Some accountants use a sales forecast combined with an after-tax profit margin, as follows:

Estimated after-tax earnings in year t =
        (Estimated sales in year t) x (After-tax profit margin expected in year t)

Estimated EPS in year t =
        Estimated earnings in year t / Number of common shares outstanding in year t

NOTE: The price model is based upon all future earnings, however, for ease of computation, assume that earnings will continue at the same inflation-adjusted level.

EXAMPLE 6

Assume that a company reported sales of $100 million, and its sales are estimated to grow at a 6 percent annual rate; the profit margin is about 8 percent. The company had 2 million shares outstanding. The company's P/E ratio was 15, which is expected to continue for the next year. Projected sales next year will equal $106 million ($100 million x 1.06).

Estimated after-tax earnings next year:

$106 million x 8% = $8.48 million

Estimated EPS next year:

$8.48 million/2 million =$4.24

If it is assumed that EPS will continue at the same inflation-adjusted level, the stock should be trading at a price of $63.60 by the end of next year:

Estimated share price next year = $4.24 x 15 = $63.60

NOTE: If you are looking for an advisory service's estimated EPS for the next year for a company, you can obtain it from publications such as Value Line Investment Survey. As noted in Chapter 16, this information is also available on the Internet.

What determines the Price-Earnings Ratio

What determines the P/E multiple is very complex. Empirical evidence seems to suggest the following factors are incorporated:

- Historical growth rate of earnings

- Forecasted earnings

- Average dividend payout ratio

- Beta of the company's systematic (uncontrollable) risk

- Instability of earnings

- Financial leverage

- Other factors, such as competitive position, management ability, and economic conditions.

HOW TO READ BETA

Beta measures a security's volatility relative to an average security. Put another way, beta is a measure of a security's return over time compared to that of the overall market. For example, if ABC's beta is 2.0, it means that if the stock market goes up 10%, ABC's common stock goes up 20%; if the market goes down 10%, ABC goes down 20%.

NOTE: Generally, the higher the beta, the greater the return expected (or demanded) by the investor and therefore, the more risky the stock is.

Figure 6-2 provides a guide for how to read betas:

FIGURE 6-2: MEANING OF DIFFERENT BETA VALUES

Beta	What It Means
0	The security's return is independent of the Market. An example is a risk-free security such as a T-bill.
0.5	The security is only half as responsive as the market.
1.0	The security has the same response, or risk, as the market (*i.e.,* average risk). This is the beta value of the market portfolio such as Standard and Poor's 500 or Dow Jones 30 Industrials.
2.0	The security is twice as responsive, or risky, as the market.

Figure 6-3 gives examples of betas.

FIGURE 6-3:   BETA VALUES FOR SELECTED STOCKS
(April 1999)

Microsoft	1.4
Pfizer	0.9
Intel	1.4
Wal-Mart	0.9
GTE	0.6
General Motors	1.1
IBM	1.3
AOL	2.5

Source: AOL Personal Finance Channel and MSN Money Central Investor, April 12, 1999.

NOTE: Betas for stocks are widely available in investment newsletters and directories like Value Line Investment Survey. They can also be found on the Internet. For example, the Yahoo! Finance site (finance.yahoo.com) offers betas as part of the profile of a company.

HOW TO READ STOCK QUOTATIONS

Financial dailies (*e.g.,* the *Wall Street Journal* and *Investor's Business Daily*) contain the most extensive security price quotations, but they can also be found in most national and regional newspapers.

NYSE and AMEX Stocks

Typical listings of a common stock could include some or all of the following information shown in Figure 6-4.

FIGURE 6-4: STOCK LISTING FOR IBM CORP.

52 Weeks				Yld			Sales				Net
High	Low	Stock	Sym	Div. %	PE	100s	Hi	Lo	Close		Chg.
137 7/8	67 1/2	IBM	IBM	.48 .51	22	266,687	94 5/8	92 1/2	93 15/16		+2 15/16
(1)	(2)	(3)	(4)	(5) (6)	(7)	(8)	(9)	(10)	(11)		(12)

Explanatory Notes:

(1) The *highest price per share* at which the stock sold during the latest 52-week period, excluding the latest day's trading; prices are quoted in dollars and eighths of dollars. IBM's highest price was 137 7/8 ($137.875).

(2) The *lowest price per share* at which the stock sold during the latest 52-week period. IBM's lowest price was 67 1/2 ($67.50).

NOTE: High and lows for new issues begin at the date of issue. Where a split or stock dividend amounting to 25 percent or more has been paid, the high-low range and dividends are shown for the new stock only.

(3) The *company's name,* which may be abbreviated. If there is a space, it is to set aside a footnote.

NOTE: Absence of a qualifier after the company name indicates a common stock; "pf" indicates a preferred stock. Other qualifiers will be explained later.

(4) *Exchange ticker symbol.* The symbol is used to identify the stock in newspapers, exchanges, and computer databases.

(5) The indicated regular *dividend* in the current year based on what the company has paid in the last quarter or six months. IBM's was estimated at $0.48 a share. Extra dividends paid in good earning years are not shown. They are identified in qualifier footnotes. In the CBS MarketWatch Internet site quotation, the dividend given is the quarterly dividend.

(6) The *current yield* is the rate of return found by dividing the current year regular dividend by the closing price of the stock.IBM's current yield is 0.51 percent, which is calculated by dividing the expected dividend ($.48) by the closing share price (93 15/16) and rounding the answer to the nearest tenth of a percent. This figure is the return an investor can expect on each share of stock owned. Compare this yield measure with those of other stocks or with the interest paid on debt securities. It is based on cash dividends only; stock dividends are not included except when a company pays only stock dividends, or has a history of paying dividends regularly.

(7) The *P/E ratio,* also called the P/E multiple, or earnings multiple, is computed by dividing the stock's selling price by the per share earnings for the most recent four quarters. It is usually rounded to the nearest whole number. There is no entry if earnings are negative. The P/E ratio suggests that investors are optimistic about the stock's prospects. Low P/E figures, on the other hand, often represent lower investor favor. Unfortunately, there is no such thing as "ideal" or "best" ratio. Reasons for high or low P/E ratios include the company's riskiness, stability of company earnings, growth outlook, or the industry of which the company is part.

(8) *Share sales.* For common stocks, sales are reported in lots of 100 shares, so 26,668,700 shares (266,687 x 100) were traded on that day. When a "z" precedes volume, the figure that follows represents the actual number of shares traded. For example, z35 means 35 shares were traded, not 3,500.

(9) The *highest price* paid for the stock that day. IBM's was 94 5/8 ($94.625).

(10) The *lowest price* paid for the stock that day. IBM's was 92 1/2 ($92.50).

(11) The *last price* paid that day. IBM's was 93 15/16 ($93.9375).

(12) *Net change* is the difference between the closing price for the reported day and the closing price of the previous day. IBM's closing price on the current day was 2 15/16 ($2.9375) higher than its closing price on the previous day.

NOTE: For more details, see "Explanatory Notes" following the stock quotations wherever you find the price quotation.

Figure 6-5 presents a sample stock quotation from the CBS MarketWatch Web site *(cbs.marketwatch.com)*. The numbered notes parallel the information in Figure 6-4.

FIGURE 6-5: STOCK LISTING FOR IBM CORP.

Open:	94 1/4	Prev Close:	91	5:01 PM	@BigCharts.com
High: **(9)**	94 5/8	52 wk High: **(1)**	137 7/8		
Low: **(10)**	92 1/2	52 wk Low: **(2)**	67 1/2		
Volume: **(8)**	26,668,700	Yield: **(6)**	0.51%		
Dividend: **(5)**	0.12	P/E Ratio: **(7)**	22.21		
Ex Date:	8/6/99	EPS:	4.23		

IBM **(3)**   IBM (NYSE) **(4)**   **(11)** 93 15/16 ⬆ **(12)** +2 15/16   +3.23%   10/22/99

Source: CBS MarketWatch

Investor's Business Daily stock quotations also provide "Smarter Numbers," to help you make better investment decisions (see Figure 6-6):

- **EPS Rank (Earnings per share Ranking).** The newspaper believes that a percentage increase in a company's EPS is a better barometer of stock price performance than P/E ratios or dividend yields. This column tracks a company's per share earnings growth over the last 5 years and ranks it against all other publicly traded issues. A ranking of 80, for example, means that the company's earnings record was in the top 20 percent, outperforming 80 percent of the companies measured.

- **Rel. Str. (Relative Price Strength).** Ranked on a scale of 0 to 99, Relative Strength column measures each stock's price movement over the last year compared to 6,000 other stocks: NYSE, AMEX, OTC/NASDAQ. A ranking of 80, for example, means that the stock was in the top 20 percent of all publicly traded issues, outperforming 80 percent of the companies measured.

• **Vol. % Chg. (Changes in Trading Volume).** This column shows how that day's volume compares with the stock's average trading volume during the last 50 days—up or down.

A listing of "+150" means the stock traded 150 percent above its normal trading volume for the day.

FIGURE 6-6: *INVESTOR'S BUSINESS DAILY* "SMART NUMBERS"

IBD *SmartSelect*™ CORPORATE RATINGS

```
┌ Earnings Per Share
│  ┌ Relative Price Strength
│  │  ┌ Industry Group Relative Strength
│  │  │ ┌ Sales+Profit Margins+ROE
│  │  │ │ ┌ Accumulation/Distribution
```

52-Week High			Stock	Symbol	Closing Price	Price Chg	Vol% Chg	Vol.Spon. 100sRank	Day's High	Low
78	17	DBB	$74^{7/16}$	CenturaBnk	CBC $46^{7/8}$+	$^{5/16}$	**+79**	1228 C	$48^{5/8}$	$46^{7/8}$ 0
90	61	BAB	49	CenturyTel	5 CTL $41^{11/16}$-	$^{1/8}$	+30	5581 B	$41^{13/16}$	41^k_o
52	9	BAD	$40^{1/2}$	Ceridian	5 CEN $20^{1/4}$+	$^{1/16}$	-45	5154 B	$20^{3/8}$	$19^{15/16}{}^k_o$

Source: Investor's Business Daily

Over-the-Counter Stock Quotations

Over-the-Counter stocks (OTC) are not listed on either national exchange. These stocks are traded by telephone, one broker to another, unlike on the national exchanges, where transactions are executed on an exchange floor.

At one time, newspaper quotations for over-the-counter stocks were less comprehensive than quotations for stocks on the national exchanges. While this is still true in some listings, quotations for what is called the National Market now cover OTC stocks as thoroughly as national exchange issues. Individual papers, of course, may omit some of the listing components, like yield, P/E ratio, or the 52-week high and low. The quotations usually appear under some version of the following headings:

• NASDAQ National Market or National Market Issues (National Association of Securities Dealers Automated Quotations service ((NASDAQ)): Traditionally, over-the-counter quotations have differed from exchange quotations in two important ways (see Figure 6-7):

1. Less information is given

2. Daily quotations list two prices, called "Bid" and "Asked" prices. Prices are both current prices but they are not necessarily the amounts of actual transactions. Bid Price is the price a dealer is willing to pay for a stock.. Bid prices quoted in the newspaper are always the highest available. Asked Price is the price at which a dealer is willing to sell a stock. Asked prices quoted in the newspaper are always the lowest available.

OTC stock quotations that are in addition to the National Market list appear in newspapers under many headings: Over-the-Counter Quotations; Over-the-Counter Market; NASDAQ Bid and Asked Quotations; NASDAQ Over-The-Counter; OTC

Many papers also carry an additional OTC list entitled additional OTC Quotes; NASDAQ Supplementary OTC. The agency that reports OTC stock price data from the market makers is NASDAQ. It is wholly owned by the National Association of Securities Dealers, is the regulatory agency for the OTC market.

FIGURE 6-7: OTC STOCK LISTING EXAMPLE

Sales Stock	Div	100s	Bid	Asked	Net Chg
AppleC	N/A	37456	73 7/8	73 15/16	-2 3/16
(1)	(2)	(3)	(4)	(5)	(6)

Explanatory Notes:

(1) The name of the company (Apple Corp.).

(2) Apple has not paid a dividend since 1995.

(3) Number of shares traded, as expressed in 100's. Apple had 3,745,600 shares (37456 x 100) traded. The "z" footnote means raw figures; thus, z15 means just 15 shares changed hands, not 1,500.

(4) Bid price is the highest prices the stock can be sold for and (5) Asked is the lowest price the stock can be purchased at the close

of the given day's trading. The bid price of 73 7/8 means you would have received $73.875 if you wanted to sell a share and the 73 15/16 asked price means that you would have paid $ 73.9375 to buy a share. The spread between the bid and the asked price is part of the broker's commission (or profit) for making a market in the stock.

(6) Net chg. is the change in the bid price from the previous day's trading. Apple stock has dropped 2 3/16 ($2.1875) a share from the bid price on the reported day versus the bid price of the previous trading day.

Figure 6-8 presents a price quotation for an OTC stock from the Yahoo! Finance Web site *(finance.yahoo.com)*. Notes correspond to those in Figure 6-7.

FIGURE 6-8: TYPICAL OTC WEB-QUOTATION

(1)	APPLE COMP INC (NasdaqNM:AAPL) - More Info: News, SEC, Msgs, Profile, Research, Insider					
Last Trade $Oct\ 22 \cdot 73\ ^{15}/_{16}$	Change (6) $-2\ ^{3}/_{16}\ (-2.87\%)$	Prev Cls $76\ ^{1}/_{8}$	Volume (3) 3,745,600	Div Date Dec 1995	
Day's Range $73\ ^{3}/_{8} - 77\ ^{1}/_{4}$	Bid (4) $73\ ^{7}/_{8}$	Ask (5) $73\ ^{15}/_{16}$	Open $77\ ^{1}/_{8}$	Avg Vol 5,802,590	Ex-Div Nov 1995	
52-week Range $31\ ^{3}/_{8} - 80\ ^{1}/_{8}$	Earn/Shr 3.69	P/E 20.63	Mkt Cap 11.895B	Div/Shr (2) N/A	Yield N/A	

AAPL 22-Oct-1999 (C) Yahoo!
80 70 60 50 40 30
Nov Jan Mar May Jul Sep
Small: [1d | 5d | 1y | none]
Big: [1d | 5d | 3m | 1y | 2y | 5y | max]

Source: Yahoo!Finance

The Fifth Letter of OTC Ticker Symbols: Ticker symbols aren't just random of letters assigned to a stock. They actually can tell you about the company itself. A ticker with three letters or fewer indicates that the company trades on the New York or American exchanges. Tickers with four or five letters trade on the NASDAQ, NASDAQ Small Cap or OTC Bulletin Board markets. When the fifth letter is assigned, it tells a tale. For example, Figure 6-9 shows a listings of Intel securities from the CBS MarketWatch Web site *(cbs.marketwatch.com)*. The W added to the Ticker Symbol on one of Intel Corporation's securities indicates that the security is a warrant. Figure 6-10 shows how to translate that fifth letter.

FIGURE 6-9: FIFTH LETTER OF OTC TICKER SYMBOL:
AN EXAMPLE

Company	Exchange	Symbol
Intel Corp	NASDAQ	INTCW
Intel Corporation	NASDAQ NM	INTC

Source: CBS MarketWatch

FIGURE 6-10: WHAT THE FIFTH LETTER OF NASDAQ
TICKER SYMBOLS MEAN

A   Class A Share
B   Class B Share
C   NASDAQ Listing Under Review
D   New Shares
E   Delinquent In Required Filings With The Securities Anti
        Exchange Commission
F   Foreign Stocks (No Longer Mandatory)
G   First Convertible Bond
H   Second Convertible Bond, Same Company
I   Third Convertible Bond, Same Company
J   Voting
K   Nonvoting
L   Miscellaneous Situations
M   Fourth Preferred, Same Company
N   Third Preferred, Same Company
O   Second Preferred, Same Company
P   First Preferred, Same Company
Q   In Bankruptcy Proceedings
R   Rights
S   Shares Of Beneficial Interest
T   With Warrants Or With Rights
U   Units
V   When Issued And When Distributed
W   Warrants
Y   ADR, Or American Depositary Receipt. (No Longer
        Mandatory)
Z   Miscellaneous Situations

Qualifiers

Stocks: A large number of alphabetic qualifiers appear throughout stock quotations. The particular qualifiers and their definitions depend on the news service applying the quotations to the newspapers. Most newspapers receive their financial quotations from the Associated Press (AP). United Press International (UPI) also supplies quotes. Some of the qualifiers used by UPI are the same as those used by the AP, some are not. Because The Associated Press supplies the majority of papers, the AP definitions are listed first. When there is a separate UPI definition, or when the UPI definition is the sole definition, it is marked in brackets: "[UPI...]." Newspapers usually provide a table of symbols. Most use the same qualifiers for over-the-counter (OTC) quotations as for the national exchanges. However, you should verify this in your own newspapers before assuming the definitions listed in Figure 6-11 also apply to over-the-counter quotations. The *Wall Street Journal* uses UPI quotations for OTC stocks and AP for the NYSE and AMEX listings.

FIGURE 6-11: QUALIFIERS AND DEFINITIONS—NATIONAL EXCHANGE

a   The Amount In The "Dividend" Column Includes One Or More Amounts In Addition To The Usual Dividend.

b   The Amount Indicated In The "Dividend" Column Is The Annual Cash Dividend Plus A Stock Divided.

c   The Amount Indicated In The "Dividend" Column Completely Liquidates The Stock (As In The Final Dividend From Income Shares Of A Dual-Purpose Fund Or The Final Payment From A Bankrupt Company).

cld   "Called," Meaning A Company Is Calling In (And Paying Off Or Perhaps Substituting New Stock For) A Particular Issue Of Preferred Stock.

d   The Price Indicated (Usually In The "Low" Column) Is A New 52 Week Low. For Example, "High-Low-Close (Or Last)." Sometimes This Applies To The Closing Price Only.

e   The Amount Indicated In The "Dividend" Column Was Declared Or Paid Within The Preceding 12 Months But There Is No Regular Rate.

FIGURE 6-11: QUALIFIERS AND DEFINITIONS—NATIONAL EXCHANGE, *Continued*

g   Following The Stock Name, It Means Dividends And Earnings Are In Canadian Currency. Trading, However, Is In U.S. Dollars. No Yield Or P/E Ratio Is Shown Unless Stated In U.S. Dollars. Dividends May Be Subject To Canadian Withholding For U.S. Citizens.

h   A Temporary Exception To NASD Qualifications Has Been Made For This Security.

i   The Dividend Indicated Was Declared Or Paid After An Earlier Stock Dividend Or Split.

j   The Dividend Amount Indicated Has Been Paid So Far This Year, But The Current Dividend Has Been Omitted Or Deferred, Or No Action Was Taken On Dividends At The Last Board Meeting.

k   The Dividend Indicated Has Been Declared Or Paid So Far This Year On A Cumulative Issue Of Preferred Stock With Dividends In Arrears.

n   This Is A New Stock Issued Within The Last 52 Weeks. The Listed 52 Week High And Low Are As Of The Inception Of Trading. Because Of Its Effect On The 52 Week High And Low Price, The "N" Is Retained In The Quotation For 52 Weeks.

nd   "Next Day" Delivery Of Stock Certificates. Settlement (Payment) Is Also Required On That Day.

pf   Preferred Stock.

pp   The Holder Still Owes One (In Some Quotations, More Than One) Installment On The Purchase Price.

r   The Amount Indicated Was Declared Or Paid In Dividends During The Preceding 12 Months, Plus A Stock Dividend.

rt   The Quotation Is For "Rights," Not Stock. Rights Are Like Warrants, Except They Are Shorter Term. Some Stocks, Particularly New Issues, First Appear In Units That Can Include Rights. After Rights Are Exercised Or Expire, The Stock Will Trade Without Them. Rights Can Be Traded Separately From Stocks.

s   Following The Stock Name, It Means That Either A Stock Split Or A Stock Dividend Within The Last 52 Weeks Has Increased The Number Of Shares Outstanding By 25% Or More. *NOTE: Because of its effect on the 52-week high and low, the "s" is retained in the quotation for 52 weeks.*

FIGURE 6-11: QUALIFIERS AND DEFINITIONS—NATIONAL
EXCHANGE, *Continued*

t   This Amount Was Paid In Stock Dividends During The
         Preceding 12 Months. Estimated Cash Value Is Of Stock On
         Ex- Dividend Or Ex-Distribution Date. (See "x-dis".)

u   The Amount Indicated (Usually In The "High" Column) Is A
         New 52 Week High. Sometimes This Applies To The Closing
         Price Only.

v   Trading Of This Issue Has Been Halted On The Primary Market
         On Which It Is Listed.

vj or vi Bankruptcy does not necessarily mean a company ceases to
         exist or that the stockholders lose their entire investment. After
         emerging from bankruptcy some companies have appreciated
         considerably. However, if the company is liquidated, then com-
         mon stockholders will be paid proportionate to the number of
         shares they hold, only after major creditors, bondholders, and
         preferred stockholders.

wd   "When Distributed." The Stock Has Been Legally Issued But
         The Certificates Are Not Yet Available. For Example, They
         May Not Have Been Printed. If The Security Trades At This
         Time, The Purchaser Will Not Receive The Certificate Until
         They Are Made Available And Are Distributed.

wi   Short For "When, As, And If Issued." The Stock Is Trading
         Before It Has Cleared All Legal Requirements For Issuance.
         Should The Stock Not Be Issued, All Trades Will Be Canceled.

wt   The Quotation Is For Warrants, Not Stock.

ww   "With Warrants." Sometimes New Issues Of Stock Appear In
         Units That Include A Number Of Warrants. These May Be
         Detached And Traded Separately Or Remain With The Stock
         Certificates As They Are Specified Here. You Must Determine
         From Your Broker Or A Stock Guide The Length Of Time
         From Which The Warrants Are Still Valid.

x   "Ex-Dividend" Or "Ex-Rights," Meaning The Security Trades
         TheDay After Dividends And Rights Were Awarded. Often
         Appears In The "Sales" Or "Volume" Column. Ex-Dividend,
         "Without Dividend," Means The Immediately Prior Dividend
         Was Paid To The Previous Owner On The Previous Day And
         The Purchaser Of Stock From This Issue Will Not Receive A
         Dividend Until The Next Payment Is Declared.

FIGURE 6-11:   QUALIFIERS AND DEFINITIONS—NATIONAL
                   EXCHANGE, *Continued*

x-dis   "Ex-Distribution," Indicating The Day After The Distribution
         Of Stock Dividends Was Made. Ex-Distribution, "Without
         Distribution," Means The Immediately Prior Stock Dividend
         Was Declared To The Previous Owner On The Previous Day
         And The Purchaser Of This Stock Will Not Receive It.
xr   "Ex-Rights," Indicating That The Stock Is Now Trading
         Without The Rights Formerly Attached To It.
xw   "Ex-Warrant," Indicating That The Stock Is Now Trading
         Without The Warrant Formerly Attached To It. (See "ww".)
y   Ex-Dividend (See "x") And Sales In Full—*i.e.,* The Actual
         Number Of Shares Traded Is Shown.
z   "Sales In Full," Meaning The Actual Number Of Shares Is
         Quoted, Not The Number Of Round Lots. It Is Done To
         Accommodate Those Stocks That Are Normally Trade In Lots
         Of Other Than 100 Shares (*i.e.,* 10-, 25-, Or 50-Shares Lots).

HOW TO READ "TOMBSTONE" ADS

A sample advertisement called a tombstone for the sale of common stock,
appears as Figure 6-12.

Explanatory Notes:

(1) This is only the total number of shares being offered *for sale.*
    Many more shares may have been authorized for sale by the cor-
    poration's charter, but the board of directors decided not to issue
    them now.

(2) Preferred shares and bonds are also offered in tombstone
    announcements. Sometimes you will see units offered which will
    consist of, for example, 1 share and 2 warrants. (The warrant is
    like an option, and can be used in the future to purchase more
    shares at a specified price after a given date).

(3) This is the price at which the security will sell for (or has been
    sold for) in advance of its issuance. Demand for these issues on
    the secondary market will determine the price, as is the case for all

FIGURE 6-12: TOMBSTONE AD, AN EXAMPLE

$1,270,750,000

7,475,000 Shares **(1)**
(2) Common Stock

Price $170 Per Share **(3)**

Upon request, a copy of the Prospectus describing these securities and the business of
the Company may be obtained within any State from any Underwriter who may legally
distribute it within such State. The securities are offered only by means of the Prospectus,
and this announcement is neither an offer to sell nor a solicitation of an offer to buy. **(4)**

(5)

Goldman, Sachs & Co.   Morgan Stanley Dean Witter

BancBoston Robertson Stephens

BT Alex. Brown
Incorporated

Donaldson, Lufkin & Jenrette

Hambrecht & Quist   Merrill Lynch & Co.   NationsBanc Montgomery Securities LLC   PaineWebber Incorporated

Prudential Securities   Salomon Smith Barney   Warburg Dillon Read LLC   Dain Rauscher Wessels
                                                                                                a division of Dain Rauscher Incorporated

Pacific Crest Securities Inc.   Volpe Brown Whelan & Company   Thomas Weisel Partners LLC   Wit Capital Corporation

April 12, 1999

outstanding securities. If there are more offers to buy than there are shares to go around in the initial offering, the stock is called a "hot issue" and the market price will rise as soon as the shares begin trading on the secondary market. Incidentally, shares of a new issue cannot be purchased "on margin," a type of credit you can get from your broker using other shares you own as collateral. The shares must be paid for in full.

(4) Standard disclaimer stating that this is not an offer to sell stock. Such offers can legally be made only through a prospectus. (See the section "How To Read A Prospectus" in chapter 5). A legal sale of a new issue cannot be made without the buyer receiving a prospectus in advance of the transaction. In fact, if you don't receive a prospectus in advance before you receive a confirmation notice of trade, you have a legal right to cancel the transaction without penalty within a reasonable amount of time. Since new issues are generally more speculative than securities already trading on the open market, the prospectus requirement prevents a broker from strong-arming you into buying a security over the phone about which you may know very little. Tombstones are for information purposes only; often the stock has already been sold out.

NOTE: There are two prospectuses. The preliminary prospectus is called a "red herring," because of a statement printed on the cover in red to the effect that the registration has not been declared effective by the SEC. The purpose of the preliminary prospectus is to stimulate sales. The SEC may or may not require revision or amendments. After the SEC has accepted the preliminary prospectus, a new prospectus, without the red lettering, is printed and used for offering the shares. The reference in the tombstone is to the second prospectus.

(5) This is the list of the investment bankers or underwriters that make up the syndicate bringing out the issue. Those with the largest number of shares to sell are listed first, and in bolder type than those with a relatively minor stake. If you wish to acquire the security at initial price, before it starts trading on the secondary market, you must get the shares through one of these firms or a firm that has contracted with one of them to sell the securities. Some will be retail brokers, selling to the general public, but some may handle only sales to large institutional buyers.

CAPSULE EARNINGS REPORT

The amount a company earns can influence the price of its stock, and many investors attempt to forecast earnings before they are released. (It is important to note, however, that a major determinant of stock prices is earnings on a per-share basis, that is, EPS, rather than total earnings.)

Take a look at a sample earnings report (Figure 6-13). Though it provides only the most basic information. Even so, note that dates are given for two years so that current performance can be easily compared to last year's.

FIGURE 6-13: COMPANY EARNINGS

For periods shown. In parenthesis, the first one to five letters before the comma are the company's stock ticker symbol. N after the comma indicates stock is listed on the New York Stock Exchange. A indicates the American Stock Exchange, NNM indicates Nasdaq National Market System, NSC indicates Nasdaq Small Capitalization, and ECM indicates Emerging Company Marketplace.

	Abbott Laboratories (1)		
	(ABT,N)		(3)
(2)	3d qrd to Sept. 30	1999	1998
(4)	Sales	3,120,662,000	3,035,767,000
(5)	Net inc.	587,159,000	531,722,000
(6)	Share earns	.38	.34
(7)	Shares outst	1,539,633,000	1.544,680,000

Explanatory Notes:

(1) Company name, is usually shortened, and the primary market on which its common shares are traded.

(2) Time period of the report. This is cumulative for the year, so a third quarter report would be, in effect, a nine-month report.

(3) Years the figures are given for. Those for the previous year are always from the same period of time (number of months) as the present report.

(4) Sales figures in dollars. The amount is always net; allowances have been made for discounts and returns.

(5) Net income in dollars is the profit after payment of all obligations except dividends for the common stock.

(6) Share earnings is the net income divided by the number of shares outstanding.

(7) Shares outstanding. This is the weighted average of the number of shares of common stock outstanding during the period.

DIVIDEND REPORT

Dividends also affect stock-price movements. Figure 6-14 shows a sample Dividend Report.

FIGURE 6-14:   DIVIDEND REPORT

REGULAR:	(2) Period	(3) Amt	(4) Payment Date	(5) Record Date
Corp Hi Yld .(1). . . .M		.1046	10/29/99	10/22/99
Corp Hi Yld II . . . . .M		.0982	10/29/99	10/22/99
Corp Hi Yld III . . . . .M		.116	10/29/99	10/22/99
Countrywide Cred . .Q		.10	11/01/99	10/14/99
Flamemaster Corp .Q		.03	11/11/99	10/22/99
Fortis Secs . . . . . . .M		.055	11/15/99	10/25/99

Source: Investor's Business Daily

Explanatory Notes:

(1) Company name.

(2) Period. Most dividends are declared quarterly and are designated by Q. Monthly is designated by M.

(3) Amount. The amount of dividend, usually in dollars per share.

(4) Payable date. The day on which this amount is payable.

(5) Record date. The day on which a shareholder must be listed as the holder of record to qualify for the dividend.

For the first company, the regular dividend is paid monthly, the dividend is 10.46 cents per share, the dividend will be paid to shareholders of record on October 22, and the actual payment will be made on October 29. On the day after the record date, the stock trades ex-dividend and usually falls a little in price to compensate for the fact that it is no longer eligible for the latest dividend.

The *Mergent Dividend Record* (formerly the *Moody's Dividend Record*) presents quarterly dividends and the date of declaration, date of record, date payable, and ex-dividend date. This is published twice a week. There is also a yearly *Mergent Annual Dividend Record.* Standard and Poor's publishes the *Standard & Poor's Dividend Record,* which provides similar information. Figures 6-15A and 15B contain excerpts from both publications.

FIGURE 6-15A: DIVIDEND RECORD

MERGENT DIVIDEND RECORD

Issue	Div.per sh.	Rec or Ex/Payable
Thursday, October 21 (cont.)		
------EX DIV DATE------		
Apogee Enterprises, Inc. Com 0.0525		Oct 25/Nov 9
Energy East Corp. Com 0.21		Oct 25/Nov 15
Goldman Sachs Group, Inc. (The) Com . .0.12		Oct 25/Nov 22
Idacorp, Inc. Com 0.465		Oct 25/ Nov 19
Idaho Power Co. 70.7% pfd 1.7675		Oct 25/Nov 19
7.68% 1st pld 1.92		Oct 25/Nov 15
Industries Amisco Lfee.Com ....bC$0.20		Oct 25/Nov 15
Marcus Corp. (The) Cl B Com 0.50		Oct 25/Nov 15
Com 0.055		Oct 25/Nov 15
Potash Corp. of Saskatchewan, Inc.		
(Canada) Com...................b0.25		Oct 25/Nov 15

Source: Mergent Dividend Record

FIGURE 6-15B: DIVIDEND RECORD

Divd $	Declared	Ex-Date	Stk Record	CUSIP Payable
21ST CENTY TELECOM GROUP INC				90130P
✧ SR PFD EXCHANGEABLE 13.75% np				603
Rate - None Pd '99- Stk '98- Stlk				
* Init Stk	—	May 18	May 01	May 15 98
† Stk	—	Aug 19	Aug 03	Aug 18 98
† Stk	Oct 13	Feb 16	Feb 01	Feb 15
*3.6667% Stk				
†3.4375% Stk				

Source: Standard & Poor's Dividend Record

Another Mergent FIS, Inc. publication related to dividends is *Moody's Handbook of Dividend Achievers,* which contains reports of more than 300 firms that have outstanding records of dividend increases.

SHORT INTEREST

Knowing the size of short positions for a stock can be helpful for investors. The short interest is the number of shares of stocks that have been sold by investors hoping to profit from a fall in the stock market. A large short interest can mean that the market is bearish on the stock because many investors expect the price of the stock to fall.

Short interest is typically given on Internet stock quotations. Yahoo! Finance *(finance.yahoo.com)* includes it as part of company profiles, and CBS MarketWatch *(cbs.marketwatch.com)* includes it as part of company fundamentals. The *Wall Street Journal* prints three short interest reports each month, one each for the NYSE, the AMEX, and the NAS-DAQ. The Company Sleuth Internet site *(www.companysleuth.com)* provides a detailed history of the short interest for stocks (Figure 6-16).

FIGURE 6-16: SHORT INTEREST

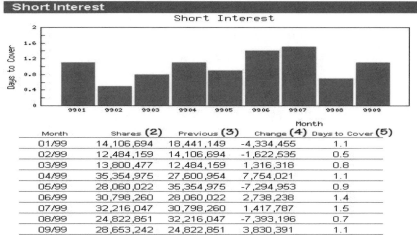

Microsoft Corporation (MSFT) [1]

Month	Shares [2]	Previous [3]	Change [4]	Days to Cover [5]
01/99	14,106,694	18,441,149	-4,334,455	1.1
02/99	12,484,159	14,106,694	-1,622,535	0.5
03/99	13,800,477	12,484,159	1,316,318	0.8
04/99	35,354,975	27,600,954	7,754,021	1.1
05/99	28,060,022	35,354,975	-7,294,953	0.9
06/99	30,798,260	28,060,022	2,738,238	1.4
07/99	32,216,047	30,798,260	1,417,787	1.5
08/99	24,822,851	32,216,047	-7,393,196	0.7
09/99	28,653,242	24,822,851	3,830,391	1.1

Source: Company Sleuth (*www.company sleuth.com*)

Explanatory Notes:

(1) The company name.

(2) The short position for the stock at mid-month. This is the number of shares currently borrowed by investors for sale.

(3) The short position for the previous month.

(4) The change in short interest between the two months.

(5) The number of days it would take to cover the short interest if trading continued at the average daily volume for the month. It is the short interest for the current month divided by the average daily volume. This is sometimes referred to as the short ratio.

WHAT IS PREFERRED STOCK?

Preferred stock is viewed as a hybrid security because it possesses features of both corporate bonds and common stocks. It's similar to common stock in that:

- It pays dividends.

- It represents owner's equity.

- It is issued without stated maturity dates.

Preferred stock is also like to a corporate bond in that:

- Its dividends are fixed for the life of the issue and are paid quarterly. The dividend is stated as a percentage of par value of the stock, or in dollar terms per share.

- It has a prior claims on assets and earnings.

- It can carry convertible and call characteristics and there are sinking fund provisions.

Preferred stocks are traded on the basis of the yield they offer to investors. Because they are viewed as fixed income securities, they are in direct competition with bonds in the marketplace. Corporate bonds, however, occupy a position senior to preferred stocks.

The advantages of owning preferred stocks are:

- They have relatively higher yields than comparably rated fixed-income securities.

- Dividends are paid quarterly. Bonds pay interest every six months.

- Safety. Preferred stocks take precedence over common stocks. The preferred stock dividend must be paid before any dividends on common stock can be paid.

- They usually cost less per share so even small investors can afford them.

- They have call protection for the first five to ten years of issuance.

- Both listed and OTC preferreds are active and fairly liquid.

The disadvantages include:

- They are vulnerable to interest rate and price level changes.

- They have restricted capital gains except for convertible preferred stock. Convertible preferred stock allows the holder to exchange your preferred shares for a fixed number of common shares.

Figure 6-17 presents major features of preferred stock.

FIGURE 6-17: CHARACTERISTICS OF PREFERRED STOCK

Voting rights	None unless dividend is not paid
Income	Fixed as long as dividend is
Capital gain/loss potential	Only if interest rates change or the company's preferred stock rating changes
Inflation hedge	None except for adjustable
Preemptive right	None
Priority of claim	Prior to common stock
Unit of purchase	Usually in units of 100 shares

Ratings of Preferred Stock

Standard & Poor's and Moody's rate the quality of preferred stocks as they do bonds. The S&P rating scheme is similar to that of as bonds, but triple Ratings are not assigned to preferred stocks. The Moody's scheme is somewhat different (see Figure 6-18). The ratings are based on the financial soundness of the issuing company and its ability to meet its payment obligations in a timely manner. Preferred stockholders come after bondholders in the event of a bankruptcy.

Calculating Expected Return from Preferred Stock

Return on preferred stock is computed as it is for bonds. The calculations depend on whether the preferred stock is issued in perpetuity or if it has a call that is likely to be exercised.

Perpetuity

Since preferred stock usually has no maturity date when the company must redeem it, you cannot calculate a yield to maturity. You can calculate current yield as follows:

FIGURE 6-18:   DESCRIPTION OF PREFERRED STOCK RATINGS

Standard & Poor's	Quality Indication
.....	Highest Quality
AA	High Quality
A	Upper Medium Grade
BBB	Medium Grade
BB	Contains Speculative Elements
B	Outright Speculative
CCC & CC	Default Definitely Possible
C	Default, Only Partial Recovery Likely
D	Default, Little Recover Likely

NOTE: *Standard & Poor's does not issue AAA ratings on preferred stock.*

Moody's	
aaa	Top Quality
aa	High Grade
a	Upper Medium Grade
baa	Lower Medium Grade
ba	Speculative Type
b	Likely To Be Already In Arrears
caa	Little Assurance Of Future Dividends

Current yield = D/P

where,   D = annual dividend, and
           P = the market price of the preferred stock.

EXAMPLE 7

A preferred stock paying $2.00 a year in dividends with a market price of $20 would have a current yield of 10 percent ($2/$20).

Yield to Call

If a call is likely, a more appropriate return measure is yield to call (YTC). Theoretically, YTC equates the present value of the future dividends and the call price with the current market price.

EXAMPLE 8

Consider the following two preferreds:

Preferreds	Market price	Call Price	Dividends	Term to Call	YTC
A	$8/share	$9	$1/year	3 years	16.06%
B	10	9	$1	3	6.89

Comparison to Bond Yields

Yields on straight preferred stock are closely correlated to bond yields, since both are fixed income securities. However, yields on preferred stock are often below bond yields, which seems unusual because preferred stock have a position junior to bonds. However, corporate investors favor preferred stock over bonds because of a dividend exclusion allowed in determining corporate taxable income.

Types of Preferred Stock

There are many types of preferred stock. Dividends can be either fixed or floating and is paid quarterly. All have no maturity date. (A maturity date is an important distinction between debt and equity.) Most issues, however, are callable at the option of the issuer after a specified period. The types of preferred stock include:

Convertible Preferred Stock

Convertible preferred stock is convertible into common shares and thus offers growth potential plus fixed income. It tends to behave differently in the marketplace than straight preferred. The market price of a convertible preferred should equal the common stock price times the conversion rate.

Cumulative Preferred Stock

With cumulative preferred stock, any dividend due that is not declared accumulates and must be paid before any common stock dividend can be declared. Most preferred stocks are cumulative.

Non-Cumulative Preferred Stock

Non-Cumulative Preferred Stock is a hangover from the heyday of the railroads and is rare today. Dividends, if unpaid, do not accumulate.

Participating Preferred Stock

Participating Preferred Stock is typically issued by firms desperate for capital. Preferred shareholders share in profits with that of common holders by way of extra dividends declared after regular dividends are paid. This type may have voting rights.

Prior Preferred Stock (or Preference Shares)

Prior Preferred Stock has priority over other preferred shares in claims on assets and earnings.

Callable Preferred Stock

Callable Preferred Stock, carry a provision that permits the company to call in the issue and pay it off at full value, plus a premium of perhaps 5 percent.

Adjustable-rate Preferred Stock (ARPS)

Adjustable-Rate Preferred Stock, which is also called floating or variable-rate preferred stock, is preferred stock with a floating dividend rate that resets each quarter. The rate is determined by using the highest of three benchmark rates: the 3-month T-bill, the 10-year T-note, and the 20- or 30-year T-bond. Thus, you are assured of a favorable dividend regardless of the shape of the yield curve.

Foreign Bank Preferred Stock

Foreign Bank Preferred Stock usually consists of American depository receipt (ADR) shares issued by foreign banks. They are SEC-registered, U.S.-dollar-denominated perpetual preferred stock with the following advantages:

- Higher fixed dividend rates than domestic preferred stock.

- Tax advantages on a portion of the dividend income in the form of a 15% to 25% tax credit. This means a higher after-tax yield than many comparable tax-exempt municipal bonds. Tax-deferred retirement accounts such as IRAs do not qualify.

- Opportunity to diversify globally without foreign currency exposure.

Money Market Preferred Stock

Money market preferred stock (MMPS), also known as auction-rate preferred stock, is the newest and most popular member of the preferred stock group. It offers the following advantages:

- Low market risk in the event of price decline

- Competitive yield

- Liquidity

MMPS pays dividends and adjusts rates up or down, depending on the current market, every seven weeks. Unlike other adjustable-rate preferred stock, the market, not the issuer, sets the rate. If no bids are placed for a stock, MMPS' dividend rate is automatically set at the 60-day AA commercial paper rate quoted by the Federal Reserve Bank. There is a possibility, however, of a failed auction if no buyers show up at the auction. You must take into account the credit quality of MMPS.

Money market preferred stock types include:

- Short-term auction-rate stock (STARS)

- Dutch-auction-rate transferable securities (DARTS)

- Market-auction preferred stock (MAPS)

- Auction-market preferred stock (AMPS)

- Cumulative auction-market preferred stock (CAMPS)

If you want to supplement your monthly cash flow, you might do so with a diversified portfolio of preferred stocks.

Preferred Stock Quotations

Preferred stocks listed on the organized exchanges are reported in newspapers in the same sections as common stocks but with the symbol "pf" after the name of the corporation. Quotations are read the same way as common stock quotations. Preferred issues are also listed in *The Bond Record.*

Figure 6-19 gives a typical preferred stock quotation found in financial pages.

FIGURE 6-19: SAMPLE PREFERRED STOCK QUOTATION

Yld High	Sales Low	Stock	Div	%	Net PE	100s	High	Low	Close	Ch
57 1/8	52 1/8	Aetna pf	4.97e **(3)** 9.3		**(1)**	10	53 1/4	43 1/8	43 1/4	-1/8
1191/2	110 1/2	A Can pf	13.75	11.8	--	5	117	117	117	-7/8
100	59	Anheus pf	3.60	3.8	**(2)**	36	96	94 1/2	96	+1
33 5/8	20 3/8	LIL pf	U	--	-- **(4)**	24	27 3/4	27 1/4	27 5/8	+1/4

Explanatory Notes:

(1) The high yield of 11.8% for A Can pf suggests a straight preferred.

(2) The low yield of 3.8% for Anheus pf is a good indication of a convertible issue.

(3) The e symbol after the dividend for Aetna pf indicates a varying dividend payment; this issue is probably adjustable rate.

(4) The lack of a yield figure for LIL pf indicates that dividends are not being paid

IMPORTANT REFERENCES FOR STOCK

Standard & Poor's Stock Guide

The *Standard & Poor's Stock Guide* is a monthly publication that gives you a preliminary look at the common and preferred stock of several thousand companies (and over 400 mutual funds).

The *Standard & Poor's Stock Guide* contains the following company information:

- The *Index Numbers.* These are a visual guide to the columnar data. Stocks with options are indicated by *; stocks in the S & P 500 are flagged with *.

- *Ticker Symbol.* Ticker symbols on listed issues are those of the exchange the stock is listed on. OTC stocks carry NASDAQ Trading System symbols. Supplementary symbols that would appear on the ticker tape after the symbol, such as "pr" for preferred stocks, etc., are indented.

- *Stock's Name.* This is not necessarily the exact corporate title of the company; because of space limitations, abbreviations may be necessary. Where the name of the company is not followed by the designation of a particular stock issue, the common or capital stock is referred to.

  The call price of preferred stock is shown in parentheses after the name of the issue: the footnoted data indicates the year in which the call price declines. The unit of trading for stocks on the NYSE and the AMEX is indicated as follows:

  –10—10 shares

  –25—25 shares

  –50—50 shares

  –All others—100 shares.

- *Com. Rank* and *Pfd Ranking* (common stock and preferred stock ratings).

- *Inst. Cos.* The number of institutional investors—banks, insurance companies, endowment funds, and "13F" money managers—that hold this stock

- *Hold Shs. (1,000).* The number of shares (000 omitted) held by institutional investors.

- *Principal Business.* Where a company is engaged in several lines of business effort is made to list the line from which it obtains the greatest proportion of revenue. The company's rank in its industry is given where possible.

- *Price Range.*

  –Historical high & low are for the calendar years indicated.

  –Last year high & low. Price ranges are not exclusively from the exchange on which the stock is currently traded, but are based on the best available data covering the period.
    Price ranges of OTC stocks are based on the best available high and low bid prices during the period, and should be viewed as reasonable approximations.

- *Month Sales in 100s.* Trading is for the month indicated in hundreds of shares. NYSE and AMEX companies are based on composite a tape, all others are for primary exchanges shown.

- *Last Month OTC-Bid Price.* Closing quotations on principal for the preceding month. For Canadian issues, prices are quoted in Canadian dollars if the first exchange listed is Canadian exchange. For NASDAQ and OTC stocks, the latest available bid price is shown under the "last" column.

- *Percentage Dividend Yield.* Yields are derived by dividing dividend rates by the price of stock; the rate is based on the latest dividend paid including (+), or excluding (e) extras as indicated by footnote. Additional symbols used: (s) including stock; and (++) extras and stock.

- *Price-Earnings (P/E) ratio.*

The *Standard & Poor's Stock Guide* contains the following information on common and convertible preferred stocks.

- *Index.* Details of stock dividends and stock splits effected during the past five years are reported by symbol # and footnotes that carry number corresponding to those in the Index column.

Adjustments are made for all stock dividends.

- *Cash Dividend.* Each Year Since. One or more cash dividends have been paid each calendar year to date, without interruption, beginning with the year listed.

- *Dividends.*

  –Latest Payment. If the latest dividend was at a regular established rate, it is noted by an M (Monthly), a Q (Quarterly), an S (Semi-Annually), or an A (Annually). Date refers to date of disbursement of the most recent payment. An extra or stock dividend is indicated by footnote. The date shown is that on which the stock sells "ex-dividend".

  –This Year. Payments made or declared payable thus far in the current calendar year, including both regular and extras, if any.

  –Total Ind. Rate. Indicated rates are usually based on the most recent quarterly or semi-annual payments or dividends paid during the last 12 months.

  –Last Year. Total dividend payments, including extras if any, made in the preceding calendar year. For preferred dividend accumulations to latest payment due date, see the next column.

- *Financial Position.*

  –Cash and Current Equity Assets. Cash & Equivalent, Current Assets (includes cash/equiv.) and Current Liabilities are given in millions of dollars (000,000) omitted: 17.0 ($17,000,000), 1.75 ($1,750,000), etc.

  –Current Liabilities. Where current balance sheet items are not of analytical significance, special calculations pertinent to the industry in which the company operates are presented; Book Value per Share for banks, Net Asset Value per Share for investment trusts, and tangible Equity per Share (stockholders) for insurance and finance companies. Intangibles such as goodwill, debt discount or preferred liquidating value have been deducted.

- *Capitalization.* Long-term debt is in millions of dollars, 25.0 ($25,000,000); 2.58 ($2,580,000); 0.20 ($200,000). It includes funded debt and long-term bank loans, etc. Preferred and common stocks are in shares to the nearest thousands (000 omitted): as 150—150,000; 30—30,000; 2—1,500 (due to rounding). Outstanding shares exclude treasury stock. The preferred shares column represents the combined total of preferred shares outstanding.

- *Annual Earnings.*

   –Year ends. Earnings in general are Primary as reported by the company including discontinued operations but excluding extraordinary items. More detailed information on method of reporting and usage of standard footnotes can be found on Page 1 of the *Stock Guide..*

   –Per Share Latest Five Years. Earnings for fiscal years ending March 31 or earlier are shown as in the preceding calendar year. Earnings estimates are the product of careful analysis by industry specialists of available relevant information. They are unofficial, however, and for their accuracy cannot be assumed. An arrow denotes changes in current estimates.

   –Last 12 Months. This is 12 months earnings through the period shown as interim earnings, when available, or annual, if not.

- *Interim Earnings.* Interim earnings are shown, when available, for the longest accounting interval since the last fiscal year-end. Also published in this column from time to time are references to sinking fund provisions and dividend arrears of preferred stock. See also the Financial Position column for such notations.

- *Index.* The index numbers are a visual guide to help you keep oriented.

S&P Corporation Records and Moody's Manuals

The six volumes Corporation Records are organized alphabetically. Each volume is updated twice during the year (one volume is updated each month), and there are daily supplements. The volumes contain historical company information, financial statements, news announcements, earnings updates, and other news of general interest. Subsidiary companies are cross-referenced to the parent corporation. *Moody's Manuals* are organized alphabetically rather than by trade categories

The statistical section in the T-Z volume includes a mutual fund summary, addresses of many no-load mutual funds, and foreign bond statistics. Special tables contained in the T-Z volume list new stock and bond offerings on a monthly basis. This volume also presents a classified index of industrial companies listed by standard industrial classification (SIC) codes. For example, if you want to find out about cereal breakfast food companies, you would first find the corresponding SIC number for cereal breakfast foods; SICs are listed in alphabetical order. The number, 2043, then leads you to the cross-listing of companies.

Moody's Manuals are widely used and present historical financial data on the companies listed, on their officers, and on the companies' general corporate condition. The Manuals are organized by category like banks and finance, industrial, municipals and government, OTC industrial, public utility, and transportation. Each manual has a biweekly news supplement that updates quarterly earnings, dividend announcements, mergers, and other news of interest. *Moody's Manuals* are comprehensive; each category takes up one or two volumes and several thousand pages.

S&P Stock Reports

Standard & Poor's *Stock Reports* is among one of their more popular publications. These reports are often mailed out from brokerage houses to customers who want basic information on a company. The information is much more detailed than the *Stock Guide,* but less detailed than *Corporation Records. Stock Reports* provides basic figures, analysis, and projections for over 6,400 publicly-held U.S. corporations. There are is contained in three separate multiple-volume sets for NYSE Stocks, AMEX Stocks, and OTC and Regional Stocks.

End-of-the-year stock reports on about 1,020 NYSE stocks are bound to the annual publication called the Standard & Poor's *Stock Market Encyclopedia*. Periodically, Standard & Poor's publishes other books that contain reports from the *Stock Reports (e.g., The S&P 500,* and *The S&P SmallCap 600)*.

Moody's Handbook of Common Stock

The *Moody's Handbook of Common Stock* is published by Mergent FIS, Inc., is similar to *S&P's Stock Reports*. This handbook is a quarterly guide to common stocks, providing organizational, operational, and financial data on over 1,000 stocks. The presentations answer five basic questions.

1. What does the company do?

2. How has it done in the past?

3. How is it doing now?

4. How will it fare in the future?

5. For what type of investor is the stock suitable?

A report begins with capsule stock information including short-term and long-term price scores (SAPS and LAPS) and an evaluation of the quality of the common stock: (1) high grade, (2) investment grade, (3) medium grade, and (4) speculative grade. In addition, the handbook discusses corporate background, recent developments, and prospects. Approximately 1,000 companies are listed. (Refer to "How To Use This Book" section of the *Handbook*).

Other Mergent FIS (Moody's) Publications

Moody's *Stock Survey* is a weekly publication that discusses the weekly investment climate and market performance. It also recommends selected stocks for purchase.

Mergent FIS, Inc. also offers CD-ROM and Internet subscription services such as Company Data Direct and Company Data Direct International. These constitute a database of all the information collected by Mergent FIS on domestic and international companies. The U.S. version covers more than 10,000 companies listed on the NYSE, AMEX, and NASDAQ.

The *Value Line Investment Survey*, Ratings and Reports

One of the investment services most widely used by individuals, stockbrokers, and small bank trust departments; the *Value Line Investment Survey,* published by Arnold Bernhard & Company, ranks each of the roughly 1700 stocks it covers from 1 (best) to 5 (worst) as to its "timeliness"—probable relative price performance over the next 12 months. These timeliness ranks, updated weekly, have been available since 1965.

Value Line is noted for its comprehensive coverage. Raw financial data are available as well as trend line growth rates, price history patterns in graphic form, quarterly sales, earnings, and dividends, and a breakdown of sales and profit margins by line of business. Value Line contains 13 sections divided into several industries each. The first few pages are devoted to an overview of the industry with company summaries following. Each section is revised on a 13-week cycle. Value Line reports contain both descriptive and analytical information. Examples of descriptive information are "company's capital structure" and "monthly price ranges—past 15 years'; examples of analytical information are: rank for timeliness" and "estimated average price range—3 to 5 years ahead."

Unique to the Value Line evaluation system depends primarily on historical relationships and regression analysis. From the valuation model, each company is rated 1 through 5, with 1 being the highest positive rating and 5 the lowest. Each company is rated on timeliness and safety. It should be noted that Value Line ties to minimize human judgment in making its evaluation. Figure 6-21 describes what is included in repports published by the *Value Line Investment Survey.*

FIGURE 6-21: *VALUE LINE INVESTMENT SURVEY* REPORTS

1. Here is the core of Value Line's advice—the rank for Timeliness; the rank for Safety; Beta—the stock's sensitivity to fluctuations of the market as a whole.

2. The projected average annual return— based on estimated 3- to 5-year price appreciation plus dividend income.

3. The record of insider decisions—decisions by officers and directors to buy or sell as reported to the SEC one month or more after execution.

4. A record of the decisions taken by the biggest institutions (over $28 billion in equity holdings)—including banks, insurance companies, mutual funds—to buy or sell during the past three quarters and the total number of shares bought or sold.

5. The capital structure as of recent date showing the percentage of capital in long-term debt (14%) and in common stock (86%); the number of times that total interest charges were earned (20 as of June 1995).

6. Current position—current assets and current liabilities, the components of working capital.

7. Annual rates of change (on a per-share basis). Actual past, estimated future.

8. Quarterly earnings are shown on a per-share basis (estimates in bold type), quarterly sales on a gross basis.

9. Quarterly dividends paid are actual payments. The total of dividends paid in four quarters may not equal the figure shown in the annual series on dividends declared. (Sometimes a dividend declared at the end of the year will be paid in the first quarter of the following year).

10. Footnotes explain a number of things, such as the way earnings are reported, wether "fully diluted", on a "primary" basis, or on an "average shares outstanding" basis.

11. The stock's highest and lowest price of the year.

12. The Value Line—reported earnings plus depreciation ("cash flow") multiplied by a number selected to correlate the stock's 3- to 5-year projected target price with "cash flow" projected out to 1995-96.

13. Monthly price ranges of the stock—plotted on a ratio (logarithmic) grid to show percentage changes in true proportion. For example, a ratio chart equalizes the move of a $10 stock that rises to $11 with that of a $100 stock that rises to $110. Both have advanced 10% and over the same space on a ratio grid.

14. Recent price—nine days prior to delivery date.

15. P/E ratio—the most recent price divided by the latest six months' earnings per share plus earnings estimated for the next six months.

16. P\E median—a rounded average of four middle values of the range of average annual price/earnings ratios over the past 10 years.

17. Relative P/E ratio—the stock's current P/E divided by the median P/E for all stocks under Value Line review.

18. Dividend yield—cash dividends estimated to be declared in the next 12 months divided by the recent price.

19. Options patch—indicates listed options are available on the stock and on what exchange they are most actively traded.

20. The 3- to 5-year target price range, estimated. The range is placed in proper position on the price chart and is shown numerically in the "1998-00 Projections" box on the left side of the price chart.

21. Relative price strength describes the stock's past price performance relative to the Value Line Composite Average of 1,700 stocks. The Timeliness rank usually predicts the future direction of this line.

22. The number of shares traded monthly as a percentage of the total outstanding.

23. Statistical milestones that reveal significant long-term trends. The statistics are presented in two ways: 1) the upper series records results on a per-share basis; 2) the lower records results on a gross basis. Note that the statistics for the current year are estimated, as are the figures for the average of the years 1998-2000. The estimate would be revised, if necessary, should future evidence require. The weekly *Summary & Index* would promptly call attention to such revisions.

24. A condensed summary of the business, significant shareholders, and the company's address and telephone number.

25. A 400-word report on recent developments and prospects—issued once every three months on a preset schedule.

26. The date of delivery to the subscribers. The survey is mailed on a schedule that aims for delivery to every subscriber on Friday afternoon.

27. Value Line's Indexes of Financial Strength, Price Stability, Price Growth Persistence, and Earnings Predictability.

Source: Value Line Investment Survey

APPENDIX 6-A: COMMON STOCK RATINGS

S & P'S EARNINGS AND DIVIDEND RANKINGS FOR COMMON STOCKS

The investment process involves assessment of various factors—such as product and industry position, corporate resources and financial policy—with results that make some common stocks more highly esteemed than others. In this assessment, Standard & Poor's believes that earnings and dividend performance is the end result of the interplay of these factors and that, over the long run, the record of this performance has a considerable bearing on relative quality. The rankings, however, do not pretend to reflect all of the factors, tangible or intangible, that bear on stock quality.

Relative quality of bonds or other debt, that is, degrees of protection for principal and interest, called creditworthiness, cannot be applied to common stocks, and therefore rankings are not to be confused with bond quality ratings which are arrived at by a necessarily different approach.

Growth and stability of earnings and dividends are deemed key elements in establishing Standard & Poor's earnings and dividend rankings for common stocks, which are designed to capsulize the nature of this record in a single symbol. It should be noted, however, that the process also takes into consideration certain adjustments and modifications deemed desirable in establishing such rankings.

The point of departure in arriving at these rankings is a computerized scoring system based on per-share earnings and dividend records of the most recent ten years—a period deemed long enough to measure significant time segments of secular growth, to capture indications of basic change in trend as they develop, and to encompass the full peak-to-peak range of the business cycle. Basic scores are computed for earnings and dividends, then adjusted as indicated by a set of predetermined modifiers for growth, stability within long-term trend, and cyclicality. Adjusted scores for earnings and dividends are then combined to yield a final score.

Further, the ranking system makes allowance for the fact that, in general, corporate size imparts certain recognized advantages from an investment standpoint. Conversely, minimum size limits (in terms of corporate sales volume) are set for the various rankings, but the system provides for making exceptions where the score reflects an outstanding earnings-dividend record.

The final score for each stock is measured against a scoring matrix determined by analysis of the scores of a large and representative sample of stocks. The range of scores in the array of this sample has been aligned with the following ladder of rankings:

A+	Highest	B+	Average	C	Lowest
A	High	B	Below Average	D	In Reorganization
A-	Above Average	B-	Lower		

NR signifies no ranking because of insufficient data or because the stock is not amenable to the ranking process.

The positions as determined above may be modified in some instances by special considerations, such as natural disasters, massive strikes, and non-recurring accounting adjustments.

A ranking is not a forecast of future market price performance, but is basically an appraisal of past performance of earnings and dividends, and relative current standing. These rankings must not be used as market recommendations; a high-score stock may at times be so overpriced as to justify its sale, while a low-score stock may be attractively priced for purchase. Rankings based upon earnings and dividend records are no substitute for complete analysis. They cannot take into account potential effects of management changes, internal company policies not yet fully reflected in the earnings and dividend record, public relations standing, recent competitive shifts, and a host of other factors that may be relevant to investment status and decision.

S & P'S PREFERRED STOCK RATINGS

A Standard and Poor's preferred stock rating is an assessment of the capacity and willingness of an issuer to pay preferred stock dividends and any applicable sinking fund obligations. A preferred stock rating differs from a bond rating in as much as it is assigned to an equity issue, which issue is intrinsically different from, and subordinate to, a debt issue. Therefore, to reflect this difference, the preferred stock rating symbol will normally not be higher than the bond rating symbol assigned to, or that would be assigned to the senior debt of the same issuer.

The preferred stock ratings are based on the following considerations:

- Likelihood of Payment. Capacity and willingness of the issuer to meet the timely payment of preferred stock dividends and any applicable sinking fund requirements in accordance with the terms of the obligation.

- Nature of, and Provisions of, the issue.

- Relative position of the issue in the event of bankruptcy, reorganization, or other arrangements affecting creditors' rights.

AAA This is the highest rating that may be assigned by Standard and Poor's to a preferred stock issue and indicates an extremely strong capacity to pay the preferred stock obligations.

AA A preferred stock issue rated AA also qualifies as a high quality fixed income security. The capacity to pay preferred stock obligations is very strong, although not as overwhelming as for issues rated AAA.

A An issue rated A is backed by a sound capacity to pay preferred stock obligations, although it is somewhat more susceptible to the adverse effects of changes in circumstances and the economic conditions.

BBB An issue rated BBB is regarded as backed by an adequate capacity to pay the preferred stock obligations. Whereas it normally exhibits adequate protection parameters, adverse economic conditions or changing circumstances are more likely to lead to a weakened capacity to make payments for a preferred stock in this category than for issues in the A category.

BB, B, CCC Preferred stock rated BB, B, and CCC are regarded, on balance, as predominately speculative with respect to the issuer's capacity to pay preferred stock obligations. BB indicates the lowest degree of speculation and CCC the highest degree of speculation. While such issues will likely have some quality and protective characteristics, these are out-weighed by large uncertainties or major risk exposures to adverse conditions.

CC   The rating CC is reserved for a preferred stock issue in arrears on dividends or sinking fund payments but that is currently paying.

C   A preferred stock rated C is a non-paying issue.

D   A preferred stock rated D is a non-paying issue with the issuer in default on debt instruments.

NR indicates that no rating has been requested, that there is insufficient information on which to base a rating, or that S&P does not rate a particular type of obligation as a matter of policy.

Plus (+) or Minus (-) To provide more detailed indications of preferred stock quality, the ratings from AA to CCC may be modified by the addition of a plus or minus sign to show relative standing within the major rating categories.

FITCH PREFERRED STOCK RATING SYMBOLS

Ratings of preferred stock should be viewed in the universe of preferred stocks and in relationship to bonds. Preferred stocks, by definition, are junior to debt obligations. Preferred capital is basically permanent capital although sinking funds that provide for repayment of capital give investors added protection. Preferred dividends are payable only when declared; they are not contractually guaranteed.

AAA   rated preferred stocks are considered of the highest quality in the universe of preferred and preference stocks. Strong asset protection, conservative balance sheet ratios and positive indications of continued protection of preferred dividend requirements are prerequisites for a AAA rating.

AA   rated preferred stocks are considered of very high quality. Maintenance of asset protection and dividend paying ability appears assured but not quite to the extent of the AAA classification.

A   rated preferred or preference issues are considered of good quality. Asset protection and coverage of preferred dividend are considered adequate and are expected to be maintained.

BBB rated preferred or preference issues are considered reasonably safe but they lack the more protective assurances of the A to AAA categories. Current results should be watched for possible signs of deterioration.

BB rated preferred or preference issues are considered speculative. The margin of protection is slim or subject to wide fluctuations. The longer-term financial capacities of the enterprises cannot be predicted with assurance.

B   rated issues are considered highly speculative. While earnings should normally cover dividends, directors may reduce or omit payment due to unfavorable developments, inability to finance or wide fluctuations in earnings.

CCC ratings indicate that the issue is hazardous. The issue should be assessed on its prospects in a possible reorganization.

APPENDIX 6-B:
SOURCES OF COMPANY DATA

U.S. COMPANIES

Public Companies: Printed Data

Moody's Manuals
Historical financials, detailed descriptions of securities outstanding, bond ratings

Standard & Poor's Stock Reports
Financial information, business segment descriptions, current information on company activities

Standard & Poor's Industry Reports
Discussion of industry trends, including company-specific information

Value Line Investment Survey
Financial information on 1,700 public companies, including forecasts

SEC filings:

- 1O-K—Detailed annual financial information

- 10Q—Quarterly financial information

- Proxy statement—Details regarding security issues

- 13D—Insider trading provides historical data on transactions by insiders

Annual reports
Audited annual reports to shareholders

Wall Street Transcript
Summaries of analyst reports, CEO speeches

Dun & Bradstreet

- Business Rankings—Ranking by sales of both public and private companies by SIC codes

- Million Dollar Directories—Listings of both public and private companies within SIC codes

- Corporate affiliations—Listing of divisions, product lines, and subsidiaries with SIC codes

Magazine Indexes

- *F&S Index*—List of recent articles about a company

- *Business Periodicals Index*—List of recent articles about a company

- The *Wall Street Journal* Index—List of the Wall Street Journal cites of a company

Public Companies: Computer-Readable Data

Datext: Compact-disk-based information on 10,000 publicly held companies, organized by groups (Technology, Industrial, Service, Consumer, Corp-Tech, and Commercial Bank); contains financials, subsidiaries, directors, stock reports, recent articles, comparable financials

    Dialog: A number of financial databases:

        –Disclosure: Historical financials, officers, subsidiary list, annual report

Moody's Corporate Profiles: Condensed financials, institutional holdings

Media General: Weekly prices, dividends, and ratios

Investext: Analysts' reports; financial abstracts

Predicast: Index of newspaper articles

Newspaper Index: News summaries

Dow Jones:

- Stock quotes—Recent stock quotes

- Current news-News wire service

- Disclosures—Historical financials, ratios, ownership information, analysts' reports

Nexis:

- Full text—Text of articles on a company

- Exchange—Search capability

Privately Held Companies: Printed Data

Dun & Bradstreet Reports
Brief financial and non-financial profiles on private companies, including sales, SIC, and number of employees

Standard & Poor's Corporate Register
List of officers, products, SIC

Thomas Register
CEO, SIC, sales, number of employees

Privately Held Companies
Computer-Readable Data

Dialog
See description under "Public companies"

Nexis
See description under "Public companies"

Dun & Bradstreet Credit Rating
Credit rating, special events, financials, officers

Newsnet
TRW business profiles

NON-U.S. COMPANIES

BARRA International produces individual company betas using a Goldman Sachs monthly rate-of-return database. The betas are computed using BARRA methodology that incorporates regression toward the mean and a multifactor approach. Currently available are:
The World Book, with 2,500 companies from the *Financial Times* list. They alos have a number of books for different countries and areas (*e.g.,* United Kingdom, Japan, West Germany, Australia).

Although BARRA produces betas, it unfortunately does not provide information on the number of shares outstanding, market risk premiums, or line-of-business breakdowns of company assets. For more information contact: BARRA International, 65 London Wall, London EC2M STU, England. Phone: 01-920-0131.

The London Business School, London, England has a share price database and a risk measurement service. The share price database, updated annually, contains monthly rate-of-return data for over 4,500 U.K. companies from 1975 to present (with some as early as 1955). It also contains indexes (dividend yields, earnings yields, exchange rates, interest rates on government bonds, and the *Financial Times* A Classified Index), shares outstanding, dividends, earnings, and adjustments (for splits, script, and rights). The LBS risk measurement service produces quarterly updates of total volatility and betas that are adjusted for thin trading and for regression toward the mean. For more information contact: London Business School, Sussex Place, Regent's Park, London NW1 4SA, England. Phone: 01-262-5050.

Karlsruhe Universitat, Karlsruhe, West Germany has the most complete German data. The Karlsruhe Kapitalmarktdatenbank has been produced, it has 7 stock market indexes, monthly rates of return for 234 German stocks, 13 foreign stocks listed in Germany, 62 call and put options, 44 warrants, and 300 government bonds. Although no commercial service for betas yet exists, the computer programs are available and the institute is willing to produce data under contract. For more information contact: Institut fur Entscheidungstheorie und Unternehmensforschung, Universitat Karlsruhe, Postfach 6980 D-7500 Karlsruhe 1, West Germany. Phone: 721-608-3427.

Morgan Stanley Capital International, New York, New York, USA
provides stock market return indexes for 19 countries as well as European
and World indexes. These have P/E, price-to-cash-earnings, and price-to-
book ratios; limited balance sheet information; shares outstanding; and
earnings and dividends per share for roughly 1,700 of the largest companies in the world (1970 to present). For more information contact:
Morgan Stanley, Inc., 1633 Broadway, New York, New York 10019.
Phone: 212-765-3114.

Compass is a very large database with heavy product/service offering
orientation but with some financial information, covering all significant
U.K. companies and major European companies (Euro-Compass).

Datastream *(www.datastream.com)* is an online database service providing equity data for

• All U.K. quoted companies

• Foreign companies quoted in Canada

• Japan

• Netherlands

• Switzerland

• U.S.

• France (190 companies)

• Germany (4,000 companies)

• Hong Kong

and company accounts information for

• Quoted companies

• 40,000 unquoted U.K. companies

Extel *(ww.primark.compfid/)* is an authoritative card-based five-year
summary (for main market, USMA, third market, and major unquoted

companies) of financial statements, capital and restructuring transactions, acquisitions and disposals, and dividends.

Hoppenstat is a German database of company financial information.

ICC is a company offering databases for UK comp;anies. Phone number: +44 (0) 181-481-8720.

Investex provides online brokers' reports, including all major U.K. brokers (and some foreign), covering all major U.K. and most major foreign corporations. Phone number: 617-345-2704; Fax: 617-330-1986.

Japan Company Handbook is a useful reference for Japanese companies in first and second section with summary financial information. Phone number: 3-32465-555; Fax: 3-32415-543.

M&A Database is based on M&A magazine data, covers all major transactions, most smaller U.K. deals, and many smaller U.S. deals.

Worldscope *(ww.primark.compfid/)* is a CD-ROM system with financial information on major global and U.S. corporations.

Chapter 7
BONDS AND OTHER FIXED INCOME SECURITIES

Fixed income securities generally stress current income and offer little or no opportunity for appreciation in value. Usually liquid, they bear less market risk than other types of investments. Fixed income investments perform well when economic conditions are stable and inflation is low. As interest rates drop, the price of fixed income investments increase. Examples of fixed income securities are corporate bonds, convertible bonds, government bonds, tax-exempt bonds, and short-term debt securities.

This chapter covers:

- Basics of corporate and government bonds and the types of bonds issued

- How to calculate the yield on bonds and how to read bond quotations

- How to select a right bond for you

- Basics about other short-term fixed income securities

- Sources of fixed income securities information

CORPORATE BONDS

A bond is a certificate or security showing that you loaned funds to a company or to a government in return for fixed future interest payments and repayment of your principal. Bonds have the following advantages:

- There is predictable income each year.

- Bonds are safer than equity securities because bondholders come before common stockholders in the distribution of earnings and of assets if there is a corporate bankruptcy.

Bonds suffer from the following disadvantages:

- They don't participate incrementally in corporate profitability.

- They carry no voting rights.

Terms and Features of Bonds

There are certain bond terms you should be familiar with, including:

- **Par value:** This is the face value, usually $1,000.

- **Coupon rate:** The nominal interest rate that determines the actual interest to be received on a bond. It's the annual interest on the par value.

EXAMPLE 1

You own a $1,000 bond with a coupon rate of 6%. The annual interest payment is: $1,000 x 6% = $60

- **Maturity date:** The date on which repayment of the bond principal is due.

- **Indenture:** This is the lengthy legal agreement detailing the issuer's obligations on the bond. It contains the terms of the bond issue as well as any restrictions on the firm, known as restrictive covenants. The indenture is administered by an independent trustee. A restrictive covenant might the company's agreement to maintain: (a) certain levels of working capital; (b) a particular current ratio; and (c) a specified debt ratio.

- **Trustee:** The third party with whom the indenture is made. The trustee's job is to see that the terms of the indenture are actually carried out.

- **Yield:** The yield is different from the coupon interest rate (Example 2). It's the effective interest rate you're earning on the bond investment. If you buy a bond below its face value (at a discount), the yield is higher than the coupon rate. If you paid more than face value (you bought at a premium), the yield is below the coupon rate. Calculations of various yields on a bond are given later in the chapter.

EXAMPLE 2

Cost of a bond with an 8% coupon rate	*Annual interest*	*Yield*
$1,000: You buy at par	$80.00	8%
$800: You buy at a discount	80.00	10%
$1,200: You buy at a premium	80.00	6 2/3%

- **Call provision:** The issuing company may redeem most bonds early, at face value or a premium. An issuer may opt to call a bond early if market interest rates decline, so that it can issue bonds to replace the old bonds at a lower interest rate. Investors are insulated from calls for a specified time after the bond is issued (usually 10 years).

- **Sinking fund:** In a sinking fund bond, the company puts aside money periodically for the repayment of debt, thus reducing the total amount of debt outstanding. A sinking fund may be required in the bond indenture to protect investors.

The Types of Bonds

Figure 7-1 describes the features of the various categories of bonds. Bonds may be further categorized as follows:

- **Secured bonds:** Specific company collateral is pledged to back the bond issue. These include:

- *Mortgage bonds:* Mortgage bonds are backed by collateralized property. In case of default, the bondholders may foreclose on the secured property and sell it to satisfy their claims. *First mortgage bonds* (senior lien bonds) have a claim against all the corporation's fixed assets; *second mortgage bonds* (junior liens), are backed by real property, but are second in priority.

FIGURE 7-1: THE WORLD OF BONDS

	Maturity	Denomination	Pricing*	Call Provision
Corporate bonds	20 - 30 years	$1,000	% of Par	Often callable
Municipal bonds	1 month - 30 years	$5,000 - $10,000	Quoted on yield-to-maturity basis	Often callable
Agency Bonds	30 days - 20 years	$1,000 - $25,000 and up	Quoted on yield-to-maturity basis	No

Marketable Government Securities

	Maturity	Denomination	Pricing*	Call Provision
Treasury bills	13, 26, or 52 weeks	$10,000 - $1 million in increments of $5,000	Issued at discount; priced in basis points	No
Treasury notes	2 - 10 years	$1,000 - $1 million	Issued at par; priced at % of par	Usually not callable
Treasury bonds	Over 10 years	$1,000 - $1 million	Priced at % of par	Usually not callable

Non-Marketable Government Securities

	Maturity	Denomination	Pricing*	Call Provision
Series EE	Adjustable	$50 - $10,000	Issued at 50% discount	No
Series HH	10 years	$500 - $10,000	Issued at par	No

Government securities are priced in 1/32s of a percentage point; corporate bonds are priced in 1/8s.

- *Collateral trust bonds* are backed by marketable securities deposited with the trustees.

- *Equipment trust certificates* are generally issued by transportation corporations (railroads or airlines). The trustee holds title to the equipment until the certificate is paid.

- **Unsecured bonds** rely the credit of the issuer with no collateral. For instance,

- *Debentures* are backed by the issuing corporation's *good faith* and *credit*. The issuer must be financially sound. High credit ratings are essential. Government bonds are examples.

- *Subordinated debentures* are honored after debentures in the case of liquidation or reorganization (though still before stocks). Junior debentures are sometimes issued by finance companies.

- **Income bonds** pay interest only if there is profit.

- **Convertible bonds** may be converted to common stock at a later date at a specified conversion price. They have features of both bonds and common stock in that they not only generate constant interest income but also capital appreciation through the related common stock. Relevant formulas are:

  Conversion ratio = Par value of a bond/Conversion price
  Parity price of a bond = Common stock price x conversion ratio
  Parity price of a stock = Price of the bond/conversion ratio

EXAMPLE 3

A $1,000 par value bond with a conversion price of $40 would imply a conversion ratio of 25:1 ($1,000/$40=25 or $40x25=$1,000). If the bond was selling at $1,150, then the parity price of the stock would be $1,150/25 = $46.

- **Zero-coupon bonds** are purchased at a discount and mature at par. Each year, the portion of the discount that is earned is taken as interest income on the tax return. Tax must be paid every year on the "earned" portion of the discount every year even though the issuer makes no payment. Zero-coupon bonds require a lower initial investment. Many corporations, municipalities, quasi-federal agencies like Fannie Mae and Freddie Mac, and the U.S. Treasury issue zero-coupon bonds.

- **Tax-exempt bonds** (also called municipals, though not all are issued by cities) have a lower interest rate than comparable corporate bonds, but the interest is not taxed. The after-tax yield is usually higher than an equivalent taxable bond.

- **U.S. government securities** include bills, notes, bonds, and mortgages. Treasury *bills* are used for near-term government financing and have a maturity of twelve months or less. Treasury *notes* mature in one to 10 years. Treasury *bonds* mature in 10 to 25 years. All these can be bought in denominations of $1,000. Interest earned on U.S. government securities is tax free for state and local returns. "Ginnie Maes" are guaranteed pools of 25- to 30-year

Federal Housing Administration (FHA) or Veterans
Administration (VA) mortgages.

- **Deep-discount bonds** are bought at a substantial discount from
  face value, either because they may be risky or because they have
  a long maturity date.

- **Junk bonds** are bonds with low credit ratings from Moody's and
  Standard & Poor's. Often issued by financially unsound companies, they offer high return but have high risk.

- **Serial bonds** mature in installments over time rather than at one
  maturity date. Some serial bonds have *balloon maturity,* usually
  maturing in one year.

- **Series bonds** are issued over a period but with the same maturity
  date.

Yields, Interest Rates, and Bond Prices

Keep in mind the daily fact of financial life: the yields of bonds—no matter what kind they are—move in the opposite direction to their prices.
And a bond's current yield is different from its interest rate (coupon rate).
While your rate of return holds steady, the yield (real return) moves up
and down as interest rates change. When interest rates rise, the price of
your bond goes down because its interest rate becomes less attractive than
the higher rates of new bonds of similar quality. Since the payments
promised by the bond issuer don't change, the market adjusts the yield by
raising or lowering the value of the bonds.

The *yield curve* graphically depicts the relationship between length of
time to maturity and the yield of a bond. Other factors, such as default
risk and tax treatment, are held constant. The curve can help you decide
whether to buy long or short-term bonds. Analysts often use the yield
curve to make judgments about the direction of interest rates, because
interest rate is so critical in determining a bond's yield and price; a yield
curve is simply a graphic presentation of the term structure of interest
rates.

How to Choose a Bond

When you choose a bond, take into consideration the five basic factors outlined in Figure 7-2.

FIGURE 7-2: FACTORS IN CHOOSING A BOND

- Investment quality rating

- Time to maturity

  –Short-term (0-5 years)

  –Medium (6-15 years)

  –Long-term (over 15 years)

- Call or conversion features

- Tax status

- Yield to maturity

Quality

The investment quality of a bond is measured by its bond rating, an evaluation of the possibility that a bond issue might go into default. The rating, which is a perception of risk, affects the interest rate you're willing to accept, the price you're willing to pay, and the maturity period you're willing to agree to.

Bond investors tend to place more emphasis on independent analysis of quality than do common stock investors. Bond ratings are done by, among others, Standard & Poor's and Mergent, F.I.S., Inc. (which now publishes the Moody's ratings). Figure 7-3 summarizes the designations used by these well-known independent agencies.

Pay careful attention to ratings because they can affect not only potential market behavior but relative yields as well. Specifically, other things being equal, the higher the rating, the lower the yield.

Ratings do change over time and the rating agencies have "credit watch lists." Try to pick only those bonds rated Baa or above by Moody's or BBB or above by Standard & Poor's, even though doing so means giving up about 3/4 of a percentage point in yield.

FIGURE 7-3: WHAT BOND RATINGS MEAN*

Moody's	Standard & Poor's	Quality Indication
Aaa	AAA	Highest quality
Aa	AA	High quality
A	A	Upper medium grade
Baa	BBB	Medium grade
Ba	BB	Contains speculative elements
B	B	Outright speculative
Caa	CCC & CC	Default definitely possible
Ca	C	Default, only partial recovery likely
C	D	Default, little recovery likely

Ratings may also have a + or - added to show relative standings in class.

Maturity

You can further control the risk element through the maturities you select. The maturity indicates how much you stand to lose if interest rates rise. The longer a bond's maturity, the more volatile its price. *There is a trade-off:* Shorter maturities usually mean lower yields. If you're a conservative investor, select bonds with maturities no further out than 10 years. The longer the maturity, the more susceptible the bond price is to changing interest rates.

Features

Check to see whether a bond has a call provision that allows the issuing company to redeem its bonds after a certain date before maturity if it chooses to. You're generally paid a small premium over par if an issue is called—but not as much as you would have received if you had been able to hold the bond until maturity. Bonds are usually called only if their interest rates are higher than the going market rate. Try to avoid bonds that have a call provision when the company may be at "event risk" (merger, acquisition, leveraged buyout, etc.).

Convertible bonds can be converted into common stock at a given date. They provide fixed income in the form of interest, but you may also benefit from the appreciation of the common stock.

Tax Status

If you're in a high tax bracket, consider tax-exempt bonds. Most municipal bonds are rated A or above, making them a good grade risk. They can be bought through mutual funds.

Yield to Maturity

Yield has a lot to do with the rating of a bond. The calculation of yield is taken up later.

Other Considerations

Think about buying a bond at a *discount* (below face value) when:

- There is a long maturity period.

- It's a risky company.

- The interest rate on the bond is less than the current market interest rate.

Buy a bond at a *premium* in the reverse circumstances:

- The maturity period is short.

- The company is very solid.

- The interest rate on the bond is higher than the current market rate.

And if you have only a small amount to invest or if you don't have time to do the necessary research yourself, think about buying shares in a bond mutual fund (see chapter 8).

Calculating Yield (Effective Rate of Return)

Bonds are evaluated on many different types of return, including current yield, yield to maturity, yield to call, and realized yield.

Current yield is the annual interest payment divided by the current price of the bond. This is reported in the *Wall Street Journal,* among other places.

The current yield is:

$$\frac{\text{Annual interest payment}}{\text{Current price}}$$

EXAMPLE 4

A $1,000 par value bond with a 12% coupon rate is selling for $960. What is the current yield?

$120/$960 = 12.5%

The problem with this measure of return is that it doesn't take into account the maturity date. A bond with 1 year to run and another with 15 years to run would have the same current yield quote if interest payments were $120 and the price were $960. Clearly, the one year bond would be preferable under this circumstance because you would not only get $120 in interest, but also a gain of $40 ($1000 - $960) within a year, and this amount could be reinvested.

Yield to Maturity (YTM) takes into account the maturity date of the bond. It's the real return you would receive from interest income plus capital gain, assuming the bond is held to maturity. The exact way of calculating this measure is too complicated for our purposes, but the approximate method is:

$$\text{Yield} = \frac{I + (\$1,000 - V)/n}{(\$1,000 + V)/2}$$

where
    V = the market value of the bond
    I = dollars of interest paid per year
    n = number of years to maturity

EXAMPLE 5

You're offered a 10-year, 8% coupon, $1,000 par value bond at a price of $877.60.

(a) What's the rate of return (yield) you could earn if you bought the bond and held it to maturity?

(b) Is the yield greater or lower than the coupon rate?

$$\text{Yield to call} = \frac{\$80 + (1{,}000 - \$877.50)/10}{(\$1{,}000 + \$877.60)/2} = \frac{\$80 + \$12.24}{\$938.80} = \frac{\$92.24}{\$938.80} = 9.8\%$$

(c) Since the bond was bought at a discount, the yield (9.8%) came out greater than the coupon rate of 8%.

Yield to Call: Not all bonds are held to maturity. If the bond may be called, calculate yield by using the yield to maturity formula but with the call price in place of the par value of $1,000.

EXAMPLE 6

A 20-year bond was issued at a 13.5% coupon rate; after two years, rates dropped. The bond is currently selling for $1,180, the yield to maturity is 11.15%, and the bond can be called at $1,090 five years after issue. Thus if you buy the bond two years after issue, your bond may be called back after three more years at $1,090. Compute the yield to call.

The yield to call figure of 9.25% is 190 basis points less than the yield to maturity of 11.15%. Thus, the return is lower.

$$\text{Yield to Call} = \frac{\$135 + (1{,}090 - \$1{,}180)/3}{(\$1{,}090 + \$1{,}180)/2} = \frac{\$135 + (\$90/3)}{\$1{,}135} = \frac{\$105}{\$1{,}135} = 9.25\%$$

Realized Yield: You may trade in and out of a bond long before it matures. How do you evaluate the investment appeal of any bonds you intend to buy and then sell? Realized yield is simply a variation of yield to maturity. Two variables are changed in the yield to maturity formula to provide this measure: Future price is used in place of par value ($1,000), and the length of planned holding period is substituted for the number of years to maturity.

EXAMPLE 7

You plan to hold a bond for only three years, and you've estimated that interest rates will change in the future so that the price of the bond will move up, so that you can buy the bond today at $877.70 and sell it issue three years later at a price of $925. Compute the realized yield.

$$\text{Realized Yield} = \frac{\$80 + (\$925 - \$877.70)/3}{(\$925 + \$877.70)/2} = \frac{\$80 + \$15.77}{\$901.35} = \frac{\$95.77}{\$901.35} = 10.63\%$$

Tax-Equivalent Yield: Yield on a municipal bond may be compared to an equivalent prior-tax yield. Munis make sense for people whose tax-equivalent yield on a tax-free bond or fund would be greater than the yield from a similar taxable alternative. Here are two equations to determine whether tax-exempt yields are right for you.

For federal tax-equivalent yields:

$$\frac{\text{Tax - free yield}}{(1 - \text{Tax rate})} = \text{Tax equivalent yield}$$

For combined effective federal/state tax rates (if you're considering buying bonds or funds holding bonds issued in your home state):

State rate x (1- federal) = Effective state rate

Effective state rate + Federal = Combined effective rate federal/state tax rate

EXAMPLE 8

If your marginal *federal* tax rate is 36% and your municipal bond investment earns 7% interest, the tax-equivalent yield on a taxable investment is .07 [7%/(1 - .36) = .1094 (10.94%)].

Thus, you could choose between a taxable investment returning 10.94% and a tax-exempt bond paying 7% and the returns would be the same.

Some states don't tax munis either. Figure 7-4 shows tax-equivalent yields if free from (a) federal taxes and from (b) selected state as well as federal taxes.

FIGURE 7-4: PERCENTAGE TAX-EQUIVALENT YIELDS*

Tax-Free Yield	Federal Tax Equivalent Yield Necessary	Federal/State Tax Equivalent Yield Necessary					
		CA	CT	FL	MA	NJ	NY
4.00	6.25	7.02	6.54	6.25	7.10	6.72	7.13
5.00	7.81	8.78	8.18	7.81	8.88	8.40	8.91
6.00	9.38	10.53	9.82	9.38	10.65	10.0	10.69
7.00	10.94	12.29	11.45	10.94	12.43	11.76	12.48

*Tax-equivalent yields are based on a federal tax rate of 36% and state rates of CA: 43.04%; CT: 38.88%; FL: 36.00%; MA: 43.68%; NJ: 40.48%; NY: 43.89% (including New York City rate).

NOTE: You can use a bond table to find the value for various yield measures. A source is Thorndike Encyclopedia of Banking and Financial Tables by Warren, Gorham & Lamont, Boston (see Table 1).

Determining Interest-Rate Risk

Interest-rate risk can be determined in two ways. One way is to look at term structure by measuring the average term to maturity—applying Macaulay's duration coefficient. The other way is to measure the sensitivity of changes in price associated with changes in its yield to maturity—the interest elasticity.

Macaulay's duration coefficient: Macaulay's duration (D) is an attempt to measure the risk of a bond by considering its maturity and the pattern of cash inflows (interest payments and principal repayment). It's defined as the number of years until a bond pays back its principal. A simple example below illustrates the duration calculations.

EXAMPLE 9

A bond pays a 7% coupon rate annually on its $1,000 face value; it has 3 years until it matures and thus a YTM of 6%. To compute duration:

1. Calculate the present value of the bond for each year.

2. Express present values as proportions of the price of the bond.

3. Multiply proportions by years' digits to obtain the weighted average time.

Year	Cash Flow	PV Factor @6%	(Step 1) PV of Cash Flow	(Step 2) PV as proportion of bond price	(Step 3) Year x step 2 PV result
1	$ 70	.9434	$66.04	.0643	.0643
2	$ 70	.8900	62.30	.0607	.1214
3	$1,070	.8396	898.37	.8750	2.6250
			$1,026.71	1.0000	2.8107

Although duration is expressed in years, think of it as a percentage change. The duration of this 3-year bond is a little over 2.8 years; 2.8 years means this particular bond will gain 2.8% of its value for each 1% drop in interest rates (or lose 2.8% for each 1% drop).

Keep in mind that

- A bond's duration is always less than or equal to its term to maturity; only a pure discount bond—one with no coupon or sinking-fund payments—has duration equal to the maturity.

- The higher the duration (D value), the greater the interest rate risk, since duration implies a longer recovery period.

- Duration will not tell you anything about the credit quality or yield of your bonds, although some bonds (or bond funds) manage to produce top returns without undue risk. For example, Harbor Bond Fund has returned a respectable return—an annualized 11.5% over the past five years. Yet, its duration is a middle-of-road 5.3 years.

Interest rate elasticity: A bond's interest rate elasticity (E) is defined as:

$$E = \frac{\% \text{ change in bond price}}{\% \text{ change in YTM}}$$

Since bond prices and YTMs move inversely, E will always be a negative number. Any bond's elasticity can be determined directly with the above formula (see Example 9). However, if we know the duration coefficient (D), we can calculate the E using the following simple formula:

$$(-1)\, E = D\, \frac{YTM}{(1+YTM)}$$

EXAMPLE 10

Using the same data as in the previous example, E is calculated as follows:

$$(-1)\; E = 2.8107\; [.06/(1.06)] = .1591$$

which means that the bond (or bond fund) will lose or gain 15.91% of principal value for each 1% point move in interest rates.

MUNICIPAL BONDS

Municipal bonds are issued by state or local governments or by any other political subdivision or public agency that is not federal. Interest income from municipal bonds is exempt from federal tax. Bonds issued by a state and bought by residents of that state are exempt from state income taxes. That's why munis pay the lowest rate of interest compared to taxable bond issues.

The minimum investment in munis is $5,000; when municipals are issued at a discount, however, the difference between the discount and par is considered interest income. Any capital gain realized in the purchase and sale of a municipal bond is subject to capital gains tax.

Municipal bonds may be categorized as either *general obligation (G.O.) bonds* or *revenue bonds*.

General Obligation (G.O.) Bonds are backed by the full faith and credit (and the taxing power) of the issuer. Local governments can collect property taxes, known as "ad valorem" taxes; most state governments collect income and sales taxes. In the event of a default, G.O. bondholders have the right to compel a tax levy or legislative appropriation to make payment on the debt.

Revenue Bonds are backed by revenues from the facilities built with the proceeds of the bond issue; sewer bonds, stadium bonds, solid waste disposal, or toll bridge bonds are examples. Since only the specified revenues back a revenue bond, this is a self-supporting debt. The flip side of this is that because revenue bonds are backed by a single source of funds, they are riskier than G.O. bonds. Because of this, most revenue bonds are issued under a trust indenture.

Municipal bonds are not traded on national exchanges but in the over-the-counter market. Generally, this confines investor interest in municipal issues to residents of the state of issuance. Another factor that limits municipal trading is that most issues are "serial" maturities: Within a single bond offering are multiple maturities, with each maturity having a relatively small principal amount. The small amount of each maturity available limits trading.

NOTE: Ask your broker if he or she has access to any on-line services, such as J.J. Kennedy Information Systems, that provides a comprehensive data basis of most municipal bonds outstanding; this is necessary for accurate portfolio analysis and the prompt answering of credit questions.

If you're considering municipal bonds for tax or income reasons, you have three investment choices for diversification: (1) personal purchases, (2) municipal bond unit investment trusts (UITs) (see below), and (3) municipal bond mutual funds (see chapter 8). If the preservation of capital is of primary importance, the UIT may be a better investment than a mutual fund. Figure 7-5 compares the three approaches.

GOVERNMENT BONDS

Government bonds are the most liquid issues traded on any market, are extremely safe, have some tax advantages (yields are not usually subject to state and local taxes), and can be used as loan collateral.

Treasury bills have a maximum maturity of one year and common maturities of three months (91 days, or 13 weeks), six months (182 days, or 26 weeks), or one year (52 weeks). They trade in minimum units of $10,000. They don't pay interest in the traditional sense; they're sold at a discount, and redeemed when the maturity date comes around, at face value. T-bills are extremely liquid in that there is an active secondary or resale market for them. T-bills have extremely low risk because they're backed by the U.S. government. Another reason for their popularity is that the interest income they produce is exempt from state and local income taxes.

FIGURE 7-5: OPTIONS FOR INVESTING IN MUNICIPAL BONDS; THREE CHOICES

	Direct Purchase	UIT	Mutual Fund
Portfolio policy and management	Your own selection	Passive; no	Active management
Payments	Twice a year	Monthly	Monthly or automatic reinvestment
Commissions	Usually some percent buy-sell spread	Some buy-sell spread plus front-end load	Load or no-load
Investor profile	Experienced, with considerable funds	Long-term (10 Years)	Smaller and short-term
Interest rate risk	High	Low	Medium
Capital gain/loss potential	High	Low	Medium

The price of a T-bill is quoted in terms of the discount yield: "March 4, bid 4.30%, asked 4.20%" is an offer to buy the bill at 95.70% of par (an offer to pay $9,570 for the bill since par value of T-bills is usually $10,000) and offering to sell at 95.80% of par.

The yield on discount securities like T-bills, called the *discount yield (d),* is calculated using the formula:

$$d = \frac{\$10,000 - P}{P} \times \frac{365}{\text{days - to - maturity}}$$

where
   P = purchase price.

The formula simply states that the yield on the discount security is equal to the gain on the bill relative to its face of $10,000, ($10,000 - P)/$10,000, times a factor that annualizes this gain, 365/days-to-maturity.

EXAMPLE 11

Assume that P=$9,800. The T-bill yield is

$$\frac{\$10,000 - \$9,800}{\$9,800} \times \frac{365}{90} = \frac{-\$200}{\$9,800} \times 4.06 = 0.0829 = 8.29\%$$

The so-called equivalent bond yield (EBY) allows you to compare the yields on discount securities with other kinds of bonds, making them comparable to bonds. The idea is to compute a yield that reflects the opportunity bond market investors have to receive and reinvest semiannual coupon payments. The formula is:

$$EBY = \frac{365 \times d}{360 - (d \times days\text{-}to\text{-}maturity)}$$

where d = discount.

EXAMPLE 12

For the 90-day instrument used in the previous example, the EBY would be

$$EBY = \frac{365 \times 0.0829}{360 - (0.0829 \times 90)} = 0.846 = 8.46\%$$

Auctions for 3- and 6-month T-bills take place weekly and for 12-month bills monthly.

Treasury notes have maturities of two to 10 years; they're available in registered form without coupons. They are not callable. They're quoted in 1/32's of a percentage point; "Maturing 11/10/90 - Bid: 99.16; Ask: 99.2" means bid at 99 16/32 or $995; ask at 99 24/32 or $997.50.

Treasury bonds have maturities ranging from 10 to 30 years. Some have optional call dates: for instance, in "Due 6/30 1992/97," the first date shown is the call date, the second the maturity date. They're quoted like T-notes.

Treasury STRIPS (Separate Trading of Registered Interest and Principal of Securities) are also called zero coupon Treasuries. These are designated Treasury notes and bonds that can be converted by dealers into zero-coupon securities. It's done by stripping the bonds of their coupons; one group of units sold represent only the repayment of principal at the maturity date. The interest payments (coupons) are also grouped and sold separately as a zero-coupon issue. All new Treasury notes and bonds of 10 years or longer are eligible for the STRIP program.

Investors are attracted to STRIPS because of their predictability, fixed rate of interest, and maturity at a known value. *One chief drawback:* Although they don't pay interest until maturity, the IRS requires you to pay taxes on each year's accrued value as though you had received a check in the mail. Note, however, that they typically outperform straight Treasuries by 15 to 50 basis points.

Buying Treasuries

You can buy Treasuries for as little as $1,000 to $10,000 (depending on the security) without paying a commission through a program called Treasury Direct. Or you can pay $50 or $60 per transaction and buy through a broker. Each of these methods has its pros and cons.

Treasury securities are sold in a variety of maturities at regularly scheduled auctions (see Figure 7-6). The dates for non-weekly auctions are announced about a week in advance. To learn the exact dates, call the nearest Federal Reserve Bank. In New York City, for example, the phone number is (212) 720-6619. You can either speak directly with a service representative or get the information you need from a recording. The office will mail you the proper investment forms to fill out and mail back.

FIGURE 7-6: U.S. TREASURY SECURITIES

Treasury Bills
What: . . . . .13 weeks and 26 weeks
When: . . . . .Every Monday, except holidays
How much: . . . .$10,000 minimum, then $1,000 increments

What: . . . . .52 weeks
When: . . . . .Every four weeks, generally on a Thursday
How much: . . . .$10,000 minimum, then $1,000 1ncrements

Treasury Notes
What: . . . . .Two years
When: . . . . .Monthly, generally on a Tuesday late in the month
How much: . . . .$5,000 minimum, then $1,000 increments

What: . . . . .Three years
When: . . . . .Quarterly, in early February, May, August, November
How much: . . . .$5,000 minimum, then $1,000 increments

What: . . . . .Five years
When: . . . . .Monthly, generally on a Wednesday late in the month
How much: . . . .$1,000 minimum, then $1,000 increments

What: . . . . .10 years
When: . . . . .Quarterly, in early February, May, August, November
How much: . . . .$1,000 minimum, then $1,000 increments

Treasury Bonds
What: . . . . .30 years
When: . . . . .Twice a year, in February and in August
How much: . . . .$1,000 minimum, then $1,000 increments

Zero Coupon Treasuries - Treasury Strips
What: . . . . .Three months to 30 years
When: . . . . .Quarterly, in early February, May, August, November
How much: . . . .$1,000 minimum, then $1,000 increments

INVESTING IN SAVINGS BONDS

U.S. Savings Bonds are another type of Treasury investment, but they're non-transferable: They can be redeemed only by the purchaser, and can be neither marketed nor used as collateral for loans. There are two types of U.S. savings bonds: Series EE and Series HH.

Series EE are bonds bought for 50% of face value. They pay no periodic interest; the interest accumulates between the purchase price (say, $100) and the bond's maturity value (which would be $200). Series EE bonds can be bought in denominations from $25 to $5,000, with a maximum limit of $15,000 annually. Early redemption is penalized with a lower interest rate than stated on the bond.

When held for at least five years, Series EE bonds earn the higher of either a guaranteed 4% return or market-based interest. Bonds with maturities of less than five years earn a lower return. The market-based rate, announced each May and November, is 85% of the market average on five-year Treasury securities. *NOTE: Since yields are adjusted every six months, the bonds offer unique opportunities in times of rising interest rates.*

Since May 1, 1995, two methods have been used to compute market-based interest.

- The short-term rate, for bonds held less than five years, is 85% of the average yields on six-month Treasury securities.

- The long-term rate, for bonds held five to 17 years, is 85% of the yields on five-year Treasury securities.

The Treasury also now offers *Series I* (inflation-protected) bonds. While close cousins of Series EE bonds, I bonds protect against the risks of inflation. This series promises a fixed rate of return for many years and semiannual adjustments for inflation.

Series HH bonds are issued only in exchange for Series E and EE bonds. They are bought at face value and pay interest semiannually until maturity. Early redemption is penalized. An HH bond can be redeemed after six months and has a maturity period of 10 years. Maximum purchase in one year is $20,000 face value. Interest on HH Series Bonds is taxable each year.

EXAMPLE 13

George Lee decided to invest $5,000 in a Series EE savings bond for his retirement. If the interest averages 8% (accrued semi-annually), how much will he have after 10 years?

The future value of $1 for 20 periods at a semiannual rate of 4% is 2.191. He will have $10,955 ($5,000 x 2.191).

Savings Bond Advantages

The interest earned on savings bond is free from state and local taxes. Federal income taxes can be deferred on Series EE bonds until they're redeemed and can be deferred even beyond rolling EE bonds over into HH bonds. Moreover, there are no service charges on purchase or redemption as there are with many other investments. Perhaps most important, they are perfectly secure, being backed by the U.S. government.

NOTE: Parents who sell EE bonds to pay for their children's college tuition don't have to pay federal income taxes on the interest earned if their income is under a certain amount (for example, in 1995, income under $63,450 for couples or $42,300 for single parents) and if the bonds are in the parents' names.

Savings Bond Disadvantages

Savings bonds lack liquidity; you can't cash them in at all for at least six months, and if you do it then, there's a penalty. Also, their yield is relatively lower yield. If you have savings bonds, you might be better off selling those paying low rates, putting the proceeds in a higher-yielding investment vehicle, but holding on to higher-yielding EE bonds.

U.S. savings bonds can be bought without fees at most banks and other financial institutions or through payroll thrift plans. They can be replaced if lost, stolen, or destroyed.

NOTES:

- *To find out what a particular savings bond is worth, obtain a redemption value from any bank that sells the bonds or from the Treasury: Savings Bond Marketing Office, 800 K. St., NW, Suite 800, Washington D.C., 20226.*

- *For details of mistakes and anxieties about them, see a new book by Daniel Pederson, U.S. Savings Bonds: A Comprehensive Guide for Bond Owners and Financial Professions (TSBI, Detroit, Michigan. (800) 927-1901).*

- *For more on the various series, check out www.publicdebt. treas.gov.*

Government Agency Bonds

The U.S. government promotes home ownership through the activities of the Federal Home Loan banks, the Federal National Mortgage Association (FNMA, "Fannie Mae"), the Government National Mortgage Association (GNMA, "Ginnie Mae"), and the Federal Home Loan Mortgage Corporation (FHLMC, "Freddie Mac"). These agencies make a secondary market in home mortgages. Their function is to add liquidity and safety to investing in the mortgage market. They buy mortgages from the banks that originated the loans, getting the funds to do this by selling bonds to the public. The U.S. government does not directly back any of these issues except those of Ginnie Mae.

Government National Mortgage Association (GNMA) is a mortgage pass-through agency. From conventional lenders it buys pools, or groups, of a large number of home mortgages insured by the Veterans Administration and Federal Housing Administration; it then issues certificates ("pass through" certificates) for these mortgage pools to GNMA investors. GNMA certificates are offered with a minimum $25,000 face amount, and $5,000 increments thereafter. They pay interest and part principal monthly. In this sense, you, as a GNMA investor, are in a position similar to a mortgage lender.

Ginnie Mae guarantees that all payments of principal and interest will be timely. Since many mortgages are repaid before maturity, investors in GNMA pools usually recover most of their principal well ahead of schedule.

Ginnie Mae is considered an excellent investment. The higher yields, coupled with the U.S. government guarantee, provide a competitive edge over other intermediate-term to long-term securities, including those issued by other government agencies.

Many mutual funds invest primarily or exclusively in Ginnie Maes. These enjoy the same advantages as regular mutual funds: diversification and professional management.

The Federal National Mortgage Association

Fannie Mae, a publicly held corporation, provides a secondary market for government-guaranteed mortgages. It finances this by selling debentures with maturies of several years and short-term discount notes from 30 to

360 days to provide investors. These are unsecured, and are not guaranteed by the government. For this reason the yields are often higher than Treasury securities.

The Federal Home Loan Mortgage Corporation

Freddie Mac also offers a secondary market for conventional mortgages, buying them for its own portfolio. It, too, is publicly held. It issues pass-through certificates like Ginnie Mae and guaranteed mortgage certificates (GMCs) that resemble bonds. Freddie Mac's securities are not guaranteed by the government; unlike Treasuries, they are also subject to state and federal taxes.

Freddie Mac also now offers collateralized mortgage obligations (CMOs). Because pass-through certificates have problems because mortgage pools have a long fixed life and mortgage prepayment risk is high, CMOs were created to eliminate or minimize these risks. There is a range of short-term (5-year) through long-term (20-year) pools. CMOs offer high current income while getting around the problem of uncertainty regarding the timing of return of principal, but in exchange for easing the uncertainty, the yield is slightly lower than pass-through securities. CMOs sell in denominations from $1,000 to $12,000.

On the basis of expected cash flows to be received over the life of the pool, separate classes of securities called tranches are created. For example, a 15-year mortgage pool may be broken up into 5 tranches:

Tranch 1	1 - 3 years
Tranch 2	4 - 6 years
Tranch 3	7 - 9 years
Tranch 4	10 - 12 years
Tranch 5	13 - 15 years

As mortgages are prepaid, the payments are applied to Tranch 1 securities. After Tranch 1 is retired, prepayments then are used to retire Tranch 2. Thus, prepayment risk is reduced. Investors can buy mortgage-backed securities with a wide range of maturities.

Even though prepayment risk is reduced, CMO pricing can be volatile. The most volatile are "zero-tranch" portions of CMOs, which receive no interest payments until the preceding tranches are retired.

OTHER FIXED-INCOME SECURITIES

Some other types of short-term debt securities are very secure; their maturities are less than one year, and they are of high quality and marketability. They may be held temporarily. Among them are:

Certificates of deposit (CDs) are high-quality bank instruments usually requiring an investment of at least $2,000. The maturity period is usually three months or more. Though a penalty is assessed for early redemption, the penalty is treated for tax purposes as a deduction from gross income.

Banker's acceptances (BAs) are time drafts (orders to pay a specified amount to the holder on a specified date), drawn on and "accepted" by a bank, which means the bank assumes the responsibility to make payment when the draft matures, thereby making the draft more readily marketable. BAs are usually used in foreign trade. They are bearer securities, and can be held to maturity or traded. The maturity is nine months or less and the security trades at a discount to face value. Only the highest quality (prime) BAs are eligible for Fed trading.

Eurodollars are the deposit liabilities, denominated in U.S. dollars, of banks located outside the U.S. Since the Eurodollar market is relatively free of regulation, banks in this market can operate on narrower margins or spreads between dollar borrowing and lending rates than banks in the U.S.

Commercial paper refers to short-term financial instruments issued by large high-quality companies on an unsecured discount basis. A typical investment is $100,000 or more.

Money market funds (see chapter 8) are a safe way to invest in high-quality liquid securities (*e.g.,* T-bills). A conservative investment, they're usually stated on a $1 per share basis.

Figure 7-7 ranks short-term investment vehicles in terms of default risk.

FIGURE 7-7: DEFAULT RISK OF SHORT-TERM INVESTMENT VEHICLES

Higher

Degree
of Risk

Eurodollar time deposits and CDs
Commercial paper (top quality)
Bank CDs (uninsured)
Bankers' acceptances (BAs)
U.S. Treasury Repos
U.S. government agency obligations
U.S. Treasury obligations

Lower

BOND FUNDS

These are the three key factors you need to check regarding the bonds in any fund portfolio.

Quality

Check the credit rating of the typical bond in the fund. Ratings by Standard & Poor's and Moody's show the relative danger that an issuer will default. AAA is the best grade; BB or lower signifies a junk bond.

Maturity

The average maturity of your fund's bonds indicates how much you stand to lose if interest rates rise. The longer the term of the bonds, the more volatile the price. For example, a 20-year bond may fluctuate in price four times as much as a four-year issue.

Premium or Discount: Some funds with high current yields hold bonds that trade for more than their face value (at a premium). Such funds are less vulnerable to losses if rates go up. Funds that hold bonds trading at a discount to face value can lose the most.

In choosing a bond fund, keep in mind the following guidelines:

- Rising interest rates drive down the value of all bond funds. For this reason, rather than thinking only of current yield, look at total return (yield plus capital gains from falling interest rates or minus capital losses if rates climb).

- All bond funds do not benefit equally from tumbling interest rates. If you think interest rates will decline and you want to increase total return, buy funds that invest in U.S. Treasuries or top-rated corporate bonds. Consider high-yield corporate bonds (junk bonds) if you believe interest rates are stabilizing.

- Unlike bonds, bond funds don't allow you to lock in a yield. A mutual fund with a constantly changing portfolio is not like an individual bond, which can be kept to maturity. If you want steady, secure income over several years or more, consider, as alternatives to funds, buying individual top-quality bonds yourself or investing in a municipal bond unit trust, which maintains a fixed portfolio.

Unit Investment Trusts

Like a mutual fund, a unit investment trust offers to investors the advantages of a large, professionally selected and diversified portfolio. Unlike a mutual fund, however, its portfolio is fixed; once structured, it's not actively managed. Unit investment trusts are available of tax-exempt bonds, money market securities, corporate bonds of different grades; mortgage-backed securities; preferred stocks; utility common stocks; and other investments. Unit trusts are most suitable for investors who need a fixed income and a guaranteed return of capital. They disband and pay off investors after the majority of their investments have been redeemed.

READING BOND QUOTATIONS

Corporate Bond Prices

Corporate bond prices are reported in the financial pages of many newspapers. Figure 7-8 presents a typical corporate bond quotation.

FIGURE 7-8: SAMPLE BOND QUOTATION

Bonds	Cur. Yld.	Vol.	Close	Net Chg.
IBM 7.7s 04	8.3	7	92 1/4	+1 5/8
NWA 71/2 10	cv.	24	104	-1/2
(1) (2)	(3)	(4)	(5)	(6)

Explanatory Notes:

(1) *Name of the issuer:* IBM is an abbreviation for International Business Machines.

(2) *Coupon rate of interest and the year of maturity:* 7.7s tells us the bond pays $77 a year interest, which is 0.077 x $1,000 (the face value of the bond); "s" is used for ease of pronunciation. The last two digits refer to the year in which the principal will be paid off. Thus, 7.7s04 means "seven-point sevens of zero-four"—7.7% bonds due in year 2004: 7.7% is the fixed interest rate the issuer is paying.

(3) *Current yield:* IBM's current yield of 8.3% is determined by dividing the annual interest of $77 by the bond's closing price of $922.50. This figure represents the *effective,* or *real* rate of return on the current market price; it describes what you, as an investor, will actually earn from a bond. The symbol cv. in this column tells us the bond is a convertible; current yields are not calculated for convertibles. The NWA bond is a convertible.

(4) *Volume* means the number of bonds traded: seven IBM bonds traded on the day being reported.

(5) *Close* is the ending price of the day: IBM's is 92 1/4. Because the report shows one-tenth the actual price, to get the actual price, you must multiply the reported price by ten:

Actual price   = 10 * Reported price
                    = 10 * 92 1/4
                    = 10 * 92.25
                    = $922.50

(6) *Net Change* means the difference between the closing price of the day being reported and the closing price of the previous day: IBM's price increased (+) by 1 5/8, which means the price was up $16.25 (10 * 1 5/8) for the day. The NWA bond was down $5.00 (10 * 0.5) for the day.

NOTE: The market price of a bond is usually expressed as a percentage of its par (face) value, which is customarily $1,000. Corporate bonds are quoted to the nearest one-eighth of a percent.

Qualifiers

Bond quotations often contain qualifiers or notes before the coupon rate that give additional information regarding the bond (see Figure 7-9).

FIGURE 7-9: ABBREVIATIONS FOR BOND QUOTATION QUALIFIERS

Qualifiers	Definitions
ct/cf	Certificate: This bond has matured but the certificate is still of value and still being traded
cv	Convertible bond: convertible into stock under certain conditions.
d	Deep discount.
f	Flat: The bond is traded without the accrued interest (*i.e.,* it won't be added to the price). Once an interest payment has been missed, the bond trades flat. After an extended period in which interest payments are met, it's possible to restore a bond to normal trading.
m	Matured: These bonds have already matured; they are no longer drawing interest, and their negotiability has been impaired. They should be redeemed.
na/nc	Non-accrual: There is no obligation to pay back interest owed.
r	Registered: The bondholder's name is registered with the company or its agent and interest payments are automatically mailed (as opposed to bonds with coupons). Most listed corporate bonds are either registered or available in either registered or coupon form. Bonds are not marked "r" unless a distinction is necessary. For example, the registered form and the bearer form may be trading at slightly different prices.
vj	(Sometimes appears, incorrectly, as "vi") The company is in bankruptcy or receivership or is being reorganized under the Bankruptcy Act. Claims of bondholders are prior to those of common or preferred stockholders in case of liquidation. However, when corporations have more than one bond issue, some may take precedence over others.
wd	When distributed: The bond certificate has not been printed and will be available at a later date.
ww	With warrants: The buyer of these bonds will also receive warrants for the purchase of stock at a specified price. The warrants are usually attached to the bond certificate.
x	Ex-interest: This is a day on which a new purchaser of a bond that normally trades flat will not qualify for the current interest payment.
xw	Ex-warrants: The buyer of the bond will not receive warrants. This indications is used for bonds that once had warrants that presumably now have expired, been sold, or exercised by a previous owner.
zr	Zero coupon.

Treasury Securities Quotations

Figure 7-10 and its notes explain how quotations on Treasury notes and bills are to be read.

FIGURE 7-10: TREASURY BILLS, BONDS AND NOTES

(1) Month		(2) Rate	(3) Bid	(4) Ask	(5) Chg	(6) Yld
Nov 00	P	5 ¾	100.02	100.04	-0.01	5.62
Nov 00	P	8 ½	102.30	103.00	-0.02	5.69

Source: New York Times, October 12, 1999

Explanatory Notes:

(1) *Month* refers to the year and month that the bond matures. The first bond shown matures in November 2000. The letter symbol p tells you that the instrument is a note rather than a bond. (It's common practice to refer to both bonds and notes as bonds.) The letter k indicates that non-U.S. citizens are exempt from withholding.

(2) *Rate* refers to coupon rate. The first bond has a coupon rate of 5 3/4% (5.75%).

(3) *Bid* is the highest price bond dealers were offering to buy the bond, quoted in 32nds of $10; thus, the first bond's fraction of .02 means 2/32 of $10, or $.0625. To find the price per $1,000 of par value, multiply the whole number by 10 and add the fractional part. Thus, 10 x $100 = $1,000; $1,000 + $0.625 = $1,000.625.

(4) *Asked* is the lowest price dealers were accepting. The last bond's asked price was 100.04 or $1,001.25.

(5) *Chg.* shows the difference in price between the day quoted and the previous day; the first bond was down .01, $.3125 (1/32 x $10).

(6) *Yld.* means yield to maturity (YTM) based on the asked price. The current yield is obtained by dividing the annual interest by the current asked price. For the first bond, the current yield is 5.74%:

$$\frac{\text{Annual interest}}{\text{Asked price}} = \frac{5\,3/4\% \times \$1,000}{\$1,001.25} = \frac{\$57.50}{\$1,001.25} = 5.74\%$$

However, the first bond has a yield to maturity (YTM) of 5.62%, as shown (Figure 7-10).

NOTE: *Keep in mind that:*

- *Prices are quoted as a percent of par.*

- *U.S. government bonds are highly marketable in keenly competitive market, so they're quoted in thirty-seconds rather than eighths. Moreover, decimals are used in quoting prices, rather than fractions. For example, a quotation of 106.17 for a treasury bond indicates a price of $1,065.31 [$1,060 + (17/32 x $10)]. See Figure 7-11 for the decimal value of the fractions.*

- *Accrued interest must be added.*

FIGURE 7-11: FRACTION EQUIVALENTS

1/32				.03125
2/32	1/16			.06250
3/32				.09375
4/32	2/16	1/8		.12500
5/32				.15625
6/32	3/16			.18750
7/32				.21875
8/32	4/16	2/8	1/4	.25000
9/32				.28125
10/32	5/16			.31250
11/32				.34375
12/32	6/16	3/8		.37500
13/32				.40625
14/32	7/16			.43750
15/32				.46875
16/32	8/16	4/8	1/2	.50000
17/32				.53125
18/32	9/16			.56250
19/32				.59375
20/32	10/16	5/8		.62500
21/32				.65625
22/32	11/16			.68750
23/32				.71875
24/32	12/16	6/8	3/4	.75000
25/32				.78125
26/32	13/16			.81250
27/32				.84375
28/32	14/16	7/8		.87500
29/32				.90625
30/32	15/16			.93750
31/32				.96875

Stripped Treasuries Quotations

Quotations for Treasury STRIPS differ somewhat from the quotations of other Treasury instruments, as you can see from Figure 7-12.

FIGURE 7-12: T-BILLS, BONDS & NOTES

(1) Mat.Date	(2) Bid	(3) Asked	(4) Bid Chg.	(5) Yield
		STRIPPED SECURITIES		
Nov 99 a	99.20	99.20	+0.01	4.86
Nov 99 c	99.20	99.20	+0.01	4.86
Feb 00 a	98.11	98.11	+0.03	5.16
Feb 00 c	98.22	98.22	+0.14	4.09

Source: *Investor's Business Daily,* October 15, 1999

Explanatory Notes:

(1) *Mat. Date:* the month and year the strip matures. The first stripped Treasury matured in August 1999. Letters next to the maturity date describe the portion of the Treasury securities being quoted:

• "a" means "stripped coupon interest," a security that represents the interest-bearing or "coupon" portion of a Treasury bond that has been separated form the bond itself.

• "b" means "Treasury bond, stripped principal."

• "c" means "Treasury note, stripped principal."

(2) *Bid:* the highest price dealers were offering to buy the strip.

(3) *Asked:* the lowest price dealers were accepting.

(4) *Bid. Chg.:* the difference between the price on the day quoted and the previous day.

(5) *Yield:* yield to maturity (YTM) based on the bid price. The first bond has a YTM of 4.86%, as shown in the quotation.

NOTE: *For stripped Treasuries, the coupon rate is always zero.*

Quotations on Government Agency Securities

Quotations for Fannie Mae, Ginnie Mae, and Freddie Mac securities are read like quotations for Treasury securities.

Tax-Exempt Bond Quotations

Figure 7-13 gives a municipal bond quotation from Bonds Online *(www.bondsonline.com)*, which provides quotes and other information for a variety of bond types (corporate, municipal, treasury, zero coupon, and CMOs). For example, it gives Moody's and S&P bond ratings and computes purchase price and accrued interest.

FIGURE 7-13: SAMPLE ON-LINE BOND QUOTATION

(1)	(2)	(3)	(4)	(5)	(6)	(7)	(8)	(9)	(10)	(11)
State	Moody	S&P	Qty	Min	Issue	Coupon	Maturity	Yld	LY	Price
CA	-	-	660		Los Rios Calif Cmnty	3.500	01-21-2000	2.065	NC	100.289
CA	NR	BBB+	75		Santa Barbara Calif	5.700	03-01-2000	3.457	NC	100.685
CA	NR	NR	10		Tuolumne Pk & Rec Di	6.500	04-15-2000	83.850	NC	75.188
CA	Aa3	NR	5		Riverside Calif Wtr	5.600	05-01-2000C	5.589		100.002
CA	NR	NR	25		Santa Margarita Cali	7.500	07-01-2000P	3.978	PRE	104.170
CA	NR	NR	10		Galt Calif Ctfs Part	7.400	09-01-2000P	3.901	PRE	104.706
CA	NR	NR	45		Vallejo Calif Pub Fi	4.650	09-02-2000	4.499	NC	100.113

Source: Bonds Online

Explanatory Notes:

(1) *State:* the state in which the issuing agency is located.

(2) *Moody:* Moody's rating for the bond (NR = no rating).

(3) *S&P:* the Standard & Poor's rating for the bond (NR = no rating).

(4) *Quantity:* the quantity being sold.

(5) *Min:* the minimum block size traded.

(6) *Issue:* the issuing agency.

(7) *Coupon:* the coupon rate (3.5% for the first bond).

(8) *Maturity:* the month, date, and year the bond matures. (A C means the bond is callable, a P that the bond is pre-refunded, which means that the bond will be replaced by a new bond offering.)

(9) *Yld.:* yield to maturity (YTM), or call date in the case of a pre-refunded bond. The current yield is not given in most quotations.

It can be calculated without difficulty. For the first bond, the coupon rate of 3.5% yields $35 per $1,000 bond. This is an 3.49% yield on the current price, $1,002.89.

$$YTM = \frac{\$35}{\$1,002.89} = 3.49\%$$

The first bond, however, has a yield to refund date of 2.065%.

(10) *LY:* notes on the bonds being traded. PRE means the bond is pre-refunded; NC that it not callable.

(11) *Price:* The trading price of the bond. Prices are quoted as a percent of par. The first bond's price was 100.289, which is $1,002.89. Accrued interest must be added to the price.

BOND OFFERING ADVERTISEMENTS

As with stocks, underwriters place ads in newspapers when there are new bond issues for sale. Figure 7-14 is typical.

Explanatory Notes:

(1) The *standard disclaimer* states that this is not an offer to sell bonds; such offers can legally be made only through a prospectus. (See the section "How to Read a Prospectus" in chapter 5). In principle, tombstone ads like this are for information purposes only; often the issue has already been sold, as is the case with this one.

(2) *Total amount of borrowing:* If the bonds are all in denominations of $1,000, the issue will consist of 1,000,000 bonds. (1,000,000 x $1,000 = $1,000,000,000).

(3) *Name* of the company or agency issuing the bonds.

(4) *Coupon rates and maturity dates.*

(5) Since the bonds have already been sold, the tombstone reports *the price* they brought. The 100% indicates that they were sold at face value with no premium or discount. Bonds are dated as of the date

FIGURE 7-14: BOND OFFERING ADVERTISEMENT

Morgan Stanley Dean Witter is a service mark of Morgan Stanley Dean Witter & Co.

(1)

These securities have not been registered under the Securities Act of 1933 and may not be offered or sold in the United States absent registration or an applicable exemption from the registration requirements. These securities having been previously sold, this announcement appears as a matter of record only.

$1,000,000,000 **(2)**

(3)

FMR Corp.

$250,000,000 7.49% Debentures Due 2019
$750,000,000 7.57% Debentures Due 2029 **(4)**

Interest payable June 15 and December 15

Price 100% and Accrued Interest **(5)**

MORGAN STANLEY DEAN WITTER **(6)**

FIDELITY CAPITAL MARKETS

GOLDMAN, SACHS & CO.

LEHMAN BROTHERS

SALOMON SMITH BARNEY

June 30, 1999

they are first offered (the bond date). Whenever bonds are sold after that date, the buyer is entitled to receive interest from the bond date. Therefore, the price of the bonds includes any interest accrued between the bond date and the purchase date.

(6) *Underwriters* marketing the bonds initially.

For comparison purposes, Figure 7-15 contains an example of a tombstone ad of a convertible bond issue.

FIGURE 7-15: TOMBSTONE ADVERTISEMENT

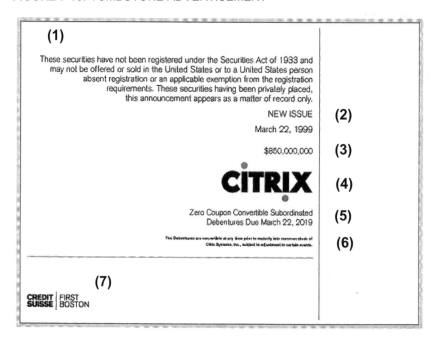

Explanatory Notes:

(1) *The standard disclaimer.* Offers to sell bonds can legally be made only through a prospectus. (See the section "How to Read a Prospectus" in chapter 5). After the SEC has accepted a preliminary prospectus, a new prospectus without the "red herring" lettering is used for offering the shares; the reference in the ad is to the second prospectus.

(2) This is a *new issue.*

(3) The *amount being borrowed.*

(4) The issuing *company.*

(5) *The type of security:* These bonds don't pay interest (they're zero coupon bonds). The return is created by selling the bonds at a deep discount. These are unsecured liabilities (subordinated debentures) that mature on March 22, 2019.

(6) *Notice of convertibility:* "The debentures are convertible at any time prior to maturity into common shares of Citrix Systems, Inc., subject to adjustment in certain events."

(7) Credit Suisse and First Boston are *underwriting* the issue. If there are numerous underwriters in the syndicate bringing out the issue, those with the largest number of bonds to sell are listed first and in bolder type than those with a relatively minor stake.

INFORMATION RESOURCES

Mergent Bond Record is a monthly publication of Mergent, F.I.S., Inc., that contains data on corporate bonds, convertible bonds, government bonds, municipal bonds, and ratings on commercial paper and preferred stock. Figure 7-16 suggests the range of data it provides.

Corporate bond information includes the interest coupon, payment dates, call price, Moody's rating, and yield to maturity. The current price as well as the yearly and historical high-low prices are presented. The total amount of a bond issue outstanding is given, with a designation for a sinking fund and the original issue date. Data on convertible bonds includes conversion price, conversion value, and conversion period. Information on industrial revenue and municipal bonds is usually limited to the Moody's rating.

The *Mergent Bond Record* also contains historical yield graphs for various types of bonds over at least 30 years. Figure 7-17 is a good example of what you can expect to find in the publication.

FIGURE 7-16: TABLE OF CONTENTS, *MERGENT BOND RECORD*

Table of Contents

Source: Mergent Bond Record

FIGURE 7-17: SAMPLE LISTING, *MERGENT BOND RECORD*

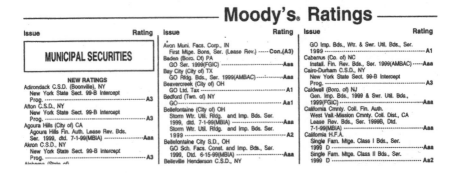

Source: Mergent Bond Record

The weekly *Moody's Bond Survey* reviews the week's activity in the bond market, rating changes, new issues, and bonds called for redemption.

Standard & Poor's Bond Guide has the same format as the *S&P Stock Guide.* A monthly publication in booklet form, it presents data on corporate and convertible bonds. Figure 7-18 (pages 240-241) shows one page on corporate bonds: The S & P rating is presented along with the bond form (either a coupon or registered bond), call prices, sinking funds, yields, prices, and other information. Figure 7-19 (page 242) shows one page on convertible bonds. You will see coupons, interest payment dates, and maturity dates as well as the S & P rating. All the conversion data are given with bond prices and common stock prices.

For these figures, note that the explanatory notes are expanded on and should be supplemented by further explanations in the *Bond Guide* itself.

Explanatory Notes:

(1) *Exchange:* Most bonds, like those in Figure 7-18 are not listed on an exchange, but a solid circle in this column means the bond is traded on the NYSE, and a solid diamond means the bond is traded on the AMEX.

(2) *Title-Industry Code & Co. Finances:* The name of the issuer, with information about control, name change, subsidiary, etc., footnoted to reference. The company's principal business is indicated by numerical reference; a directory of these numbers appears elsewhere in the volume.

(3) *Individual Issue Statistics:* Description of individual issues ; for the meaning of the abbreviations see elsewhere in the *Bond Guide.*

(4) *Interest Dates:* Dates are indicated by first letter of alternate six months in which interest is payable. (An) or (Q) precedes dates on which interest is payable either annually or quarterly. Unless otherwise noted, dates are the first day of the month. Month of maturity is indicated by a capital letter. Symbols following interest dates note foreign issues payable in U.S. funds or currency of issuing country; and issues in default. The entries are fully explained elsewhere in the *Bond Guide.*

FIGURE 7-18: CORPORATE BONDS

(2)	(6) Fixed Charge Coverage			(8)	(10) Corporate Bonds		
(3)					-------------Millions $-------------		
Title-Industry Code & n				Year	Cash &	Curr.	Curr.
Co. Finances d	1996	1997	1998	End	Equiv.	Assets	Liab.
					-------------------Redemption Provisions-------------------		
(1) (4) Individual Issues Statistics	(5) Date of (7) Last		Eligible	(9)	(11) ----------Regular--------- (Begins)		(12)-Sinking Fund------- (Begins)
Exchange Interest	S&P	Rating	Prior	Bond			
Dates	Rating	Change	Rating	Form	Price	Thru	Price	Thru

ADVANTA Corp. (Cont.)									
M-T Nts"C" 7⅜s 2000 . . . a016	BB–	2/98	BB	Y	BE	NC	. . . .	. . . .	. . . .
M-T Nts 'D' 7½s 2000 . . . 1A28	BB–	2/98	BB	Y	BE	NC	. . . .	. . . .	. . . .
Nts 7s 2001 . . . . Mn	BB–	2/98	BB	Y	BE	NC	. . . .	. . . .	. . . .
Advanced Restaurant Grp. . 27c	n/a	n/a		. . . .	Dc	146.9	218.6	365.8	3-31-99
Sr Sub Nts² 11¼s 2008 . . . Jj15	B	4/98	NR	Y	BE	105.625	(1-15-03)	. . . .	. . . .

(5) *S&P Debt Rating:* S&P's rating definitions appear in the front of the *Bond Guide.*

(6) *Fixed Charge Coverage:* Represents the number of times available earnings (before income taxes and extraordinary charges or credits) cover fixed charges like interest on funded debt, other interest, or amortization of debt discount and expense.

(7) *Eligibility:* Eligible for bank purchase.

(8) *Year End:* The month the company fiscal year ends. For fiscal years ending March 31 or earlier, figures are shown under the preceding calendar year.

(9) *Bond Form:* C = coupon only; CR = coupon or registered, interchangeably; R = registered only.

(10) *Million $- Cash & Equiv., Curr. Assets, Curr. Libs., Bal. Sheet Date:* Figures are reported in millions of dollars (000,000 omitted): 1275 = $1,275,200,000; 17.5 = $17,500,000. Data is updated from annual and interim reports information of which is shown. Utilities with a reasonable debt-to-property ratio may often report current liabilities in excess of current assets. This is rarely of real significance as utilities have constant tax deferrals, high current debt maturity, and the ability to forecast revenues.

FIGURE 7-18: CORPORATE BONDS, *Continued*

Balance Sheet Date **(14)**	L Term Debt (Mil$) Refund/Other ----Restriction---		Capital- ization (Mil$) **(16)**	Total Debt % Capital **(18)**	**(19)** Price Range 1999		**(20)** Mo. End Price Sale(s)	**(21)** Curr.	Yield to
	Price	(Begins) Thru	Outst'g (Mil $)	Underwriting Flm Year	High	Low	or Bid	Yield	Mat.
	. . . .	. . . . .	25.0	B7 '97	$97\frac{3}{8}$	$95\frac{1}{8}$	$95\frac{1}{2}$	7.72	11.44
.	. . . .	. . . . .	50.0	M2 '97	$97\frac{3}{4}$	$95\frac{3}{4}$	$96\frac{1}{8}$	7.80	11.41
	. . . .		200	S1 '96	$95\frac{7}{8}$	$92\frac{3}{8}$	$92\frac{3}{4}$	7.55	11.68
	1136	*1364*		87.2					
	ⁱZ110	1-15-01	592	Exch. '98	$103\frac{3}{4}$	94	94	11.97	12.41

ADV-AIR 27 appears above columns 19-21 in the header area, and (13) (15) (17) appear above the L Term Debt, Capitalization, and Total Debt % Capital columns respectively.

Source: Standard and Poor's *Bond Guide*

(11) *Redemption Provisions:* Regular call price with beginning or ending date.

(12) *Sinking Fund,* if any, is reported together with price and date.

(13) *L Term Debt (Mil $):* These are obligations due after one year, including bonds, debentures, mortgages, and capitalized leases. Increased debt resulting from new financing and offered after the latest balance sheet date is indicated by "*".

(14) *Refund/Other Restriction:* Refund restrictions are denoted by "x," giving date at which restriction expires. Redemption provision may include the symbol NC, which means non-callable, and others (+ , Z, *) explained in the Bond Guide.

(15) *Capitalization (Mil $):* The sum of the stated values of common shareholders' equity, preferred and preference stock, total debt, and minority interest.

(16) *Outstanding (Mil. &):* Amount of issue outstanding, in millions of dollars, as of the latest complete balance sheet.

(17) *Total Debt % Capital:* Total debt (including short-term debt) of the company divided by total capital; provides a measure of the company's leverage.

(18) *Underwriting- Firm, Price & Year.* Keyed to the Directory of Underwriters elsewhere in the *Bond Guide,* this shows the original underwriter, usually the head of the syndicate, the price, and the year the issue was originally offered.

(19) *Price Range:* For current calendar year to date.

(20) *Mo. End Price Sale(s) or Bid:* Last sale price for listed issues, and latest bid price or S&P valuation for over-the-counter issues or listed issues not traded last day of the month. "Flat" means the issue is traded without accrued interest. A = Ask price.

(21) *Curr. Yield-Yield to Mat.Yields* (current and to maturity): Computed on month-end price shown in preceding column.

FIGURE 7-19: CONVERTIBLE BOND QUOTATIONS

		(1)		(2)			(3)		
					Shares		Div.		
Exchange		B F			Conv.	Price	Income	1999	
↓	Issue, Rate, Interest Dates	o o S&P n r	Outstdg	Ex-	per $1,000	per	per	–Price Range–	
	and Maturity	Rating d m	Mil$	pires	Bond	Share	Bond	High	Low
Aames Financial 5½s Ms15 2006	NR	R	114	2006	53.56	18.67	. . . . .	40%	33$^{1/8}$
Acclaim Entertainment . . . . . 10s Ms 2002	NR	R	50.0	2002	193.05	5.18	. . . . .	251	120$^{1/8}$

FIGURE 7-19: CONVERTIBLE BOND QUOTATIONS, *Continued*

			(4)	(5)				(6)			
Curr			Stock		Stock			Earnings Per Share		Last	
Bid		Yield	Value		Data					12	
Sales(s)	Curr	to	of	Conv	Month	P/E	Yr.				
Ask(A)	Yield	Maturity	Bond	Patiry	End	Ratio	End	1998	1999	Mos.	
39$^{3/8}$	13.97	24.39	9$^{1/8}$	7$^{3/8}$	•1$^{11/16}$	d	Je	v1.23	. . . .	^{3}d7.00	
131$^{5/8}$	7.60	. . . . .	131$^{5/8}$	6$^{7/8}$	6$^{15/18}$	12	Au	v0.37	E0.54	^{5}0.55	

Source: Standard and Poor's *Bond Guide*

Explanatory Notes:

1) *Bond Form:* C = coupon only; CR = coupon or registered, interchangeably; R = registered only.

(2) *Conv. Expires:* The year in which the option to convert expires.

(3) *Div. Income per Bond:* If a $1,000 bond were converted, the annual dividend the company is expected to pay on the stock based on the most recent annual rate of payment.

(4) *Stock Value of Bond:* The price at which the bond must sell to equal the price of the stock (number of shares received on conversion x price of the stock).

(5) *Conv. Parity:* The price at which the stock must sell to equal the bond price (price of bond divided by number of shares received on conversion).

(6) *Last 12 Mos.:* Earnings through period indicated by superior number preceding figure: 1 for Jan., 2 for Feb., etc. Figure without superior number indicates fiscal year end. The letter "d" means dilution, indicating earnings on a fully diluted basis.

Yields on Short-Term Debt Securities

Newspapers and other sources of financial information provide information on key interest rates (or yields) on short-term debt securities. Interest rates are reported from the standpoint of both the institutional investor and the individual investor. This information is also available free on the Internet (*e.g., www.bankrate.com*).

The daily "Credit Markets"" column in the *Investor's Business Daily* and the *Wall Street Journal* provides a capsule view of current conditions and future prospects in the bond market.

APPENDIX 7-A: USEFUL WEB SITES

Web Address	Primary Focus
www.aaii.org/fxdincme	This American Association Of Individual Investors site has some interesting articles on fixed-income investments
www.bondsonline.com	Site is dedicated to fixed-income securities
www.bradynet.com	Dedicated totally to bonds, particularly strong in emerging markets
www.fed.fil.com/convertibles/glossary.htm	Definitions of terms related to convertible bonds plus links to current bond market news and events
www.fitchibca.com	Free access to Fitch ratings
www.moneyline.com/mlc_bond.html	Descriptions of municipal, Treasury, and agency bonds
www.moneypages.com/syndicate	Bond information and links to related sites, with a glossary of municipal bond terms
www.netspace.org/users/david/finance.html	A large number of links to sites that offer information on bonds
www.psa.com	The Bond Market Association home page with links to bond web sites
www.publicdebt.treas.gov/bpd/bpdindex.htm#speindex	A wealth of information about all types of U.S. Treasury debt instruments
www.smartmoney.com	A wealth of information about bonds, including interactive bond yield and asset allocation tools
www.standardandpoors.com	Primarily information on bond ratings and other S&P services
www.worth.com/articles/B01.html	*Worth* magazine article on the benefits of convertible securities

APPENDIX 7-B:
SOFTWARE FOR BOND AND FIXED-INCOME
SECURITIES ANALYSIS

Fixed income analysis software analyzes the quality and maturity structures of bond and other fixed income securities. Below is a list of popular fixed income analysis software.

Bondeye (DOS)
Ergo, Inc., (805) 969-9366

Bonspec (DOS)
Interactive Data Corp., (617) 863-8295

Bondcalc (DOS, Windows, OS/2)
Bodcalc Corp., (212) 587-0097

Bond Calculator and MBS/ABS Calculator (DOS)
Bond-Tech, Inc., (513) 836-3991

Bond Portfolio and Bond Pricing (Windows, Mac)
Baarns Publishing, (800) 377-9235 or (818) 837-1441

Bonds and Interest Rates Software (DOS)
Programmed Press, (516) 599-6527

APPENDIX 7-C: BOND RATING SERVICES

There are three major rating services: Moody's, Standard & Poor's and Fitch. Moody's and Standard &Poor's ratings can be accessed free at the Bonds Online Internet site *(www.bondsonline.com)*. The Fitch Internet site *(www.fitchibca.com)* makes the Fitch ratings available free to visitors who register with the site (registration is free).

MOODY'S

Aaa   Bonds, which are rated Aaa, are judged to be of the best quality. they carry the smallest degree of investment risk and are generally referred to as "gilt edge." Interest payments are protected by a large or by an exceptionally stable margin and principal is secure. While the various protective elements are likely to change, such changes as can be visualized are most unlikely to impair the fundamentally strong position of such issues.

Aa   Bonds, which are rated Aa, are judged to be of high quality by all standards. Together with the Aaa group, they comprise what are generally known as high-grade bonds. They are rated lower than the best bonds because the margins of protection may not be as large as in Aaa securities or fluctuation of protective elements may be of greater amplitude or there may be other elements present which make the long term risks appear somewhat larger than in Aaa securities.

A   Bonds that are rated A possess many favorable investment attributes and are to be considered as upper medium grade obligations. Factors giving security to principal and interest are considered adequate but elements may be present which suggest a susceptibility to impairment sometime in the future.

Baa   Bonds that are rated Baa are considered as medium grade obligations, (*i.e.,* they are neither highly protected nor poorly secure). Interest payments and principal security appear adequate for the present but certain protective elements may be lacking or may be characteristics and in fact have speculative characteristics as well.

Ba   Bonds that are rated Ba are judged to have speculative elements; their future cannot be considered as well assured. Often the protection of interest and principal payments may be very moderate and thereby not well safeguarded during both good and bad times over the future. Uncertainty of position characterized bonds in this class.

B   Bonds that are rated as B generally lack characteristics of the desirable investment. Assurance of interest and principal payments or of maintenance of other terms of the contract over any long period of time may be small.

Caa   Bonds that are rated Caa are poor standing. Such issues may be in default or there may be present elements of danger with respect to principal or interest.

Ca   Bonds that are rated Ca represent obligations which are speculative in a high degree. Such issues are often in default or have other marked shortcomings.

C   Bonds, that are rated C are the lowest rated class of bonds and issues so rated can be regarded as having extremely poor prospects of ever attaining any real investment standing.

STANDARD AND POOR'S

AAA   Bond rated Aaa has the highest rating assigned by Standard and Poor's. Capacity to pay interest and repay principal is extremely strong.

AA   Bond rated AA has a very strong capacity to pay interest and repay principal and differs from the higher rated issues only in small degree.

A   Bond rated A has a strong capacity to pay interest and repay principal although it's more susceptible to the adverse effects of changes in circumstances and economic conditions than higher rated categories.

BBB   Bond rated BBB is regarded as having an adequate capacity to pay interest and repay principal. Whereas it normally exhibits adequate protection parameters, adverse economic conditions or changing circumstances are more likely to lead to a weakened capacity to pay interest and repay principal for bonds in this category than in higher rated categories.

BB, B, CCC, CC   Bond rated BB, B, CCC, and CC is regarded, on balance, as predominantly speculative with respect to capacity to pay interest and repay principal payments in accordance with the terms of the obligation. BB indicates the lowest degree of speculation and CC the highest degree of speculation. While such bonds will likely have some quality and protective characteristics, they are outweighed by large uncertainties or major risk exposures to adverse conditions.

C   The rating C is reserved for income bonds on which no interest is being paid.

D   Bond rated D is in default, and payment of interest and /or repayment of principal is in arrears.

Plus (+) or Minus (-)   The ratings from AA to B may be modified by the addition of a plus or a minus sign to show relative standing within the major rating categories.

S & P'S CORPORATE AND MUNICIPAL RATING DEFINITIONS

A Standard & Poor's corporate or municipal debt rating is a current assessment of the credit worthiness of an obligor with respect to a specific obligation. This assessment may take into consideration obligers such as guarantors, insurers, or lessees.

The debt rating is not a recommendation to purchase, sell or hold a security, inasmuch as it does not comment as to market price or suitability for a particular investor.

The ratings are based on current information furnished by the issuer or obtained by Standard & Poor's from other sources it considers reliable. Standard & Poor's does not perform any audit in connection with any rating and may, on occasion, rely on unaudited financial information. The ratings may be changed, suspended or withdrawn as a result of changes in, or unavailability of, such information, or for other circumstances.

The ratings are based, in varying degrees, on the following considerations:

- Likelihood of default-capacity and willingness of the obligor as to the timely payment of interest and repayment of principal in accordance with the terms of the obligation;

- Nature of and provisions of the obligation;

- Protection afforded by, and relative position of, the obligation in the event of bankruptcy, reorganization or other arrangements under the laws of bankruptcy and other laws affecting creditors' rights.

Provisional Ratings

The letter "p" indicates that the rating is provisional. A provisional rating assumes the successful completion of the project being financed by the debt being rated and indicates that payment of debt service requirements is largely or entirely dependent upon the successful and timely completion of the project. This rating, however, while addressing credit quality subsequent to completion of the project, makes no comment on the likelihood of, or the risk of default upon failure of such completion. The investor should exercise his own judgment with respect to such likelihood and risk.

The letter "L" indicates that the rating pertains to the principal amount of those bonds where the underlying deposit collateral is fully insured by the Federal Savings and Loan Insurance Corp. or the Federal Deposit Insurance Corp. The continuance of the rating is contingent upon S&P's receipt of an executed copy of the escrow agreement or closing documentation confirming investments and cash flows.

NR indicates that no rating has been requested, that there is insufficient information on which to base a rating, or the S&P does not rate a particular type of obligation as a matter of policy.

Debt Obligations of issuers outside the United States and its territories are rated on the same basis as domestic, corporate, and municipal issues. The ratings measure the creditworthiness of the obligor but don't take into account currency exchange and related uncertainties.

Bond Investment Quality Standards

Under present commercial bank regulation issued by the Comptroller of the Currency, bonds rated in the top four categories (AAA, AA, A, BBB, commonly known as "Investment Grade" ratings) are generally regarded as eligible for bank investment. In addition, the Legal Investment Laws of various states may impose certain ratings or other standards for obligations eligible for investment by savings banks, trust companies, insurance companies and fiduciaries.

FITCH'S

AAA Bonds rated AAA are considered to be investment grade and of the highest quality. The obligor has an extraordinary ability to pay interest and repay principal, which is unlikely to be affected by reasonably foreseeable events.

AA Bonds rated AA are considered to be investment grade and of high quality. The obligor's ability to pay for interest and repay principal, while very strong, is somewhat less than the AAA rated securities.

A Bonds rated A are considered to be investment grade and of good quality. The obligor's ability to pay interest and repay principal is considered to be strong, but may be more vulnerable to adverse changes in economic conditions and circumstances than bonds with higher ratings.

BBB Bonds rated BBB are considered to be investment grade and of satisfactory quality. The obligor's ability to pay interest and repay principal is considered to be adequate. Adverse changes in economic conditions and circumstances, however, are more likely to weaken this ability than bonds with higher ratings.

BB   Bonds rated BB are considered speculative and of low investment grade. The obligor's ability to pay interest and repay principal is not strong and is considered likely to be affected by adverse changes in economic conditions.

B   Bonds rated B are considered speculative. Bonds in this class are lightly protected as to the obligor's ability to pay interest over the life of the issue and repay principal when due.

CCC   Bonds rated CCC may have certain characteristics which, with the passage of time, could lead to the possibility of default on either principal or interest payments.

CC   Bonds rated CC are minimally protected. Default in payment of interest and/or principal seems probable.

C   Bonds rated C are in actual or imminent default in payment of interest or principal.

DDD, DD, D   Bonds rated DDD, DD, and D are in default and in arrears in interest and/or principal payments. Such bonds are extremely speculative and should be valued only on the basis of their value in liquidation or reorganization of the obligor.

Plus (+) or minus (-) signs after bond rating symbols (from AA to BB) indicate relative standing within a rating category. They are refinements more closely reflecting strengths and weaknesses and are not to be used as trend indicators.

KEY TO FITCH'S RATING PROCESS

The rating process begins with a request to Fitch by an issuer or their authorized representative, or an institutional investor. After all pertinent financial and operating data relating to the issuer and the security are submitted, the rating request is assigned to an analyst specializing in the issuer's industry.

The entire process takes approximately two weeks, depending on the complexity of the issue. Once the relevant data have been examined, analysts review their findings and their rating recommendations with the Rating Committee. Before a rating is approved it must have the support of a majority of the committee's members.

In the event a rating is contested, there are appeal procedures. During an appeal, additional information and /or a more detailed explanation of previously submitted information will be considered. Once the appeal is completed, the final decision is then made by the Rating Committee.

Fitch ratings are widely accepted by regulatory agencies in states that require ratings on investments by banks, pension funds, and savings and loan institutions.

Key to Fitch's Rating Symbols

Fitch's ratings provide a guide to investors in determining the investment risk attached to a security. The rating represents its assessment of the issuer's ability to meet the obligations of a specific debt issue.

Fitch's ratings are not recommendation to buy, sell or hold securities since they incorporate no information on market price or a yield relative to other debt instruments.

The rating takes into consideration special features of the issue, its relationship to other obligations of the issuer, the record of the issuer and of any guarantor, as well as the political and economic environment that might affect the future financial strength of the issuer.

Securities that have the same rating are of similar but not necessarily identical investment quality since the limited number of rating categories cannot fully reflect small differences in the degree of the risk. Moreover, the character of the risk factor varies from industry and between corporate, health care and municipal obligations.

Fitch's Demand Bond or Note Ratings

Certain demand securities empower the holder at his option to require the issuer, usually through a remarketing agent, to repurchase the security with notice (which is customarily seven days to thirty days with accrued interest at par). This is also referred to as a put option. The ratings of both the long term and the demand provision may be changed or withdrawn at any time if, in Fitch's sole judgement, changing circumstances warrant such action.

Fitch demand provision ratings carry the same symbols and related definitions as for commercial paper and long-term bonds. For example, AA/F-1.

SHORT TERM DEBT RATINGS

MOODY'S

Moody's short-term debt ratings are opinions of the ability of issuers to repay punctually senior debt obligations that have an original maturity not exceeding one year.

Among the obligations covered are commercial paper, Eurocommercial paper, bank deposits, bankers' acceptances, obligations to deliver foreign exchange, and insurance company senior policyholder and claims obligations. Obligations relying upon support mechanisms such as letters-of-credit and bonds of indemnity are excluded unless explicitly rated.

Moody's employs the following three designations, all judged to be investment grade, to indicate the relative repayment ability of rated issuers:

- Issuers rated Prime-1 (or supporting institutions) have a superior ability for repayment of senior short-term debt obligations. Prime-1 repayment ability will often be evidenced by many of the following characteristics:

  –Leading market positions in well-established industries.

  –High rates of return of funds employed.

  –Conservative capitalization structure with moderate reliance on debt and ample asset protection.

  –Broad margins in earnings coverage of fixed financial charges and high internal cash generation.

  –Well-established access to a range of financial markets and assured sources of alternate liquidity.

- Issuers rated Prime-2 (or supporting institutions) have a strong ability for repayment of senior short-term debt obligations. This will normally be evidenced by many of the characteristics cited above but to a lesser degree. Earnings trends and coverage ratios, while sound, may be more subject to variation. Capitalization characteristics, while still appropriate, may be more affected by external conditions. Ample alternate liquidity is maintained.

- Issuers rated Prime-3 (or supporting institutions) have an acceptable ability for repayment of senior short-term obligations. The effect of industry characteristics and market compositions may be more pronounced. Variability in earnings and profitability may result in changes in the level of debt protection measurements and may require relatively high financial leverage. Adequate alternate liquidity is maintained.

- Issuers rated NOT prime don't fall within any of the Prime rating categories.

Obligations of a branch of a bank are considered to be domiciled in the country in which the branch is located. Unless noted as an exception, Moody's rating on a bank's ability to repay senior obligations extends only to branches located in countries that carry a Moody's sovereign rating. Such branch obligations are rated at the lower of the bank's rating or Moody's sovereign rating for bank deposits for the country in which the bank is located.

When the currency in which an obligation is denominated is not the same as the currency of the country in which the obligation is domiciled, Moody's ratings don't incorporate an opinion as to whether payment of the obligation will be affected by actions of the government controlling the currency of denomination. In addition, risks associated with bilateral conflicts between an investor's home country and either the issuer's home country or the country where an issuer's branch is located are not incorporated into Moody's short-term debt ratings.

Moody's makes no representation that rated bank or insurance company obligations are exempt from the registration under the U.S. Securities Act of 1933 or issued in conformity with any other applicable law or regulation. Nor does Moody's represent that any specific bank or insurance company obligation is legally enforceable or a valid senior obligation of a rated issuer. If an issuer represents to Moody's that its short-term debt obligations are supported by the credit of another entity or entities, then the name of names of such supporting entity or entities are listed within the parenthesis beneath the name of the issuer, or there is a footnote referring the reader to another page for the name or names of the supporting entity or entities. In assigning ratings to such issuers, Moody's evaluates the financial strength of the affiliated corporations, commercial banks, insurance companies, foreign governments or other entities, but only as one factor in the total rating assessment. Moody's makes no representation and gives no opinion on the legal validity or enforceability of any support arrangement.

Moody's ratings are opinions, not recommendations to buy or sell, and their accuracy is not guaranteed. A rating should be weighed solely as one factor in an investment decision and you should make your own study and evaluation on any issuer whose securities or debt obligations you consider buying or selling.

NOTES:

- *Moody's ratings are subject to change. Because of the possible time lapse between Moody's assignment or change of a rating and your use of this publication, we suggest you verify the current rating of any security or issuer in which you're interested.*

- *Moody's applies numerical modifiers, 1, 2, and 3 in each generic rating classification from Aa through B in its corporate bond rating system. The modifier 1 indicates that the security ranks in the higher end of its generic rating category; the modifier 2 indicates a mid-range ranking; and the modifier 3 indicates that the issue ranks in the lower end of its generic rating category.*

Moody's bond ratings, where specified, are applied to senior bank obligations and insurance company senior policyholders and claims with an original maturity in excess of one year. Among the bank obligations covered are bank deposits and obligations to deliver foreign exchange. Obligations relying upon support mechanisms such as letters-of-credit are excluded unless explicitly rated.

Obligations of a branch of a bank are considered to be domiciled in the country in which the branch is located. Unless noted as an exception, Moody's rating on a bank's ability to repay senior obligations extend only to branches located in countries, which carry a Moody's sovereign rating.

Such branch obligations are rated at the lower of the bank's rating or Moody's sovereign rating for the bank deposits for the country in which the branch is located.

When the currency in which an obligation is denominated is not the same as the currency of the country in which the obligation is domiciled, Moody's ratings don't incorporate an opinion as to whether payment of the obligation will be affected by the actions of the government controlling the currency of denomination. In addition, risk associated with bilateral conflicts between an investor's home country and either the issuer's home country or the country where an issuer branch is located are not incorporated into Moody's ratings.

Moody's makes no representation that rated bank or insurance company obligations are exempt from registration under the U.S. Securities Act of 1933 or issued in conformity with any other applicable law or regulation. Nor does Moody's represent any specific bank or insurance company obligation is legally enforceable or a valid senior obligation of a rated issuer.

FIGURE 7C-1: STANDARD ABBREVIATIONS

–	Deficit, loss.
NA or N	Not available.
NR	Not rated by Moody's.
CP E-O-Q	Commercial paper outstanding at end of quarter.
QT	Fiscal quarter.
CTN's	Collateral Trust Notes.

MOODY'S MUNICIPAL RATING DEFINITIONS
NOTE AND DEMAND FEATURE RATINGS

Purpose

Moody's short-term ratings are designated Moody's Investment Grade or MIG 1 or VMIG 1 through MIG 4 or VMIG 4. As the name implies, when Moody's assigns a MIG or VMIG rating, all categories define an investment grade situation. The purpose of the MIG or VMIG ratings is to provide investors with a simple system by which the relative investment qualities of short-term obligations may be evaluated.

Such ratings recognize the differences between short-term credit risk and long-term risk. Factors affecting the liquidity of the borrower and short-term cyclical elements are critical in short-term ratings, while other factors of major importance in bond risk, long-term secular trends for example, may be less important over the short run.

A short-term rating may also be assigned on an issue having a demand feature generally as a variable rate demand obligation (VRDO). Such ratings will be designated as VMIG or, if the demand feature is not rated, as NR. Short-term ratings on issues with demand features are differentiated by the use of the VMIG symbol to reflect such characteristics as payment upon periodic demand rather than fixed maturity dates and payment relying on external liquidity. Additionally, investors should be alert to the fact that the source of payment may be limited to the external liquidity with no or limited legal recourse to the issuer in the event the demand is not met. A VMIG rating may also be assigned to commercial paper programs. Such programs are characterized as having variable short-term maturities but having neither a variable rate nor demand feature.

In the case of VRDOs, two ratings are assigned; one representing an evaluation of the degree of risk associated with scheduled principal and interest payment, and the other representing an evaluation of the degree of risk associated with the demand feature. The short-term rating assigned to the demand feature of VRDOs is designated as VMIG. When no rating is applied to the long- or short-term aspect of a VRDO, it will be designated NR.

Definition of Short-Term Loan Ratings

MIG 1/VMIG 1   This designation denotes best quality. There is present strong protection by established cash flows, superior liquidity support, or demonstrated broad-based access to the market for refinancing.

MIG 2/VMIG 2 This designation denotes high quality. Margins of protection are ample although not so large as in the preceding group.

MIG 3/VMIG 3 This designation denotes favorable quality. All security elements are accounted for but there is lacking the undeniable strength of the preceding grades. Liquidity and cash flow protection may be narrow and market access for refinancing is likely to be less well established.

MIG 4/VMIG 4 This designation denotes adequate quality. Protection commonly regarded as required of an investment security is present and although not distinctly or predominantly speculative, there is specific risk.

Issues or the features associated with MIG or VMIG ratings are identified by date of issue, date of maturity or maturities or rating expiration date, and description to distinguish each rating from other ratings. Each rating designation is unique as to any other similar issue of the same obligor. MIG ratings terminate at the retirement of the obligation while VMIG rating expiration will be a function of each issue's specific structural or credit features.

COMMERCIAL PAPER RATINGS

Standard And Poor's

Standard & Poor's commercial paper rating is a current assessment of the likelihood of timely payment of debt having an original maturity of no more than 365 days. Ratings are graded into four categories, ranging from "A" for the highest quality obligations to "D" for the lowest. The four categories are as follows:

A Issues assigned this highest rating are regarded as having the greatest capacity for timely payment. Issues in this category are delineated with the numbers 1, 2 and 3 to indicate the relative degree of safety.

A-1   This designation indicates that the degree of safety regarding timely payment is either overwhelming or very strong. Those issues determined to possess overwhelming safety characteristics are denoted with a plus (+) sign designation.

A-2   Capacity for timely payment on issues with this designation is strong. However, the relative degree of safety is not as high as for issues designated "A-1".

A-3   Issues carrying this designation have a satisfactory capacity for timely payment. They are, however, somewhat more vulnerable to the adverse effects of changes in circumstances than obligations carrying the higher designations.

B   Issues rated "B" are regarded as having only an adequate capacity for timely payment. However, such capacity may be damaged by changing conditions or short-term adversities.

C   This rating is assigned to short-term debt obligations with a doubtful capacity for payment.

D   This rating indicates that the issue is either in default or is expected to be in default upon maturity.

The commercial paper rating is not a recommendation to purchase or sell a security. The ratings are based on current information furnished to Standard & Poor's by the issuer or obtained from other sources it considers reliable. The ratings may be changed, suspended, or withdrawn as a result of changes in or unavailability of such information.

Fitch

Fitch Commercial Paper Ratings are assigned at the request of an issuer to debt obligations with an original maturity not in excess of 270 days. The ratings reflect Fitch's current appraisal of the degree of assurance of timely payments of such debt.

The use of the word Fitch in our commercial paper rating symbol may be abbreviated, for example Fitch-1 may be expressed F-1.

Fitch commercial paper ratings are grouped into four categories as defined below:

Fitch-1 (Highest Grade) Commercial paper assigned this rating is regarded as having the strongest degree of assurance for timely payments.

Fitch-2 (Very Good Grade) Issues assigned this rating reflect an assurance of timely payment only slightly less in degree than the strongest issues.

Fitch-3 (Good Grade) Commercial paper carrying this rating has a satisfactory degree of assurance for timely payment but the margin of safety is not as great as the two higher categories.

Fitch-4 (Poor Grade) Issues carrying this rating have characteristics suggesting that the degree of assurance for timely payment is minimal and is susceptible to near-term adverse change due to less favorable financial or economic conditions.

MUNICIPAL NOTES RATINGS

Standard & Poor's

A Standard & Poor's note rating reflects the liquidity concerns and market access risks unique to notes. Notes due in three years or less will likely receive a note ratings. Notes maturing beyond three years will most likely receive a long-term debt rating. The following criteria will be used in making that assessment.

- Amortization schedule (the larger the remaining term relative to remaining terms of similar instruments the more likely it will be treated as a note).

- Source of Payment (the more dependent the issue is on the market for its refinancing, the more likely it will be treated as a note).
  Note rating symbols are as follows:

SP-1 Very strong or strong capacity to pay principal and interest. Those issues determined to possess overwhelming safety characteristics will be given a plus (+) designation.

SP-2 Satisfactory capacity to pay principal and interest.

SP-3 Speculative capacity to pay principal and interest.

S & P's Tax-Exempt Demand Bonds

Standard & Poor's assigns "dual" ratings to all long-term debt issues that have as part of their provisions a demand or double feature.

The first rating addresses the likelihood of repayment of principal and interest as due, and the second rating addresses only the demand feature. The long-term debt rating symbols are used for bonds to denote the long-term maturity and the commercial paper rating symbols are used to denote the put option (for example, "AAA/A-1+"). For the newer "demand notes," S&P's note rating symbols, combined with the commercial paper symbols, are used (for example, "SP-1+/A-1+").

KEEFE'S DOMESTIC AND FOREIGN BANK RATINGS

Keefe BankWatch ratings are based upon a quantitative analysis of all segments of the organization including, where applicable, holding company, member banks or associations, and other subsidiaries. Keefe BankWatch assigns only one rating to each company, based on consolidated financials. While the ratings are intended to be equally applicable to all operating entities of the organization, there may, in certain cases, be more liquidity and/or credit risk associated with doing business with one segment of the company versus another (*i.e.,* holding company vs. bank).

It should be further understood that Keefe BankWatch ratings are not merely an assessment of the likelihood of receiving payment of principal and interest on a timely basis. As importantly, they incorporate Keefe's opinion as to the vulnerability of the company to adverse developments, which may impact the market's perception of the company, thereby affecting the marketability of its securities.

Keefe BankWatch ratings don't constitute recommendations to buy or sell securities of any of these companies. Further, Keefe BankWatch does not suggest specific investment criteria for individual clients.

In those instances where disclosure, in its opinion, is either incomplete and/or untimely, a qualified rating (QR) is assigned to the institution. These ratings are derived exclusively from a quantitative analysis of publicly available information. Qualitative judgments have not been incorporated.

Generally, banks with assets of less than $500 million are assigned a numerical "score" based exclusively on a statistical model developed by BankWatch. These "scores," which are compiled from regulatory reports, represent a performance evaluation of each company relative to a nation-wide composite of similar sized banks. The score indicates the bank's percentile ranking, *i.e.,* a score of 75 suggests that the company has out-performed 75% of its peer group. If a bank of this size is associated with a holding company that is not rated by BankWatch, an asterisk (*) may appear before the holding company name. This indicates that the analysis ("score") on that company has been done on a "bank only" basis and is not reflective of the consolidated company's financial performance.

A Company possesses an exceptionally strong balance sheet and earnings record, translating into an excellent reputation and unquestioned access to its natural money markets. If weakness or vulnerability exists in any aspect of the company's business, it's entirely mitigated by the strengths of the organization.

A/B Company is financially very solid with a favorable track record and no readily apparent weakness. Its overall risk profile, while low, is not quite as favorable as for companies in the highest rating category.

B A strong company with a solid financial record and well received by its natural money markets. Some minor weaknesses may exist, but any deviation from the company's historical performance levels should be both limited and short-lived. The likelihood of a problem developing is small, yet slightly greater than for a higher-rated company.

B/C Company is clearly viewed as good credit. While some short-comings are apparent, they are not serious and/or are quite manageable in the short-term.

C Company is inherently a sound credit with no serious deficiencies, but financials reveal at least one fundamental area of concern that prevents a higher rating. The company may recently have experienced a period of difficulty, but those pressures should not be long-term in nature. The company's ability to absorb a surprise, however, is less than that for organizations with better operating records.

C/D While still considered an acceptable credit, the company has some meaningful deficiencies. Its ability to deal with further deterioration is less than that for better-rated companies.

D The company's financials suggest obvious weaknesses, most likely created by asset quality considerations and/or a poorly structured balance sheet. A meaningful level of uncertainty and vulnerability exists going forward. The ability to address further unexpected problems must be questioned.

D/E The company has areas of major weakness, which may include funding/liquidity difficulties. A high degree of uncertainty exists as to the company's ability to absorb incremental problems.

E Very serious problems exist for the company, creating doubt as to its continued viability without some form of outside assistance — regulatory or otherwise.

Qualified Rating Characteristics

QR-A Exceptionally strong company as evidenced by its recent financial statements and its historical record.

QR-B Statistically a very sound institution. Financials reveal no abnormal lending or funding practices, while profitability, capital adequacy and asset quality indicators consistently rank above peer group standards.

QR-C Statistical credentials should be viewed as average relative to peer group norms. A sound credit with one or more concerns preventing a higher rating.

QR-D The company's financial performance has typically fallen below average parameters established by its peers. Existing earnings weakness, exposure to margin contraction, asset quality concerns and/or aggressive management of loan growth raise serious questions.

QR-E Several problems of a serious nature exist. Key financial indicators and/or abnormal growth patterns suggest significant uncertainty over the near term. The institution may well be under special regulatory supervision, and its continued viability with outside assistance may be at issue.

Country Rating

An assessment of the overall political and economic stability of a country in which the bank is domiciled.

I.   An industrialized country with a long history of political stability complemented by an overall sound financial condition. The country must have demonstrated the ability to access capital markets throughout the world on favorable terms.

II. An industrialized country that has had a history of political and economic stability but is experiencing some current political unrest or significant economic difficulties. It enjoys continued ability to access capital markets worldwide but at increasingly higher margins. In the short run, the risk of default is minimal.

III. An industrialized or developing country with a wealth of resources, which may have difficulty servicing its external debt as a result of political and/or economic problems. Although it has access to capital markets worldwide, this cannot be assured in the future.

IV. A developing country that is currently facing extreme difficulty in raising external capital at all maturity levels.

V.   A country that has defaulted on its external debt payments or which is in a position where a default is highly probable.

FITCH INVESTMENT NOTE RATING SYMBOLS

Fitch Investment Note Ratings are grouped into four categories with the indicated symbols. The ratings on notes with maturities generally one to three years reflect Fitch's current appraisal of the degree of assurance of timely payment, whichever the source.

FIN-1 + Notes assigned this rating are regarded as having the strongest degree of assurance for timely payment.

FIN-1 Notes assigned this rating reflect an assurance of timely payment only slightly less than the strongest issues.

FIN-2 Notes assigned this rating have a degree of assurance for timely payment but with a lesser margin of safety than the prior two categories.

FIN-3 Notes with this rating have speculative characteristics, which suggest that the degree of assurance for timely payment is minimal.

Chapter 8
MUTUAL FUNDS

If you want a variety of investments and you have limited resources, you can get diversification by investing in a mutual fund. A mutual fund is a company in the business of managing and investing other people's money. When you buy shares in a mutual fund, you become part owner of a portfolio of securities.

Mutual fund investing is characterized by:

- **Diversification.** Your investment may be used to buy a broad range of equity, debt, and other securities. Diversification reduces your risk.

- **Automatic reinvestment.** Dividends, interest, and capital gains may be reinvested into the fund, usually at no charge.

- **Ease of withdrawal.** Funds may be withdrawn as needed, usually at no charge.

- **Liquidity.** You can redeem your shares at any time.

- **Ability to change investments.** You can go from one fund type to another in a family of funds.

- **Small minimum investment.** You can buy into some mutual funds for less than $1,000.

INVESTING IN MUTUAL FUNDS

A mutual fund is managed by professionals who use the money invested to buy a variety of securities. Ownership is in the form of proportionate shares.

EXAMPLE 1

Mutual Fund X has the following securities:

Stock	Number of Shares
GE	200
AT&T	300
Intel	500

If you own 3% of the fund, your share would be equivalent to:

6 shares of GE
9 shares of AT&T, and
15 shares of Intel.

Net Asset Value (NAV)

The price of a mutual fund share is stated as net asset value (NAV), computed as follows:

$$\frac{\text{Fund's total assets - debt}}{\text{Number of shares outstanding in the fund}}$$

EXAMPLE 2

Assume that on a given date, the market values in a fund are as shown. The fund has liabilities of $4,500. The NAV of the fund is calculated as:

GE: $100 per share x 200 shares	$20,000
Gap: $50 per share x 300 shares	15,000
CBS: $75 per share x 100 shares	7,500
Total assets (gross)	$42,500

Liabilities of the fund's portfolio	<u>4,500</u>
Total assets (net)	$38,000
Number of fund shares outstanding	<u>1,000</u>
Net asset value (NAV) per share	
[Net total assets /Number of shares]	$ 38

Thus, if you own 3% of the fund, your investment is worth:
3% x 1,000 shares = 30 shares; 30 shares x $38 = $1,140

Services Offered by Mutual Funds

A major reason that mutual funds are attractive is the many convenient services offered to their shareholders. Some can be used in your investment strategy. Common services are summarized in Figure 8-1.

FIGURE 8-1: MAJOR SERVICES OF MUTUAL FUNDS·

- Accounting and reporting for tax purposes·
- Safekeeping and custodian services
- Automatic reinvestment·
- Exchange privileges
- Periodic withdrawals
- Checking privileges
- Acceptance of small investments·
- Tax-sheltered plans (*e.g.,* IRA and Keogh)
- Guardianship under the Uniform Gift to Minors Act·
- Pre-authorized check plan

Making Money in Mutual Funds

You make money from dividends and capital gains due to changes in NAV.

Dividends: Mutual funds typically pay out a large percentage of their income. You're fully taxed on dividends.

Capital gains: Capital gains are distributed each year to fund holders. You're taxed at the maximum capital gains rate of 28%. NAV shows only the current market value of your portfolio. Look, too, at the number of shares you own and how their total value has increased over time from dividends and capital gains reinvestment into more shares.

Multiply the number of shares you own by the net asset value per share to determine value.

Total return equals:

(Dividends + Capital gains distributed + Price appreciation in fund shares)

The percentage return equals:

$$\frac{(\text{Dividends} + \text{capital gain distributions} + (\text{ending NAV} - \text{beginning NAV}))}{\text{Beginning NAV}}$$

where (ending NAV - beginning NAV) is price appreciation.

EXAMPLE 3

Your mutual fund paid dividends of $1.00 per share and capital gain distributions of $.40 per share this year. NAV per share at the beginning of the year was $10.00 and at year end was $12. Percentage return equals:

$$\text{Percentage return} = \frac{\$1.00 + \$.40 + (\$12 - \$10)}{\$10} = \frac{\$3.40}{\$10} = 34\%$$

The Cost of Mutual Funds

If you invest in a mutual fund, a fee will be charged. When shopping for funds, take a close look at these charges. Charges are classified as load, management fees, 12b-1 fees, back-end loads, deferred loads, and reinvestment loads.

Load: A *load* is the fee to buy shares, a form of sales charge that may range from 1% to 8.5% (maximum legal limit) of the amount invested. That means that if you invested $1,000 in a fund with an 8.5% load, only $915 would go into the fund.

Mutual fund prices are stated in "bid" and "ask" form. The bid is the price at which the fund will buy back its shares. The ask or "offer" is the price the investor must pay to buy shares. The difference between the offer and the bid is the load. *No-load* mutual funds have no sales fees, so the bid and ask prices are the same. *NOTE: A sales fee does not mean the fund will perform better. The fee will reduce your net return rate.*

Management and Expense Fees: All funds (load and no-load) pay the portfolio manager a fee. It typically ranges from 0.5% to 1% of the fund's assets.

12b-1 Fees: These charges are for advertising and promotion. They typically range from 0.25% to 0.30%, but some run as high as 1.25%.

Back-end Loads, or Redemption Fees: These are charged when you sell your shares. They are based on a percentage of the NAV. Steep back-end loads can reduce your profits or increase your losses.

Deferred Load, or Contingent Deferred Sales Fees: These are deducted from your original investment if you sell shares before a specified time.

Reinvestment Loads: These fees are taken out of reinvested interest, dividends, and capital gains. For example, if you receive a capital-gains distribution of $150 and the reinvestment fee is 7%, the fund will keep $10.50 and reinvest $139.50.

Taxation of Mutual Funds

Unless you're investing in a tax-deferred IRA or a tax-free bond fund, the capital gains from mutual fund investing are taxable. Capital gains distributions usually come once during the year, typically in December. If you buy shares right before a distribution, you can be caught in a tax bind: A portion of the price you paid will be returned to you as a taxable gain.

In general, a fund that turns over securities often in pursuit of a high return may generate more taxable gains than one that hold onto securities that are climbing in value. For this reason, *Consumer Reports* has recently added to its ratings a new column: "Tax Efficiency." Here are some tax tips in connection with mutual fund investing.

- Never buy shares of a mutual fund late in the year without checking its distribution, or "ex-dividend," date.

- Try to sell those shares that had the highest original cost.

- Check out tax consequences when you have to move your money from one fund to another. The IRS views such switches as a taxable event.

- Use tax efficiency as an added screening device. Try to pick the fund showing the highest tax efficiency.

THE KINDS OF MUTUAL FUNDS

Mutual funds are categorized by type depending on purpose, structure, fees, switching privileges, return potential, and risk. You can invest in virtually any type of fund, depending on your investment goals. The two basic types of funds are *open-end,* which can sell an unlimited number of ownership shares, and *closed-end,* which can issue only a fixed number.

In open-end funds, you buy from and sell shares back to the fund. You can redeem them whenever you desire. Shares are bought at NAV plus service fee, and redeemed at NAV less a commission. In closed-end funds there is a fixed number of shares you buy like stocks on the exchanges or in the OTC market. Share price is determined independently of NAV by factors of supply and demand.

Figure 8-2 summarizes the difference between open-end funds, (which are commonly known as mutual funds) and closed-end investment companies.

Mutual funds may be further categorized as:

Money market funds, which invest solely in short-term debt securities. Because their price of the fund is constant, these funds are very conservative. You can buy and sell shares at $1.00. Money market funds offer high-interest income with protection of principal.

Growth funds look for high return via capital gains. They usually invest in companies with growth that exceeds the inflation rate whose stocks have constant current income over the long term. Like other growth investments, the aim of these funds is to increase share value, not pay dividends.

FIGURE 8-2: OPEN-END AND CLOSED-END FUNDS COMPARED

	Mutual fund	**Closed-end funds**
Number of shares	Fluctuates	Fixed
Traded at net asset value (NAV)	Yes	No—a discount or premium from NAV
Liquidity	Almost immediate	3 business days
Dividends and Capital gain	Can be reinvested	Some offer automatic reinvestment
Accessibility	Yes; via a toll-free phone; check writing privileges	Check-writing privileges limited
Method of purchase	Direct from fund or on-line	Stock exchange or OTC
Flexibility	Yes, exchange privileges	No
Commission	Load or no-load	Yes

Aggressive growth (capital appreciation) funds take greater risk for higher capital appreciation. Dividend income is secondary at best. These funds concentrate on new, high-tech businesses. They offer the greatest potential for growth, but also greater risk.

NOTE: These funds are appropriate if you're not especially worried about near-term variability in return but want long-term appreciation. Their aggressive strategies may consist of leveraged purchases, short selling, call options, and put options, as well as buying stock.

Income funds generate current income through investments in securities that pay interest or cash dividends, such as dividend-paying stocks, corporate bonds, and government securities. Generally, the higher the income sought, the riskier the underlying investments. These funds offer current income, but the risk may vary from low to high, depending on the fund.

Growth and income funds emphasize current dividend or interest and capital appreciation. They offer moderate growth potential and moderate risk. The objective is long-term growth. Their share value should be stable.

Balanced funds seek preservation of capital along with growth and income. The aim of these funds is to *balance* the portfolio with the best ratio of stocks and bonds within the funds' investment objective guidelines, adjusted to prevailing market conditions. Balanced funds tend to underperform all-stock funds in strong bull markets.

Index funds model a specific sector of the investment markets. Different index funds model the performance of large domestic companies, small domestic companies, international stocks, government bonds, and tens of other market segments. Big-cap stock index funds generally target the S&P 500 index, which is currently the most visible and popular of index funds. Broad market index funds might target the Wilshire 5000 index, while mid-sized index funds may track the S&P MidCap 400 index or the Wilshire 4500 index. Small-stock index funds might track the Russell 2000 index.

Sector (specialized) funds invest by industry. The risk is high because the fortunes of the fund depend of the performance of the industry. If an industry such as pharmaceuticals takes a hit, the losses can be huge.

International funds invest in securities of overseas (foreign) companies. Some invest in only one geographic area, such as Fidelity Canada Fund. Others, like Vanguard Trustees Commingled International Portfolio, are broader. Fund values increase if the dollar decreases due to exchange rates.

Municipal tax-exempt funds seek current tax-free income by investing for the most part in tax-exempt bonds issued by municipalities to build schools, highways, and public projects. They offer current tax-exempt income with low to high risk depending on the yield sought and individual investments.

Just as there are many different kinds of mutual funds, there are many ways to buy them, depending on your financial status and investment objectives. Among them are:

- **Accumulation plan:** You invest periodically, (usually monthly). Minimum investments may be required (*e.g.,* $100 per month). This approach is advisable for long-term investors.

- **Withdrawal plan:** You make periodic payments (*e.g.,* quarterly) of a given sum.

- **Life insurance-mutual fund plans:** This combines life insurance with shares of the mutual fund. If the fund performs well, it pays your insurance premiums. If not, you must pay the premium.

- **Automatic dividend reinvestment:** Fund proceeds (dividends and capital gains) are automatically reinvested.

- **Individual retirement account (IRA):** You contribute $2,000 before-tax-income each year. When you take out money at retirement, hopefully you will be in a lower tax rate.

- **Payroll deduction plans:** Amounts are withheld from your salary and used to buy fund shares, often through a 401(k) (or a 403(b) plan for those who work at nonprofits).

DOLLAR COST AVERAGING

Dollar-cost averaging is an investment strategy designed to take advantage of the market's long-term upward bias while reducing risk over time. It simply means that you invest the same amount of money at regular intervals, whatever the market price of a stock is. It eliminates the need to predict share-price movements and to figure out the right time to buy, and it protects you from putting too much money into the market at the wrong time. With this strategy, your installment buys more shares when the share price of your fund is down, and fewer shares when the price of the fund is high, which can potentially lower your average cost per share and allow you to buy more shares. Lowering your cost can also reduce your downside risk. It ensures that the entire portfolio will not be purchased at temporarily inflated prices. Note, however, that dollar-cost averaging can result in high transaction costs that can lower returns over time. That is why buying mutual funds, which often charge either no sales fee or a flat commission, is a popular way to implement this strategy.

In mutual fund investing, the typically small investment minimums allow you to implement this strategy easily in a cost-effective way. Many funds and brokerages make this process easy by accepting direct deductions from checking accounts or paychecks.

You may unknowingly be using this strategy as part of employer-sponsored savings plans like a 401(k) retirement program. Many of these benefit plans routinely make equal purchases of assets at set periods, quietly accomplishing dollar-cost averaging.

Dollar-cost averaging will work as long as fund prices rise over the long haul. Figure 8-3 shows how dollar cost-averaging works for a no-load mutual fund and compares it with two other investment strategies: lump-sum up-front investment and lump-sum investment after saving (see Figure 8-4).

FIGURE 8-3: DOLLAR-COSTING BASED MUTUAL FUND PURCHASE PLAN

Period	Amount Invested	Share Price	Shares Purchased
1	$ 100	$ 12.50	8
2	100	8.00	12.5
3	100	10.00	10
4	100	8.00	12.5
5	100	10.00	10
6	100	12.50	8
7	100	14.28	7
8	100	12.50	8
9	100	16.67	6
10	100	20.00	5
	$1,000	$124.45	87.0

Average share price = $124.45/10 = $12.45
Total shares owned = 87
Average share cost = $1,000/87.0 shares = $11.49
Total market value now = 87 shares x $20 = $1,740

FIGURE 8-4: LUMP SUM INVESTMENT STRATEGIES COMPARED

Lump-Sum Up-Front Investment

Period	Amount Invested	Share Price	Shares Purchased
1	$1,000	$12.50	80
2	0	10.00	0
⋮			
⋮			
10	0	20.00	0

Average share price = $12.45
Total shares owned = 80
Average share cost = $1,000/80 shares = $12.50
Total market value now = 80 shares x $20 = $1,600

Lump-Sum Up-Front Investment after $1,000 is Saved

Period	Amount Invested	Share Price	Shares Purchased
10	$1,000	$20.00	50

Average share price = $20.00
Total shares owned = 50
Average share cost = $1,000/50 shares = $20.00
Total market value now = 50 shares x $20 = $1,000

With dollar-cost averaging, you bought 87 shares, now worth $20 apiece (a total market value of $1,740: $20 x 87 shares). You invested only $1,000 over the period. Your average share cost of $11.49 is lower than the average ($12.45) of the market price of the fund's shares during the periods in which they are accumulated. So you've actually made money through this process. It works because you bought more shares when they were cheap and fewer shares when they were not.

EVALUATING MUTUAL FUND PERFORMANCE

Mutual funds, like any other investments, are evaluated on the basis of return and risk. The return on a mutual fund equals: (1) dividend (interest) income, plus (2) capital gains, plus (3) change in NAV of the fund. Using the data in Figure 8-5 as a comparison, take the statement you get from the mutual fund and complete the form in Figure 8-6.

FIGURE 8-5: YOUR MUTUAL FUND INC.

Date	Transaction	Dollar Amount	Share Price	Shares	Shares Owned
	Beginning balance	0.00			
07/19	Purchase	$2,500.00	$10.16	246.063	246.063
08/17	Purchase	2,500.00	10.87	229.991	476.054
11/30	Purchase	1,000.00	11.27	88.731	564.785
12/22	Dividend reinvestment, .09	50.83	11.91	4.268	569.053
12/22	Short-term change reinvest- ment, .07	39.53	11.91	3.319	572.372
12/22	Reinvested capital gain, .13	73.42	11.91	6.165	578.537
12/22	Ending Balance	$6,890.38	11.91		578.537

FIGURE 8-6: FIGURING YOUR PERSONAL RATE OF RETURN

Step	Example	Your Fund
1. The number of months for which your fund's performance is being measured.	5	_____
2. Your investment at the beginning of the period (multiply the total number of shares owned by the NAV) [(0 + 246.063) x $10.16].	$2,500.00	_____
3. The ending value of your investment (multiply the number of shares you currently own by the current NAV) (578.537 x $11.91).	$6,890.38	_____
4. Total dividends and capital gains received in cash— not reinvested ($0).	0.00	_____
5. All additional investments (any redemptions subtracted) ($,2500 + 1,000).	$3,500.00	_____
6. Computation of your gain or loss:		
—*Step (a):* Add line 2 to half of the total on line 5 [$2,500 + 1/2($3,500)]	$4,250.00	_____
—*Step (b):* Add line 3 and line 4, then subtract 1/2 of the total on line 5 [($6,890.38 + $0) - 1/2($3,500)]	$5,140.38	_____
—*Step (c):* Divide the answer from step (b) sum by the step (a) answer ($5140.38/$4250)	1.2095	_____
—*Step (d):* Subtract the numeral 1 from the result of step (c), then multiply by 100 [(1.2095 - 1) x 100].	20.95	_____
7. Compute your annualized return (divide 12 by the number of months on line 1; multiply the result by the percentage found in line 6, step (d) [(12/5) x 20.95].	50.28	_____

Measuring Risk or Volatility

In evaluating how the fund did, consider the published measures of risk or volatility of the funds to ascertain the amount of risk. The three popular measures of risk are beta, R-squared, and standard deviation.

Beta shows how volatile a mutual fund is compared with the market as a whole, as measured against the S&P 500 Index on the equity side and the Lehman Aggregate Bond Index on the bond side. By definition, the beta of the market index is 1.00.

Fund Beta	**Meaning**
1.0	Fund price fluctuations track the market.
>1.0	The fund goes higher in bull markets and lower in bear markets than the market.
<1.0	The fund will gain less in bull markets and lose less in bear markets.

EXAMPLE 4

A fund with a 1.50 beta is significantly more volatile that its benchmark. It's expected to perform 50% better than the market in up markets, and 50% worse in down markets. By the same token, a fund with a beta of 0.75 should capture 75% of the market gains in a rally and lose only 75% as much in a decline.

R-squared and standard deviation

Some analysts, like those preparing Morningstar's Mutual Fund Values, prefer to use R-squared ("R^2") or standard deviation ("Std. Dev.") as a risk measure in mutual fund tables. R-squared, ranging from 0 to 100, gives you an idea about well a fund's performance correlates with that of the benchmark like the S&P 500 Index. An R-squared of 0 means that a fund's returns have no correlation; an R-squared of 1.00 indicates that a fund's returns are completely in sync—up and down—with the benchmark. An R-squared of less than 0.70 is considered a low correlation between the fund and its benchmark.

R-squared also provides a context for beta. Beta may not mean much if the R-squared is low. For example, Vanguard Gold and Precious Metals Fund has a relatively low beta of 0.79, but the fund is hardly a low-risk investment. The fund's R-squared of 0.14 reveals that its returns are weakly correlated with those of the S&P 500 Index, so its beta versus a broad index tells you little about its volatility. *The higher the R-squared, the higher the relationship between the funds and the benchmark and thus the more relevant is the beta figure.*

Standard deviation compares a fund not with a benchmark but with its own past record. It says that in 95 cases out of 100, the fund's period-ending price will be plus or minus a certain percentage of its price at the beginning of the period, usually a month. This uses the degree to which a fund's returns have fluctuated above or below its mean, or average, return over the previous period (say, like 36 months). In general, the higher the standard deviation, the greater the volatility, and thus the risk.

NOTE: If you're using beta, R-squared, or standard deviation to help pick a fund, make sure your review covers at least three years so you get an accurate picture of the risk and stability of the fund. All these numbers, of course, should be weighed with other indicators, including total return over at least five years, performance in the up or down market, and the experience of the fund manager.

Risk measures such as beta, R-squared, and standard deviation for mutual funds are published in *Value Line Mutual Fund Survey, Morningstar's Mutual Fund Values* and other publications. They are also available on the Internet. Figure 8-7 is a mutual fund report from CBS MarketWatch *(cbs.marketwatch.com)* prepared from data supplied by Lipper, Inc. Figures 8-8A, 8-8B, and 8-8C are a mutual fund report from Yahoo!Finance *(finance.yahoo.com)* prepared from data provided by Morningstar, Inc. The Morningstar Web site also reports the data *(www.mornstar.net).*

The Alpha Value

Alpha value of a security, also called the "average differential return," is the difference between the actual return and the return predicted by the overall mutual fund beta. Generally, a positive alpha (excess return) indicates superior mutual fund performance, a negative value inferior performance.

FIGURE 8-7: MARKETWATCH MUTUAL FUND REPORT

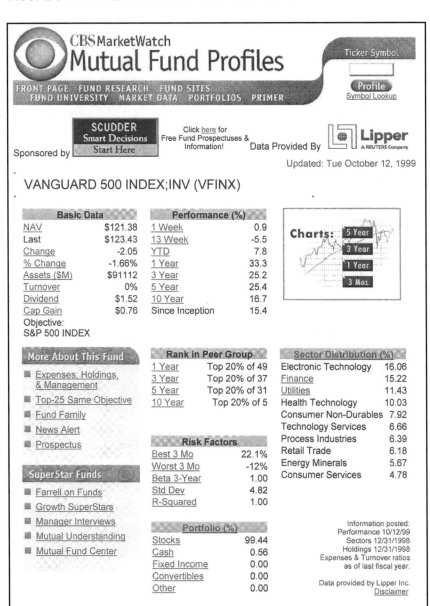

Source: CBS MarketWatch

FIGURE 8-8A: YAHOO! MUTUAL FUND REPORT, Part 1

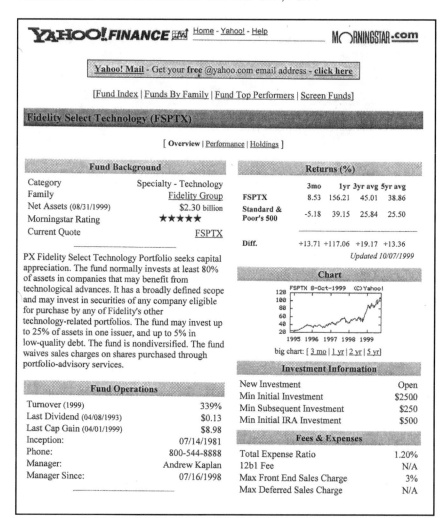

FIGURE 8-8B: YAHOO! MUTUAL FUND REPORT, Part 2

Fidelity Select Technology (FSPTX)

[Overview | **Performance** | Holdings]

Yearly Total Returns (%)

Year	Return
1998	74.16
1997	10.37
1996	15.63
1995	43.67
1994	11.13
1993	28.65
1992	8.72
1991	58.97
1990	10.51
1989	16.99

Return Statistics

Number of Years Up	13
Number of Years Down	4
Best 1 Yr Total Ret	74.16%
Worst 1 Yr Total Ret	N/A
Best 3 Yr Total Ret	30.52%
Worst 3 Yr Total Ret	N/A

Risk (MPT Statistics)

	3 Yr	5 Yr	10 Yr
Alpha	9.06	3.03	7.46
Beta	1.48	1.46	1.41
R-Squared	61	55	58
Std. Deviation	48.30	38.17	32.29
Sharpe Ratio	0.92	0.92	0.92
Treynor Ratio	33.61	24.88	20.62

Returns Comparison (%)

	FSPTX	Index*	Diff.
Year To Date	51.23	8.24	42.99
1 Month	0.86	-2.11	2.97
3 Mo	8.53	-5.18	13.71
1 Year	156.21	39.15	117.06
3 Year Avg	45.01	25.84	19.17
5 Year Avg	38.86	25.50	13.36
10 Year Avg	29.08	17.24	11.84
15 Year Avg	17.70	18.23	-0.53
Last Bull Market	83.95	26.16	57.79
(10/01/1998 to 06/30/1999)			
Last Bear Market	-3.09	-8.961	5.87
(07/31/1998 to 09/30/1998)			

* = Index means Standard & Poor's 500

Updated 10/07/1999

Rank in Category
(By Total Return)

1 Year	31 / 77 = 40%
3 Year	5 / 47 = 8%
5 Year	4 / 27 = 12%
10 Year	3 / 12 = 16%
15 Year	6 / 7 = 71%

Top 10 in Category

Last Updated: 8-Oct-99

Source: Yahoo!Finance

FIGURE 8-8C: YAHOO! MUTUAL FUND REPORT, Part 3

Fidelity Select Technology (FSPTX)

[Overview | Performance | Holdings]

Portfolio Composition (%)	
Stocks	87.23
Bonds	0.00
Preferred	0.00
Convertibles	0.00
Cash	12.76

Sector Weightings (%)	
Consumer Durables	1.45
Services	6.00
Retail	0.43
Technology	92.13

Updated 2/28/1999

Top Equity Holdings (%)		
NOKA	Nokia Cl A ADR	8.56
MOT	Motorola Inc	6.31
CSCO	Cisco Systems Inc	4.34
MSFT	Microsoft Corp	4.17
TXN	Texas Instruments Inc	3.92
ADCT	ADC Telecommunications Inc	3.86
EBAY	eBay Inc	3.67
MU	Micron Technology Inc	3.33
AMAT	Applied Materials Inc	3.06
ASM	Authentic Fitness Corp	2.91

Quotes for Top Holdings

Updated 2/28/1999

Equity Holdings	
Avg. Price/Earnings	53.01
Avg. Price/Book	11.93
Median Market Cap	31.30 B

Updated 2/28/1999

Source: Yahoo!Finance

EXAMPLE 5

Assume that the market return (rm) is 8% and the risk-free rate (rf) is 5%. XYZ fund, with a beta of 1.5, returned 7.5%. The expected return, then, is 9.5% (5% + 1.5(8% - 5%)]. That means the fund has a negative alpha of 1.5% (9.5% - 8%).

NOTES:

- *"Keep your alpha high and your beta low" is a basic strategy for those who want good investment performance.*

- *A key question to ask is: Can a fund consistently perform at positive alpha levels?*

- *Morningstar's Mutual Fund Values (Figure 8-8B) shows the alpha value as well as beta, R^2, and standard deviation.*

CHOOSING A MUTUAL FUND

To pick the "right" mutual fund:

- Prepare a listing of the characteristics of a fund that would be appropriate for your risk tolerance and investment needs and objectives.

- Read the prospectuses of several funds that satisfy your requirements. The prospectus includes the fund's purpose, securities selection criteria, performance, fees, and financial condition. Read the statement of objectives as well as the risk considerations and investment constraints. Look at the Statement of Additional Information to check out charges and portfolio holdings. Review for annual and quarterly financial information.

- Ask yourself whether the fund matches your requirements.

With this information in hand, ask:

- *How has the fund performed in both good and bad times over the past 10 years?* Compare its performance fund to comparable funds and market averages of the same type. Examine its standard deviation in financial publications. What's the trend in per-share and dollar values? (Many magazines, including *Business Week, Kiplinger's Personal Finance, Worth, Consumer Reports, Financial World, Forbes* and *U.S. News* and *World Report* publish mutual fund performance statistics. Investment newsletters like those of Morningstar and Lipper Analytical publish fund rankings (to be discussed later), which may be a place to start.

- *How good is the fund management?* Your fund is only going to do as well as the person or people who run it. (The *Value Line Mutual Fund Survey* has recently added a Manager Ratings box to its one-page fund reviews.)

- *What is the quality of the portfolio?* How diversified is it? (Morningstar Mutual Funds has recently added a special securities section to its fund-data page to show what percentage of a fund's assets were invested in derivatives, which are regarded as risky.)

• *What is the fund's expense ratio,* the percentage of its net assets going annually to cover management fees, transaction costs, administrative overhead, legal and auditing fees, and marketing costs (12b-1 fees)? This information is in the prospectus under the heading "Annual Fund Operating Expenses." Compare expense ratios in similar funds (see Figure 8-9), because they can affect overall performance. One recent study of fund performance found that a $10,000 investment in two no-load funds, each earning 9% over 20 years, would grow to $30,475 in the fund with a 3% expense ratio and $45,840 in the fund with a 1% expense ratio.

FIGURE 8-9: AVERAGE EXPENSE RATIOS

Stock Funds	Average Expense Ratio	Bond Funds	Average Expense Ratio
Aggressive growth	1.80%	Corporate	0.70%
Growth	1.30%	General	0.80%
Growth & income	1.00%	Government	0.70%
Balanced	1.00%	Mortgage-backed	0.70%
Index	0.50%	High-yield	0.90%
Small capitalization	1.40%	Tax-exempt	0.60%
International	1.60%	International	1.70%
Gold	1.80%		

• *How high are sales and redemption fees, and how extensive are shareholder services?*

• *How is the fund ranked by such services as Lipper and Morningstar?* Performance benchmarking can also help you to objectively measure a fund's performance.

Performance Benchmarking

One way to objectively measure a fund's performance is to compare it to groups of similar investments—mutual fund peer groups and market indexes. Mutual fund peer group rankings report performance for funds with similar asset classes, strategies, objectives, and risk.

Typically, funds are first sliced into categories based on their investment goals. Then each fund is ranked according to such criteria as five-year total return, risk, or risk-adjusted return by where it falls among all funds in its category. Among ranking sources:

Morningstar offers a risk measurement system for comparing long-term performance of more than 2,000 mutual funds. The system rates stock and bond funds from 5 stars (the best) to no stars (the worst or unrated). Morningstar uses a proprietary system that measures fund price and dividend performance as well as the risks taken by fund management to get those results. The fund is then compared both to its own category and against the industry as a whole. Thus, the best performing fund in a category that is in a weak market sector might get only 2 or 3 stars.

Investors can use Morningstar rankings to find potentially better-performing investments. Many brokerages and financial planning firms limit their clients' investments to 5-star and 4-star funds; this is not always the correct choice. For one, Morningstar's rankings reflect past performance and that often slants the reviews toward funds with recently successful investment styles.

In addition, within each category—especially a sector not performing well—the highest-rated fund may have succeeded by limiting its exposure to certain risks. An investor who believes that an out-of-favor market sector is ready to return might want to buy a fund with a lower rating that is more fully invested in that sector. Morningstar rankings can be accessed free at *www.morningstar.com. Lipper Mutual Fund Rankings* and *Value Line Mutual Fund Survey* are two other important sources. Lipper rankings can be accessed free at the CBS MarketWatch Web site *(cbs.marketwatch.com)*. Value Line Rankings can be accessed free at the Quicken Web site *(quicken.excite.com)*.

Magazine rankings

Business Week, Fortune, Forbes, and *Money* magazines all print periodic analyses of individual funds and their rankings, as do many newsletters and newspapers.

Using Market Indexes as Benchmarks

Each fund describes its strategy and objective and also lists relevant market indexes (see Figure 8-10). These market indexes are also found in the *Wall Street Journal, Barron's,* and *Investor's Business Daily.* To use them effectively, first find the total average annual return for the 1-, 5-, and 10-year periods for the benchmark and compare those figures with the fund's returns for the same periods before making a decision about getting into or staying in the fund.

FIGURE 8-10: TYPICAL MARKET INDEXES USED AS PERFORMANCE
           BENCHMARKS

	Funds	**Index**
Domestic		
	Growth	S&P 500
	Aggressive growth	Value Line
	Small company	Russell 2000
	Government bond	Lehman Bros. Government/Corporate Bond Indexes
	Municipal bond	Lehman Bros. Municipal Bond Index
International		
	Global	Morgan Stanley International World Index, Morgan Stanley Europe, Australia, and the Far East (EAFE), Index
	Foreign bond	Solomon Bros. Non-U.S. Dollar World Bond Index
	Global bond	Shearson World Bond Index

REDUCING THE RISK OF INVESTING IN MUTUAL FUNDS

In a bearish market, minimizing or spreading risk is particularly important, but it's a good idea any time. Below are five popular strategies for reducing risks and making money in mutual funds.

- *Find low-cost funds.* Especially in difficult times, fees and expenses will loom larger, deepening losses and delaying recoveries.

- *Build a balanced, diversified portfolio.* Sensible diversification will minimize risks.

- *Use dollar-cost averaging.* Investing a fixed amount of money at regular intervals keeps you from committing your whole savings at a market peak.

- *Divide your money among fund managers with different styles and philosophies.* Funds with differing styles will take turns outperforming and being outperformed by those with other styles. In a nutshell, diversify across mutual funds.

- *Concentrate on short- or intermediate-term bond funds.* Typically, the longer the maturity for bonds in a fund's portfolio, the greater the fund's return—but also the deeper its losses as interest rates rise.

What to Look for in a Mutual Fund Prospectus

Mutual fund prospectuses are too often confusing and-to-read documents, though the SEC goes under the impression that every investor reads them. In reality, however, few do.

Why read the prospectus? Because it can help you avoid many problems. For instance:

- Knowing the fund's minimum initial investment can help you avoid selecting a fund you can't afford.

- Knowing how mutual fund switching generates taxable transactions can help you avoid problems with the IRS.

- Knowing that your mutual fund investment will be made at the price prevailing at the end of the day you invest, rather that the previous day's close, can save you unpleasant surprises.

- Knowing the proper form you have to fill out to gain the telephone redemption privilege can help avoid the frustrating experience of needing your money and not being able to get it.

- Knowing that you can file a "letter of intent" and qualify multiple investment amounts in the same fund for a quantity discount can save you broker's commissions.

What else do you need to read in a prospectus?

- *The date.* Make sure you have the latest information. Prospectuses are updated at least annually.

- *The minimum.* Make sure you can qualify to invest.

- *The investment objective.* Is this the right fund for you? A lot of people say they are invested in a Puritan fund, but when you ask which Puritan fund, they don't know. All mutual funds are not alike. You need to know that the fund's investment objectives match yours.

- *Performance.* How has the fund done in the past? Is it good enough? How does the fund do in good and bad markets? How much does the fund's return vary?

- *Risk.* Don't panic reading these frightening lists but do understand which risks you're exposed to. Discuss the risks with your accounting, tax, and financial advisers. Risk analysis and evaluation is crucial. The risk of the fund should correspond to your risk preferences.

- *Services.* Know what services you may need. Apply to use all the services that are free. You never know when you might need them.

- *Fees.* A lot of people bought a no-load fund only to discover that it was a rear-end-loaded fund (you pay when you redeem the shares). This is important to ask about. Find out what the normal or average fee is, and then evaluate if it's worth it to you.

You also will want to know if your fund is at least an average performer among similar funds. (The prospectus is described in more detail later in the chapter.)

Picking the Right Fund with a PC

A personal computer can be useful in picking a mutual fund. For example, CompuServe has seized upon the mutual fund boom by developing an array of in-depth databases for small investors. Its FundWatch On-line by *Money* magazine allows you to quickly screen over 1,700 mutual funds using criteria that mirror your investment philosophy to find only those that are consistent with your goals; you then obtain a detailed report on a fund by entering its name or ticker symbol. GO MONEYMAG is the command at any CompuServe! prompt. Screening criteria include:

- Investment objective (for example, aggressive growth, growth, international, municipal, etc.)

- Fees (no-load or load) and expense ratio

- Performance ratings and rankings

- Total asset size

- Management company

- Dividend yield

- Risk ratings (for example, beta and alpha)

A menu of funds found by CompuServe can be displayed on your screen ranked by return over one of seven different time periods, including the latest bull and bear markets. From this menu, you simply select the funds you'd like to investigate, and detailed reports for each will be provided. These detailed reports include comprehensive descriptive and performance information, along with sector and portfolio holdings for many funds.

NOTE: Computer software for mutual funds picking is getting easier and easier to use. Programs include Mutual Fund Selector by Intuit (619) 550-5002, the maker of Quicken and TurboTax.

TYPES OF FUNDS ANALYZED

Index Funds: The No-Brainer Investment Method

If you want the returns of the stock or bond market, but not the risk that your fund manager makes the wrong bet, consider an index fund. This is a sensible method for investors who aren't interested in the ongoing process of evaluating funds and wish to obtain the market's return with minimal effort and expense.

Index funds simply hold the stocks that their index represents, in proportion to their index weightings. For example, an S&P index fund actually holds all the stocks in that index. There are many mutual funds based on the S&P 500 index, which represents approximately 70% of the market value of all outstanding U.S. common stocks. Other index funds emulate the broader Wilshire 5,000-Stock Index and the Russell 2000. According to a study by Lipper Analytical Services of New York, over 90% of the basic stock mutual funds did not beat the S&P 500 index for the year 1999. In fact, stock fund managers have been beaten by the S&P 500 in 15 of the past 20 years.

The Advantages of Index Funds

- Performance can be tracked simply by checking the index. The fund guarantees the same annual return as the market as a whole.

- Management costs typically are lower. Index funds are cheap to run because there's no need for research staff. The average index-fund charges about 0.5%, or $5 for every $1,000 invested.

- Index funds usually have all their money in stocks or bonds with no cash cushion needed. The typical actively managed fund keeps a cash cushion of 3 to 10% of the portfolio, which is used to handle investor withdrawals and to seek new opportunities. Cash, being the worst performing asset, is a drag on long-term performance.

- There are tax savings. Since index funds rarely trade the securities they hold, capital gains are significantly less and thus taxes are lower.

NOTE: There are also index funds that track foreign securities markets. They typically emulate the EAFE (Europe and Far East) index. These are excellent vehicles for obtaining the profit opportunities from international diversification at reduced risk. Vanguard has the widest selections of stock, bond, and EAFE index funds.

Here are some points to keep in mind if you're building index funds into your asset mix:

- *Examine the expense ratio.* Except for the international portfolios, stick with index funds that have expense ratios below 0.5%—otherwise you're not gaining the main advantage of indexing.

- If you're planning to invest the minimum, *be aware of any fixed account maintenance fees.* Some funds charge a $10 annual account maintenance fee.

- *Examine portfolio turnover.* True, passive index funds do have turnover rates of 5% to 10%, but the composition of some benchmarks—particularly bond indexes—change often and higher turnovers are normal as the manager adjusts the make-up of the fund to that changing composition.

- *Note redemption fees and switching limitations.* Make sure there is no conflict between these restrictions and your time frame. Index funds are not recommended for in-and-out traders.

- *The ratio of net investment income to average assets* (see the "Financial Highlights" table in the prospectus) is an important determinant of the tax efficiency of any fund, including indexed portfolios. This ratio would be lower for a small-stock portfolio than for an S&P 500 portfolio, making the former more tax-efficient, all else being equal.

- *If you invest in a mix of index and actively-managed funds,* index funds are best-suited for your taxable accounts, and your less tax-efficient holdings are better suited for tax-deferred retirement plans. A tax-managed index fund could be particularly appropriate for a large investor in the highest tax bracket.

- *Be wary of "enhanced" index funds.* If you see a portfolio that calls itself an index fund but doesn't have all the major characteristics of one, it's probably not true-blue. Some enhanced index funds may strive to beat a particular index by trying to predict which stocks in the benchmark will deliver the best performance and overweight those issues while underweighting or excluding others. If an index fund tries to outperform its benchmark, it can't be a true passive portfolio. Make sure you understand what you're buying.

Money Market Funds

Money market funds are a special form of mutual funds allowing you to own a portfolio of high-yielding CDs, T-bills, and similar short-term securities without investing a large amount. There is a great deal of liquidity; funds can be withdrawn by check. They are therefore called *cash equivalents.*

Money market funds are considered very conservative, because most of the securities purchased by the funds are quite safe. The yield, however, fluctuates daily. Despite the myth that all money funds perform about the same, some regularly offer significantly higher yields than others, chiefly because they keep their expenses low.

The advantages of money market mutual funds are that:

• Interest is earned.

• There is no load.

• Small deposits are possible.

• Some let you write checks.

The disadvantage over CDs and savings accounts is that money market funds aren't federally insured.

Questions to ask in picking a money market fund:

• What's the average maturity? The shorter it is, the safer the fund is likely to be, and the faster it will begin offering competitive yields if interest rates rise.

• Can you write checks against your fund without charge?

• What's the minimum check amount: $200? $250? $500? The smaller the amount, the more often you can use your fund as a parking place for future investment or for emergency.

- How much do you need to open an account?

- What's the expense ratio? Money market fund expense ratios can range from 0.3% a year to 2%.

Information on Money Market Funds

Most mutual fund families offer a money market fund to investors. Current yield quotes and average maturity can be found weekly in the *Wall Street Journal, Barron's,* and other daily newspapers. For in-depth information, see *IBC/Donoghue's* weekly and annual reports; these track the performance and portfolio holdings of 750 money market mutual funds. Current and historical quotes are also available in on-line services such as Prodigy, Compuserve, Dow Jones News/Retrieval, and Telescan Analyzer. For example, CompuServe's Rategram (!GO RATEGRAM is the command) ranks the highest-yielding taxable and tax-exempt money market funds available. In addition, each report provides the fund's telephone number, minimum required deposit, safe index rating, average maturity, and yields.

IBC Financial Data, Inc. provides data on money market funds that is published in Barron's and on the IBC Web site *(www.ibcdata.com)* (Figure 8-11). It issues several publications giving extensive information on money market funds *(e.g., IBC's Money Fund Reporter, IBC's Money Fund Expenses Report, IBC's Rated Money Fund Report,* and *IBC's Offshore Money Fund Report).*

FIGURE 8-11: IBC'S MONEY FUND SELECTOR

Taxable Retail Money Fund Tables

from *IBC's Money Fund Report*™

Alphabetical Listings as of Tuesday October 12, 1999

(1)	(2)	(3) Assets ($mil)	(4) 7 Day Yield	(5) 30 Day Yield	(6) Compound 7 Day Yield	(7) Average Maturity (days)
59 Wall Street MMF		1,162.7	4.83	4.82	4.95	40
59 Wall Street US Treasury MMF		147.6	4.12	4.13	4.20	45
AAL Money Market Fund/Cl A	r	311.3	4.76	4.64	4.87	60
AAL Money Market Fund/Cl B	kr	2.0	3.80	3.57	3.87	60
AARP High Quality Money Fund		424.5	4.68	4.61	4.79	41
AARP Premium Money Fund		170.8	5.09	5.06	5.22	41
ABN AMRO Govt MMF/Common Cl	k	463.9	4.95	4.95	5.07	64
ABN AMRO Govt MMF/Investor Cl	k	83.3	4.63	4.63	4.74	64

Source: IBC Web site

Explanatory Notes:

(1) *The name of the fund.*

(2) *Facts about the fund:* "k" means that all or a portion of fund's expenses are being waived or reimbursed; "r" means that investment restrictions apply.

(3) *Assets:* The value of the fund's assets in millions of dollars (to the nearest $100,000).

(4) *7 Day Yield,* also called the 7-day average, current, or simple yield. It's the fund's total return (minus management fees and expenses) for a particular week, annualized as a percentage of the average share price. This yield measure does not reflect compounded earnings.

(5) *30 Day Yield,* the average for the previous 30 days. This is considered more reliable than 7-day yields for projecting longer-term performance.

(6) *Compounded 7 day Yield,* also called the compound effective yield. This represents the current yields after compounding interest over a 12-month period:

$$\text{Compound average} = [1 + \frac{7 \text{ - day average yield}}{(100 \times 52.142857)}]$$

(7) *Average Maturity (Days)* This represents the average maturity for the entire investment of the fund. Because money market funds invest exclusively in short-term debt securities, average maturity is short. Generally, the shorter the maturity, the swifter the fund responds to changing interest rates. Change in the average maturity figure is construed as an excellent predictor of the direction of short-term interest rates. If average maturity increases by several days for several weeks, the manager expects short-term interest rates to drop; and vice versa.

SELECTING A BOND (INCOME) FUND

In selecting a bond fund, consider:

- *Quality:* How is the fund rated by Standard & Poor's and Moody's?

- *Maturity:* What is the life of the bond? What effect will changing interest rates have? A longer maturity means wider price fluctuation. For example, a 10-year bond varies more in price than a 5-year bond.

  NOTE: *Some bond funds manage to produce top returns without undue volatility. For example, Harbor Bond Fund has returned a respectable return: an annualized 11.5% over the past five years. Yet, the average maturity of its portfolio is a middle-of-the-road 5.3 years.*

- *Premium or discount* funds have high return bonds with prices more than their par value (premium). Such funds are less susceptible to losses if interest rates increase. Funds selling at a discount sell below face value; these can lose most.

- *Total return:* Will the shares of the bond fund generate more than interest payouts? Capital gains or losses can make a huge difference in performance. Total return reflects both interest and price changes.

- *Commissions, loads, or fees:* The difference between yields on the best and worst bond funds is often slight. Fees can be more important to total return than the money manager. Check out the expense ratio.

- *Prepayment and currency risk:* There is a *prepayment* risk for funds that invest in mortgage-backed securities, such as Ginnie Maes. Mortgage prepayments accelerate when interest rates decline, and can appreciably shorten your expected long-term string of high payments. *Currency* risk exists with international bond funds. For example, some international funds frequently generate handsome returns, not because of higher interest abroad, but because of a fall in the value of the U.S. dollar.

Guidelines for Investing in a Bond Fund

- Increasing interest rates mean lower NAV for bond funds. Instead of concentrating just on current yield, consider total return (yield plus capital gains from declining interest rates or less capital losses if interest rates increase)

- All bond funds do not react the same way when interest rates decline. If you believe interest rates will drop, buy funds that invest in U.S. Treasuries or high quality corporate bonds. Consider high-yield junk bonds if you think interest rates will stay stable or go up. Consider the duration of the fund in measuring interest rate risk.

- Bond funds vary greatly. Some are aggressively managed and have high risks; others buy only government issues and are best suited for conservative investors. Read the prospectus.

- Consider the taxability of interest payments. Interest payments on municipal bonds are generally free from federal income tax and from the taxes of the state of the buyer's residence, which is particularly important for investors living in states with high tax rates.

Tax-Exempt Municipal Bonds

Increases in tax rates have brought tax-free income more attention lately. But you don't need to be in the top brackets to benefit from municipal bonds. As long as your marginal federal rate is at least 28%, you should give serious consideration to municipal bond funds. When trying to decide how much better (or worse) off you would be with a tax-exempt rather than a taxable bond fund, it's useful to examine your taxable equivalent yield, which was discussed earlier.

If similar but taxable bond funds yield less than your taxable equivalent yield, then you're better off in the muni fund, while if taxable funds yield more, you're better off in the taxable fund. What do we mean by "similar"? It's important to compare bond funds with a similar average maturity and credit quality. Comparing, for example, the taxable equivalent yield of a short-term muni portfolio with a long-term high-yield corporate fund is not meaningful. ***NOTE:*** *Muni-bond funds have call risk, the danger that a bond carrying a relatively high coupon will be called in for early redemption by its issuer. Nearly all municipal bonds have some sort of call provision.*

In picking a muni bond fund, you should consider:

- *Portfolio composition.* What sectors does the fund invest in? Is it diversified enough?

- *Credit quality.* The larger the proportion of investment grade bonds, the lower the credit risk.

- *Duration.* The longer the duration, the greater the interest rate risk.

- *Standard deviation.* This is the most common statistical indicator of an assets risk.

- *Yield.* The yield is based on the standardized SEC 30-day yield and total return.

- *Expense ratio.*

UNIT INVESTMENT TRUSTS

Like a mutual fund, a unit investment trust gives investors the benefits of a professionally managed diversified portfolio. Unlike a mutual fund, the portfolio stays constant. After the initial selections are done, there is no active management. Unit investment trusts include tax-free municipals, corporate bonds, preferred stock and common stock. Unit trusts are good for those on fixed income; they're guaranteed a return on capital. After the fund ceases, investors shares are redeemed.

CLOSED-END FUNDS

Closed-end funds have features similar to both mutual funds and common stocks. They differ from open-end funds in two ways:

1. They operate with a fixed number of shares outstanding; these trade among individuals in secondary markets, just like common stocks. If you wish to invest in a closed-end fund, you must buy shares from someone willing to sell, and in order to sell shares,

you must locate a buyer. Transactions in closed-end mutual funds are easy to arrange, however, since most of these funds are traded on the NYSE or AMEX or on the OTC market.

2. The price of a closed-end fund is based on a demand/supply relationship. New shares are not issued. Therefore, the NAV of the fund may be more or less than its current market price of stock. A major point of closed-end funds is the size of discount or premium. When the market price is above the NAV, the fund said to be selling at a premium; when market price is below the NAV, it's selling at a discount. Many funds of this type sell at discounts, which enhances their investment appeal. A number of publications such as the *Wall Street Journal* and *Barron's* report the premiums or discounts of closed-end funds.

The advantages of closed-end funds are:

• Professional management

• Diversification

• The opportunity to buy at a discount.

   NOTE: Closed-end funds are well suited for income investors and those seeking international diversification.

The disadvantages are:

• High management fees, ranging from 0.5% to 1.5%.

• Wide variations in brokerage commissions. (Negotiate or use a discount broker if you can.)

   NOTE: Herzfeld Closed-End Average tracks 20 closed-end mutuafunds accounting for about 50% of the value of all the funds traded on the exchanges. It's published in Barron's. An upward trend is a positive sign in a bullish market.

Sources of Information on Closed-end Funds

In addition to the *Wall Street Journal* and *Barron's,* you can find current and historical data on closed-end funds in:

- *Morningstar Closed-End Funds* (Morningstar Inc., 800-876-5005)

- *S&P Stock Reports and S&P Stock Guide* (Standard & Poor's Corp., 212-208-8800)

- *International Encyclopedia of Mutual Funds, Closed-End Funds, and REITs* (Glenlake Publishing Co., Ltd., 773-262-9765)

Current and historical quotes are also available in on-line services like Prodigy, Compuserve, Dow Jones News/Retrieval, and Telescan Analyzer.

HOW TO READ MUTUAL FUND QUOTATIONS

Mutual-fund quotations regularly appear in newspapers under the headings "Mutual Funds" and "Money-Market Funds." Figure 8-12 shows how quotations of mutual funds appear a newspaper.

FIGURE 8-12: SAMPLE MUTUAL FUND QUOTATIONS

Fund (1)	NAV (2)	Offer Price (3)	NAV change (4)
ABT Midwest Funds:			
Emerg Gr	10.00	10.93	-0.04
Growth	13.62	14.89	-0.10
Int Gov't	10.63	N.L. (5)	+0.04

Explanatory Notes:

(1) *The fund name abbreviated.* Several names under one heading indicate a fund family. Emerg Gr and Growth are load funds; the offer price is higher than NAV—the difference is the load.

(2) *The net asset value (NAV) of a share at the close of the preceding business day.* This column may also be called "Sell" or "Bid." This is the price you would have received (less any end-load fee or redemption charge) if you sold your shares back to the mutual fund on that business day. You can figure the most recent value of your holdings by multiplying the NAV by the number of shares you own.

(3) *The offering price,* also called "Buy" or "asked." It's the price you would have paid to buy shares at the close of the preceding business day. N.L. indicates a no-load fund.

NOTE: *The difference between NAV and the offer price is the front-end load. It should be viewed in percentage terms: 9.3% for the two load funds:*

NAV	Offer Price	Load		Load %
Emerg Gr	10.00	10.93	.93	0.93/10.00 = 0.093 (9.3%)
Growth	13.62	14.89	1.27	1.27/13.62 = 0.093 (9.3%)

(4) *Change from the previous day;* Emerg Gr was down 4 cents per share.

Qualifiers for Mutual Funds:

- **e** Ex-capital gain distribution
- **f** Previous day's quotation
- **p** Fund assets are used to pay distribution costs. 12b-1 plan.
- **r** Redemption charge or contingent sales fee may apply
- **s** Stock dividend or split
- **t** Both **p** and **r** apply
- **x** Ex-dividend
- **NL** No-load fund

Figure 8-13 is a typical newspaper listing for a closed-end fund.

FIGURE 8-13: SAMPLE CLOSED-END FUND QUOTATION

				(1)
Funds	Stock Exch	NAV Value	Strike Price	% Diff
Adams Express	NYSE	17.81	16 3/8	-8.06
Global Growth Income	NYSE	9.37	5/8	+2.72

Explanatory Note:

(1) *A negative difference* means the shares sell at a discount; *a positive difference* means they sell at a premium.

SOURCES OF MUTUAL FUND INFORMATION

With more than 6,000 mutual funds in existence today, no single source will satisfy your information needs completely, but the following important sources may help. For more sources information, see chapter 15 (Investment Advisories and Newsletters).

Mutual Fund Fact Book and A Guide to Mutual Funds (The Investment Company Institute, 1775 K Street NW, Suite 600, Washington, D.C. 20006). These cover most mutual funds by investment objective, statistics on specific funds, and background on trends in the mutual fund industry; they also provide brief mutual fund term definitions.

The Individual Investor's Guide to No-Load Mutual Funds (American Association of Individual Investors, 625 N. Michigan Ave., Department NLG, Chicago, IL 60611, 312-1280-0170). This classic guide provides investment objective, operating statistics, and various performance measures for close to 450 mutual funds.

Investor's Directory and No-Load Mutual Fund Resource List No-Load Mutual Fund Association, P.O. Box 2004, JAF Station, New York, NY 10116). These publications offer a bibliography of newsletters, magazines, books, other publications and organizations, including advisory services.

Mutual fund guidebooks are available at your local bookstore or public library, or you can order them by phone. Some other popular publications are:

- Gerald Peril, *The Mutual Fund Encyclopedia* (1-800-326-6941)

- Gordon Williamson, *The 100 Best Mutual Funds You Can Buy* (1-800-748-5552)

- *IBC/Donoghue's Mutual Fund Almanac* (1-800-343-5413)

- Sheldon Jacobs, *The Handbook for No-Load Fund Investors* (1-800-252-2042).

You can get help in selecting mutual funds from a number of other sources, including investment advisory services that charge fees. Among the other options are *Money, Forbes, Barron's, Business Week,* and *The Kiplinger Personal Finance Magazine.* The Fund Watch column appears in each issue of *Money;* it ranks about 450 mutual funds twice a year, reporting each fund's 1-, 5-, and 10-year performances and its risk rating. It compares funds within broad categories on a risk-return basis. *Money* also annually publishes *The Best 100 Mutual Funds,* a list of recommended mutual funds. The list is available at the Money Web site *(www.money.com).*

Business Week also categorizes mutual funds by risk (very high, high, average, low, and very low) based on 5-year risk-adjusted performance relative to the S&P 500. These ratings are available at *www.businessweek.com* (see Figure 8-14).

FIGURE 8-14: MUTUAL FUND RATINGS

Fund Family/Name	Rating	Category	Cat. Rating	1-Mo.	3-Mo.	YTD	12-Mo.	3-yr.	5-yr.	10-yr.
										Next 50 Funds ->
ACCESSOR GROWTH ADV	A	Large-cap Growth	B+	-1.80	-5.40	4.00	32.70	29.30	27.00	NA
ALLEGHANY/CHICAGO TR GR & IN	A	Large-cap Growth	A	.0	-4.30	8.40	34.10	25.00	26.50	NA
AMERICAN BALANCED	A	Domestic Hybrid	B+	-2.30	-5.20	3.30	12.20	13.50	14.80	11.70
AMERICAN CENT EQUITY GR INV	A	Large-cap Value	A	-1.50	-3.70	4.10	28.20	25.10	24.80	NA
AMERICAN CENT INC & GROW INV	A	Large-cap Value	A	-2.70	-5.50	3.60	26.60	24.80	24.70	NA
BARCLAYS GLBL INV LP 2010	A	Domestic Hybrid	B+	.40	-1.70	2.20	12.50	13.10	13.60	NA
BRIDGES INVESTMENT	A	Large-cap Blend	B+	-.10	-4.00	8.40	28.90	21.10	20.40	13.80
BT INVESTMENT EQUITY 500 IDX	A	Large-cap Blend	A	-2.80	-6.30	5.00	27.50	24.90	24.80	NA
BT INVESTMENT LIFECYCLE LONG	A	Large-cap Blend	A	-1.10	-3.10	2.50	14.60	17.50	16.90	NA

Source: Business Week Web site

NOTE: *Past yields are not necessarily indicative of future yields.*

Investors Business Daily ranks the 36-month relative performance of all mutual funds. No adjustment is made for risk or type of fund. This ranking is reported as part of their mutual fund quotations. The use of rankings is becoming a common practice. For example, the *Orange County Register,* a better quality, regional newspaper provides weekly rankings of mutual funds (based upon three-year and five-year returns) as part of their mutual fund quotations.

Forbes, a biweekly, rates investment company performance every year in its early September issue (Figure 8-15). It also publishes a quarterly supplement on mutual funds that contains performance data compiled by Lipper, Inc. The magazine's ratings can be accessed free at *www.forbes.com.* Both risk and return aspects are considered, and performance is related to fluctuations in the overall market. If a market rise is expected, you might use the *Forbes* ratings to select a fund that has done extremely well during such periods, regardless of its performance in a declining market. On the other hand, if you're risk-averse you might prefer a fund that has performed reasonably well in both good and bad markets. In Figure 8-15, on the left-hand margin are performance ratings: In up markets, 5% of the funds rated by *Forbes* receive a rating of A+; the next 15%, an A; the next 25%, a B; the next 25%, a C; the next 25%, a D; and the bottom 5%, an F. Down markets show a similar distribution.

FIGURE 8-15: INVESTMENT COMPANY PERFORMANCE

Market Performance		Fund/800 phone	5-year annualized total return	Assets 6/30/98 ($mil)	Weighted average P/E	Median market cap ($bil)	Tax efficiency	Annual expenses per $100	Minimum initial investment
UP	Down	STOCK							
B	B	Vanguard US Growth Portfolio/835-1510	24.1%	$10,722	31.3	$66.7	A	$0.38	$3,000
B	B	Vanguard/Windsor II/835-1510	22.3	30,606	20.1	25.5	C	0.40	3,000
D	A+	T Rowe Price Capital Appreciation/638-5660	14.5	1,090	32.5	5.0	C	0.64	2,500
		T Rowe Price Dividend Growth/638-5660	21.3	1,069	26.4	8.5	A	0.80	2,500

Source: Forbes Web site

Morningstar Mutual Funds covers over 1,200 funds, load and no-load, equity and fixed-income. Morningstar reports on current happenings at the fund, holdings, rankings, and performance data. It has a five-star system rating both return and risk. Morningstar rankings can be accessed free at *www.morningstar.net.*

The Value Line Mutual Fund Survey, like its stock service, provides analyses, ratings, and reports on some 2,000 mutual funds; they include a bull v. bear market comparison and a comparison of each fund with others of the same type and with the S&P 500 Index. Value Line rankings can be accessed free at quicken.excite.com.

A new magazine, *Mutual Funds Magazine,* is a very good source of information, with interesting articles.

Of course, the rapid expansion of the Internet has made available a considerable amount of information. Many funds, such as Fidelity and Vanguard, have extensive Web sites. Popular magazines that cover mutual funds can be accessed online. Recent performance results and evaluations of mutual funds are also available through services like America Online, CompuServe, MSN, and Prodigy.

Standard & Poor's Corporation, Lipper, Inc., Morningstar, Inc., Value Line, and Wiesenberger Investment Companies publish widely used sources of such information available by subscription. Mutual fund newsletters provide financial information to subscribers for a fee. All of these sources are rather expensive, but their reports may be available at brokerage firms or libraries.

Most funds have toll-free telephone services where you can get detailed information on each family of funds. These numbers can easily be obtained by calling the toll-free directory service: 800-555-1212.

CTA Research Corporation publishes the *Mutual Fund Consistency Index Newsletter* (see Figure 8-16). Its Web site *(www.mutualfund-index.com)* gives mutual fund profiles that contain the Sharpe ratio for each fund. The Sharpe ratio is also reported by Morningstar (www.morningstar.net). This measure developed by William Sharpe is computed as follows:

$$\text{Sharpe Ratio} = \frac{\text{Excess returns}}{\text{Fund standard deviation}} = \frac{\text{Total fund return - Risk - free rate}}{\text{Fund standard deviation}}$$

This gives you a view of returns per unit of risk. For example, if a fund has a return of 10%, the risk-free rate is 6%, and the fund standard deviation is 18%, the Sharpe measure will be:

$$\text{Sharpe measure} = \frac{10\% - 6\%}{18\%} = \frac{4\%}{18\%} = .22$$

This measure can be compared with other funds or the market in general to assess performance.

FIGURE 8-16: *MUTUAL FUND CONSISTENCY NEWSLETTER*

Mutual Fund Consistency Index Newsletter

| CTAs | MUTUAL FUNDS | STOCKS-BONDS | HEDGE FUNDS | HIGH INCOME | BRIDGE LOANS |
| HOME | NEWSLETTERS | PROFILES | RESOURCE CENTER | CONTACT US | LINK TO US |

Vanguard US Growth Portfolio   **A MUTUAL FUND Consistency Index Profile**

Market Focus:

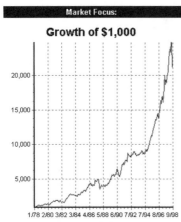

Growth of $1,000

1/78 2/80 3/82 3/84 4/86 5/88 6/90 7/92 7/94 8/96 9/98

Minimum Account Size: $3,000		
	%	$ Results
Total Return	2155.5%	$64,666
Avg. Annual Return	16.2%	$486
Maximum Drawdown	29.9%	$898
Return/Max. Drawdown	0.5	

An offering can only be made by a disclosure document. To receive a Mutual Fund Disclosure or more info, click here.

Time Window Total Returns (%)					
	36mo	18mo	12mo	6mo	3mo
Avg	58.5	27.4	17.8	8.7	4.3
High	132.3	70.78	77.96	48.95	29.04
Low	5.05	-20.23	-21.62	-24.41	-29.93

Monthly Performance															
Year	Jan	Feb	Mar	Apr	May	Jun	Jul	Aug	Sep	Oct	Nov	Dec	Year Max Draw	Mill $ Under Mgt.	Dollar Return
1988	3.2	4.6	-4.0	-0.7	0.4	5.7	-2.5	-3.2	6.0	0.4	-2.1	1.3	8.8 5.7	132.2	263
1989	7.1	-1.9	3.0	5.7	5.2	-1.9	10.8	1.8	1.6	-1.0	1.6	1.5	38.2 1.9	198.2	1,147
1990	-6.3	2.3	4.6	-0.6	10.9	2.3	-2.3	-8.2	-5.9	-2.7	7.6	4.4	4.2 17.9	355.9	126
1991	8.6	7.5	3.1	-1.1	5.0	-5.0	5.6	4.1	-1.7	0.9	-2.7	16.5	46.8 5.0	978.1	1,403
1992	-2.3	-1.4	-1.4	0.4	0.6	-2.1	3.8	-0.9	1.5	-0.1	4.8	-0.1	2.8 6.0	1,820.5	82
1993	-0.5	-3.7	1.2	-4.4	1.8	0.5	-1.0	2.1	-0.4	2.2	-0.1	1.1	-1.4 7.3	1,847.2	-44
1994	3.1	-1.2	-4.5	1.5	2.0	-2.9	2.2	4.2	-1.7	2.5	-2.1	1.4	3.9 5.7	2,109.3	116
1995	2.8	3.8	2.4	3.7	3.5	3.0	2.1	-0.4	5.6	2.4	3.9	0.3	38.4 0.4	3,624.1	1,153
1996	4.0	3.1	-0.4	1.8	2.9	2.2	-4.8	1.9	7.2	1.0	7.2	-2.3	26.1 4.8	5,532.0	782
1997	5.6	0.7	-5.4	6.7	6.5	2.7	7.0	-7.0	3.6	-1.9	4.5	1.5	25.9 7.0	8,054.6	778
1998	2.9	7.8	4.1	2.4	-1.5	6.4	-0.6	-14.1	6.1				12.2 14.6	9,587.0	366

Reward To Risk					
Avg Annual Return	16.2%	Total Return	2155.5%	Annual Sharpe ratio	0.55
Maximum Drawdown	29.9%	Total of Drawdowns	221.4%	Avg 12 mo. Ret/Max DD	0.8
Avg Ret/Max. Draw.	0.5	Tot Ret/Tot Draw.	9.7	% of Positive Months	62.7%

Largest Drawdowns and Recovery Period					
	1st	2nd	3rd	4th	5th
Drawdown	29.9	19.2	17.9	14.6	13.2
Mos. To Low	3	14	4	2	11
Mos. To Recovery	20	3	3	2	8

Source: Investor's Consistency Index Web site

S&P on Mutual Funds

The *Standard & Poor's Stock Guide* includes a *Mutual Fund Summary* designed to give subscribers a comprehensive statistical reference of mutual funds in a single alphabetical arrangement (see Figures 8-17A and 8-17B). The presentation, covering a broad cross-section of the industry, features the factual information necessary for an intelligent approach to mutual fund investment.

Because of the varying fund types and objectives, based on their stated aims, the information has to be evaluated in the light of your own goals and of the prospectus. Figures shown for percentage return, or change in net asset value, represent records for past periods and are based on calculations explained in the *Summary*.

Standard & Poor's rates bond funds on the basis of the creditworthiness of the investments the fund holds. The ratings do not take into account fund activities, including the allocation of expenses, the possible sale of investments before maturity at a loss, or hedging operations, or the extent to which interest rate fluctuations might affect share price.

Funds rated AAAf are composed exclusively of investments with a AAA S&P rating or short-term investments issued by entities whose long term, unsecured debt is so rated.

Other Publications

A report entitled *Investment Companies* is published annually with quarterly updates by Warren, Gorham and Lamont, Boston. It provides numerous statistics for over 500 mutual funds, including a history, investment objectives, sales charges, statistical history, and, for many funds, a 10-year performance analysis. It also discusses background, management policy, and financial records for all leading U.S. and Canadian mutual funds.

Find A Fund *(www.findafund.com)* provides Wiesenberger rankings free. The Wiesenberger firm also publishes *Management Results,* a quarterly update on the long-run performance of many funds, and *Current Performance and Dividend Record,* a monthly report on short-run performance (plus dividends).

Lipper, Inc. compiles the *Lipper Mutual Fund Investment Performance Averages,* ranking all mutual funds quarterly and annually

FIGURE 8-17A: MUTUAL FUND SUMMARY

PERFORMANCE OF S&P SUPER COMPOSITE 1500, S&P MIDCAP 400 AND THE SMALLCAP 600

	% Change From Previous Dec. 31 At Dec. 31						Dividends paid		$10,000 Invested 12-31-93	1999 Range	
	1994	1995	1996	1997	1998	July 30 1999	1998	1999	Now Worth	High	Low
S&P 500	+1.32	+37.58	+22.96	+33.36	28.58	8.87	16.20	9.36	31,999	1420.33	1211.89
MIDCAP 400	-3.58	+30.95	+19.20	+32.25	19.11	4.60	4.17	2.73	24,798	428.66	352.35
SMALLCAP 600	-4.77	+29.96	+21.32	+25.58	-1.31	4.11	1.40	0.79	24,166	190.24	154.14
S&P SUPER COMP 1500	.....	+36.52	+22.41	+32.93	26.35	8.37	3.31	1.93	.....	298.47	254.39

Source: Standard & Poor's *Stock Guide*

FIGURE 8-17B: MUTUAL FUND SUMMARY

Ticker Symbol	Fund	Year Offered	Prin. Obj	Type	June 30, 1999 Total Net Assets (Mil. $)	Cash & Equiv (Mil. $)	See Foot-notes	Net Assets per Share % Change from Previous Dec. 31 At 1995	Dec. 31 1996	1997	1998	July 30, 1999	Min. Unit	Max. Sales Chg. %	Distributions Per Share from Invest. Income 1998	1999	Security Profits 1998	1999	$10,000 Invested 12-31-93 Now Worth	PRICE SHARE 1999 High	Low	NAV Per Sh 07-30-99 NAV Per Shr	Offer Price	% Yield From Inv. Inc.
AGNMX	AARP GNMA & US Treasury...*84		I	GB	4341.1	n/a	.....	+ 12.5	+ 4.2	+ 7.7	+ 6.1	- 4.5	$500	None	0.904	.....	.....	.....	12,588	15.25	14.56	14.56	14.56	6.2
AGIFX	AARP Growth & Income Fund..*84		GI	C	7009.7	n/a	.....	+ 31.4	+ 21.4	+ 30.6	- 5.0	+ 8.5	$500	None	0.91	0.58	.....	.....	22,138	56.17	47.70	53.16	53.16	1.7

Source: Standard & Poor's *Stock Guide*

by type of fund. It publishes indexes for growth funds, growth&income funds, and balanced funds (see Figure 8-18). Lipper rankings can be accessed free at the *cbs.marketwatch.com.*

FIGURE 8-18: WEEKLY FUND CATEGORY RANKING

Major equity fund categories as defined by Lipper Inc., ranked by weekly average percentage return, including dividends, through Thursday (all returns include dividends):

Category	No. of funds	Week	Year to date	12 months
Science and technology	119	+5.15%	+49.58%	+153.72%
Health and biotechnology	59	+3.84	+0.59	+32.74
European	159	+3.02	+1.72	+28.81
Emerging markets	181	+2.95	+28.39	+54.50
Growth	1,226	+2.71	+9.00	+49.15
Pacific (ex Japan)	54	+2.67	+48.63	+79.63
Capital appreciation	288	+2.54	+12.23	+58.53
International	635	+2.51	+14.32	+40.87
Mid-cap	435	+2.43	+9.75	+59.00
Global	260	+2.42	+12.38	+44.37
Utilities	105	+2.02	+5.63	+17.65
Growth and income	962	+1.80	+4.08	+31.14
Equity income	242	+1.33	+1.13	+19.97
Gold	46	+1.18	+16.14	+0.89
Balanced	443	+0.98	+1.99	+19.22
Small companies	782	+0.64	+6.70	+52.07
Latin American	58	+0.24	+15.93	+32.06
Natural resources	62	−3.45	+23.97	+25.20
General stock fund avg.	**4,087**	**+1.95**	**+7.37**	**+45.40**
S&P 500 Index		**+3.73**	**+7.19**	**+37.33**

Source: Los Angeles Times

Morningstar's Mutual Fund Values is a biweekly publication about the operating characteristics, investment holdings, and market behavior of almost 1,000 mutual funds (similar information is available free at *www.morningstar.net).* It covers:

- Risk-adjusted ratings computed over 3, 5, and 10 years.

- Beta, alpha, R-squared (R^2), and standard deviation

- Annual total return for the past 10 years

- Total return for past 3 months, 6 months, 1 year, 3 years, 5 years, and 10 years

- Portfolio composition

- Annual net assets, expense ratio, income ratio, and turnover ratio for the past 10 years

- Weighted average P/E ratio

UNDERSTANDING MUTUAL FUND STATEMENTS*

One of the advantages of mutual fund investing is the wealth of information funds must provide to current and prospective investors.

To new mutual fund investors, the information may seem over-whelming. However, regulations governing the industry have standardized the reports: Once you know where to look for information, the location will hold true for almost all funds.

A mutual fund produces five types of statements: the prospectus; the Statement of Additional Information; annual, semiannual, and quarterly reports; marketing brochures; and account statements—and the Statement of Additional Information is actually part of the prospectus. The SEC has allowed mutual funds to streamline the prospectus by dividing it into two parts: Part A, which all prospective investors must receive, and Part B, the Statement of Additional Information, which the fund must send only to investors who specifically request it. In practice, when most people (including the funds) refer to the prospectus, they are referring to Part A. That's what we'll do here as well.

The Prospectus

The prospectus is the single most important document produced by the mutual fund, and it's *must* reading *before* you invest. The law requires that prospective investors receive a prospectus before the fund can accept an initial order. In addition, current shareholders must receive new prospectuses when they are updated, at least once every 14 months.

Although the prospectus must cover specific topics, the overall structure may vary among funds. The cover usually gives a quick synopsis of

---

*This section has been adapted from the American Association of Individual Investors' *The Individual Investor's Guide to No-Load Mutual Funds.*

the fund: investment objective, sales or redemption charges, minimum investment, retirement plans available, address, and telephone number. More detailed descriptions are in the body of the prospectus.

Fee Table: The SEC requires that all mutual fund prospectuses to have a table near the front that delineates all charges to the investor. The first section of the table lists all transaction charges, including front-end and back-end loads and redemption fees; the second section lists all annual fund operating expenses, including management fees and any 12b-1 charges, as a percentage of net assets; and the third section illustrates the total cost of these charges to an investor over time. Figure 8-19, assuming an initial investment of $10,000 and a 5% growth rate for the fund, and states the total dollar cost if an investor were to redeem shares at the end of 1 year, 3 years, 5 years, and 10 years. A no-load fund must provide this table even though there may be no fees.

Condensed Financial Information: One of the most important parts of the prospectus is the condensed financial information section, which provides statistics on income and capital changes per-share of the fund (see Figure 8-20). Per-share figures are given for the life of the fund or 10 years, whichever is less. Also included are statistical summaries of investment activities throughout each period. Occasionally these financial statements are only referred to in the prospectus and are actually contained in the annual report, which must then accompany the prospectus.

The per-share section summarizes the financial activity over the year to arrive at the end-of-year NAV for the fund. The financial activity summarized includes increases in NAV due to dividend and interest payments and capital gains. Decreases in NAV are due to capital losses from investment activity, investment expenses, and payouts to fund shareholders in the form of distributions.

FIGURE 8-19: SAMPLE TABLE OF COSTS

Summary of Expenses

Shareholder Transaction Expenses*

Sales Load on Purchases	None
Sales Load on Reinvested Dividends	None
Deferred Sales Load	None
Electronic Funds Transfer Fee on Redemption	$2 each
Exchange Fee and Transaction Fee on Redemption by Mail or by Telephone	$5 each
Wire Transaction Fee on Redemption	$10 each
Checkwriting Fee on Redemption	$2 each
Account Closeout Fee	$5**

The fees listed above (other than the account closeout fee) are waived if your account balance is $100,000 or more at the time of the transaction.

The individual transaction fees paid by shareholders of a Fund will accrue to the benefit of that Fund. The fees will be used to offset transfer agency and out-of-pocket expenses of a Fund, which should benefit all Fund shareholders by helping to reduce the Fund's expenses.

---

* Investment dealers and other firms may independently charge additional fees for shareholder transactions or for advisory services; please see their materials for details. The table does not include the $1.00 monthly small account fee. See "How to Make a Redemption."

** There is a $10 fee for closing an account within one year of opening the account. For individual retirement accounts, there is a $5 fee for closing an account within one year of opening the account, but there is no closeout fee for accounts closed one year or more after opening the account.

Annual Fund Operating Expenses

(as a percentage of average net assets after management fee and expense reduction)

	Money Fund	Government Money Fund	Muni Money Fund
Management Fees	0.39%	0.07%	0.00%
12b-1 Fees	None	None	None
Other Expenses(1)	0.05%	0.09%	0.09%
Total Operating Expenses	0.44%	0.16%	0.09%

(1) "Other Expenses" for the Government Money Fund and the Muni Money Fund have been estimated for the current fiscal year.

FIGURE 8-19: SAMPLE TABLE OF COSTS, *Continued*

Example

You would pay the following expenses on a $1,000 investment, assuming a 5% annual return and redemption by mail at the end of each time period:

Fund	1 year	3 years	5 years	10 years
Money Fund	$10	$19	$30	$60
Government Money Fund	$7	$17	N/A	N/A
Muni Money Fund	$6	$16	N/A	N/A

The purpose of the preceding table is to assist you in understanding the various costs and expenses that an investor in a Fund will bear directly or indirectly. As discussed more fully under "Investment Manager," the Adviser has agreed to temporarily reduce its management fee and reimburse or pay operating expenses of each Fund as follows: (i) with respect to the Money Fund, the Adviser has agreed to waive its management fee and absorb operating expenses to the extent necessary to maintain the Fund's total operating expenses at no more than 0.45% until January 1, 2000; (ii) with respect to the Government Money Fund, the Adviser has agreed to waive its management fee and absorb operating expenses to the extent necessary to maintain the Fund's total operating expenses at no more than 0.10% through at least June 1, 1999 and, thereafter, has agreed to waive its management fee or absorb operating expenses to the extent necessary to maintain the Fund's total operating expenses at no more than 0.34% until June 1, 2000; and (iii) with respect to the Muni Money Fund, the Adviser has agreed to waive its management fee and absorb 100% of the Fund's other operating expenses through at least June 1, 1999 and, thereafter, has agreed to waive its management fee and absorb operating expenses to the extent necessary to maintain the Fund's total operating expenses at no more than 0.34% until June 1, 2000. Without such fee reductions and expense reimbursements, "Management Fees" would be 0.39%, 0.50% and 0.50%, "Other Expenses" would be 0.05%, 0.09% and 0.09% and "Total Operating Expenses" would be 0.44%, 0.59% and 0.59% for the Money Fund, the Government Money Fund and the Muni Money Fund, respectively. "Other Expenses" for the Government Money Fund and the Muni Money Fund have been estimated for the current fiscal year. The Example assumes a 5% annual rate of return pursuant to requirements of the Securities and Exchange Commission. This hypothetical rate of return is not intended to be representative of past or future performance of the Fund. *The Example should not be considered to be a representation of past or future expenses. Actual expenses may be greater or less than those shown.*

Source: Zurich YieldWise Funds

FIGURE 8-20: CONDENSED FINANCIAL INFORMATION

The financial highlights table is intended to help you understand the Fund's financial performance for the life of the Fund. Certain information reflects financial results for a single Fund share. The total returns in the table represent the rate that an investor would have earned or lost on an investment in the Fund assuming reinvestment of all dividends and distributions. This information has been audited by PricewaterhouseCoopers LLP, whose report, along with the Fund's financial statements, is included in the Fund's annual report, which is available upon request by calling 800-223-0818.

Financial Highlights

		Year Ended March 31,		November 17, 1995 (commencement of operations) to March 31, 1996
		1999	1998	1997	
(1) Net asset value, beginning of period	$16.27	$12.34	$10.55	$10.00
(2) Income (loss) from investment operations:				
Net investment income (loss)	(.13)	(.08)	.12(1)	.07(1)
(3) Net gains on securities (both realized and unrealized)	3.61	4.80	1.82	.52
Total from investment operations	3.48	4.72	1.94	.59
(4) Less distributions:				
Dividends from net				
(5) investment income	—	—	(.14)	(.04)
Distributions from capital gains	—	(.79)	(.01)	—
Total distributions	—	(.79)	(.15)	(.04)
(6) Net asset value, end of period	$19.75	$16.27	$12.34	$10.55
Total return	21.39%	39.17%	18.36%	5.93%†
Ratios/Supplemental Data:				
(7) Net assets, end of period (in thousands)	$34,103	$29,675	$18,081	$12,448
(8) Ratio of expenses to average net assets	1.58%(4)	1.69%(4)	1.97%(2)(3)	2.45%*(2)(3)
Ratio of net investment income (loss) to average net assets	(0.76)%	(0.60)%	(0.64)%(2)(3)	(0.32)%*(2)(3)
(9) Portfolio turnover rate	36%	49%	56%	17%†

(1) Net of custody fee credits, expense reimbursement and fees waived by the Adviser. Had these expenses been fully paid by the Fund for the periods ended March 31, 1997 and 1996, net investment loss per share would have been $(.07) and $(.001), respectively.
(2) Due to the reimbursement of expenses and waiver of fees by the Adviser, data are not indicative of future periods.
(3) Before custody fee credits, expense reimbursement and fees waived by the Adviser. After expense reimbursement and fees waived for the periods ended March 31, 1997 and 1996, ratio of expenses to average net assets was 0.40% and 0%*, respectively; and ratio of net investment income to average net assets was 0.93% and 2.13%*, respectively.
(4) Before offset of custody credits. The ratio of expenses to average net assets would not have changed net of custody credits.
* Annualized.
† Not annualized.

Source: Value Line U.S. Multinational Company Fund, Inc.

Explanatory Notes:

(1) *NAV at Beginning of Year* is the value of one share of the fund.

(2) *Net Investment Income* is investment income less expenses.

NOTE: *This line is important because it reflects the stability of net income over the time period. High net investment income would most likely be found in funds that have income rather than growth as their investment objective. Since net investment income must be distributed to shareholders to avoid direct taxation of the fund, high net investment income may translate into into high tax liability for the investor.*

(3) *Net Realized and Unrealized Gain (Loss)* is the change in the value of investments that were sold during the year or that continue to be held by the fund.

(4) *Dividends from Net Investment Income* will include dividends in the current fiscal period; tax law requires that all income earned must be distributed in the calendar year earned.

(5) *Distributions from Capital Gains* are realized net capital gains distributions to fund shareholders.

(6) *NAV at End of Year* reflects the value of one share of the fund at the end of the year. It's calculated by dividing the total assets of the fund by the number of shares outstanding. The figure will change for a variety of reasons, including changes in investment income, expenses, gains, losses and distributions.

NOTE: *A decline in NAV may or may not be due to poor performance. For instance, it may be due to a significant distribution of realized gains on securities.*

(7) *Ratio of Expenses to Average Net Assets* is one indicator of fund performance and strategy. The expense ratio relates operating expenses incurred by the fund to average net assets. Total net assets for the year are divided by two to find the average. Operating expenses include the investment advisory fee, legal and accounting fees, and 12b-1 charges to the fund; they do not include brokerage fees, loads, or redemption fees. A high expense ratio

detracts from your investment return. In general, common stock funds have higher expense ratios than bond funds, and smaller funds have higher expense ratios than larger funds. The average for common stock funds is 1.4%, and for bond funds about 1.1%. An expense ratio above 1.5% is high; funds with expense ratios above 2.0% should be carefully scrutinized.

(8) *Ratio of Net Investment Income to Average Net Assets,* which is like dividend yield, is a comparison between earnings (dividends, interest, and capital gains) and average net assets. This, too, should reflect the investment objective of the fund. Common stock funds with income as part of their investment objective would be expected to have a ratio of about 3% under current market conditions, and aggressive growth funds would have a ratio closer to 0%. Bond funds would have ratios normally more than twice those of common stocks funds.

(9) *Portfolio Turnover Rate,* a measure of the volatility of a fund, relates the number of shares bought and sold by the fund to the total number of shares held in the portfolio; a high turnover rate (more than 100%) would mean the fund is doing a lot of trading. The turnover rate is the lower of purchases or sales divided by average net assets. (A rate of 100% or more does not mean a fund replaces its holdings entirely. Some holdings may be replaced twice in a year; others may remain in the portfolio for several years.)

In determining the turnover rate for common stock funds, fixed-income securities with a maturity of less than a year are excluded, as are all government securities, short or long-term. For bond funds, however, long-term U.S. government bonds are included.

The higher the turnover, the greater the brokerage costs incurred by the fund. Brokerage costs are reflected not in the expense ratio but in a decrease in NAV. In addition, funds with high turnover rates generally have higher capital gains distributions, which are taxed in the year of distribution.

Aggressive growth funds are most likely to have high turnover rates, as do some bond funds. A 100% portfolio turnover rate indicates that securities in the portfolio have been held for one year on average; a 200% portfolio turnover indicates that they have been held only six months. The portfolio turnover rate for the average mutual fund is around 100%, but varies with market conditions.

Investment Objective/Policy: The investment objective section of the prospectus elaborates on the brief statement on the cover. It describes the type of investments the fund will make—whether bonds, stocks, convertible securities, options, etc.—and gives general guidelines as to the proportions these securities will represent in the fund's portfolio. Common stock funds usually state the orientation toward either capital gains or income.

The management will also briefly discuss here approaches to market timing, risk assumption, and anticipated portfolio turnover rate. Some prospectuses may indicate investment restrictions they on the fund, such as limits on purchasing securities on margin, selling short, concentration in firms or industries, trading foreign securities, and lending securities; this section may also state the allowable proportions in certain investment categories. Restrictions are usually detailed more fully in the Statement of Additional Information.

Fund Management: The fund management section names the investment advisor and gives the advisory fee schedule. Most advisors charge a management fee on a sliding scale that decreases as assets under management increase. Occasionally, some portion of the fee is tied to the fund's performance relative to the market.

Some prospectuses will describe the fund's officers and directors, with a short biography of affiliations and relevant experience. For most funds, however, this information is provided in the Statement of Additional Information. The board of directors is elected by fund shareholders; the fund advisor is selected by the board of directors. The advisor is usually a firm operated by or affiliated with officers of the fund. Information on fund officers and directors is not critical to fund selection.

Rarely mentioned in either the prospectus or the Statement of Additional Information, however, is the portfolio manager for the fund. The portfolio manager employed by the fund advisor is responsible for the day-to-day investment decisions of the fund. To find out who the portfolio manager is and how long he has been in the position usually requires a telephone call to the fund.

Other Important Sections: Other sections in a mutual fund prospectus that you should be aware of may appear under various headings, but they are not difficult to find:

- Mutual funds that have 12b-1 plans, also known as distribution plans, must describe them clearly and prominently in the prospectus. The distribution plan details how the marketing of the fund relates to fund expenses. For instance, advertising, distribution of fund literature, and any arrangements with brokers would be included; the 12b-1 plan pays for these distribution expenses. Sometimes, these plans do not charge the fund for the expenses but rather allow the advisor to pay for them. (The actual cost to the fund of a 12b-1 plan will be listed in the fee table.)

- The capital stock, or fund share characteristics, section summarizes shareholder voting rights, participation in dividends and distributions, and the number of authorized and issued shares of the fund. Often, a separate section will discuss the tax treatment that will apply to fund distributions, which may include dividends, interest, and capital gains.

- The how-to-buy-shares section gives the minimum initial investment and any minimums for additional investments; it will also give load charges or fees; information on how to buy by mail, wire, and telephone; distribution reinvestment options; and any automatic withdrawal or retirement options.

- The how-to-redeem-shares section discusses telephone, written and wire redemption options, with a special section on signature guarantees and documents that may be needed. Also detailed are any fees for reinvestment or redemption. Shareholder services are usually outlined here, with emphasis on switching among funds in a family of funds. This will include any fees for switching and any limits on the number of switches allowed.

Statement of Additional Information

This document elaborates on the prospectus. It lists and describes investment restrictions; expands on any 12b-1 plan; and gives brief biographies of directors and officers, with the number of fund shares they own directly and beneficially. The investment advisor section, while reiterating the major points made in the prospectus, gives all the expense items and contract provisions of the agreement between the advisor and the fund.

The Statement of Additional Information will often include much more information on the tax consequences of mutual fund distributions and investment than the prospectus, including conditions under which federal income tax will be withheld. Financial statements are incorporated only by reference to the annual report. Finally, the independent auditors give their opinion on the financial statements.

Annual, Semiannual, and Quarterly Reports

All funds must send their shareholders audited annual and semiannual reports. Mutual funds are may combine their prospectus and annual report. Some do this, many do not.

The annual report describes the fund activities over the past year, listing all investments of the fund at market value as of the end of the fiscal year (sometimes giving the cost basis for each investment). Though looking in-depth at individual securities held by the fund is probably a waste of time, it's helpful to be aware of the general categories of investment. Look, for instance, at the percentage invested in common stocks, bonds, convertible bonds, or any other holdings that interest you. Then look at the types of common stocks held and the percentage of fund assets by industry classification to assess how the portfolio will fare in various market environments.

The annual report will also have a balance sheet listing all assets and liabilities of the fund by general category. This holds little interest for investors.

The statement of operations, which is like an income statement, is of interest only for the breakout of fund expenses. For most funds, the management fee is by far the largest expense; the expense ratio in the prospectus conveys much more useful information. The statement of changes in net assets is very close to the financial information in the prospectus, but the information is not on per share—per share information may be detailed in a separate section. Other than any pending litigation against the fund, footnotes to the financial statement are usually routine.

The quarterly or semiannual reports are current accounts of the investment portfolio, and provide more timely views of the fund's investments than does the annual report.

Marketing Brochures and Advertisements

The most important bit of information in brochures and advertisements will be the telephone number to call to receive the fund prospectus and annual report, if you have not received them already.

A new SEC ruling has tightened and standardized the rules about mutual fund advertising. All mutual funds that use performance figures in their ads must now include 1-, 3-, 5-, and 10-year total return figures. Bond funds that quote yields must use a standardized method for computing yield, and must also include total return figures. Finally, any applicable sales commissions must be mentioned in the advertisement.

Account Statements

Mutual funds send out periodic account statements detailing reinvestment of dividend and capital gains distributions, new purchases or redemptions, and any other account activity such as service fees. This statement provides a running account balance by date with share accumulations, account value to date, and a total of distributions made to date. These statements are invaluable for tax purposes and should be saved. The fund will also send out, in January, a Form 1099-Div for any distributions made the previous year, and a Form 1099-B if any mutual fund shares were sold.

APPENDIX 8-A: USEFUL WEB SITES

Web Address	Primary Focus
finance.yahoo.com	General business information; includes fund profiles
quicken.excite.com	General business information; includes fund profiles
www.aol.com/finlist/perform	Discusses the Sharpe, Treynor, and Jensen performance measures
www.businessweek.com	General business articles; includes fund ratings
cbs.marketwatch.com	General business information; includes fund profiles
www.forbes.com	General business articles; includes fund ratings
www.fundsinteractive.com/newbie.html	Educational material for beginning mutual fund investors
www.ibcdata.com	Money market fund information
www.mfea.com	Mutual fund investors' center has a variety of educational and historical information on funds
www.morningstar.net	Home page for the premier mutual fund reporting company; fund profiles are available
www.mutualfund-index.com	Mutual fund profiles including Sharpe ratio
www.schwab.com/Schwab NOW/Snlibrary/Snnlib014/SN014.html	Very good fund profiles from Charles Schwab
www.findafund.com	General mutual fund information, including fund profiles
www.stocksmart.com/mutualfundspro.html	Basic data on all funds sorted by fund family

Chapter 9
WARRANTS, OPTIONS, AND FUTURES

Warrants, stock rights, options, and futures are called leveraged investments because you can participate in these investment vehicles with a small sum of money. The value of these instruments is derived from the value of the underlying securities. In this chapter, we discuss:

- The different types of options

- How to determine the value of an option and its rate of return

- The advantages of receiving stock rights as dividends

- The use of stock warrants in connection with debt instruments

- Option quotations

- How hedgers and speculators use stock options

- Straddles and spreads

- The functions of an option writer

- Commodity and financial futures

- How hedgers and speculators use futures

- Futures quotations

- Sources of information on options and futures.

OPTIONS

Options give you the right to buy a security at a specified price for a stated period of time. Because they have their own inherent value, they're traded in secondary markets. You may want to acquire an option to take advantage of an expected rise in the price of the underlying stock. Option prices relate directly to the prices of the stock that's optioned. Options include stock rights, warrants, and calls and puts. Investing in options is very risky; it requires specialized knowledge.

Stock Rights

In a stock rights offering, current stockholders have the first right to buy new shares and thus to maintain their present ownership interest. This is known as a preemptive right.

EXAMPLE 1

Assume that you own 3% of XYZ Company. If the company issues 5,000 additional shares, you may receive a stock rights offering: a chance to buy 3%, 150 shares, of the new issue.

This right enables you to buy more common stock at a subscription price (sometimes called an exercise price) for a short time, usually no more than several weeks. This subscription or exercise price is lower than the current market price of the stock.

EXAMPLE 2

A company has 2 million shares outstanding and wants to issue another 100,000 shares. Each existing stockholder receives one right per share owned. A stockholder would thus need 20 rights in order to buy one new share.

NOTE: Stockholders who don't want to buy additional stock can sell their rights in the secondary market before the expiration date, after which it no longer has value.

One advantage of a stock rights option is, of course, the lower exercise price. Another is that you don't have to pay a brokerage fee when you buy the additional stock.

The Value of a Right

The value of a right depends on whether the stock is traded "rights-on" or "rights-off." In a rights-on trade, the investor who buys a share receives the attached stock right. In a rights-off or ex-rights trade, the stock and its rights are separated from each other and traded in different markets. Regardless of the form of the rights, the value of the right equals

$$\frac{\text{Market price of current stock} - \text{Subscription price of new stock}}{\text{Number of rights to buy one share}}$$

EXAMPLE 3

Assume the current market price of a stock is $30 a share. The new share has an exercise price of $26. An investor needs two rights to obtain one new share. The right equals:

$$\frac{\$30 - \$26}{2} = \frac{\$4}{\$2} = \$2$$

As long as the stock price holds at around $30 a share, the right has a value of $2.

Rights Quotation

Stock rights are reported as part of the regular stock quotation (see Figure 9-1).

FIGURE 9-1: RIGHTS QUOTATION

$13^{1/2}$	$2^{25/32}$	−69.3	CstDntl	4	$3^{1/4}$	$3^{1/18}$	$3^{3/16}$	...
$10^{6/18}$	$23/32$	−89.2	CstFedl rt		$1^{5/32}$	$11/16$	$23/32$	_$23/32$

Source: Los Angeles Times

The qualifier "rt" after the company name says that the company "CstFedl" has stock rights.

WARRANTS

A warrant is an option to buy a certain number of shares at a stated price for a specified time period at a subscription price that's higher than the current market price. A warrant may or may not come in a one-to-one ratio with stock already owned. Unlike an option, a warrant is usually good for several years; some, in fact, have no maturity date.

Warrants are often given as sweeteners for a bond issue. This allows the firm to float the debt or issue the bond at a lower interest rate. Warrants may also be included with a bond when an acquiring company offers cash plus warrants in exchange for the voting common stock of the acquired business. Warrants may also be issued with preferred stock.

Generally, once the bond has been issued, the warrants are detachable. Detachable warrants have their own market price. Even though warrants are exercised, the debt with which they were first issued still exists. Most warrants are traded on the AMEX; some are traded on the NYSE.

Warrants are not issued often and are not available for all securities. They pay no dividends and carry no voting privileges. The warrant allows the holder to take part indirectly in price appreciation of common stock and to obtain a capital gain. One warrant usually equals one share, though sometimes more than one warrant is needed to get one share.

Warrants can be bought from a broker. The price of a warrant is quoted along with the price of the common stock. Brokerage fees for warrants, like stocks, depend on the market price of the security.

When the price of the common share goes up, the holder of the warrant may either sell it (since the warrant also increases in value) or exercise it and get the stock. Trading in warrants is speculative; there is potential for high return, but the risk is high because the stock price may drop instead of rise.

EXAMPLE 4

Assume a warrant of XYZ Company stock lets you buy one share at $25. If the stock increases past $25 before the expiration date, the warrant increases in value. If the stock goes below $25, the warrant loses its value.

Though the exercise price for a warrant is usually set, the price of some warrants may rise as the expiration date approaches. Exercise price is adjusted for stock splits and large stock dividends.

Return on a Warrant

The return on a warrant for a holding period of no more than one year equals:

$$\frac{\text{Selling price} - \text{Acquisition price}}{\text{Acquisition price}}$$

EXAMPLE 5

Assume that you sell a warrant at $21 that had cost you only $12. The return is:

$$\frac{\$21 - \$12}{\$12} = \frac{\$9}{\$12} = 75\%$$

The return on a warrant for a holding period in excess of one year equals:

Selling price – Acquisition price / Years / Average investme

NOTE: *Warrants are speculative because their value depends on the price of the common stock for which they can be exchanged. If stock prices fluctuate widely, so will the value of the warrant.*

The Value of a Warrant

A warrant's value is greatest when the market price of the related stock is equal to or greater than the exercise price of the warrant. The value of a warrant thus equals:

Market price of common stock - Exercise price of warrant) x
Number of common stock shares bought for one warrant

EXAMPLE 6

A warrant has an exercise price of $25. Two warrants equal one share. The market price of the stock is $30. The warrant has a value of:

$$(\$30 - \$25) \times 0.5 = \$2.50$$

Usually the market value of a warrant is greater than its intrinsic value, or premium, because warrants are speculative. Typically, as the value of a warrant goes up, the premium goes down. (*Premium* is the market price of the warrant minus its intrinsic value.) If the warrant in Example 6 has a market price of $4.00, the premium is $1.50.

EXAMPLE 7

Assume that 100 bonds ($100,000 worth) are issued. Each bond has eight warrants attached. Each warrant permits the investor to buy one share of stock at $12 until one year from the date the bond was issued. The warrant will have no value at the issue date if the stock is selling below $12. If the stock increases in value to $25 a share, the warrant will be worth about $13. The eight warrants would thus be worth about $104.

EXAMPLE 8

Assume XYZ common stock is selling at $40 per share. One warrant can be used in the next three years to buy one share at $34. The intrinsic (minimum) value per warrant is $6 = ($40 - $34) x 1. Because the warrant has three years left and can be used for speculation, it may be trading for more than $6. Assuming the warrant was selling at $8, it has a premium of $2, the difference between the price and the intrinsic value.

Even when the stock is selling for less than $34 a share, the warrant may be marketable because speculators may expect an attractive increase in the stock price in the future.

EXAMPLE 9

If the XYZ common stock was at $30, the warrant has a negative intrinsic (minimum) value of $4, but the warrant might have a dollar value of, say, $1 because of an expected rise in stock value.

Leverage Effect of a Warrant

You may use the leveraging effect of warrants to boost your dollar returns.

EXAMPLE 10

Let's say you have $7,000 to invest. If you buy common stock when the market price is $35 a share, you can buy 200 shares. If the price increases to $41 a share, you would have a capital gain of $1,200. But if you invest the $7000 in warrants priced at only $7 a share, you can acquire 1,000 of them. (One warrant equals one share.)

If the price of the warrants increases by $6, your profit will be $6,000. In this instance, you would earn a return of only 17.1% on the common stock investment, whereas on the warrants you would get a return of 85.7%.

On the other hand, assume the price of the stock drops by $6. If you invest in the common stock, you could lose $1,200; you would still have equity of $5,800. However, if you invest in the warrant you could lose everything.

NOTE: To get maximum price potential from a warrant, the market price of the common stock must equal or exceed the warrant's exercise price. Lower-priced issues offer greater leverage opportunity. Furthermore, a warrant with a low unit price generates higher price volatility and less downside risk, and thus is preferable to a warrant with a high unit price.

Warrants can be used to protect a speculative transaction. For example, assume an investor sells a stock short and the price rises. The speculator can't keep the short position continually open, and it may be too costly to wait till the stock goes down. To protect the short sale the investor may buy a warrant fixing the buy price and limiting the potential loss on the trade.

EXAMPLE 11

Assume that you sell short 100 shares at $15 each. Then you buy warrants for 100 shares at $13 a share. The cost of the option is $3, or 3 points a share, a total of $300. In effect, you're buying the stock at $16 a share. Thus, if the stock rises above $15, your loss is limited to $1 a share.

The advantages of warrants are that:

• The price of a warrant tracks the price of the common stock, making a capital gain possible.

- The low unit cost gives you leverage in the form of lowering the capital investment without damaging capital appreciation. This increases the potential return.

- Downside risk potential is lower because of the lower unit price.

The disadvantages of warrants are that:

- If the price of the stock doesn't rise the expiration date, the warrant loses its value.

- The warrant holder receives no dividends.

- Investment in warrants requires extensive study and experience.

Warrant Quotations

The warrant quotation is part of the regular stock quotation. In Figure 9-2, the qualifier "wt" after the company name means that "ChlPza" has issued a warrant.

FIGURE 9-2: WARRANT QUOTATIONS

$15^{3/4}$	$9^{1/2}$	−9.0	CherryCp		$12^{7/8}$	$12^{1/2}$	$12^{9/8}$	$−^{1/4}$
$36^{3/4}$	$9^{1/2}$	+12.9	ChiRex	39	$26^{1/4}$	$23^{7/8}$	$24^{1/8}$	−2
5/32	1/54	+500.0	ChlPza wt		3/32	1/16	3/32	$+^{1/32}$

Source: Los Angeles Times

Warrant Offerings

Figure 9-3 is an announcement of the issuance of subordinated debt coupled with detachable warrants.

Explanatory Notes:

(1) Unlike the tombstones we have seen so far, there is only one underwriter/investment banker/lender in this transaction.

(2) Subordinated debt is being issued with detachable warrants. The warrants were issued in partial compensation (*e.g.,* additional interest) for the loan.

FIGURE 9-3: WARRANT OFFERING

(3) This is the name of the company issuing the subordinated debt and warrants.

(4) This is the amount of the loan.

CALLS AND PUTS

You can buy and sell calls and puts, another type of sock option, in round lots, usually 100 shares.

When you buy a call, you're buying the right to acquire stock at a fixed price. You do this when you expect the price of that stock to rise. Buying a call gives you a chance to make a significant gain from a small investment—but you also risk losing your full investment if the stock price doesn't rise. Calls come in bearer negotiable form; they have a life of one to nine months.

Buying a put gives you the right to sell stock at a fixed price. You might buy a put when you expect a stock price to fall. Buying a put gives you an opportunity to make a considerable gain from a small investment—but you'll lose the entire investment if the stock price doesn't fall. Like calls, puts come in bearer-negotiable form and have a life of one to nine months.

Calls and puts are typically written for stock actively traded on organized exchanges.

Though they carry no voting privileges, ownership interest, or dividend income, option contracts are adjusted for stock splits and stock dividends. Calls and puts are like warrants in that they're an alternative way to invest in common stock, use leverage, and speculate.

Calls and puts are not issued by the company with the common stock but rather by option makers (writers). The maker receives the price paid for the call or put minus commission costs. The option trades on the open market. Calls and puts can be acquired through brokers and dealers. The maker must buy or deliver the stock when requested.

Holders of calls and puts don't necessarily have to exercise them to earn a return. They can trade them in the secondary market. The value of a call increases as the underlying common stock goes up in price. The call can be sold on the market before its expiration date.

Calls and puts are traded on option exchanges, secondary markets like the Chicago Board Options Exchange, American Stock Exchange, Philadelphia Stock Exchange, and Pacific Stock Exchange. They're also traded in the OTC markets. *Listed* options are traded on organized exchanges. *Conventional* options are traded in the OTC market.

The Options Clearing Corporation issues calls listed on the options exchanges. Orders are placed with this corporation, which then issues the calls or closes the position. Because no certificates are issued for options, you must have a brokerage account to trade in options. A holder who exercises a call goes through the Clearing Corporation, which picks at random a writer from member accounts. A call writer would be required to sell 100 shares of the common stock at the exercise prices.

Exchanges permit general order (*i.e.,* limit) and orders applicable only to options (*i.e.,* spread order).

The strike price (exercise price) is the price per share for 100 shares, which the buyer of a call may buy or the buyer of a put may sell. The strike price is set for the life of the option on the options exchange. When the stock price changes, new strike prices are introduced for trading purposes, reflecting the new value.

For conventional calls, there are no restrictions on what the strike price should be. However, it's usually close to the market price of the stock. In the case of listed calls, stocks priced lower than $50 a share must have striking prices in $5 increments. Stocks between $50 and $100 have striking prices in $20 increments. Striking prices are adjusted for material stock splits and stock dividends.

An option expires on the last day it can be exercised. For conventional options, the expiration date can be any business day; listed options have a standardized expiration date.

The cost of an option is referred to as a premium. It's the price the buyer of the call or put has to pay the writer. (With other securities, the premium is the excess of the buy price over a determined theoretical value.)

The premium for a call depends on:

- The dividend trend of the related security

- The market price of the stock it relates to

- How much the price of the related security varies (high variability means a higher premium because the option has greater speculative appeal)

- Prevailing interest rates

- The spread between the price of the stock and the option's exercise price (a wider spread means a higher price)

- The volume of trading in the option

- The exchange on which the option is listed

- How much time remains before the option expires (the longer the time, the higher the premium)

In-the-Money and Out-of-the-Money Call Options

When the market price exceeds the strike price, the call is said to be "in-the-money." But when the market price is less than the strike price, the call is "out-of-the-money" (see Figure 9-4).

FIGURE 9-4: XYZ PUTS AND CALLS AT 50 STRIKE PRICE

	Stock Price	
	Puts	**Calls**
In-the-money	Over 50	Under 50
At-the-money	50	50
Out-of-the-money	Under 50	Over 50

Out-of-the-money call options have no intrinsic value. In-the-money call options have an intrinsic value equal to the difference between the market price and the strike price.

Value of call = (Market price of stock - Exercise price of call) x 100

EXAMPLE 12

The market price of a stock is $45; the strike price of a call is $40. The call has a value of $500.

If the total premium (price) of an option is $7 and the intrinsic value is $3, the additional premium of $4 arises from other considerations. The total premium consists of the intrinsic value plus speculative premium (time value) based on factors such as risk, variability, forecasted future prices, expiration date, leverage, and dividend.

Total premium = Intrinsic value + Speculative premium

In-the-Money and Out-of-the-Money Put Options

Because puts permit the owner to sell stock at the strike price, when the option strike price exceeds the market price of the stock, we have an in-the-money put option with its value determined as follows:

Value of put = (Exercise price of put - Market price of stock) x 100

EXAMPLE 13

The market price of a stock is $53; the strike price of the put is $60. The value of the put is $700.

When the market price of stock exceeds the strike price, the put is out-of-the money, which has no intrinsic value.

The value for calls and puts is the price at which the options should be traded, but typically they trade at higher prices than true value when the expiration date is far off. This difference is the investment premium.

$$\text{Investment premium} = \frac{\text{Option premium - Option value}}{\text{Option value}}$$

EXAMPLE 14

A put has a theoretical value of $1,500 and a price of $1,750. It's therefore traded at an investment premium of 16.67% [($1,750 - $1,500)/$1,500 = $250/$1,500].

Calls

The call buyer takes the risk of losing the entire price paid for the option if the stock price doesn't rise.

EXAMPLE 15

A two-month call option allows you to acquire 500 shares of XYZ Company at $20 per share. You exercise the option when the market price is $38, making a gain of $9,000 before paying the brokerage commission. If the market price had declined from $20 you would not have exercised the call, and you would have lost what you paid for it.

Calls cost significantly less than common stock; a little change in common stock price can result in a major change in the call's price. An element of the price of the call is the speculative premium attributable to the time remaining on the call. Calls can also be viewed as a means of potentially controlling 100 shares of stock without a large dollar investment.

Significant percentage gains on call options are possible because the investment is low compared to the related common stock.

EXAMPLE 16

A stock has a present market price of $35. A call can be bought for $300, allowing you to acquire 100 shares at $35 each. The more the price of the stock increases, the more the call will be worth.

The stock is at $55 when the call expires. The profit is $20 on each of the 100 shares of stock in the call, or a total of $2,000 on an investment of $300. You could thus earn a return of 667% if you exercise the call for 100 shares at $35 each, and then immediately sell them at $55 per share. (You would have earned the same amount by investing directly in the common stock, but you would have been risking $3,500, so the rate of return would have been significantly lower.

EXAMPLE 17

You can buy ABC Company stock at $30 a share, or $3,000 for 100 shares. You can acquire a $33 three-month call for $400. You buy the call and decide to invest your $2,600 in a three-month CD earning 14% interest. The CD will return $91 (14% x $2,600 x 3/12). If the ABC Company stock goes to $16, the option will be worthless but you will not have lost $1,400 ($14 a share). Rather, the loss is limited to $309 ($400 - $91). By not buying a stock you may have foregone a dividend, but it's unlikely to have reduced your loss by much.

If the stock went up to $43, you could exercise the call at $33—a sizable gain with little investment.

EXAMPLE 18

Here's another example of call trading: A call gives you the right to acquire 100 shares of $30 stock at $27. The call trades at about $3 a share. If you believe the stock price will increase but you have a current cash flow problem, you can buy a call so as not to lose a good investment opportunity.

EXAMPLE 19

On February 6 you buy a $32 June call option for $3 a share. If the stock has a market price of $34.50, the speculative premium is $0.50. In June, when the stock price is $37, you exercise the option. The cost basis of the 100 shares of stock for tax reporting is the strike price ($32) plus the option premium ($3), or $35.

Puts

The put holder may sell 100 shares at the strike price for a given period to the put writer. Buy a put when you expect a price decline. The maximum loss is the premium cost, which will be lost if the stock price doesn't drop.

EXAMPLE 20

A stock has a market price of $35. For $300 you acquire a put to sell 100 shares of stock at $35 per share. At the exercise date of the put, the price of the stock has gone $15 a share. As the holder of the put, you simply buy on the market 100 shares at $15 each and then sell them to the writer of the put for $35 each. You realize a gross profit of $20 per share, or $2,000. The net gain is $1,700.

EXAMPLE 21

The price of a stock was $55 on March 2. You buy a $56 June put for $4. (The speculative premium is therefore $3.) On June 7, the stock price has fallen to $47 and the price of the June put to $8. The intrinsic value is $9 and the speculative premium is $1. As the put holder, you now have a gain of $4 if you want to sell the put rather than delivering the stock.

Naked or Covered Options

Options may be "naked" (uncovered) or "covered." *Naked* options are options on stock that the writer doesn't own. The investor writes the call or put for the premium and will keep it if the price change is in his favor or too small for the buyer to exercise the option. But the writer's loss exposure is unlimited.

    Covered options are written against stocks the writer owns, so they are not quite as risky (a call can be written for stock the writer owns or a put can be written for stock already sold short). This is a conservative mechanism to obtain positive returns. The goal is to write an out-of-the-money option, keep the premium paid, and have the market price of the stock equal but not exceed the option exercise price. Writing a covered call option is like hedging a position, since if the stock price falls, the writer's loss is partly netted against the option premium.

Option Writing

The writer of a call agrees to sell shares at the strike price. Investors write options because they believe that a price increase in the stock will be less than what the call buyer expects. They may even expect the price of the stock to remain static or to decrease. If the option is not exercised, the writer keeps the price paid for it (minus transaction costs). However, when an option is exercised, the writer can suffer a loss, sometimes quite a significant one.

The writer of a call must come up with the stock at the agreed price if the option is exercised. An investor selling an option expects that it will not be exercised. The risk is that the writer must buy stock or, if he or she already owns it (is "covered"), lose the gain. The writer can buy back an option to eliminate the exposure.

EXAMPLE 22

The strike price is $40; the premium for your call is $5. If the stock is at less than $40, the call would not be exercised, and your gain is the $5. If the stock exceeds $40 and the buyer exercises the call, you must provide 100 shares at $40. However, you lose money only if the stock price exceeds $45.

Call and Put Investment Strategies

You can use calls and puts for: (1) hedging; (2) straddles; and (3) spreads.

You can hedge by holding two or more securities to lower risk and at the same time make some profit. It may involve buying a stock and later buying an option on it.

For example, you can buy a stock along with writing a call on it. Also, if you already hold stock that has risen in price, you can buy a put for protection against downside risk.

EXAMPLE 23

As an example of hedging, let's say you buy 100 shares of XYZ at $26 each and a put for $200 on the 100 shares at an exercise price of $26. If the stock remains static, you lose the $200. If the price decreases, your loss on the stock will be offset by your gain on the put. If the price rises, you earn a capital gain on the stock, offset by the loss of what you spent on the put. To get the benefit of a hedge, you have to take the loss on the put. (Also, note that the hedge expires with the put.)

You can also buy a put to hedge your position after making a profit on the stock.

EXAMPLE 24

You hold 100 shares of XYZ stock bought at $60 a share. When the price increased to $80, you can take a profit of $20 a share. To guarantee your profit you buy a put with an $80 exercise price at a cost of $300. No matter what happens later, you have a minimum gain of $1,700. If the stock falls, your minimum profit will be $1,700; if it rises, you'll realize an additional profit.

Some other time you might buy a call as a hedge to protect a short sale from the risk of increasing stock price. When you use a call, you as a short lower your profit by the cost of the call.

Calls and puts may also be used to speculate as an alternative to investing in stocks. You acquire options when you think you can earn a higher return than you would by investing in the underlying stock. In general, you can obtain a higher return at lower risk with out-of-the-money options, though the price consists only of the investment premium, which you can lose if the stock doesn't rise.

EXAMPLE 25

A speculator buys a call for 100 shares at $25 a share. The option costs $150. The stock price rises to $33 a share. The speculator exercises the option and sells the shares, realizing a gain of $650 ($33 - $25 - $1.50 = $6.50 x 100 shares). The speculator could also choose to sell the option itself rather than exercising it, making a profit because of its increased value. Note that if the stock price declines, the loss to the holder is limited to $150 (the cost of the option), plus brokerage fees. In effect, this call option permitted the speculator to buy 100 shares worth $2,500 for $150 for a short period.

"Straddling"—buying a put and call on the same stock with the identical strike price and exercise date—is used by speculators who hope for significant movement in stock price in one direction that will make a gain that exceeds the cost of both options. If the price doesn't move as expected, the loss will be the cost of the options. The straddle holder may also choose to widen risk and profit potential by closing one option before closing the other.

EXAMPLE 26

You buy a call and a put for $4 each on September 30 when the stock price is $42. They both expire in four months. The total investment is $800 at ($4 x 2 x 100 shares). By the time the options expires, the stock price has risen to $60. The call earns a profit of $14 ($18 - $4) and the loss on the put is $4. Your net gain is $10 per share, $1,000 total.

A "spread" is buying a call (long position) and writing (selling) a call (short position) in the same security. Sophisticated investors may write many spreads to gain from the differences in option premiums. Though the return potential is significant, the risk is very high. There are different types of spreads:

- A *vertical* spread is the buying and selling two contracts with the same expiration date but at different strike prices.

- A *horizontal* spread is the buying and selling of two options with the same strike price but with different expiration dates.

- A *diagonal* spread combines the horizontal and vertical.

The gain or loss from a spread depends on changes in the two option prices as the price of the stock increases or decreases (the price spread).

The speculator who uses a *vertical bull spread* anticipates an increase in price of stock, but this strategy reduces the risk. Here there is a ceiling on the gain or loss.

A speculator using a *vertical bear spread* expects the stock price to decline. This investor sells short the call with the lower strike price and caps upside risk by buying a call with a higher strike price.

Puts, straddles, and spreads may be bought either to maximize return or to minimize risk. They're not traded on listed exchanges but must be acquired through brokerage houses and members of the Put and Call Brokers and Dealers Association.

Those who employ straddles, spreads, and other similar strategies often use computers for analysis. These investment approaches are appropriate only for very sophisticated investors.

OPTION QUOTATIONS

Figure 9-5 is a sample of how options are quoted on the S&P 100 index.

FIGURE 9-5: INDEX OPTIONS

(2)	(3)	(1)		(4)	Close: 672.04 (5)	
S&P	**100**	**(CBOE)**				
Strike		**Calls**			**Puts**	
Price	**Oct**	**Nov**	**Dec**	**Oct**	**Nov**	**Dec (6)**
600	r	80	r	1/16	$4^{1/4}$	$8^{1/2}$
610	s	s	s	1/16	$5^{1/2}$	s
620	r	r	r	1/16	$6^{1/4}$	$10^{3/4}$
.						
.						
.						
745	r	$^{1/2}$	r	s	s	s

Prev call vol. 97,473 **(7)**   Call open int. 236,239 **(8)**
Prev put vol 169,567   Put open int. 267,538

Source: New York Times

Explanatory Notes:

(1) *Name of the exchange:* Chicago Board Option Exchange (CBOE)

(2) *Name of the index.*

(3) *Prices or premiums of options.* Quoted price is the price per point. Note that there are two groups of three prices, one set for calls [see (4) below], one for puts [see (6) below]. Note that the market value of an option equals 100 x the quoted price. For example, the S&P

100 Index (October maturity) would cost $3,200 ($32 x 100) for the 640 call.

(4) *The closing prices, or premiums, for calls.* Index options expire in about three months at most. You would pay 8 3/4, or $875.00 per contract, for the deep in-the-money October 665 calls because the index closed at 672.04 (item #5), making its value $67,204.00. The call holder with a strike price of 665 ($66,500) has an option with an intrinsic value of $704 (the difference between $67,204 and $66,500) and hopes that the value will rise even higher so the option can be sold or exercised at a profit after transaction costs. In the meantime, the 685 strike price call options have no intrinsic value since they're out-of-the-money and thus cheap. An October 680 costs only 1, or $100.00 per contract, since it gives the buyer the right to pay $68,000 for an investment worth only $67,204.

An "s" means an option was not offered for sale on the reporting date. An "r" means a given option was not traded during the period reported.

(5) *The closing price of the underlying stock (S&P 100 index).*

(6) *The closing prices, or premiums, for puts.* Premiums on puts move in the opposite direction to calls. October puts with a 700 strike price are expensive ($2,800 per contract) because they're deep in the money; they give the holder the right to demand $70,000 for an index that's worth only $67,204.

(7) *The number of call contracts traded during the session* and the number of contracts still open (open interest). These figures reflect investment optimism, since calls are gambles that the market will rise.

(8) *The number of put contracts traded during the session* and the number of contracts still open (open interest). These figures measure investment pessimism, since puts are gambles that the market will fall.

FUTURES CONTRACTS

A future is a contract to buy or sell a given amount of an item for a given price by a certain date (in the future—thus the name "futures market"). The seller of a futures contract agrees to deliver the item to the buyer of the contract, who agrees to buy the item. Futures investors trade in commodities and financial instruments. The contract specifies the amount, valuation, method, quality, month and means of delivery, and the exchange to be traded in. The month of delivery is the expiration date—the date on which the commodity or financial instrument must be delivered.

Commodities contracts are guarantees by a seller to deliver a commodity, like cocoa or cotton. Financial contracts are a commitment by the seller to deliver a financial instrument, like a Treasury bill, or a specific amount of foreign currency. To invest in futures, you will need specialized knowledge, and great caution. Figure 9-6 and 9-7 show the kinds of commodity and financial futures available. Quotations for futures can be obtained from the Commodity Charts & Quotes—Free Web site *(tfc-charts.w2d.com)*.

FIGURE 9-6: COMMODITIES FUTURES

Grains & Oilseeds	Livestock & Meat	Food, Fibre & Wood	Metals & Petroleum
Barley	Broilers	Butter	Copper
Canola	Beef--Boneless	Cheddar Cheese	Gold
Corn	Cattle--Feeder	Cocoa	Palladium
Flaxseed	Cattle--Live	Coffee	Silver
Oats	Cattle--Stocker	Cotton #2	Silver--1000 oz
Peas--Feed	Hogs--Lean	Lumber	Light sweet crude
Rice--Rough	Pork bellies--Fresh	Milk bfp	Heating oil
Rye	Pork bellies--Frozen	Milk--Non-fat dry	Natural gas
Soybeans	Turkeys	Orange juice	Platinum
Soybean meal		Oriented strand board	High-grade copper
Soybean oil		Potatoes	Mercury
Wheat--Durum		Rice	Propane
Wheat		Shrimp--Black tiger	Unleaded gasoline
Wheat--Feed		Shrimp--White	Palo Verde electricity
Wheat--Spring		Sugar	Twin City electricity
Wheat--White		Sugar--World	
Wheat--Winter			

FIGURE 9-7: FINANCIAL FUTURES

Currencies	Interest Rates	Securities	Indexes
Australian dollar	Eurodollars	Bank CDs	Dow Jones Industrials
Brazilian real	Federal funds–30 days	GNMA pass-through	Eurotop l00 Index
British pound	Libor–1 month	Stripped Treasuries	Goldman Sachs
Canadian dollar	Treasury bills		Major Market
Euro	Treasury bonds–30-year		Municipal Bond Index
French franc	Treasury notes–10-year		NASDAQ 100
German mark	Treasury notes–2-year		Nikkei 225
Japanese yen	Treasury notes–5-year		NYSE Composite
Mexican peso			PSE 100 Tech
Russian ruble			Russell 1000
South African rand			Russell 2000
Swiss franc			S&P 400 MidCap
Thai baht			S&P 500
U.S. dollar			SP 500–Mini
			S&P Barra–Growth
			S&P Barra–Value
			Value Line
			Value Line–Mini

A long position is buying a contract in the hope that its price will rise. A short position is selling a contract in anticipation of a price drop. You can terminate each position by reversing the transaction. For instance, the long buyer can later take a short position for the same amount of the commodity or financial instrument. Almost all futures are offset (canceled out) before delivery.

Hedgers and speculators trade in futures. Hedgers protect themselves with futures contracts in the commodity they produce or in the financial instrument they hold. For instance, a producer of wheat who anticipates a decline in wheat prices can sell a futures contract to guarantee a higher current price when delivery is made.

Speculators use futures contracts for capital gain on price rises of the commodity, currency, or financial instrument.

Futures contracts are traded through specialized brokers; certain commodity firms deal only in futures. The fees for futures contracts are based on the amount of the contract and the price of the item; commissions vary. Trading in futures is basically the same as in stocks, except that you must establish a commodity trading account.

Futures trading can help you cope with inflation. However, futures contracts are specialized and high-risk area because of the numerous variables, including the international economic situation. Futures prices can be quite volatile.

COMMODITIES FUTURES

In a commodity contract, the seller promises to deliver a given commodity by a certain date at a predetermined price. The contract specifies the item, the price, the expiration date, and the unit to be traded (*e.g.,* 50,000 pounds). Commodity contracts may run up to one year. Investors must continually evaluate how market activity is affecting the value of the contract.

EXAMPLE 27

You buy a futures contract for the delivery of 1,000 units of corn five months from now at $4.00 per unit. The seller of the contract doesn't have to have physical possession of the item, and you as the contract buyer need not take custody of the commodity at the "deliver" date. For instance, as the initial buyer of 1,000 bushels of corn, you enter into a similar contract to sell the same quantity, thus in effect closing out your position.

NOTE: A person can invest in a commodity directly or through a mutual fund. A third method is to buy into a limited partnership involved in commodity investments. The mutual fund and partnership strategies are more conservative, since risk is spread and management know-how provided.

Investors trade commodities in the hope of high return rates and as a hedge against inflation. In inflation, commodities move favorably because they're tied into economic trends. But risk and uncertainty are high because commodity prices vacillate and because there is so much high-margin investing. Commodities investors must have plenty of cash available to answer margin calls and to cover their losses. To reduce risk, commodities investors should hold a diversified portfolio, and they should be assured of the integrity and reliability of the salesperson.

The buyer of a commodity always has the option of letting the contract run to gain possible higher profits or of terminating it and using the earnings to put up margin on another futures contract. (This is referred to as an inverse pyramid.)

Commodity futures exchanges let buyers and sellers negotiate cash (spot) prices. Cash is paid for immediate physical possession of a commodity. Prices in the cash market rely to some degree on prices in the futures market. The price of a commodity may rise over time as it incorporates holding costs and anticipated inflation.

Commodity and financial futures are traded primarily on the Chicago Board of Trade (CBT), though there are other large exchanges, some of which specialize. Examples are the New York Cotton Exchange, the Chicago Mercantile Exchange, and the Amex Commodities Exchange. Since there is a chance of significant gains and losses, exchanges restrict the daily price movements for a commodity. The commodities exchanges are regulated by the federal Commodity Futures Trading Commission (CFTC), not the SEC.

Return on a Futures Contract

The return on a futures contract comes from capital gain (selling price minus buy price) since no current income is involved. High capital gain is possible due to price volatility of the commodity and the effect of leverage from the low margin requirement. However, if things go sour, the entire investment in the form of margin could be lost quickly. The return on investment when dealing in commodities (whether a long or short position) equals:

$$\frac{\text{Selling price - Purchase price}}{\text{Margin deposit}}$$

EXAMPLE 28

You buy a cotton contract for $60,000, putting up an initial deposit of $5,000. You later sell the contract for $64,000. The return is:

$$\text{Return} = \frac{\$64,000 - \$60,000}{\$5,000} = 80\%$$

Margin requirements for commodity contracts are relatively low, usually ranging from 5% to 10% of the contract's value. (For stocks, you will remember, the margin requirement is 50%.) In commodities trading, no money is really lent, and so no interest is paid.

An *initial margin* is required as a deposit on the contract. The purpose of the deposit is to cover a market value decline on the contract. The amount of the deposit depends on the type of contract and the exchange where it's traded.

The *maintenance deposit* is lower than the initial deposit and provides the minimum margin that must always by maintained in the account. It's usually about 80% of the initial margin ($4,000 in example 28).

EXAMPLE 29

You make an initial deposit of $10,000 on a contract and the maintenance deposit is $7,500. If the market value of the contract decreases by no more than $2,500, you have no problem. However, if the market value of the contract declines by $4,500, the margin on deposit will go to $5,500, and you will have to deposit another $2,000 in order to keep the sum at the maintenance deposit level. If you don't come up with the additional $4,500, the contract will be canceled. Commodity trading may be in the form of hedging, speculating, or spreading.

Investors use *hedging* to protect their position in a commodity. For example, a citrus grower (the seller) will hedge to get a higher price for his products while a processor (or buyer) of the item will hedge to obtain a lower price. By hedging, an investor minimizes the risk of loss but loses the prospect of sizable profit.

EXAMPLE 30

A commodity is currently selling at $120 a pound, but a manufacturer that needs the commodity expects the price to rise. To guard against higher prices, the buyer acquires a futures contract at $135 a pound. Six months later, the price of the commodity moves to $180. The futures contract price is now $210. The buyer's profit is $75 a pound. If 5,000 pounds are involved, the total profit is $375,000. At the same time, the cost on the market rose by only $60 a pound, or $300,000. In effect, the manufacturer has hedged his position, coming out with a profit of $75,000, and has kept the rising costs of the commodity under control.

Some people invest in commodities to *speculate*.

EXAMPLE 31

You buy an October futures contract for 37,500 pounds of coffee at $5 a pound. If the price rises to $5.40, you'll gain $0.40 a pound for a total gain of $15,000. If you only put up an initial margin requirement of 10%, your gain is 80% ($0.40/$0.50 a lb.). If the transactions occurred within two months, your annualized gain would be 480% (80% x 12 months/2 months). This resulted from a mere 8% ($0.40/$5.00) gain in the price of coffee.

Spreading attempts to take advantage of wide swings in price and at the same time cap loss exposure. As in stock option trading, the spread investor buys one contract and sells the other in the hope of achieving a minimal but reasonable profit. If the worst happens, the spread helps to minimize the investor's loss.

EXAMPLE 32

You acquire Contract 1 for 10,000 pounds of commodity Z at $500 a pound. At the same time, you sell short Contract 2 for 10,000 pounds of the same commodity at $535 a pound. Subsequently, you sell Contract 1 for $520 a pound and buy Contract 2 for $543 a pound. Contract 1 yields a profit of $20 a pound; Contract 2 takes a loss of $8 a pound. You have netted a profit of $12 a pound, so your total gain is $120,000.

FINANCIAL FUTURES

Financial futures trading, similar in many ways to commodity trading, now constitutes about two-thirds of all contracts. Because of the instability in interest and exchange rates, financial futures can be used to hedge. They can also be used as speculative investments because of the potential for significant price variability. Financial futures have an even lower margin requirement than commodities. The margin on a U.S. Treasury bill, for example, may be a low as 2%.

Financial futures are traded on the New York Futures Exchange, the AMEX Commodities Exchange, the International Monetary Market (part of Chicago Mercantile Exchange), and the Chicago Board of Trade. The basic types of financial futures are: (1) interest rate futures; (2) foreign currency futures; and (3) stock-index futures.

An *interest rate futures* contract gives the holder the right to a given amount of the related debt security at a later date (usually no more than three years). The security may be Treasury bills and notes, certificates of deposit, commercial paper, or Ginnie Mae certificates, among others.

Interest rate futures are stated as a percentage of the par value of the underlying debt security. As interest rates decrease, the value of the contract increases. As the price of the contract goes up, the buyer has the gain while the seller loses. A change of one basis point in interest rates causes a price change. (A basis point is 1/100 of 1%.)

Those who trade in interest rate futures don't usually take possession of the financial instrument but are more interested in hedging. For instance, if a company will issue bonds in 90 days, the underwriters are now working on the terms, and interest rates are expected to rise before the issue, investors can hedge by selling short Treasury bills. A rise in interest rates will result in a lower price to repurchase the interest rate future, with resulting profit. This will net against the increased interest cost of the debt issuance.

Speculators find financial futures attractive because of their potentially large return on a small investment. If you're a speculator hoping for increasing interest rates, you will want to sell an interest rate future, since it will soon decline in value. With large contracts (say, a $1,000,000 Treasury bill), even a small change in the price of the contract can provide significant gain. However, the risk is equally significant; these can be volatile securities with great gain or loss potential.

A *currency futures contract* gives you a right to a specified amount of a foreign currency at a future date. Because the contracts are standardized, they trade on secondary markets. Currency futures are expressed in dollars or cents per unit of the foreign currency. They typically have a delivery date of no more than one year.

Currency futures can be used for either hedging or speculation. The purpose of hedging in a currency is to lock into the best money exchange possible.

EXAMPLE 33

Here's an example of hedging an exposed position: A manager agrees to accept francs in four months. If the franc decreases compared to the dollar, the manager gets less value. To hedge his exposure, the manager can sell a futures contract in francs by going short. If the franc declines in value, the futures contract will make a profit, thus offsetting the loss when the manager receives the francs.

EXAMPLE 34

As an example of speculation, in February you buy a currency futures contract for delivery in June. The contract price is $1, which equals 2 pounds. The total value of the contract is $50,000, and the margin requirement is $6,000. The pound strengthens until it equals 1.8 pounds to $1. Hence, the value of your contract increases to $55,556 ($50,000 x 2/1.8), giving you a return of 92.6% ($5,556/$$6,000). If the pound had weakened to 2.2, you would have taken a loss on the contract.

A *stock-index futures* contract is tied into a broad stock market index. Introduced in 1982, futures contracts apply to the S & P 500 Stock Index, New York Stock Exchange Composite Stock Index, and Value Line Composite Stock Index; smaller investors can avail themselves of the S & P 100 futures contract that involves a smaller margin deposit.

Stock-index futures allow you to participate in the general change in the entire stock market: You can buy and sell the market as a whole rather than a specific security. If you anticipate a bull market but are unsure which stocks will rise, you should buy a stock-index future. Because of the risks, trade in stock-index futures only for the purpose of hedging or speculation. Figure 9-8 compares stock index futures contracts.

BUYING AND SELLING FUTURES

You may invest in a commodity directly, through a mutual fund, or by buying a limited partnership. The mutual fund and partnership approaches are more conservative, because risk is spread and the management is professional.

Futures may be directly invested as follows:

- *Commodity pools* managed by professional traders (these are filed with the CFTC).

- *Full service brokers* will give you recommendations.

- *Discount brokers:* You decide on your own when and if to invest.

FIGURE 9-8: STOCK INDEX FUTURES CONTRACTS
SPECIFICATION

Index and Exchange	Trading Hours	Index	Contract Size and Value	Contract Months
S&P 500 Index				
Index and Options Market (IOM) of the Chicago Mercantile Exchange (CME)	10:00 am to 4:15 pm (NYT)*	Value of 500 selected stocks Traded on NYSE, AMEX, and OTC, weighted to reflect market value of issues	$500 × the S&P 500 Index	March, June, September, December
NYSE Composite Index				
New York Futures Exchange (NYFE) of the New York Stock Exchange	10:00 am to 4:15 pm (NYT)*	Total value of NYSE Market: 1550 listed common stocks, weighted to reflect market value of issues	$500 × the NYSE Composite Index	March, June, September, December
Value Line Index				
Kansas City Board of Trade (KCBT)	10:00 am to 4:15 pm (NYT)*	Equally-weighted average of 1700 NYSE, AMEX, OTC, and regional stock prices expressed in index form	$500 × the Value Line Index	March, June. September, December
Major Market Index				
Chicago Board of Trade (CBT)	10:00 am to 4:15 pm (NYT)*	Price-weighted average of 20 blue-chip companies	$250 × MMI Index	March, June, September, December

*New York Time

- *Managed futures:* You deposit funds in an individual managed account and choose a commodity trading advisor (CTA) to trade it.

If you'd like information on managed futures:

- ATA Research Inc. provides information on trading advisors and manages individual's account via private pools and funds.

- Barclay Trading Group publishes quarterly reports on trading advisers.

- *CMA Reports* monitors the performance of trading advisers and private pools.

- *Management Account Reports,* a monthly newsletter, tracks funds, giving information on their fees and track records.

- *Trading Advisor* follows more than 100 CTAs.

There are several drawbacks to managed futures, including:

- High cost, which ranges from 15 to 20% of the funds invested.

- Substantial risk and inconsistent performance of fund advisors. *NOTE: Despite their recent popularity, management futures are still a risky choice and should only be done apart from a well-diversified portfolio.*

FUTURES QUOTATIONS

Commodity Futures

The financial pages of some newspapers, including the *Wall Street Journal,* provide the beginning, high, low, and ending (settle) prices for each day, along with the daily change for the commodity, plus the all-time high and low, open interest (the number of outstanding futures contracts for the commodity) and the expiration dates.

To determine the price of each contract, multiply the unit price by the contract size. The contract size is usually stated after the name of the commodity (see Figure 9-9).

Explanatory Notes:

(1) *Commodity.*

(2) *Exchange:* the Chicago Board of Trade.

(3) *Quantity of commodity to be delivered.*

(4) *Season:* the lifetime of the contract.

FIGURE 9-19: COMMODITIES QUOTATIONS

Season High	Open Low		Interest	Open	High	Low	Close	Chg.
(4)			**(5)**	**(6)**			**(7)**	**(8)**
(1)	**(2)**			**GRAINS**				
WHEAT	(CBOT) --	**(3)** 5,000		bu	minimum -- cents		per	bushel
352.00	250.50 Dec 99		87,397	254.00	255.00	250.50	253.50	-1.25
340.00	267.00 Mar 00		30,368	269.75	271.00	267.00	269.75	-0.75
322.00	277.00 May 00		4,101	279.00	281.00	277.00	280.00	+0.50
347.00	286.50 Jul 00		11,866	289.00	291.00	286.50	290.00	+0.25
335.00	298.00 Sep 00		317	. . .	. . .	. . .	298.00	. . .
345.00	305.00 Dec 00		429	308.00	309.00	305.00	308.00	-0.50
353.00	317.50 Jul 01		51	320.50	320.50	320.50	320.50	-1.00
352.00	350.00 Jul 02		2	. . .	. . .	. . .	348.00	. . .

Est. Vol. 15,000 Vol. 32,895 open int. 134,532 + 3,315   **(9)**

(a)   *(b)*   *(c)*   *(d)*

Source: Investor's Business Daily

(5) *Open Interest:* the number of positions reported by the clearing house.

(6) *The price the contract opened at on the reported day,* and the high and low prices for that day. Prices are in cents per bushel; 253.5 = $2.535. At $2.535, the close in the December future made the contract worth $12,675 ($2.535 per bushel x 5,000 bushels).

(7) *Close:* the last price of the day, used for daily resettlement of investors' margin accounts.

(8) *Chg.:* the difference between close prices on the reported day and the previous day.

(9) (a) Estimates of the number of contracts that changed hands during this session.

(b) Volume of the previous session.

(c) Total open interest of the two previous days.

(d) Change in the number of open contracts.

Figure 9-10 shows ho commodity futures prices are quoted on the PBS Nightly Business Report.

FIGURE 9-10: COMMODITY QUOTATIONS

Settlement Prices

(1)	COPPER:(JUNE)	7640	−10
(2)	SUGAR:(JUNE)	1188	+12
(3)	COTTON:(JUNE)	6358	+33

Explanatory Notes:

(1) *June copper futures at 7640.* The price 7640 means $0.764 per pound, quoted to a hundredth of a cent: 7640/10,000 = $0.764; -10 means that the price is down $0.0100 from the previous day's settlement price.

(2) *June sugar futures at 1188,* $0.1188 per pound, up $0.012 from the previous day's settlement price.

(3) *June cotton futures at 6358,* $0.6358 per pound, up $0.033 from the previous day's settlement price.

In Figure 9-11 we see financial futures prices as quoted on the PBS Nightly Business Report.

Here we see:

FIGURE 9-11: FINANCIAL FUTURES

Settlement Prices

(1)	GNMA:(JULY)	6116	−7/32
(2)	T-BONDS:(JULY)	6226	−5/32
(3)	T-BILLS:(JULY)	8475	UNCH

Explanatory Notes:

(1) *July Ginnie Mae futures at 6116.* The first two numbers are percent of par value (61%) and the second two are thirty-seconds of a percent (16/32%, which equal 0.5%). The settlement price is therefore 60.5% of par. This price is down 7/32nds from the previous day's settlement price.

(2) *July T-bond futures at 6226.* The first two numbers are percent of par value (62%) and the second two are thirty-seconds of a percent (26/32% which equal 0.8125%). The settlement price is therefore 62.8125% of par value, down 5/32nds.

(3) *July T-bills futures at 8475.* This figure is a straight percent of par value carried to a hundredth of a percent. The price is therefore 84.75%, unchanged from the previous day's settlement price.

Currency Futures Quotations

Figure 9-12 shows a currency quotation from Commodities, Charts & Quotes—Free *(tfc-charts.w2d.com):*

FIGURE 9-12: CME AUSTRALIAN DOLLAR

Commodity Futures Price Quotes For **(1)**

(2) CME Australian Dollar

(Price quotes for this commodity delayed at least 10 minutes as per exchange requirements)

(3)   **(4)**   Click here to refresh data

Month Click for chart	Open	High	Low	Last (5)	Time	Sett (6)	Chg (7)	Sett	Vol	O.Int	Options
								Prior Day			
Dec 99	6362	6410	6350	DN 6386	15:09	6388	+8	6378	82	22197	Call Put
Mar 00	6375	6412	6370	UP 6375	08:31	6398	-13	6388	1	112	Call Put
Jun 00	-	-	-	UC 6398	12:43	6408	-	6398	2	11	Call Put
Sep 00	-	-	-	UC 6408	09:28	6418	-	6408	-	1	Call Put

Source: Commodity Charts & Quotes

Explanatory Notes:

(1) *The currency:* the Australian dollar.

(2) *The exchange:* the Chicago Mercantile Exchange.

(3) *The delivery date* (closing date for the contract).

(4) *The opening, high, and low prices for the trading day.* The trading unit's 100,000 Australian dollars. The price is $10 per point. Therefore, the settlement price for the trading unit's $63,620, and each Australian dollar being delivered in December is worth $0.6362.

(5) *The last price at which the contract traded.*

(6) *The official daily closing price of a futures contract* is set by the exchange for the purpose of settling margin accounts.

(7) *The change in the price* from the previous settlement price to the last price quoted.

Figure 9-13 is an example of a newspaper quotation on T-bonds.

FIGURE 9-13: T-BOND QUOTATIONS: AN EXAMPLE

Season		Open					
High	Low	Interest	Open	High **(1)**	Low	Close	Chg.
US TREASURY BONDS (CBOT) - (8 pct -- $100,000 -pts & 32nds of 100 pct)							
128-28	111.29 Dec 99	579,305	112-17	112-18	111-29	112-07	-0-11
101-08	92-10 Mar 00	40,588	92-20	92-22	92-10	92-19	-0-11 **(3)**
99-15	92-06 Jun 00	101	...**(2)**	...	...	92-05	0-11
93-26	91-25 Sep 00	70	...	...	...	91-21	...
Est. Vol. 225,000 open int 608,733 - 11.331							

Source: Investor's Business Daily

Explanatory Notes:

(1) *Face value of bonds* to deliver if they were 8% coupon, 20-year maturity.

(2) *Prices* are in thousands and 32nds of a thousand; so 112-07 = $112,000 + 7/32 (1,000) = $112,218.75.

(3) *Change in settlement price* between the reported trading day and the previous day. The contract's value was down $343.75 (11/32 x $1,000).

Figure 9-14 is an example of a newspaper quotation on Treasury bill futures.

FIGURE 9-14: TREASURY BILL FUTURES QUOTATION: AN EXAMPLE

Season High	Low	Open Interest	Open (1)	High	Low	Close	Chg.
US T. BILLS (1MM)	-	($1	million	-	pts	of 100 pct)	
95.38	94.86	Dec 99	410	94.95	94.95	94.95	-0.01

Est. Vol. 12 open int 410

1475.0	1428.9	Sep 01	2	. . .	**(2).** . .	1450.0	-21.3

Source: Investor's Business Daily

Explanatory Notes:

(1) *Face value of bills* to be delivered.

(2) *Settlement price plus yield* always equal 100.00 (94.95 + 5.05 = 100.00). This is an index number, not a price (value). To determine price, you must use the formula below:

$$\begin{aligned}
\text{Price} &= \$1{,}000{,}000 - [(\text{yield} * \$1{,}000{,}000 * 90)/360] \\
&= \$1{,}000{,}000 - [(.0505 * \$1{,}000{,}000 * 90)/360] \\
&= \$1{,}000{,}000 - 12{,}625 \\
&= \$987{,}375
\end{aligned}$$

where we assume delivery of 90-day bills.

Figure 9-15 is an example of an index futures contract quotations.

FIGURE 9-15: INDEX FUTURES QUOTATIONS

Season High	Low (1)	Open Interest	Open	High	Low	Close	(2) Chg.
DJ INDUSTRIAL (CBOT)		$10 X	Dow Jones Industrial Average				
11515	7987.0 Dec 99	21,245	10675	10694	10480	1048	-213.0
11561	10172 Mar 00	1,517	10758	10758	10610	10614	-214.0
11587	10172 Jun 00	47	. . .	. . .		10733	-215.0
11610	8100.0 Dec 00	117	. . .	. . .		10968	-217.0
10210	10210 Dec 01			. . .	. . .	11523	-222.0

Vol. 5,202 open int 22,926 -383

Source: Investor's Business Daily

Explanatory Notes:

(1) *Value of a contract* = 500 x Index. Therefore,

Value = 10 x $10498 = $104,980

(2) *Settlement* is always in cash.

SOURCES OF FURTHER INFORMATION

Guides

There are several guides to help you understand the risks and uses of warrants, options, and futures.

Value Line Options and Convertibles, a book published by Arnold Bernhard and Company, Inc. (711 Third Avenue, New York, NY 10017), presents basic price and maturity information on warrants, options, and convertibles. It also computes such measures as price volatility (in the case of a warrant) and payback years and current yield (in the case of convertible issues).

"Understanding the Risks and Uses of Listed Options" is a 50-page booklet, written with the premise that options are not for everyone, that gives a plain language explanation of the "risk-reward" arithmetic of some of the most common options trading strategies. The AMEX, the CBOT, the NYSE, the Pacific Stock Exchange, the Philadelphia Stock Exchange, and the Options Clearing Corporation have jointly prepared this booklet. A copy can be obtained by writing to the Consumer Information Center, Pueblo, CO 81009.

"Before Trading Commodities—Get the Facts," a 9-page booklet prepared by CFTC (2033 K Street, NW, Washington, DC 20581) is an easy-to-read guide to commodity futures investing.

"Understanding Opportunities and Risks in Futures Trading," a 45-page booklet published by the National Futures Association (200 West Madison St., Suite 1600, Chicago, IL 60606) gives a plain language explanation on opportunities and risks associated with futures investing. It can be obtained by writing to the Consumer Information Center, Pueblo, CO 81009.

The Commodity Yearbook runs feature articles covering commodities or issues currently in the forefront of commodity trading. It also covers each traded commodity from alcohol to zinc. For example, corn is covered in six pages. The first page describes the corn crop and occurrences for the current year, and the next five give data in tabular form for the last

13 years. The book is supplemented three times a year by the *Commodity Yearbook Statistical Abstract.*

Other publications about commodities come from main-line brokerage houses and specialty commodity brokers. In addition, the commodities exchanges publish educational booklets and newsletters. The International Monetary Market (IMM) publishes the IMM Weekly Report, which discusses the interest rate markets, gold, and selected cash market information such as the federal funds rate and the prime rate. The Chicago Board of Trade (CBT) publishes the Interest Rate Futures Newsletter.

Chart Services and Software

There are many printed chart services, including:

Future Charts
Commodity Trend Service, (800) 331-1069 or (407) 694-0960.

Also, there are many computer software programs for futures analysis and charting service, including:

Strategist (DOS)
Iotinomics Corp., (800) 255-3374 or (801) 466-2111

Futures Pro (Windows)
Essex Trading Co., (800) 726-2140 or (708) 416-3530

Futures Markets Analyzer (DOS)
Investment Tools, Inc., (702) 851-1157

Commodities and Futures Software Package
Foreign Exchange Software Package (DOS)
Programmed Press, (516) 599-6527

APPENDIX 9-A: USEFUL WEB SITES

Web Address	Primary Focus
Tfc-charts.w2d.com	Futures quotations
www. cboe.com	The home page for the Chicago Board Options Exchange
www. cbot.com	The home page for the Chicago Board of Trade
www. kcbt.com	The home page for the Kansas City Board of Trade
www. options-iri.com/options/basic/basic.htm	An excellent comprehensive site for learning about options
www. adtrading.com	Applied Derivatives Trading magazine has articles on options and other derivatives; its Beginners Corner is for new investors
www. pacificex.com/options	Good information on specific options, such as LEAPS and index options
www. optionscentral.com	Both education and trading material, as well as links to other option sites
www. worldlinkfutures.com/trad.htm	Provides and electronic course on futures and options for beginners
www. eftc/gov/cftc_information.html	This CTFC site has information on the regulation and trading of futures
www. ahandyguide.com/cat1/f/f263/htm	Provides multiple links to a variety of Web sites on futures trading
www. margil.com/mrg1101.htm	Educational resources and links on futures trading

Chapter 10
TANGIBLE INVESTMENTS

Investing in tangibles like real estate, precious metals, and collectibles is considered an inflation hedge. Real estate still provides some tax shelters. Collectibles include coins, stamps, baseball cards, and antiques. This chapter discusses:

- The advantages and pitfalls of real estate investing

- Indirect forms of investing in real estate, such as real estate investment trusts (REITs), limited partnerships, and mortgage-backed securities

- Sources of information about real estate

- Basics of precious metals

- Sources of information on collectibles

REAL ESTATE

The kinds of real estate you can invest in include:

- Undeveloped land

- Residential rental property (ranging from single family houses to multi-unit apartments)

- Commercial property (*e.g.,* office buildings, shopping centers, and industrial property)

- Real estate investment trusts (REITs)

Your own home is not considered an investment property.

In choosing a real estate investment, consider:

- Location

- Method of financing the purchase of the property

- Before-tax cash flow

- After-tax cash flow

- Vacancy rate for rental property

- Gain or loss for tax purposes

- Management problems

The I.D.E.A.L. Investment?

It has often said that real estate is the IDEAL investment. Each of the five letters in the acronym stands for an advantage real estate has as an investment:

- "I" is for *interest deduction* (it could also mean *inflation* hedge or *income tax benefits*).

- "D" is for *depreciation.* The building on your land depreciates in book value each year and you can deduct this depreciation from your taxable gross income. (This is true only for investment property, not residential.)

- "E" is for *equity buildup.* This is like putting money in the bank: As you amortize a mortgage, the value of your equity investment rises steadily. With income-producing property, your tenants help you build your estate.

- "A" is for *appreciation:* Your property value (hopefully) goes up every year—though this is not guaranteed.

- "L" is for *leverage.* When you buy a house, you make a down payment of, say, 10% and you borrow the balance. From the beginning, you get the benefit of all 100% even though you put up only 10% of your own money. You're maximizing return with other people's money (OPM). The use of mortgage plus OPM means that you can use small amounts of cash to gain control of large investments and earn large returns on the cash invested.

You could also add the following advantages of investing in real estate:

- *Tax-free refinancing:* Mortgage proceeds even from refinancing are not taxable income to you. Therefore, refinancing is a way to recover your cash investment and in some cases, you profit tax-free.

- *Pride of ownership.* You may find greater personal satisfaction in owning property than stock certificates.

- *Investment and consumption.* Certain types of real estate, such as land and vacation homes, can serve both as investments and as sources of pleasure.

Disadvantages of Real Estate

Real estate investing is not free from problems. Watch out of:

- *High transaction costs,* such as brokerage commissions and closing expenses. These costs eat up short-term profits.

- *Negative cash flow* with little down (too much leverage). In jargon, we call it the alligator.

- *Balloon payments*: The balloon payment is the unpaid balance of a mortgage loan paid off in a lump sum at the end of the loan term. This is typically a large amount. If you cannot make the final payment of refinance, you lose the property.

- *Limited marketability:* Lack of a central market or exchange makes real estate investments less liquid than, say, stocks.

- *Management headaches,* such as unreliable tenants or high professional management fees.

  WARNING: *If you might need your money in a hurry, do not invest in real estate.*

Enhancing the Value of Real Estate

You may enhance the value of real estate by:

- Buying below market

- Making cosmetic improvements

- Getting beneficial zoning changes

- Making financing available

- Increasing rents

- Subdividing the property

However, watch out for schemes that lack economic reality. A beginning investor in real estate should keep the following in mind:

- Buy a property you can easily manage.

- Buy a property at a price you can afford.

- Select a good location, preferably an "emerging" attractive area.

- Buy a residential property containing from one to four units. A single-family house is generally preferable to start with.

- Buy a property that's in good condition.

- If a property needs work, make sure the problems are "curable" at a cost below the incremental value of the improvements.

- Try to buy a property that will generate revenue to cover your annual cash outlay.

NOTE: Since real estate is typically not a liquid investment, maintain at least three months' living expenses in liquid funds as a precaution in case of emergency.

Indirect Ways to Invest in Real Estate

In some situations, a direct investment in real estate is impractical, and yet you may be aware of the advantages of a real estate investment and want some of its qualities in an investment portfolio. There are three indirect ways to invest in real estate through pooled real estate investment arrangements: REITs, limited partnerships, and mortgage-based investments.

Real Estate Investment Trusts

Like closed-end mutual funds, REIT's are traded on the stock exchanges and in the OTC market. REITs invest money they obtain from selling shares in diversified real estate or mortgage portfolios rather than stocks or bonds.

As long as REITs distribute 95% of their profit to shareholders, they are exempt from corporate taxes on income or capital gains. Since REIT earnings are not taxed before they are distributed, you get a larger percentage of the profits than with stocks. REIT yields are traditionally high. The other pros and cons of REITs are summarized in Figure 10-1.

FIGURE 10-1: WHAT YOU SHOULD KNOW ABOUT REITs

Where to buy:	Stockbrokers
Pluses:	• Dividend income with competitive yields·
	• Potential appreciation in price·
	• A liquid investment in an area that's otherwise illiquid
	• A means of portfolio diversification, with participation in a variety of real estate types with minimal cash outlay
Minuses:	• Possible glut in real estate or weakening demand·
	• Market risk: possible decline in share price
Safety:	Low
Liquidity:	Very high; shares are traded on major exchanges or OTC and therefore can be bought and sold at any time.
Taxes:	Investor's income is subject to tax upon sale of REIT shares.

Picking a REIT

Before buying shares in any REIT, be sure to read the latest annual report, the Value Line Investment Survey, Audit Investments Newsletter, or Realty Stock Review. For each REIT you're considering, look at:

- *Track record:* How long has it been in business? Is the dividend record solid?

- *Cash flow:* Make sure that operating cash flow covers the dividend.

- *Adequate diversification:* Beware of REITs investing in only one type of property.

- *Property location:* Beware of concentration in economically depressed areas.

- *Type of property:* Nursing homes, some apartment buildings, and shopping centers are presently favored; "seasoned" properties are preferred.

- *Leverage:* Leverage influences the safety of the investment and the cash flow it generates. It can also magnify the capital gains and losses from rising and declining real estate property values.

- *Condition of the properties:* Avoid REITs that do not invest in upgrading properties.

- *Earnings:* Monitor earnings regularly; be prepared to sell when the market or property location weakens.

Sources of REIT Information

Since REITs are traded on the national exchanges, you can find out about them from many of the same sources you would use for listed stocks, such as *S&P's Stock Guide* and *Value Line Investment Surveys. Moody's Bank and Finance Manual,* published annually with twice-weekly supplements and available on CD-ROM, gives detailed financial information on 109 REITs. The National Association of Real Estate Investment Trusts (202-785-8717) publishes the *REIT Fact Book.* This annual reviews 25 years of the REIT industry: who, when, and how. It contains historical and year-end statistics and current industry information.

Limited Partnerships

A limited partnership (or syndicate) is another way for you to buy into real estate projects too large for a single investor. For example, to buy or build a large project like an apartment complex or a shopping mall, a group of investors form a partnership, each putting up a specified amount of money.

Syndicates have both general and limited partners. The *general* partner (or partners) usually originates and manages the project for a fee; the *limited* partners invest funds and are liable only for the amount of their investment. A limited partnership allows you to:

- Invest in part of a larger, more "prestigious" real estate project than you could otherwise afford to do.

- Obtain professional management of the project.

- Obtain a tax-sheltered cash flow.

- Diversity your investments by investing in several limited partnerships.

- Avoid the double taxation of distributions faced by a corporate structure. A limited partnership does not have to pay taxes on the income it receives as long as it is passed through.

The disadvantages of a limited partnership are:

- High management costs (typically 15% to 30%)

- Illiquidity from lack of a secondary market, unlike, for example, REITs. You would be likely to lose money if you wanted to sell your interest before the partnership liquidates its assets.

    NOTE: In recent years a new securities market—the limited partnership secondary market—has emerged. See chapter 11 for further discussion.

Mortgage-Backed Investments

A third way to get into the real estate market is through mortgage-backed securities. A mortgage-backed security is a share in an organized pool of residential mortgages, the principal and interest payments of which are passed through to shareholders, usually monthly. The several kinds of mortgage-backed securities include:

- *Ginnie Maes:* The Government National Mortgage Association (GNMA) is the largest pass-through security issuer. It packages and sells pools of Federal Housing Administration (FHA) and Veterans Administration (VA) mortgages.

- *Freddie Macs:* The Federal Home Loan Mortgage Corporation (FHLMC) is the major issuer of participation certificates (PCs). It offers pools containing conventional mortgages. Though government-sponsored, it has no government guarantees.

- *Fannie Maes:* The Federal National Mortgage Association offers a pass-through security like a PC. A privately owned corporation sponsored by the government, Fannie Mae also has no government guarantees.

- *Collaterized Mortgage Obligations* are mortgage-backed securities that separate mortgage pools into short-, medium-, and long-term portions.

Mortgage-backed securities enjoy liquidity and a high degree of safety because they are either government-sponsored or otherwise insured. Most of them are sold, however, in minimum amounts of $25,000—out of reach for most small investors.

PRECIOUS METALS

Investments in gold, silver, and other precious metals have gained popularity in the last decade. They offer:

- A hedge against inflation

- An opportunity to diversity holdings

• Psychic pleasure

This type of defensive investment doesn't produce current income. Further, it's not easily converted into cash. Appreciation may take years. Resale may not be easy.

Gold and silver are two highly volatile tangible assets in which price movements often run counter to events in the economy and the world. Bad news is good news (and vice versa) for precious metal investors. Gold and silver may be generally bought in bullion or bulk form, as coins, in the commodities futures market, indirectly through securities of firms specializing in gold or silver mining, or through mutual funds. The little-known metal palladium has also been lighting up Wall Street as a potential new energy source.

Many experts agree:

• *Platinum* is perhaps the most desirable precious metal because it has the greatest opportunity to yield substantial profits, and it's the most liquid.

• *Gold* is a good investment because it's the world's monetary metal; if inflation or monetary crisis hits, it will be the first to move.

• *Silver* is the metal for the long-term investor, for people who are willing to wait for it to go up.

  NOTE: Precious metals can move violently in response to news events that could alter supply or demand; platinum and palladium are the prime recent examples.

Figure 10-2 summarizes the basics on precious metals in terms of their sources, uses, and the news events that are likely to affect their prices.

GEMS AND COLLECTIBLES

Precious gems and other collectibles like art, antiques, stamps, Chinese ceramics, and rare books have attracted the attention of investors. Though profits can be very high, don't invest in these tangibles unless you have considerable product and market knowledge.

FIGURE 10-2: WHAT DRIVES STRATEGIC METALS

Principal sources and uses of strategic metals, and news events that are likelyto affect their prices.

Metal	Sources	Uses	Event
Gold*	South Africa, Chile, Australia	Investment, jewelry, hedge against infla-tion, dental, orna-mentation	Monetary instability, Third World debt default, Middle East confrontation
Silver*	Mexico, Russia, Peru, Canada, US, Australia	Photography, elec-tronics, jewelry, invest-ment, ster-ling, mirrors	Inflation spurs its use as "poor man's gold"
Platinum*	South Africa, Russia, Canada	Catalytic convert-ers, aerospace, oil refining, investment, jewelry, coins	Inflation, use as a conductor in Ford's catalytic converters
Palladium*	Russia, Canada, South Africa, Australia	Aerospace, dental, catalytic converters, possibly nuclear fusion	Government unrest, nuclear fusion news
Aluminum	US, Russia,Canada, Japan	Building materials, packaging, trans-portation	Mining strikes, tech-nological replace-ment (*e.g.,* low cost tubing)
Nickel	Russia, Canada, Australia	Electroplating, stainless and heat-resistant steel alloy for copper	US confrontation with Russia, tech-nological replace-ment
Cooper	US, Chile, Russia, Peru, Mexico, Zam-bia, Zaire, Canada	Electrical tubing and wiring, alloy, construction piping, jewelry, pots and pans	Mining strike or political unrest, par-ticularly in Chile or Peru
Lead	Russia, US, Canada, Australia	Batteries, solder, gas additive, ammunition	Increased use of lead-free gas in Europe, battery source industry strikes
Zinc	Russia, US, Canada, Australia	Galvanizer in paints, metals and alu-minum, brass alloy	Mining strikes

*Precious metals, unlike base metals, are in limited supply on a per tonnage or ore bassis. Precious metals do not corrode easily and have high endurance.

Source: Monex International, *A-Mark Precious Metals*

Tangibles are inflation hedges. In the 1970s oil, gold, U.S. coins, silver, and stamps had the highest compound returns, above 20%. From 1980 to 1985, a period of rapid disinflation, securities like bonds, stocks, and T-bills had higher returns than every category of tangible assets. In fact, gold and silver suffered huge losses (more than 11%) in the early 1980s.

Sources of Information on Collectibles

Periodicals: Much information on collectibles may be obtained from the *Wall Street Journal* and periodicals like *Money* and *Business Week.* The *Collector/Investor* also provides excellent articles on the collectible market, as do specialization periodicals such as *Antique Monthly, Coin Prices, Coin World, Coins, Linn's Stamp News, Numismatic News, sports Collector's Digest, Stanley Gibbons' Stamp Catalog,* and *World Coin News.*

Scott Stamp Catalog: The Scott Publishing Company has long served the philatelic (stamp) market. Its well-known *Scott Stamp Catalog* carries price data and pictures with descriptions. Recently Scott has added a *Stamp Market Update,* a quarterly report on current trends featuring prices of major U.S. stamps and popular foreign stamps, information for specialized collectors, investment opportunities and strategies suggested by recognized experts, and specialized articles, statistical tables, and graphs. The Scott Index values for "fine" stamps are used as a basis for comparison in a study of quality-adjusted rates in stamp auctions.

Kovel's Antiques and Collectibles Price List is an 800-page comprehensive guide to prices of various antiques and collectibles. The 23rd edition prepared by Ralph and Terry Kovel is published by Crown Publishers in New York City.

A Guide Book of United States Coins is the best seller for coin hobbyists. Also called the Red Book, it features the latest price and auction records, official A.N.A. Grading Standards, value changes from the previous year, and a bullion table for instant updating of gold and silver coin prices. It's published by Western Publishing Co., Inc. (M.S. 438, Racine, WI 53401).

World Coins, published by Krause Publications (700 E. State St., Iola, WI, 54990), provides a comprehensive listing of all world legal tender, current market valuation, and identification numbers, with cross-referencing.

Leonard's Annual Price Index of Art Auctions, published by Auction Index, Inc. (30 Valentine Park, Newton, MA 02165), reveals the shifting who, what, where, and how much of every art auction sale conducted in America by the 74 major auction houses the previous year.

10th Blue Book: Dolls & Values, prepared by Jan Foulke (Hobby House Press, Inc., Dept. CX, 900 Frederick St., Cumberland, MD 21502-3770, 301-759-3770), contains descriptions and value estimate ranges for 1,600 antique, collectible, and modern dolls, along with their photographs. It's considered the "bible" of doll collecting. Hobby House Press also published numerous other books on dolls, including *Cloth Dolls, Ginny 1991 Price Guide, French Dolls, Madame Alexander Price Guide for Dolls #16, and Collector's Encyclopedia of Dolls* (in 2 vols.).

For more about investing in dolls, you can also write to the National Antique Doll Dealers Association (Box 143, Wellesly Hills, MA 02181).

APPENDIX 10-A: USEFUL WEB SITES

The following are examples of general information Web sites that can be used to learn the basics of real estate investing.

Web Address	Primary Focus
www.101percent.com/education/ business/investing/realestate.html	Information primarily on personal real estate purchasing, including access to amortiza tion and other interactive calculators
www.austincoins.com/srv08.htm	Information on collecting old coins
www.ccim.com	The Commercial Real Estate Network has general information about the real estate market and certain professional certifica tions
www.nareit.com	The National Association of Real Estate Investment Trusts has a variety of informa tion on REITs and a screening model for selecting an REIT
www.wealthnetwork.com	Dedicating to providing a variety of informa tion on real estate

Chapter 11
TAX-ADVANTAGED INVESTMENTS

Investments designed specifically to provide tax benefits can be especially excellent investment vehicles for retirement planning. They include limited partnerships, various plans such as individual retirement accounts (IRAs), and annuities.

THE TAX RULES THAT APPLY

Some important tax rules are that:

- Portfolio income is considered either "investment income" or loss and capital gain or loss. Expenses associated with earning investment income are generally deductible only to the extent of investment income. Capital losses are generally deductible only to the extent of capital gains.

- Dividend income is fully taxed.

- A capital gain is the excess of net proceeds on sale over the initial cost of stock owned more than one year. A capital loss is the opposite. Net capital gains (capital gains less capital losses) are taxed at the lower of your tax rate or the maximum capital gains tax rate (varies with investments and income).

- Net capital losses are tax-deductible up to $3,000 ($1,500 for married individuals filing separately). Anything over $3,000 can be carried forward to be deducted in future years.

- Capital losses reduce ordinary income. An ordinary gain or loss results from the sale of stock owned less than one year. The tax rate for ordinary and capital gains or losses is the same under present law.

- Gains and losses from the sale of securities are reported on the trade date (the date on which you sell the stock) not the settlement date (three business days later, when the broker pays you). The settlement date may be in the following tax year.

- A way to delay the tax on the gain from the sale of stock, while assuring that gain is to sell short. You may sell short close to year-end, delivering the security to the brokerage firm and reporting the gain the following year.

- "Passive" income is income received from real estate investments and limited partnership interests. Expenses associated with managing real estate or the limited partnership are deductible only against passive income.

- The wash sale rule is that the IRS will disallow the loss if a position is sold at a loss and repurchased within 30 days of the sale date. Furthermore, the IRS considers a transaction to be a wash sale if an equivalent security such as a convertible is purchased; if a call option, warrants or rights are purchased; or if the customer sells a deep-in-the-money put.

If you rely excessively on tax preference items to reduce your regular tax liability, the alternative minimum tax (AMT) requires you to add back the preference items to taxable income and applies a flat 24% tax rate to the "alternative" income.

LIMITED PARTNERSHIPS

Limited partnerships (syndicates), now usually referred to as direct investments or private investments, are an investment strategy traditionally used for tax benefits. They can be used to invest in real estate, oil and gas, equipment leasing, and cable partnerships, and the like. For example, real estate partnerships (see chapter 10) enable investors to buy into projects too costly for one investor. A group of investors each invest money to buy a large project like a shopping mall or an apartment house.

Tax relief comes with real estate because the investor can deduct depreciation, mortgage interest, and other expenses. When the investment is made through a limited partnership or similar entity there is no double taxation of the profits. Unfortunately, the tax laws generally consider real estate to be a passive activity. As a result, any losses generated by real estate cannot be used to offset income from activities other than similar passive activities. You may be able to deduct up to $25,000 of losses generated by real estate if you have materially participated in the real estate's management (*e.g.,* selected tenants or negotiated leases and other contracts). Limited partners do not generally qualify for this provision.

There are both general and limited partners. The general partner typically originates and manages the property for compensation. The limited partners are liable just for their investments.

The advantages of limited partnerships are that they:

- Enable you to invest in large projects with professional management.

- Offer possible price appreciation.

- Let you invest in different limited partnerships because the investment required is traditionally smaller, thereby diversifying your investments.

- Help you obtain tax-sheltered cash flow.

- Avoid the double taxation of distributions faced by a corporate structure. A limited partnership functions as a pass-through agency, so it doesn't have to pay taxes on the income it receives.

The disadvantages, or risks, of syndicates are:

- *High management fees and expenses:* Limited partnerships typically assess management fees against initial investments but may also contract for part of the profit expected from activities in the program.

NOTE: Review especially the Use of Proceeds section in a limited partnership prospectus before investing. Total fees should not exceed 15%. Also carefully read the Sharing Arrangement section. In some cases, the general partner is entitled to a substantial share of capital gains and other income, although you and the other limited partners put up all or most of the money.

- *Complexity:* It's difficult for average investors to understand the fine print in terms of the complex risks and rewards associated with limited partnerships.

- *Illiquidity:* There is no active secondary market, although a limited partnership secondary market has been emerging in recent years. Secondary market liquidity softens what has perhaps been the principal negative of limited partnership investing—the long-term illiquid nature of the security. You can get information on the limited partnership secondary market from:

- *Partnership Profiles* (P.O. Box 7938, Dallas, TX 75209; 817-488-6115, which provides quarterly research reports on actively traded partnerships.

- *The Perspective,* a newsletter that carries news and analysis of the partnership market including secondary market trading prices.

- *The Stanger Report: A Guide to Partnership Investing* (Robert A. Stanger & Company, 1129 Broad Street, Shrewsbury, NJ 07702-4790; 908-389-3600, which reviews the partnership market and list both partnerships traded in the secondary market and new partnerships currently being marketed.

Figure 11-1 shows how limited partnerships are announced.

Explanatory Notes

(1) *The total number* of units being offered for sale.

(2) *Name* of the limited partnership.

(3) *The type of security being offered:* Limited partnerships can have different classes of partnership interests.

FIGURE 11-1: LIMITED PARTNERSHIP ANNOUNCEMENT

October 15, 1999 **(1)**

2,600,000 Common Units

 **(2)**

Plains All American Pipeline, L.P.

Representing Limited Partner Interests
(3)
Price $18 per Unit
(4)

(5)

(6) Salomon Smith Barney
Goldman, Sachs & Co.
A.G. Edwards & Sons, Inc.
First Union Securities, Inc.

Plains All American Pipeline, L.P. is a publicly traded Delaware limited partnership engaged in interstate and intrastate crude oil transportation, terminalling and storage, as well as crude oil gathering and marketing activities.

(7)

This announcement constitutes neither an offer to sell nor a solicitation of an offer to buy these securities. The offering is made only by the Prospectus, copies of which may be obtained in any State from such of the underwriters and others as may lawfully offer these securities in such State.

Source: Wall Street Journal, October 15, 1999

(4) *The price* at which one unit of the partnership will sell (or has been sold) in advance of its issuance. Demand on the secondary market will determine the price, as is the case for all outstanding issues. If there are more offers to buy than there are units to go around in the initial offering, the security is called a "hot issue," and the market price will rise as soon as the units begin trading.

(5) *The business of the limited partnership:* The description notes that the partnership interests will be publicly traded; limited partnership interests often are not.

(6) *The investment bankers or underwriters* that make up the syndicate bringing out the issue. Those with the largest number of units to sell are listed first, and in bolder type than those with a relatively minor stake. If you wish to acquire the security before it starts trading on the secondary market, you must get the units through one of these firms or a firm contracted by one of them to sell the securities.

(7) *Standard disclaimer:* An offer to sell stock can legally be made only through a prospectus. In principle, tombstones are only for information purposes; often the stock has already been sold out.

Oil and Gas Limited Partnerships

These include:

- Drilling programs: exploratory (wildcat) drilling in an unproven area and development drilling in or near proven fields.

- Income programs: acquiring producing properties.

- Oil and gas programs: these may deduct intangible drilling costs and a depletion allowance" reflecting the using up of estimated reserves.

Any tax breaks allocated to the limited partners may be used only to offset passive income, and tax breaks are "recaptured" by the IRS when the asset is sold. For example, if tangible property is sold, all depreciation is recaptured and taxed.

RETIREMENT PLANS

Retirement plans are either *tax qualified* or *non-tax qualified.* Contributions to tax qualified plans are deductible from your taxable income. Earnings in the plan build up, tax-deferred. Distributions taken from the plan are taxable when taken.

Contributions to non-tax qualified plans are not deductible from your taxable income. Earnings in the plan build up, tax-deferred. When distributions are taken, only the portion of the distribution that represents the build-up is taxable.

Tax-deferred investments are important to any retirement planning. Earnings, including dividends and capital gains, compound tax-deferred until they are distributed. To see how tax deferred growth can make a significant difference over the years, consider the following example.

EXAMPLE 1

Assume that your IRA account will earn 8% return on your investment annually and that your current income tax rate is 15%, while you will be taxed at a 31% rate 30 years from now when you retire. If you make annual tax-deferred contributions of $2,000 for 30 years, you could build a nest egg of $226,566; the same investment in a taxable account may produce $145,376.

Two prime receipts of pension funds income are company and individual plans.

Company-Sponsored Pension Plans

These include:

- Qualified company retirement plans

- Profit-sharing plans

- 401(k) salary reduction plans

- Tax-sheltered annuities (TSA)

- Employee stock ownership plans (ESOP)

- Simplified employee pension plan (SEP)

Individual retirement plans include:

- Individual retirement accounts (IRAs)

- Keoghs

- Annuities

Each of these types of pension plans is now discussed.

Qualified Company Retirement Plans

The IRS allows a company to contribute to a pension plan that is *qualified. Qualified* means the plan satisfies certain criteria making contributions tax deductible. Investment income also accumulates tax-free.

- *Profit-sharing plans* are defined contribution plans, but unlike with other qualified plans, you need not retire to obtain payments. Note that because contributions are made only if there is profit, there is uncertainty as to the amount of the actual retirement benefit.

- *401(k) salary reduction plans* postpone part of your salary until you retire. Each salary payment is lower. Employers often match a percentage of an employee's contributions (50% matches are common at many companies). With a 401(k), you can put away up to $10,500 tax-deferred each year. Interest accumulates tax-free until you retire. The untaxed compounding effect enhances your retirement savings.

EXAMPLE 2

You save 15% of your $60,000 annual salary in a 401(k) plan.

	Take-home Pay with 401(k) Plan	Take-home Pay without 401(k) Plan
Base pay	$ 60,000	$60,000
Salary reduction	9,000	None
Taxable income	$ 51,000	$60,000
Federal and FICA taxes	10,000	12,000
Savings after taxes	None	9,000
Take-home pay	$41,000	$39,000
Incremental take-home pay under plan = $2,000		

- *Tax-sheltered annuities (TSA)* are available is you work for a non-profit entity. It's like a 401(k), but you may take out money at any age and not incur a tax penalty, though withdrawals are subject to ordinary tax rates.

- *Employee stock ownership plans (ESOP)* are stock-bonus plans in which employer contributions are tax-deductible.

- *The simplified employee pension (SEP)*, sometimes referred to as a "super IRA," is a plan for an employer who can't afford or doesn't want the administrative burden of establishing a Keogh plan (discussed below); the employer makes annual payments for the employee to an IRA established by the employee. A contribution made to a SEP nonforfeitable: The money belongs to the employee. If employment is terminated, the entire balance in the SEP account belongs to the employee. As with most qualified plans, employers can take a deduction for contributions made to a SEP plan. SEPs have higher contribution limits than 401(k)s: You may contribute up to 15% of each employee's annual compensation or $30,000, whichever is less, to a SEP accounts.

When you retire, how much you will have depends on such factors as interest rates and whether you've placed funds for the best return. The following example illustrates the power of tax-deferred compounding.

EXAMPLE 3

Assume a $2,000 annual tax-deferred investment at the beginning of each year, an 8% fixed return, and a 39.6% tax bracket. After 30 years, the after-tax dollar amount upon withdrawal at retirement (assuming that contributions were not deductible) would be $226,566, while a taxable investment would have grown to only $129,107 (see Figure 11-2).

A couple of percentage points mean a lot. A $50,000 tax-free pension fund earning 6% will grow to $287,150 after 30 years. The same amount invested at 9% will give you $663,400 after 30 years.

EXAMPLE 4

You invest $10,000. At 10%, 12%, or 15%, what is accumulated after 30 years?

FIGURE 11-2: THE POWER OF TAX-DEFERRED GROWTH

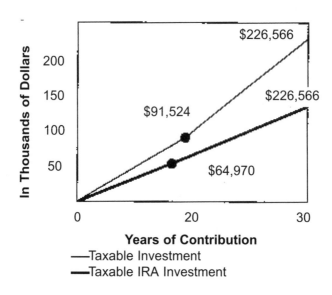

Years of Contribution
—Taxable Investment
—Taxable IRA Investment

	10%	12%	15%
Amount invested	$ 10,000	$ 10,000	$ 10,000
Future value of $1	x 17.449	x 29.960	x 66.212
Compound amount after 30 years	$174,490	$299,600	$662,120

Even if your pension is professionally managed, you may select different investments based on rate of return and risk. You may apportion your savings, with the privilege of periodic switching, say from stocks to bonds. The interest rate should exceed the inflation rate. Compound tax-free interest will make your pension grow.

Individual Retirement Accounts

If you are not covered through a company pension plan or want to save privately, you may set up your own IRA, Keogh, or annuity plan.

The IRA is a retirement savings plan that individuals set up themselves. If you do not have a company retirement plan, you can take an IRA tax deduction from adjusted gross income (AGI) of up to $2,000. A married couple may contribute up to $4,000 provided each earns $2,000 (the maximum joint contribution is $2,250 if one spouse does not work). If you work for yourself, you can establish a Keogh or similar plan that has higher contribution limits. IRA contributions accumulate tax-free and are also either tax deductible or exempt from your income. Several things to remember:

- An individual covered by an employer's pension plan, or whose spouse is covered by such a plan (assuming the spouses file a joint tax return) may qualify for only a partial deduction or no deduction based on AGI. The deduction phases out (allowable deductions are reduced $1 for each $5 increase in income) as the taxpayer's income increases over a specified amount; eventually it's eliminated (see Figure 11-3).

FIGURE 11-3

Filing Status	Deduction Is Reduced if AGI Is:	Deduction Is Eliminated if AGI Is:
Single, or head of household	$25,000 - $35,000	$35,000 or more
Married--joint return, or qualifying widow(er)	$40,000 - $50,000	$50,000 or more
Married--separate return	$ 0 - $10,000	$10,000 or more

EXAMPLE 5

You are single and have an adjusted gross income of $28,000. You can deduct an IRA contribution of:

$2,000 - [($28,000 - $25,000)/$5 x $1] = $1,400

- Withdrawals before age 59½ incur a 10% penalty except under special circumstances; the premature withdrawal is also taxed as ordinary income.

- Distributions need not begin until the age of 70½. If you don't need the income, let the account accumulate past age 59½; this can add considerably to the corpus of an IRA.

- If you don't start withdrawing at 70½, you incur a 50% penalty on the minimum amount that should have been withdrawn.

- If you're over 70½ years of age, you are not allowed to contribute to an IRA.

Keogh Plans

A Keogh pension plan, also called an HR 10 plan, is tax-deferred for self-employed people who satisfy specified criteria. It can take three forms: a profit sharing plan, a money purchase pension plan, or a combination of both. The maximum contribution rate is 25% of "after Keogh deduction" earnings or $30,000, whichever is less. Thus, the effective contribution rate is 20%.

EXAMPLE 6

Net earnings	$100,000	
Keogh contribution	20,000	(effective 20%)
After Keogh earnings	$ 80,000	

The Keogh contribution of $20,000 is 25% of the "after Keogh deduction" earnings of $80,000.

Annuities

Annuities are insurance contracts. You can pay a single large premium, an annual premium, or flexible premiums and at retirement, you obtain periodic payments for a stated time (the maximum being a lifetime) or take periodic withdrawals. The periodic withdrawals have limits set by the insurance company. Payments accumulate tax-free and are subject to tax only when withdrawn, when your tax rate is likely to be lower. Annuity payments begin at retirement.

- **Fixed (Guaranteed) Annuities** (see Figure 11-4) guarantee your principal plus a minimum interest for a year or more. There are **no** capital gains (or appreciation) potential with fixed annuities. There is low risk with this policy. You get both a minimum interest rate and an extra interest rate based on prevailing rates in the market.

FIGURE 11-4: FEATURES OF FIXED ANNUITIES

Tax-deferred income	Yes
Price stability	Yes
Capital gain (or loss) potential	No
Different payout options	Yes
Different payment options	Yes
Contribution limits	No (except based on age)
Source of funds	Not restricted to earned income
Choice of underlying investments	No
Federal deposit insurance	No
Surrender charge	Yes
IRS early withdrawal penalty	Yes
Mandatory withdrawals	Typically by age 85
Rate-guaranteed periods	For 1, 3, 5, 7, or 10 Years

Like a bond or a bond fund, a fixed annuity not be a satisfactory inflation hedge, and may therefore subject you to the risk of reducing purchasing power after retirement.

- **Variable Annuities** (see Figure 11-5) have no guarantees as fixed
  annuities do. The policy values, variable rates, changes with the performance of an underlying investment fund, much like a mutual
  fund within a family of funds. You carry the investment risk. Many
  insurance companies let you change to a different fund of a variable
  type and you can change the percentage mix of the funds as often as
  the annuity contract allows. You pay taxes on the amount distributed from the capital appreciation of the annuity value.

FIGURE 11-5   FEATURES OF VARIABLE ANNUITIES

Tax-deferred income	Yes
Price stability	No
Capital gain (or loss) potential	Yes
Different payout options	Yes
Different payment options	Yes
Contribution limits	No (Except based on age)
Source of funds	Not restricted to earned income
Choice of underlying investments	Yes
Federal deposit insurance	No
Grace period	Yes
Surrender charge	Yes
IRS early withdrawal penalty	Yes
Mandatory withdrawals	Typically by age 85
Rate-guaranteed periods	No

The main *advantages* of annuities are:

- Tax-deferred compounding of interest.

- Amount of annual contributions unrestricted, unlike retirement plans.

- Another form of savings plan.

The *disadvantages* of annuities are:

- The commission is often high (usually 7% or 8%).

- You can't withdraw funds before age 59½ without incurring a tax penalty. Also, the insurance carrier imposes penalties called surrender charges if you cash in the policy early. However, no penalty would apply if you become disabled or die. (One way to avoid the early withdrawal penalty is to annuitize, taking regular payments for the remainder of your life.) Charges may start around 7% for withdrawals in the first year and phase down by one percentage point each year after that.

- The interest earned may not keep up with or may be less than the return on alternative investment opportunities.

- Annuity income is taxed as income, not as capital gains; this can hurt if you're in a high tax bracket.

- Annuities are non-qualified, except for those that fund pension plans.

The types of annuities include:

- **Life annuity:** The annuity continues for the life of the annuitant. This usually results in the highest periodic payment.

- **Life annuity with period certain:** The annuity covers the life of the annuitant, but if that person dies early, the annuity, payable to another beneficiary, continues for a specified minimum period.

- **Joint and last survivor annuity:** If the annuitant dies, the annuity continues for the life of another person (usually the spouse).

You can invest in variable annuity contracts by making lump-sum investments or by signing a long-term investment contract (contractual plans). The plan custodian is required to send investors a statement of total charges within 60 days after the plan certificate is issued, and inform you of the right to withdraw within 45 days from the date the notice is mailed. Sales charges may be:

- **Front-end load:** Up to 50% of the sales charges may be deducted from the first 12 monthly payments (in equal amounts). If the plan is liquidated within 18 months, you receive a refund of sales charges paid in excess of 15% of the total invested.

- **Spread-load:** Up to 64% of all sales charges over the first four years can be deducted, but no more than 20% in any one year.

Buying Annuities

If you're thinking about buying an annuity:

- Be wary of unusually high "teaser" rates; these are a sign of a financially weak company. Deal with a firm that is financially sound and strong.

- Buy annuities only from highly rated insurance companies. Check them out in *Best's Insurance Reports,* Standard & Poor's, Moody's, or Duff & Phelps publications.

- Diversify among insurance companies to get a blending of rates and maturities. Dozens of mutual fund families manage variable annuity portfolios.

- Evaluate the insurance company's investment performance.

- Consider all service charges as well as contract features and terms.

- Closely review the prospectus.

   NOTE: *For comparison-shopping, refer to the monthly Morningstar Variable Annuity/Life Performance Report, 800-876-5005, and the Lipper Mutual Fund Quarterly on Variable Annuities and Life Accounts that appears in* Barron's.

Is an Annuity Right for You?

Consider an annuity if you:

- Do not have other tax-free pension plans or Keoghs

- Want to be priced to save.

- Want the assurance of a guaranteed check when you retire.

- Aren't comfortable with selecting your own investments.

Don't consider annuities if you:

- Have access to an alternative tax-deferred savings plan.

- Expect to have adequate income and savings from other sources in retirement.

APPENDIX 11-A: USEFUL WEB SITES

The following Internet sites offer critical information about tax-advantaged investments:

Web Address	Primary Focus
www.401k.com/401k/	Fidelity Investments information on 401(K) plans
www.investorguide.com/Retirement.htm#IRAs	Provides multiple links to information about 401(k) and IRA plans, including interactive retirement planning calculators
www.irs.ustrea.gov/prod/cover.html	The home page for the Internal Revenue Service

Chapter 12
INTERNATIONAL
INVESTING

As you learn more about portfolio management and mutual funds, it becomes increasingly clear that there are advantages to holding a broad range of investments. In this chapter, you will see that risk can further be reduced by holding securities issued in foreign markets.

Interest in overseas equities has risen notably in recent years, spurred by the strong performance of markets abroad and the increasing availability to U.S. investors of overseas investment vehicles.

THE ADVANTAGES OF GLOBAL INVESTING

You can derive important benefits from expanding your portfolio beyond your home country: a far greater universe of stocks, potentially greater returns, and an opportunity to reduce risk exposure. Changes in currency relationships, while a double-edged sword, sometimes enhance appreciation and offset part of the impact of price declines in foreign equities.

Broader stock Selection

Global investment gives you a much bigger pool of investment opportunities from which to choose. As Figure 12-1 illustrates, as of June 1994, U.S. stocks accounted for only 36.2 of the world's total stock market capitalization. An investor focused solely on domestic issues would thus miss nearly two-thirds of the investment opportunities in the world.

Possibility of Higher Returns

Non-U.S. stocks now account for more than half the value of all global equity securities. Recent financial studies show that investors who hold a blend of foreign and U.S. stocks receive higher returns—at lower risk— than those who are fully invested in U.S. stocks.

FIGURE 12-1: CAPITALIZATION OF WORLD EQUITY MARKETS
(as of June 1994)

Country	Percentage of the Total
United States	36.2%
Japan	28.9%
Europe	26.4%
Others	8.5%
Total	100.0%

Source: Morgan Stanley Capital International Perspective, June 1994.

Figure 12-2 compares average annual total returns of the major world stock markets (as measured by the Morgan Stanley World Index) for 10 years. Figure 12-4 shows that certain overseas stock markets have out-paced U.S. markets at certain periods. In fact, foreign stocks have led in 14 of the last 23 years, and the U.S. has been the top-performing market only since 1976.

FIGURE 12-2: U.S. AND FOREIGN STOCK RETURNS COMPOUND
ANNUAL RETURN IN U.S. DOLLARS
(annualized over 10-year periods)

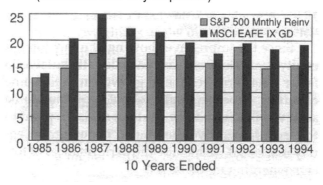

Source: Micropal, Inc.

Since the impressive showing of many foreign equity markets is at least partially attributable to faster long-term economic growth in their home countries, superior returns are, in many cases, likely to continue.

FIGURE 12-3: AVERAGE ANNUAL TOTAL RETURNS BY COUNTRY
(for the period ended 6/30/94)

Country	Percentage Return
Hong Kong	31.42%
Belgium	25.01
Austria	24.05
Netherlands	21.33
Spain	21.13
Switzerland	20.76
France	20.13
Japan	18.81
Italy	18.02
Germany	17.84
Sweden	17.68
United Kingdom	17.39
Australia	15.10
Denmark	15.05
Singapore/Malaysia	13.66
Norway	13.59

Source: Lipper, Inc.

Reduction of Risk

Adding international investments to a portfolio of U.S. securities reduces your risk by diversifying it. International investments are much less influenced by the U.S. economy, and the correlation to U.S. investments is much less. Foreign markets sometimes follow different cycles than the U.S. market, and from each other.

Although foreign stocks can be riskier than domestic issues, supplementing a domestic portfolio with a foreign component can actually reduce your portfolio's overall volatility. The reason is that by being diversified across many different economies that are at different points in the economic cycle, downturns in some markets may be offset by superior performance in others. There is considerable evidence that global diversification reduces systematic risk (beta) because of the relatively low correlation between returns on U.S. and foreign securities.

Figure 12-4 illustrates this, comparing the risk reduction through diversification within the United States to that obtainable through global diversification. A fully diversified U.S. portfolio is only 27% as risky as a typical individual stock, while an globally diversified portfolio appears to be about 12% as risky as a typical individual stock—and about 44% less risky than domestic diversification alone.

Figure 12-5 demonstrates the effect over ten years. Notice how adding a small percentage of foreign stocks to a domestic portfolio actually decreased its overall risk while increasing the overall return. The lowest level of volatility came from a portfolio with about 30% foreign stocks and 70% U.S. stocks. A portfolio with 60% foreign holdings and only 40% U.S. holdings actually approximated the risk of a 100% domestic portfolio, yet the average annual return was more than two percentage points higher.

The Risks

The advantages must be balanced against risks unique to foreign securities: currency and political risks as well as the risks of emerging markets, economies, and companies.

Currency (Foreign Exchange) Risk

When you invest in a foreign market, the return on the foreign investment in terms of the U.S. dollar depends not only on the return on the foreign market but also on the exchange rate between the local currency and the U.S. dollar. Since the exchange rates among major currencies have been volatile in recent years, exchange rate uncertainty has often been mentioned as a potential barrier to international investment.

A strong dollar—meaning that a unit of foreign currency buys fewer dollars—would push down the foreign returns of a U.S. investor.

EXAMPLE 1

You buy bonds of a German firm paying 12% interest. You will earn that rate in marks. What if you're paid in dollars? As Figure 12-6 shows, you must convert marks to dollars before the payout has any value to you.

Suppose the dollar appreciated 10% against the mark during the year after you bought the bonds. (A currency appreciates when acquiring one of its units requires more units of a foreign currency than previously.)

FIGURE 12-4:   RISK REDUCTION TRHOUGH NATIONAL AND
                   INTERNATIONAL DIVERSIFICATION

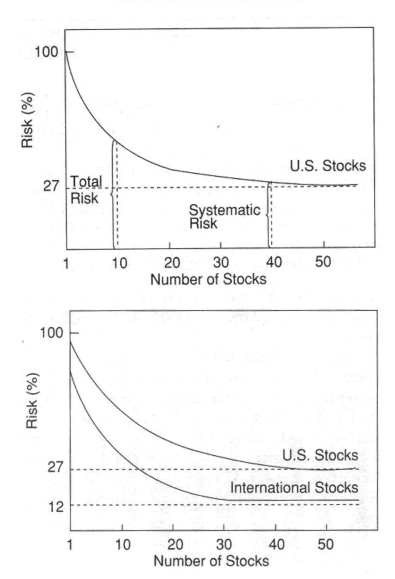

Source: B. Solnik, "Why Not Diversify Internationally Rather Than Domestically?" *Financial Analysts Journal,* July 1974, p.17.

FIGURE 12-5:   HOW FOREIGN STOCKS HAVE BENEFITTED A
                    DOMESTIC PORTFOLIO

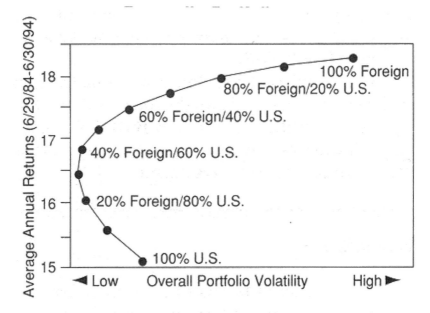

Source: Micropal, Inc.

When you bought, 1 mark acquired .616 dollars; a year later, 1 mark acquired only .554 dollars; at the new exchange rate it would take 1.112 (.616/.554) marks to acquire .616 dollars. Thus, the dollar has appreciated while the mark has depreciated. Your return in dollars is only 10.91%. The adverse movement in the foreign exchange rate—the dollar's appreciation—reduced your actual yield.

FIGURE 12-6: EXCHANGE RISK AND FOREIGN INVESTMENT YIELD

Transaction	Marks	Exchange Rate Dollars per 1 Mark	Dollars
1/1: Bought one German bond with a 12% coupon rate	500	$.6051	$302.55
12/31: Interest to be disbursed	60	$.6051	36.31
Expected yield	12%		12%
12/31: Actual interest received	60	$.5501*	33.01
Realized yield	12%		10.91%**

* $.6051/(1 + .1) = $.6051/1.1 = $.5501
**$33.01/$302.55 = .1091 = 10.91%

Currency risks can be hedged by borrowing in local currency or selling it forward. However, hedging is too costly and impractical for individual investors.

NOTE: Choosing countries with strong currencies and investing in international mutual funds can minimize currency risk.

Besides, currency swings work both ways. A weak dollar would boost the foreign returns of U.S. investors. Figure 12-7 is a quick reference to judge how currency swings may affect your foreign returns.

FIGURE 12-7: CURRENCY CHANGES AND FOREIGN
RETURN IN U.S. DOLLARS

		The Dollar			
	20%	**10%**	**0%**	**−10%**	**−20%**
20%	44%	32	20	8	−4
10	32	21	10	−1	−12
0	20	10	0	−10	−20
−10	8	−1	−10	−19	−28
−20	−4	−12	−20	−28	−36

(left axis label: **Foreign**)

Political (Sovereign) Risk

Political or sovereign risk is viewed by many as a major obstacle to international investment. Clearly, political factors are a major determinant of the attractiveness of investment in any country. Countries viewed as likely candidates for internal political upheaval or with a pronounced trend toward elimination of the private sector will be unattractive to all investors, foreign or domestic. When political risks increase significantly, local investors will attempt to diversify from the home market as rapidly as foreigners, pushing prices down.

Political instability, limited track records, poor statistics--they all make gauging risk a risky business in itself. Listed at the end of this chapter are sources of country risk information.

But if domestic investors cannot liquidate their domestic holdings or buy foreign assets because of national regulations or moral suasion, the market prices may not reflect the general local opinion. If foreign investors are constrained by the same regulations, all investors lose. A careful evaluation of the relative flexibility of domestic and foreign investment, therefore, is a key element in determining whether political risks jeopardize cross-border holdings. The risk of currency controls, for instance, is one of the few political risks that is borne primarily by foreign investors.

In some cases, political risks might even favor foreign investors relative to domestic investors because these risks will have a greater impact on the risk of a domestic investor whose portfolio is concentrated in home assets than a globally diversified investor. Accordingly, domestic shares in some countries might well be more attractive to foreign than domestic investors in periods of high political uncertainty.

Institutional Obstacles

A recurrent objection to global diversification is that the practical scope for foreign investing is limited. Many markets seem to be small, less liquid, and less efficient than those of the United States. Undoubtedly, there are many foreign stocks whose total capitalization and turnover are too limited for them to be of interest to most U.S. institutional investors. Further, in many markets—particularly the Japanese and West German— market capitalizations are often misleading indicators of an issue's marketability because a large proportion of the shares might be owned by banks, holding companies, or other concerns.

However, these considerations do not necessarily make these markets less attractive to foreign investors. In fact, just the opposite might be the case. International investors who, through diversification, can virtually eliminate the non-market risk unique to individual companies even if they hold only a small number of shares in each market. Because foreign investors do not have to rely on any single market for liquidity, they can take a longer view in regard to each market and security—even though they wish to realize profits within a reasonable period in each market and currency.

Another concern is the efficiency of foreign markets. An efficient market is one where new information is quickly reflected in prices of securities, making it unlikely that any single investor will beat the market. Although less efficiency can be desirable from an active investment manager's perspective because it implies the possibility of superior performance, it also puts the international investor at a disadvantage relative to the domestic investor, who has greater knowledge and better information. Studies of foreign markets suggest that they generally can be considered efficient in the sense that prices adjust rapidly to new information and that most professional managers are unable to consistently outperform the market.

Institutional obstacles that can make international investing costly, undesirable, or, in some cases, impossible include formal barriers to international transactions, such as exchange controls, double taxation of portfolio income in certain countries, and restrictions on ownership of securities according to the nationality of the investor. Informal barriers include the difficulty of obtaining information about a market, differences in reporting practices that make international comparisons difficult, and subtle impediments to foreign investment based on traditional practice.

Even if one assumes an integrated, efficient world capital market, investors with different legal domiciles or tax situations might want to hold different investments. However, it is difficult to determine by how much such portfolios should differ from the world optimal market portfolio in the absence of such obstacles. This would depend on the effect of the obstacles versus the gains from more complete diversification.

HOW TO INVEST GLOBALLY

You can reap the advantages of international investing in international money and capital markets, both directly and indirectly.

Buying Foreign Stock Directly

You can buy some foreign securities through U.S. brokerage firms. One advantage of owning ordinary foreign shares is the much larger selection of stocks from which to choose. Also, trading is usually more active, resulting in greater liquidity.

But buying foreign securities directly is not without difficulty:

- Transaction costs—brokerage commissions and the additional costs associated with the international clearing process—are high.

- Information and research costs more. Further, the information is often difficult to obtain and its reliability is questionable.

- You must be familiar with the financial reporting and disclosure standards of the country in which the stock is issued.

- When you own foreign shares, you're subject to the regulations of the foreign stock exchanges. Settlement can be delayed. Figure 12-8 shows stock market rules in major foreign markets.

FIGURE 12-8: STOCK MARKET RULES IN MAJOR MARKETS

Country	Settlement Date	Is Insider Trading Illegal?	Percent Stake that Must be Disclosed
Australia	Negotiable	Yes	10
Britain	Every 2 or 3 weeks	Yes (infrequent enforcement)	5
France	Monthly	Yes	5
Germany	2 business days	No (but barred by voluntary code)	25
Hong Kong	Next business day	Yes	n.a.
Italy	Monthly	Yes	2
Japan	3 business days	Yes (infrequent enforcement)	5
Netherlands	3 business days	Yes (only for directors)	10
Singapore	5 business days	Yes	n.a.
Switzerland	1 business days	Yes (no enforcement body)	5
U.S.	5 business days	Yes	5

Your Account

As with domestic stock purchases, foreign stock may be registered in your name or in street name—the name of the broker who initiates the transaction. In the former case, however, you must open custodial accounts at banks in the countries in which you plan to buy securities. This process can be simplified by opening a global custody account with a multinational commercial bank, which allows you to use the foreign subsidiaries of a single institution. Many U.S. brokers have their own custody accounts overseas to act as receiving and delivery agents.

Many foreign nations impose withholding taxes of various degree on dividends. U.S. investors can file for a refund of this tax if the U.S. has a tax treaty with the other nation. Most foreign shares can be held in either registered or bearer form, though in some countries foreign investors may only own stock in bearer form. If the shares are registered, the investor will receive dividends in local currency (less withholding taxes) and notices from the company in the local language. If the securities are held in bearer form, the investor can receive dividends (after deduction of withholding taxes) in U.S. dollars through the agent bank.

FOREIGN STOCK QUOTATIONS

- Newspapers often provide two listings associated with foreign securities: (1) Foreign securities in U.S. dollars (Figure 12-9), and (2) foreign exchange rates (Figure 12-10). Typically, the current exchange rate and the rate for the previous trading day are both given. These rates, however, are interbank rates. As a rule of thumb, we add 2% to the interbank rate to determine the rate for stock transactions. To determine a rough price for foreign securities in U.S. dollars, multiple the price by the exchange rate. For example, ANA closed at 1270 yen; the latest exchange rate for the Japanese yen is $.007605. Adding 2 percent, gives you an estimated exchange rate of $.007757. Multiplying the yen price by the approximate U.S. equivalent gives you a rough per-share price of the stock in U.S. dollars:

NOTES:

- *These rates, however, are interbank rates. As a rule of thumb, we add 2% to the interbank rate to determine the rate for stock transactions.*

- *To determine a rough price for foreign securities in U.S. dollars, you must multiple the price by the applicable exchange rate. For example, in the case of ANA closing at 1270 yen, we note that for the Japanese yen, the latest exchange rate is $.007605 as shown. Two percent added to this gives you an estimated exchange rate of $.007757. Multiplying the price of the stock in foreign currency by the approximate U.S. equivalent of yen we obtain a rough per-share price of the stock in U.S. dollars.*

1270 Yen	*(price of stock)*
x $.007757 U.S.$	*(rough exchange value of $1)*
$ 9.85 U.S.$	*(price of stock in U.S. dollars)*

FIGURE 12-9: FOREIGN SECURITIES IN U.S. $

Stock	Price	Chg
ARGENTINA (Arg. Pesos)		
Banco Frances	6.54	-0.11
Ban Galicia BA	5.15	-0.11
City Equity	3.02	-0.06
Massalin Part	8.50	nt

Source: New York Times

FIGURE 12-10: FOREIGN EXCHANGE RATES

New York prices, Rates for trades of $1 million minimum.

	Foreign currency in dollars		Dollar in foreign currency	
	Yesterday	Prev. day.	Yesterday	Prev. day.
Argent	1.0002	1.0001	.9998	.9999 Peso
Australia	.6465	.6475	1.5468	1.5444 Dollar
Austria	.9787	.0786	12.702	12.715 Schilling

Source: Long Beach Press Telegram

FOREIGN STOCK INDEXES

Foreign stock markets have indexes like those in the United States that let you easily gauge the general performance of the foreign markets and their sectors. Major newspapers and the financial media regularly report changes in these indexes. Figure 12-11 is an example of these listings from the Bloomberg Internet site *(www.bloomberg.com)*. The CBS MarketWatch Internet site *(cbs.marketwatch.com)* also reports foreign market indexes. The ING Barings Internet site *(www.ingbarings.com/ pweb/research/research_frame.htm)* contains an extensive list of links to sites dealing with financial markets in foreign countries.

FIGURE 12-11: FOREIGN EXCHANGE INDEXES

World Indices
Fri, 12 Nov 1999, 8:19pm EST

SPONSORED BY Qwest **UNLIMITED Internet Access** click>>

North/Latin America

Index	Value	Chg	Pct Chg	Date
DOW JONES INDUS. AVG (INDU)	10769.32	174.02	1.64%	16:03
S&P 500 INDEX (SPX)	1396.06	14.60	1.06%	16:59
NASDAQ COMB COMPOSITE IX (CCMP)	3221.15	23.86	0.75%	17:15
TSE 300 Index (TS300)	7526.20	37.74	0.50%	17:02
MEXICO BOLSA INDEX (MEXBOL)	6034.76	-51.54	-0.85%	16:02
BRAZIL BOVESPA STOCK IDX (IBOV)	13114.01	-75.26	-0.57%	15:14

Europe/Africa

Index	Value	Chg	Pct Chg	Date
BLOOMBERG EUROPEAN 500 (EURO500)	239.62	-0.32	-0.13%	13:00
FT-SE 100 Index (UKX)	6511.60	-39.80	-0.61%	11:31
CAC 40 INDEX (CAC)	5141.51	9.43	0.18%	11:24
DAX INDEX (DAX)	5791.05	-11.31	-0.19%	11:45
IBEX 35 INDEX (IBEX)	10469.90	-27.20	-0.26%	11:00
MILAN MIB30 INDEX (MIB30)	33930.00	-177.00	-0.52%	11:51
BEL20 INDEX (BEL20)	3354.22	69.80	2.13%	11:01
AMSTERDAM EXCHANGES INDX (AEX)	589.87	-4.93	-0.83%	10:30
SWISS MARKET INDEX (SMI)	7421.20	62.00	0.84%	11/11

Asia/Pacific

Index	Value	Chg	Pct Chg	Date
NIKKEI 225 INDEX (NKY)	18258.55	-68.73	-0.38%	1:05
HANG SENG STOCK INDEX (HSI)	14189.67	83.96	0.60%	3:05
ASX ALL ORDINARIES INDX (AS30)	3010.20	27.40	0.92%	0:07
SING: STRAITS TIMES INDU (STI)	2185.82	32.15	1.49%	4:02

Source: Bloomberg Internet site

A number of investment banking firms that follow foreign stocks issue foreign stock indexes that chart the change in the values of foreign stocks in different countries. These include:

- FTSE International produces a number of foreign stock indexes. These can be obtained free on the Web at *www.ft-se.co.uk.*

- ING Barings produces the Barings Emerging Markets Indexes. These can be accessed free at *cbs.marketwatch.com.*

- HSBC Holdings Group issues the HSBC James Capel Indexes. These can be accessed free at *cbs.marketwatch.com.*

- Morgan Stanley Capital International produces a number of global indexes, including the EAFE Index. These indexes can be accessed free from the company Web site *(www.msci.com)* or from *cbs.marketwatch.com.*

- Standard & Poor's issues S&P Global Indexes that can be accessed free on the Web at *www.spglobal.com.*

- Stoxx, Ltd., a joint venture of Dow Jones and European investment banking firms, issues the the Dow Jones Stoxx and the Dow Jones Euro Stoxx Indexes. Some of these can be accessed free at the UBS Internet site *(www.ubs.ch)* or from cbs.marketwatch.com.

AMERICAN DEPOSITORY RECEIPTS (ADRs)

In the United States, two alternatives are available for trading internationally listed foreign securities. One is for the shares to be traded directly, exactly like a U.S. company. The second alternative is via American Depository Receipts (ADRs).

ADRs are certificates that represent stock in foreign companies. Here's how it works: A foreign company places shares in trust with a U.S. bank, which in turn issues depository receipts to U.S. investors. The ADRs, then, as claims to shares of stock, are essentially the same as shares. The depository bank performs all clerical functions—issuing annual reports, keeping a shareholder ledger, paying and maintaining dividend records, and what not—allowing the ADRs to trade just like domestic securities. An ADR is traded on the NYSE, AMEX, and OTC markets as a share in stock, minus the voting rights. Examples of ADRs are Toyota, Sony, Glaxo, Cannon, and Smithkline Beecham. Prices are quoted, and dividends are paid, in dollars.

ADRs have become an increasingly convenient and popular vehicle for investing internationally. Investors do not have to go through foreign brokers and information on company operations is usually available in English. If you don't want to buy mutual funds, ADRs are good substitutes for direct foreign investment. Further, the trading and settlement costs that apply in some foreign markets are waived.

To buy ADRs, contact your stockbroker or contact Bank of New York, which is the largest seller of ADRs, at *www.bankofny.com/adr.*

The Problem with ADRs

ADRs, however, are not for everyone:

- ADRs carry an element of currency risk. For example, an ADR based on the stock of a British company would tend to lose value when the dollar strengthens against the British pound, if other factors were held constant; as the pound weakens, fewer U.S. dollars are required to buy the same shares of a U.K. company.

- Some thinly traded ADRs can be harder to buy and sell, making them more expensive than the quoted price.

- You may have problems getting reliable information on some foreign companies. For one thing, there is a shortage of data: the annual report may be all that is available, and its reliability may be questionable. Furthermore, foreign financial reporting and accounting standards are often substantially different from those accepted in the U.S.

- ADRs can be either sponsored or unsponsored. Many ADRs are not sponsored by the underlying companies. Non-sponsored ADRs oblige you to pay certain fees to the depository bank, reducing your return.

- There are a limited number of issues available, for only a small fraction of foreign stocks trade internationally. Many interesting and rewarding investment opportunities exist in shares with no ADRs.

Bank of New York maintains indexes of how ADRs perform; they can be retrieved at the bank Web site *(www.bankofny.com)* (see Figure 12-12). J.P.Morgan also maintains an Internet site providing ADR market performance *(adr.com).* Stock City maintains the ADR City Internet site *(www.cyberhost3.com/stockcit/adr/index.html),* which provides the name, exchange and ticker symbol for ADRs.

FIGURE 12-12: COMPARISON OF THE BANK OF NEW YORK ADR INDEXES

Index	High	Low	Close	Prev Close	% Change	Year To Date % Change
ADR Index	133.66	132.65	132.65	133.36	-0.53%	16.99%
Europe	139.70	138.48	138.48	139.68	-0.86%	8.99%
Asia	130.66	129.30	130.01	129.34	0.52%	41.15%
Latin America	88.43	86.89	86.89	88.43	-1.74%	15.90%
Emerging Markets	123.06	121.17	121.17	122.97	-1.46%	41.79%

Source: Bank of New York Web site

FOREIGN BONDS

All international bonds fall within two generic classifications, Eurobonds and foreign bonds. The distinction is based on whether the borrower is a domestic or a foreign resident, and whether the issue is denominated in the local currency or a foreign currency.

Eurobonds and Foreign Bond

A Eurobond, which is underwritten by an international syndicate of banks and other securities firms, is sold exclusively in countries other than the country in whose currency it's denominated. For example, a bond issued by a U.S. corporation, denominated in U.S. dollars, but sold to only investors in Europe and Japan (not in the United States) would be a Eurobond. Eurobonds are issued by multinational corporations, large domestic corporations, sovereign governments, governmental enterprises, and international institutions. They may be offered simultaneously in a number of different national capital markets, but not in the capital market of the country, nor to residents of the country, in whose currency the bond is denominated. Almost all Eurobonds are in bearer form, with call provisions and sinking funds.

A foreign bond is underwritten by a syndicate composed of members from a single country, sold principally within that country, and denominated in the currency of that country. The issuer, however, is from another country. A bond issued by a Swedish corporation, denominated in dollars and sold in the U.S., to U.S. investors by U.S. investment bankers, would be a foreign bond. Foreign bonds have nicknames; those sold in the U.S. are Yankee bonds; those sold in Japan are Samurai bonds; and those sold in the United Kingdom are Bulldogs.

Figure 12-13 looks at foreign bonds from a U.S. investor's perspective.

FIGURE 12-13: FOREIGN BONDS TO U.S. INVESTORS

	Sales	
	In the U.S.	**In Foreign Countries**
Domestic	Domestic bonds	Eurodollar bonds
Issuer		
Foreign	Yankee bonds	Foreign currency bonds Eurodollar bonds

Foreign currency bonds are issued by foreign governments and foreign corporations in their own currency. As with domestic bonds, their prices move inversely to the interest rate of the country in whose currency the issue is denominated: the values of German bonds fall if German interest rates rise. Values of bonds denominated in foreign currencies will also fall if the dollar appreciates or rise if it depreciates relative to the denominated currency. Indeed, investing in foreign currency bonds is really a play on the dollar. If both the dollar and foreign interest rates fall, investors in foreign currency bonds could make a nice return. Of course, if both the dollar and foreign interest rates rise, the investors will be hit with a double whammy.

Foreign Convertibles

Besides allowing you to participate in the appreciation of overseas stocks, foreign convertibles let you earn greater current returns while incurring less risk compared with the underlying common stocks. Their yields are usually higher than the dividends of the underlying stocks. Moreover, the conversion premium (the difference between (a) the cost of acquiring the underlying stock by converting the bond and (b) the current share price) is normally quite low, allowing you to pick up this yield advantage at a relatively low cost. Most Japanese convertibles, for instance, are issued with 5% premiums.

Convertible bonds have less downside risk than the underlying common: The fixed coupon provides a price floor determined by the yields available on comparable straight debt issues. If the company goes bankrupt, holders of convertible securities have priority over stockholders in claiming the assets of the firm. And coupon payments on Euroconvertibles are not subject to withholding taxes, while the dividend payments on the common stocks usually are.

Your yield on a foreign bond will depend both on the local market of the issuing company and on how the currency in which the bond is denominated performs against the U.S. dollar. International bond funds are an excellent route for you to get diversification benefits.

The Standard & Poor's *Bond Guide* shows the following information.

- *Exchange.* New York Stock Exchange; American Stock Exchange.

- *Individual Issue Statistics.* Descriptions of individual issues; for abbreviations, see page 2 of the *Bond Guide.*

- *Interest Dates.* Interest dates are indicated by first letter of alternate six months in which interest is payable. (An) or (Q) precedes dates on which interest is payable either annually or quarterly. Unless otherwise noted, dates are the first day of the month. Month of maturity is indicated by a capital letter. Symbols following interest dates note foreign issues payable in U.S. funds or currency of issuing country; and issues in default. *S&P Debt Rating.* S&P debt rating definitions appear in the front section of the *Bond Guide.*

- *Redemption Provisions.* Regular call price with beginning or ending date. Sinking fund, if any, is reported together with applicable price and date. Refund restrictions are denoted by the symbol x, giving date at which restriction expires. Redemption provision may include the symbol NC, which means non-callable, and others (+, Z, *), which are explained in the *Guide.*

- *Underwriting.* Keyed to the Directory of Underwriters in the *Bond Guide;* the original underwriter, usually the head of the syndicate, the price and the year the issue was originally offered.

- *Outstanding (Mil. &).* Amount of issue outstanding, in millions of dollars, as of the latest available complete balance sheet.

Foreign Bond Indexes

A number of subscription services track the performance of these bonds; several issue indexes. The CBS MarketWatch Internet site *(cbs.market-watch.com)* provides access to many of the indexes.

Subscription services that follow foreign bonds include:

- J.P. Morgan's Government Bond Indexes for the United States and other countries, which can be accessed free at *cbs.marketwatch.com* or at the company Web site *(www.jpmorgan.com).* The indexes are followed in both U.S. dollars and the local currency.

- There are Salomon Smith Barney World Government Bond Indexes for the United States and sixteen other countries, also reported in both U.S. dollars and local currency. These indexes can be accessed free at *cbs.marketwatch.com.*

- The Swiss-based UBS Group issues UBS Benchmark Bond indexes in local currency and U.S. dollars; these are also available at cbs.marketwatch.com.

INTERNATIONAL MONEY MARKETS

A market for short-term financial claims performs the essential service of enabling financial investment to be transformed into real investment. A well-developed money market can channel savings to their most efficient uses, making funds more cheaply and freely available to business. Every country with banks that accept short-term deposits (time deposits) has a money market of sorts. As an economy grows, so does the demand for a wider range of financial instruments, such as commercial paper, acceptances, and government securities; these would be traded in a secondary market where financial claims could be freely bought and sold. As an economy becomes open through international transactions, the national money market becomes linked to international money markets, just as the national capital market has its linkages with international capital markets.

There are three major ways to invest in international money markets:

1. Buy foreign short-term money market instruments directly. Investing in foreign money market assets denominated in the foreign currency allows the full impact of currency variation to be reflected in returns, along with the yield of the money market investments. If, for example, interest rates are higher in England and you think sterling will strengthen or remain on the same exchange rate with the dollar, an investment denominated in sterling would make sense.

2. Invest through the Eurocurrency market, where funds are intermediated outside the country of the currency in which the funds are denominated. Thus, the Eurocurrency market comprises financial institutions that compete for dollar time deposits and make dollar loans outside the United States, as, for instance, when a U.S. investor buys Eurodollar CDs from a bank in London. Eurocurrency banking is not subject to domestic banking regulation, such as reserve requirements and interest-rate restrictions, allowing Eurobanks to operate more efficiently, cheaply, and competitively than their domestic counterparts and to offer slightly better terms to both borrowers and lenders. Therefore, Eurodollar deposit rates are somewhat higher, and effective lending rates a little lower, than they are in the U.S. money market.

3. Place foreign currency deposits with U.S. banks in the United States. This enables you to conveniently take advantage of the expected weakness of the dollar relative to the currency in which the deposit is denominated.

BUYING SHARES OF U.S. MULTINATIONALS

Many investors achieve a reasonable degree of global diversification without recognizing it because many U.S. multinational corporations (MNCs) like IBM, Coca Cola, and General Motors do a considerable portion of their business outside the U.S. Buying shares of MNCs not only achieves global diversification, it avoids high transaction costs and the information problems faced by investors buying foreign securities directly.

An MNC owns, controls, and manages income-generating assets in a variety of countries. Thus, an MNC itself represents a portfolio of globally diversified cash flows originated in different countries and currencies. The cash flows of a MNC are likely to be strongly influenced by foreign factors, giving you achieve global diversification indirectly.

However, the share price behavior of MNCs is nearly indistinguishable from that of purely domestic firms. MNC share prices are far more sensitive to the index of their home markets than to foreign market indices. Thus, investing in domestic MNCs would not be an effective means of global diversification, though it would be cheap and convenient.

INTERNATIONAL MUTUAL FUNDS

You may find mutual funds attractive generally because they offer regular full-time professional management, safekeeping of securities, the chance to invest regular dollar amounts (funds offer both full and fractional shares), and the ability to reduce the amount invested without reducing diversity. There has been a significant increase in the number of international mutual funds as more investors are diversifying globally.

International mutual funds are probably the best way for you to achieve global diversification, either on a broad basis or by targeting specific countries or geographical regions. They are a relatively easy, low-cost way, and takes a lot of the risk out of investing in foreign securities.

Global and International Stock Funds

Foreign stock funds can be divided into four groups, ranging from highly diversified geographically to highly focused; they are global, international, regional, and single-country funds.

Global funds can invest anywhere in the world, including the United States. However, most global funds keep the majority of their assets in foreign markets. Global funds are worth considering if you aren't sure how much to allocate to foreign markets.

International (or foreign) funds invest only in foreign stocks. Because these funds focus only on foreign markets, they allow investors to control the portion of their personal portfolio they want to allocate to non-U.S. stocks.

International funds with a *regional* focus allow investors to narrow their sights to a particular region: Europe, Asia-Pacific, or Latin America, for instance. Most regional funds are closed-end, although there are some open-end. There are even some international index funds.

Single-country funds, as the most focused, are by far the most aggressive foreign stock funds. Almost all single-country funds are closed-end funds (exceptions are the Japan Fund and the French Fund). This exaggerates their aggressiveness because single-country (and regional) closed-end funds have been known to sell at both large discounts and premiums to their net asset value. Thus, closed-end single-country funds are suited only for the most sophisticated investors who are confident of their ability to assess the potential for a specific market as well as the trends in the fund's stock price versus its net asset value.

The typical single country fund is closed-end, but Wright Investor's Services, a small company, has several open-end country funds. Each of these funds is actively managed.

The most important new trend in international investing via investment companies is *passively managed country funds* geared to a major stock index of a particular country. Each of these offerings will typically be almost fully invested, have little turnover, and offer significantly reduced expenses to shareholders.

Morgan Stanley has created *World Equity Benchmark Shares (WEBS),* which track a predesignated index (one of Morgan Stanley's international capital indexes) for 17 countries. These closed-end funds trade on the AMEX. Deutsche Morgan Grenfell has created *CountryBaskets,* designed to replicate the Financial Times/S&P Actuaries World Indices, for nine different countries. Unlike WEBS, which attempt to match the performance of a particular index without owning all the stocks in the index, CountryBaskets own every stock in the index for that country.

Because of their broad focus, global and international funds are less risky and therefore a better choice for the average investor than a single country or a regional fund.

International Bond and Money Market Funds

Compared with international stock funds, the number of international bond funds is limited, as is their performance history. In selecting international bond funds, consider the following factors: open-end vs. closed-end, average maturity, country focus, and currency risk. It is often suggested that you stay short-term (typically, four years or less) and locate a fund that hedges some of its foreign exchange risk and invests in countries with currencies that move with the U.S. dollar.

International money market funds are a relatively recent phenomenon. Many of them invest only in dollar-denominated foreign money market instruments, thereby eliminating the currency risk.

If you are averse to currency risk investor, put your money here.

To minimize exposure to currency risk, many funds try to hedge. It's a matter of degree. In general, international short-term bond funds usually hedge most of the currency risk; longer-term funds have substantial exposure. Funds use currency options, futures, and elaborate cross currency hedges, but the most effective hedges are expensive.

Choosing a Mutual Fund

In evaluating a mutual fund, domestic or foreign, look at the objectives of the fund, its management and track record, its expense ratio, and so on. A big part of what you're buying in any mutual fund is management. Therefore, continuity of management is important, as evidenced by consistent track records for at least five years.

The performance of foreign mutual funds must be measured against their peers and the correct market benchmarks. For example, a broadly-diversified international fund should be compared with the EAFE index. On the other hand, a Japanese fund should be judged against other Japanese funds and with the Nikkei average.

With closed-end funds, look for a well-diversified, multi-country fund that sells at a discount; if you do buy at a premium, make sure that it's at least at the low end of its range. Look at the fund's expense ratio relative to comparable funds and to its premium or discount level. Figure 12-14 shows quotes of some international closed-end funds.

FIGURE 12-14: QUOTES ON INTERNATIONAL CLOSED-END FUNDS

Fund Name (Symbol)	Exch	Stock NAV	Market Price	Prem /Disc	52-week Market Return
Jardine Fl China (JFC)	♣N	9.18	$6^{13/16}$	− 25.8	41.5
Jardine Fl India (JFI)-c	♣N	13.21	$9^{13/8}$	− 29.0	92.4

Source: Barron's

SOURCES OF INFORMATION

Country Risk

- *Euromoney* magazine's annual *Country Risk Rating* measures the access of different countries' to international credit, trade finance, political risk, and the country's payment record. The rankings are generally confirmed by political risk insurers and top syndicate managers in the Euromarkets.

- The Economist Intelligence Unit, a New York subsidiary of the Economist Group, London, bases its ratings on such factors as external debt and trends in the current account, the consistency of government policy, foreign-exchange reserves, and the quality of economic management.

- *International Country Risk Guide,* published by a U.S. division of International Business Communications, Ltd., London, offers a composite risk rating as well as individual ratings for political, financial, and economic risk. The political variable—which makes up half the composite index—includes factors such as government corruption and how economic expectations diverge from reality. The financial rating looks at such things as the likelihood of losses from exchange controls and loan defaults. Finally, the economic rating considers such factors as inflation and debt-service costs.

- *Data Book* (quarterly), published by Thompson BankWatch, Inc. (61 Broadway, New York, NY 10006) provides a country rating assessing overall political and economic stability of the country in which a bank is domiciled.

Foreign Firms

The following list of sources provides addresses, phone number, area of business, officers, directors, and financial data for foreign corporations:

- *Moody's International Manual,* published by Moody's Investment Service annually in two volumes with weekly updating.

- *International Directory of Corporate Affiliations,* published twice a year by National Register Publishing Co.

- *The International Corporate 1000,* published by Monitor Publishing Co. with annual updating.

APPENDIX 12-A: USEFUL WEB SITES

Web Address	Primary Focus
adr.com	ADR quotations
cbs.marketwatch.com	General financial market information, with extensive list of global market, sector and bond indexes
www.bankofny.com/adr	Educational material on the definition and trading of ADRs, with a list of all ADRs in the U.S. markets
www.bloomberg.com	General financial market information, with list of world indexes
www.cyberhost3.com/stockcit/adr/index.html	List of ADRs
www.ft-se.co.uk	International investment information and extensive global index lists
www.healthwealthsolutions.com/globaltrading	Good site on the need for and approach to global investing
www.ingbarings.com/pweb/research/research-frame.htm	International investment site with links and index listings
www.msci.com	Global investment information and index listings
www.spglobal.com	List of S&P global indexes

Chapter 13
PORTFOLIO
CONSTRUCTION AND
ASSET ALLOCATION

The key question for every investor is: How do I structure an investment portfolio to achieve my financial goals? That depends on many factors: what your investment goals are; the level of risk you are willing to assume without losing your sleep; your tax bracket; and so on.

FIGURE 13-1:   A SYSTEMATIC APPROACH TO PORTOFIO CONSTRUCTION

Assess risk attitude and capacity

Set investment objectives
(age, liquidity, income needs, tax situation,
retirement, new house, college education)

Evaluate and select investment vehicles
by technical and/or fundamental screening and valuation

Decide on asset allocation/portfolio construction

Stocks	Bonds	Cash
_____%	_____%	_____%

Decide whether to do it yourself or invest through mutual funds

Monitor portfolio

Review objectives	Evaluate investment performance and risk	Assess market and economic environment

Revise portfolio

No matter what your goal, proper diversification—allocating investment assets among different types of investments in order to balance risk
and return—is a major element of structuring a successful portfolio.
Figure 13-1 shows how it's done.

ALLOCATING ASSETS WITH MUTUAL FUNDS

Asset allocation weighs various types of investments in a portfolio.
Undoubtedly, one of the best ways to allocate assets is with mutual funds;
using several types of mutual funds may be an even better way to go.

Different segments of the market react differently to the same economic conditions. For example, a cut in interest rates may lower yields on
your bond funds—but that news could spark a stock rally that would benefit your stock funds. A poor economy that tends to depress the domestic
markets may be offset by international funds. Spreading your investment
money among a family of funds is strongly recommended. More specifically,

- Diversify among different classes of investments: for example,
  cash and cash equivalents (such as money market funds), stock
  funds, bond funds, etc.

- Diversify within each class of funds: small company stock funds,
  large company stock funds, sector funds, international funds, etc.

- Go further: tax-exempt funds, taxable funds, etc.

As an alternative to constructing your own portfolio, many mutual
fund companies offer a variety of *asset allocation funds*. An asset allocation fund is a mutual fund seeking to reduce risk by investing in the right
securities at the right time. These funds stress consistent performance at
the expense of spectacular gains.

Some funds, such as Vanguard's Star Fund, use fixed weightings; others, such as Fidelity's Asset Manager, have weights that are altered within pre-defined limits. In fact, Fidelity offers several asset allocation funds
designed for various investment objectives (*i.e.,* Fidelity Asset Manager,
Asset Manager-Growth, and Asset Manager-Income.).

DO-IT-YOURSELF PORTFOLIO CONSTRUCTION

Constructing your own portfolio is difficult. Asset allocation, a time-tested approach to portfolio management, would distribute the funds within your portfolio among several asset categories or classes, typically cash and cash-equivalents (investments with maturities of less than one year such as CDs or money market funds), equities (stocks and stock funds), and fixed income securities (bonds and bond funds). Diversification within the stock market is also critical, spreading your money across several broad sectors: large-company, small-company, and foreign stocks, for instance.

The mix of instruments will depend on your financial goals, resources, total return (yield plus price change), and your tolerance of risk. The highly personalized process of asset allocation first takes into account each of your unique investment needs and objectives, your earnings ability, and the financial resources you have available. Your age may be a big factor. For example:

- Do you need to build funds for retirement or a child's college education?

- Is reducing your tax liability a priority?

- Do you need to generate current income (or yield), need funds soon, or will at some point in the future? Which is more important to you, current income or capital appreciation?

Your answers to these questions will determine how your portfolio should be split among three classes of investment vehicles:

- **Liquidity investments** can be turned into cash as needed with minimum risk or penalty. They include short-term CDs, money market funds, and money market deposit accounts.

- **Income investments** can provide present or future income. They include corporate bonds and tax-free municipal bonds, fixed annuities providing tax-deferred future income, and U.S. savings bonds.

- **Growth investments** are intended to appreciate in value over a given period. They include growth stocks, stock funds, and variable annuities.

Calculating Your Allocation Mix

Asset allocation must take into account your risk comfort level. Ask yourself: Am I conservative, moderate, or aggressive? Where is my sleeping point? (Do you want to eat well, or sleep well?)

One approach is based on your time frame. Longer-term portfolios let you assume additional risk. You can increase the amount you invest in stocks, precious metals, etc. The asset mix will change as your time horizon decreases or as gains or losses alter the composition of the portfolio.

Another approach is to time changes in asset allocation to market changes, preferably in step with market cycles. In bull markets, be heavily into stocks, for instance. In bear markets, allocate more to cash, bonds, or precious metals. Note, though, that there is controversy whether investors can profitability time market waves.

To determine your current asset allocation mix, add up your holdings of stocks, bonds, and cash, and divide each sum by the total value of the portfolio. Unfortunately, in today's complex investment world, determining what asset class certain investments belong to can be confusing. You will have to give some thought to how you allocate mixed investments such as balanced mutual funds that own both stocks and bonds or how to treat convertible securities, which are half-bond and half-stock.

The calculation can be done by hand or by using a software spreadsheet program. Personal finance software such as Meca's Managing Your Money can also help. The Dreyfus Group mutual funds and the Shearson Lehman Brothers brokerage will do the calculation for no charge. Fidelity has developed *Fidelity PortfolioMatch,* a guidebook that defines a process for evaluating your existing investment, as well as action steps tailored to your individual needs. A grid serves as an easy way to calculate asset allocation. Figure 13-2 provides a filled-out grid as an example and a blank grid for your own use.

FIGURE 13-2: ASSET ALLOCATION GRIDS

INVESTMENT	(A) AMOUNT	(B) %STOCK	(C) % BOND	(D) % CASH	$$ IN STOCK (A*B)	$$ IN BONDS (A*C)	$$ IN CASH (A*D)
BLT common	$10,000	100%	0	0	$10,000	0	0
Jaytown Balanced Fund	$15,000	60%	30%	10%	$9,000	$4,500	$1,500
Certificate of deposit	$,8,000	0	0	100%	0	0	$8,000
Burgh Water District bond	$5,000	0	100%	0	0	$5,000	0
TOTAL	(E) $38,000				(F) $19,000	(G) $9,500	(H) $9,500
ASSET ALLOCATION					(F÷E) 50%	(G÷E) 25%	(H÷E) 25%

For you to do your own:

INVESTMENT	(A) AMOUNT	(B) %STOCK	(C) % BOND	(D) % CASH	$$ IN STOCK (A*B)	$$ IN BONDS (A*C)	$$ IN CASH (A*D)
TOTAL	(E)				(F)	(G)	(H)
ASSET ALLOCATION					(F÷E) %	(G÷E) %	(H÷E) %

Fine-Tuning Your Asset Mix

The beauty of asset allocation is that as such factors as your financial circumstances and goals and your age change, your allocations can change as well. What are four reasons for fine-tuning or rebalancing your asset mix? They are:

- When external events, such as stock market correction or low yields, have thrown off your original target allocation.

- When you experience a major life event (such as having a child, losing a spouse, getting married, or retiring) that alters your investment goals.

- When the weight of one investment class in your portfolio surges or shrinks significantly.

- When you are within a year or so of achieving a particular goal.

    NOTE: If you intend to rebalance your asset mix often, consider sticking with mutual funds that have no front- and back-end loads.

GETTING HELP IN CONSTRUCTING YOUR PORTFOLIO

There are a number of sources you refer to when trying to construct a portfolio, including the following:

- Most major brokerages maintain a recommended asset allocation (or model portfolio) that is updated as the investment climate changes (see Figures 13-3 and 13-4). One of these will tell you how much you should have in each sector of the economy.

- Each quarter the *Wall Street Journal* tracks Wall Street firms' recommendations of asset allocation.

- Many market newsletters and money management firms also tell investors what they believe are good allocations for the times.

- Every issue of *Worth* magazine gives you a breakdown of what sectors and companies you should own.

FIGURE 13-3: T. ROWE PRICE PORTFOLIO SUGGESTIONS

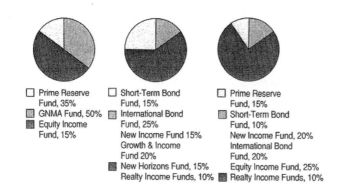

☐ Prime Reserve
Fund, 35%
▨ GNMA Fund, 50%
▨ Equity Income
Fund, 15%

☐ Short-Term Bond
Fund, 15%
▨ International Bond
Fund, 25%
New Income Fund 15%
Growth & Income
Fund 20%
▨ New Horizons Fund, 15%
Realty Income Funds, 10%

☐ Prime Reserve
Fund, 15%
▨ Short-Term Bond
Fund, 10%
New Income Fund, 20%
International Bond
Fund, 20%
Equity Income Fund, 25%
▨ Realty Income Funds, 10%

Source: T. Rowe Price

FIGURE 13-4: MERRILL LYNCH ASSET ALLOCATION

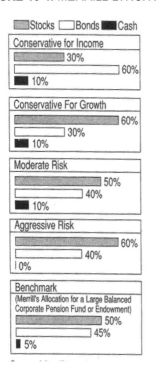

Source: Merrill Lynch

- Surveys by *Money* magazine, the American Association of Individual Investors (AAII), and others give you some idea on what other investors are doing. (These are briefly described later in this chapter.) AAII surveys periodically where individuals commit their assets, as shown in Figure 13-5.

FIGURE 13-5: AAII ALLOCATION SURVEY

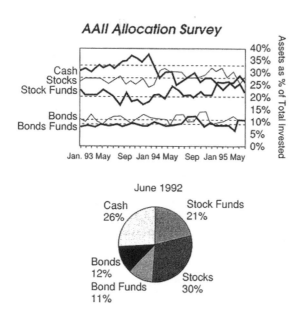

Source: AAII Journal, August 1992

USING BETA FOR ASSET ALLOCATION

You can construct or adjust your own portfolio based on beta coefficients. If you desire higher returns and can take high risk, pick securities with higher betas (or at least mix high and low beta securities so that the overall beta is higher than 1.0). The beta of a portfolio can be estimated by weighting the individual securities that comprise the portfolio. Figure 13-6 illustrates the calculation of a portfolio's beta.

FIGURE 13-6: CALCULATION OF A PORTFOLIO BETA

Stock	Beta	Percent of Portfolio (%)	Portfolio Beta
Coca Cola	1.10	30	.33
Calif. Water	.50	20	.10
Liz Clairborne	1.50	50	.75
		100	1.18

Adding a security with a high beta will increase the portfolio's beta; adding a low beta stock will reduce the risk. The higher the beta or risk, the higher the expected return. Thus, to get a higher long-run rate of return, just increase the beta of your portfolio.

THE LIFE-CYCLE GUIDE

Investment strategy must be tailored to a life cycle that depends to a large extent on the following factors:

- Do you have a stomach for risk? How much loss can you take? What's your sleeping point? Some people just can't sleep at night knowing their assets might take a dip, no matter how small.

- What are your income needs? Or do you desire growth? A retiree or someone close to retirement might look for a steady income; younger people might have the luxury of waiting for long-term growth. There is a trade-off between income and growth.

- How soon do you need results? By and large, longer time horizons allow you to take on greater risks—with greater return potential. As retirement approaches, a large percentage of assets needs to be shifted into more conservative, less risky investments.
  RULE OF THUMB: Subtract your age from 100. The result is the percentage that stocks should account for in your portfolio.

- What's your tax exposure? The bottom line for every investor is not how much you earn, but how much you keep—what's left after taxes. Investors in higher income tax brackets need to be concerned with the tax implications of their investments. Figure 13-7 is a capsule summary of the elements of the individual investment profile; Figure 13-8 shows how an investor's profile may change with age, given the assumptions that: (1) Everybody is essentially risk averse, and (2) the young have more capacity for risk than the old. Your own profile may be very different. Figure 13-9 is a suggested allocation mix.

FIGURE 13-7: INDIVIDUAL INVESTMENT PROFILE

Elements	Degree/level	Investment vehicles identifiedSith each category
Risk Tolerance	Low (0 - 5% Loss)	Cash, CDs, money market funds
	Moderate (6 - 15%)	Conservative high dividend stocks, bonds
	High (16 - 25%)	Growth stocks
Income Needs	Income	Bonds, preferred stocks
	Growth/Income	Growth/income funds, high-dividend stocks
	Growth	Growth stocks
Time/Age Factor	Short (1 - 2 Years)	Cash, CDs, money market funds, short-term bonds
	Medium (3 - 5 Years)	Intermediate-term bonds, growth stocks
	Long	(Over 5 Years) Aggressive growth stocks
Tax Exposure	Low	Bonds and other fixed-income securities
	Moderate	High-dividend stocks, preferred stocks
	High	Municipal bonds, non-dividend-paying growth stocks

FIGURE 13-8: LIFE CYCLE INVESTING: AN EXAMPLE OF A CHANGING PROFILE

	20s	30s	40s-50s	60s
Risk Tolerance	High	High	Moderate	Low
Return Needs	Growth	Growth	Growth/income	Income
Time Horizon	Long	Long	Short/long	Short/long
Tax Exposure	Lower	Higher	Lower	Lower

FIGURE 13-9: SUGGESTED ASSET MIX

	20s	30s	Midlife	60s
Money market funds	5%	5%	5%	10%
Bond funds, zero-coupon T-bonds, high grade	25%.	35%	45%	60%
Stocks funds: Growth, income, income & growth	70%	60%	50%	30%

In addition to your age, your family situation may dictate investment goals and strategies. Figure 13-10 provides some general conditions of typical goals at various family situations.

FIGURE 13-10: EFFECT OF FAMILY SITUATION ON FINANCIAL GOALS

Family Situation	Typical Financial Goals	Conditions
1. Young, single, working	Start a Business; Buy a car	Stress on capital growth No great need for liquidity Time horizon: 3-5 years Capacity for substantial risk
2. Young couple, no children	Buy a house	Similar to situation 1
3. Young couple, two children	College education fund	Similar to situation 1 Time horizon: 10-15 years
4. Middle-aged married couple, no children	Retirement fund	Moderate risk preferred Balance between growth and income Time horizon: 5-10 years
5. Divorced mother, working, children	Supplement income	Similar to situation 4 Low risk preferred
6. Married couple, retired	Supplement retirement	Stress on preservation of capital Need for liquidity and current income Low risk

USING YOUR PC FOR ASSET ALLOCATION

There are software programs designed to perform asset allocation. They try to show how to allocate funds among assets in a portfolio to minimize risk and maximize return using the Markowitz procedure. They also evaluate the potential risks and returns on different types of investments, such as cash, stocks, and bonds, so that you can allocate your funds among them for maximum returns at acceptable levels of risk. These are popular asset allocation programs.

Asset Allocator and Stock Portfolio Allocator
Portfolio Software, 617-328-8248

Asset Allocation Expert
Sponsor-Software Systems, Inc., 212-724-7535

AAT (Asset Allocation Tools)
Scientific Press, 415-366-2577

Asset Mix Optimizer
CDA Investment Technologies, Inc., 301-590-1330

Services like CompuServe, Prodigy, and America Online offer portfolio management on-line. They give you built-in access to on-line services so you can update prices on the securities in your portfolio.

On-line or not, portfolio management programs can help you monitor your investments and provide detailed reports of security and portfolio betas and dividend yields, a calendar listing maturity dates of bonds, options, and futures, along with expected dividend amounts and payment dates, a breakdown of the industries and asset classes of your securities, and your asset allocation. Popular portfolio management software programs include.

Managing Your Money
MECA Software, Inc., 203-255-1441

Financial Navigator
Financial Navigator International, 800-468-3636 or 415-962-0300

Quicken
Intuit, 800-624-8742 or 415-322-0573

WealthBuilder by Money Magazine
Reality Technologies, Inc., 800-346-2024 or 215-277-7600

CAPTOOL and Global Investor
Techserve, Inc., 800-826-8082 or 206-865-0249

Centerpiece and Performance Monitor
Performance Technologies, Inc. 800-528-9595 or 919-876-355

Equalizer and Streetsmart
Charles Schwab & Co., Inc., 800-334-4455 or 415-627-7000

Fidelity On-line Xpress
Fidelity Investments, 800-544-0246

Market Manager Plus
Dow Jones & Co., Inc., 800-815-5100 or 609-520-4641

Mutual Fund Investor
American River Software, 916-483-1600

Personal Portfolio Analyzer
Charles L. Pack, 415-949-0887

Pulse Portfolio Management System
EQUIS International, 800-882-3040 or 801-265-8886

Money Fund Vision
IBC/Donoghue, Inc., 800-343-5413 or 508-881-2800

APPENDIX 13-A: USEFUL WEB SITES

Web Address	Primary Focus
mail.coos.or.us/~wbern/eff/index.shtm	Journal dealing exclusively with efficient asset allocation using modern portfolio theory techniques
www.aol.com/finlist/perform	Discusses the Sharpe, Treynor, and Jensen performance measures
www.columbiafunds.com/maximizing_return.html#1	Useful article on matching investor objectives and asset allocation
www.healthwealthsolutions.com/globaltrading	Good site on the need for and approach to global investing
www.investools.com/cgi-bin/f/1	Register for free portfolio monitoring
www.slu.edu:80/department/finance/363class.htm	Links to many useful sources of investment information; very good links to the specific assets included in over 40 market indexes
www.wellsfargo.com/investing/assetall	Wells Fargo Bank site with pages on portfolio planning and asset allocation

Chapter 14
ON-LINE DATA SERVICES AND INVESTMENT SOFTWARE

As an investor with a modem-equipped personal computer (PC), you can now dial a data base like America Online that's oriented to investors and provides financial data, current and historical information on stock quotes, commodity quotes, access to *Disclosure's* SEC reports, and much more.

There has been a geometric explosion of information at both the library and the Internet. The investment information available on-line falls into two basic categories. One is raw data: stock quotes, market reports, corporate filings, and news releases. The other is analytical tools: research reports, portfolio services, and investment forums.

The raw data can be downloaded onto a floppy disk or into your computer memory to be analyzed later, or it can be read directly into a software program designed to perform calculations on raw data.

ON-LINE DATABASES AND NEWS RETRIEVAL

To be really useful to investors, PCs need news/retrieval capabilities and databases. Databases are organized collections of information, both historical and current. Investment analyses require considerable amounts of economic and financial information; the more current, the better.

Many investors buy or sell securities almost automatically when important events take place. You can use this same news to update your PC database.

All databases don't have the same information. The following discusses the variations in on-line databases.

Numbers

Throughout the day, you can get current prices on securities, generally only 15 to 20 minutes behind the market. If you pay a little more, though, you can get up-to-the minute quotes.

Databases give you information on trading volume, low and closing stock prices, and other technical data going back many years. You can obtain financial data, including historical, current, and projected information.

Some databases give current and historical data on mutual funds, corporate and municipal bonds, commodities and options, indexes, and the state of the economy.

Information and News

You can get information on an industry, any company you're interested in, or the economy as a whole; the information ranges from a company's profile and product lines to important industry developments.

It's true you may get this kind of information by reading the *Wall Street Journal* or by looking at the *Value Line Investment Survey,* but databases make it available more quickly and often cover more companies than Value Line's 1600. A database lets you zero in on a particular company or a particular item that you might otherwise miss.

Shortly after the market's close, you can get closing prices and also the kind of commentary on the day's activity that you find in tomorrow's paper. Getting a jump on the market this way can help you act quickly.

Analysis and Advice

Some databases will analyze their data for you or dispense their own advice or that of experts. Some databases provide on-line fundamental or technical analysis. They produce charts or do screening on-line instead of supplying data to be used by your fundamental or technical analysis software. For instance:

• **CompuServe** can select from 46,000 securities those that meet your criteria. The database offers a limited list of criteria, or you can use its Coscreen service to more thoroughly screen 9,500 stocks using the *Disclosure II* database and 24 screening categories. This service also includes FundWatch Online, which you can use to check existing and prospective mutual fund investments based on eight investment goals. Results are presented in a choice of seven ways, such as 10-year annualized return.

• **Telescan Analyzer** graphs a wide range of fundamental and technical indicators, with up to 13 years of data on 2,000 mutual funds, more than 8,000 stocks, and 150 market indices. You can compare the performance of stocks with the performance of their industry group, or the performance of the industry group with any of several overall market averages. This saves you time, but you may lose some control over the output.

A large number of databases relay the advice and analysis of others. For example:

• **Dow Jones News-Retrieval (DJN/R)** (800-832-1234) provides recommendations from S&P market analysis, and research reports from the financial press. It includes full-text articles from the *Wall Street Journal* and *Barron's,* along with access to 1,500 other business periodicals. In addition, this service includes entry to 60 databases of business and financial information.

• **Equalizer** provides access to recommendations and analysis from S&P's MarketScope (a source used by pros)

An example of a database that organizes your investment accounts is:

• **Investment Record (Claude E. Cleeton, 122 109th Avenue S.E., Bellevue, WA 98004; 206-451-0293),** which tracks up to 10 accounts, each having up to 150 investments in 10 categories. Two reports are generated: (a) a personal income statement describing in detail the investor's actual and estimated financial performance for the year, including yield and tax status, and (b) a capital asset statement detailing all investment assets.

Many discount brokers think databases make their services more attractive because they provide the research and investment data investors would otherwise miss out on by not using a full-service broker. Typical programs are the *Equalizer* program of Schwab and Co., which offers a full range of investment services as well as on-line trading through Max Ule & Co., and Quickway through Quick & Reilly.

On the Equalizer only, there is no on-line charge for checking up on your account or entering orders. There is an $8 per month account fee by Fidelity and time charges of 30 cents per minute in prime time and 10 cents in nonprime time.

Some database services can help you place buy and sell orders directly to a broker from your computer. You do this by sending the same information electronically that you would have given your broker by phone. This lets you place your orders on weekends or at night and have them executed when the market opens.

POPULAR ON-LINE SERVICES

Some major on-line sources of data are available on an interactive, time-sharing basis. Almost all on-line services provide stock quotes, investor bulletin boards where members can exchange information, and general market updates such as the Dow Jones Industrial Average. Here are a few of them:

- America Online (800-827-6364) offers a wide range of financial planning services such as investment information, stock quotes, on-line shopping, and access to recent articles from magazines ranging from *Consumer Reports* to *Worth*. Users may download personal finance programs created by other AOL subscribers. The service also includes information about retirement planning, mutual funds, and portfolio management from AAII and the Morningstar Mutual Fund rating service. Other services include:

- Nightly Business Report Online: information from the TV program, and scheduled interviews with investment experts.

- Reuters: financial news service

- Tax Forum: subscribers can ask tax questions on message boards and download files from the software library

- AOL also allows you to do a lot of your own investment research, using:

  –AOL investment research *(research.web.aol.com)*

  –AOL stock screening tool *(research.web.aol.com/ pages/screen.htm)*

  –AOL mutual fund screening tool *(research.web.aol.com/ pages.fscreen.htm)*

  –AOL financial statements and disclosure *(research.web.aol.com/ pages/disclosure.htm)*

  –AOL ratio comparisons *(research.web.aol.com/pagse/market-guide2.htm)*

Some of these services require that you become a subscriber; but AOL also has a public site with considerable investment information.

- **CompuServe (800-848-8199)** gives you access to current stock prices, on-line shopping, and software for financial planning activities such as calculating net worth, determining loan payments, and researching potential investments. The service includes FundWatch Online, which you can use to check your present and prospective mutual fund investments based on eight investment goals. Results are presented in a choice of seven ways (one is 10-year annualized return). Other services include:

  • *CoScreen:* financial information on publicly traded companies

  • *Citibank Global Report:* foreign exchange and commodity quotes

  • *E Trade Securities:* on-line discount brokerage through Quick & Reilly

  • *MMS International:* financial forecasts, including interest-rate trends and major economic indicators

  • *Executive News Service:* news coverage of specific companies

- **Delphi Internet Services Corp. (800-695-4005)** offers current stock prices, financial news, mutual fund values, mortgage and certificate of deposit rates, investment advice forums, and the UPI business news service. Other services include:

  –Trendvest Portfolio Analysis: a stock rating system

  –MarketPulse: snapshots of the market

  –RateGram: reports on certificates of deposit

  –News Services: Business Wire, Dow Jones Averages, UPI Business News, and Reuters

  –Donoghue Money Fund Reports

- **Genie (800-638-9636)** offers stock market quotes, current business articles, software, and tax advice designed for small-business owners and managers. It also has a forum for subscribers to exchange legal opinions, questions, and answers.

- **Prodigy (800-776-3449)** gives you access to financial advice from Kiplinger's Personal Finance Magazine and other resources, on-line banking services, investment information, and on-line shopping for products and services such as airline reservations, hotel rooms, electronic equipment, flowers, and gourmet foods. The CNBC Market Update has current quotes for investments, including the NYSE, AMEX, and NASDAQ, bonds, mutual funds, and world stock markets. Other services include:

  –PCFN or the PC Financial Network: discount brokerage and investment reports

  –Wall Street Edge: summaries of information collected from security analysts' newsletters

  –Strategic Investor: information (such as important ratios and research) on more than 5,000 companies and over 3,400 mutual funds

–*Money Talk:* electronic bulletin board where members can exchange information and ideas

–*Online banking:* For paying bills and managing bank and investment accounts

- **Dow Jones News Retrieval Service (800-832-1234)** includes full-text articles of the *Wall Street Journal* and *Barron's,* along with access to 1,500 other business periodicals. The service also includes entry to 60 business and financial databases.

- **Reuters Money Network (800-346-2024)** focuses on investment news and financial advice. It provides access to software for graphing investment portfolios and can be connected to financial planning software such as Quicken and Microsoft Money.

Most on-line services provide a wide variety of other services, including access to current news and sports, homework hotlines, reference materials, and discussion forums on a wide range of financial, economic, and political topics. Current information about on-line services is available in computer magazines such as *PC Computing, PC Magazine, Computer Life, Internet World, Net Guide,* and *Windows.* Many books and other publications are available to get you cruising the information highway or doing financial planning in cyberspace.

THE WORLD WIDE WEB

Though most use the terms interchangeably, the Web is the portion of the Internet that uses menus and graphics to display information. The two best sites for investors to visit are Edgar (Electronic Data Gathering, Analysis, and Retrieval) and NETworth.

Edgar is a database of the documents that publicly traded companies file with the SEC. NETworth is an investor service supported by companies that want exposure for their products. It has a variety of information, including reports from market experts, stock quotes and fundamentals, and a weekly market update. One of the latest additions is from Disclosure Inc., which provides SEC document and database services.

INVESTMENT DATABASES OF PARTICULAR INTEREST

Some databases are fundamental and technical screening devices that are easily accessible through PCs. Though not all databases offer the same information, most are useful for analyzing large numbers of companies in a short time. You can create, analyze, and compare ratios. You can do trend and regression analysis. You can implement searches for specific kinds of companies. For example, you could screen for companies meeting certain parameters, such as:

- Dividend yield greater than 7%

- Earnings growth greater than 20% per year

- P/E ratio less than 10 times

- Market price less than book value

Some databases provide useful data on the U.S. economy; others contain international economic and company data.

- **Value Line Database II** provides financial and statistical information for over 1,600 companies, representing 95% of the dollar value of stocks traded on major U.S. companies. This database can be accessed through CompuServe.

- **Stock Investor** (AAII, 625 North Michigan Avenue, Department NLG, Chicago, IL 60611; 312-280-0170) is an easy and convenient way to screen over 7,000 stocks using a menu-driven program. You can research stocks using over 100 predetermined financial variables or you can create your own variables. The program data, updated quarterly, covers all stocks on the NYSE, AMEX, OTC, and OTC Small-Cap; earnings estimates are from IBES.

- **CompuServe's FundWatch Online** by *Money* magazine allows you to screen over 1,700 mutual funds using criteria that mirror your investment philosophy to find ones that are consistent with your goals; you can get a detailed report on a fund by entering its name or ticker symbol. This service lets you conduct in-depth research on a particular stock using Disclosure II, S&P On-line, and Value Line Data Base II.

- **Prodigy's Strategic Investor** lets you screen, select, and evaluate over 5,200 stocks and 4,000 mutual funds. Prodigy also has the following on-line services:

- **TradeLine:** price and volume charts and data on virtually any security or mutual fund

- **Company Reports:** comprehensive data on over 6,000 public companies

- **Mutual Fund Center:** detailed information on funds

- **CompuServe's RATEGRAM** ranks the highest yielding taxable and tax-exempt money market funds, giving the telephone number, the minimum required deposit, and a safety index rating.

- **IBES (Institutional Brokers Estimate System Summary)** is a company investigation feature of CompuServe. It contains consensus earnings forecasts compiled from estimates made by over 3,400 analysts at 130 brokerage and research firms, comparing the estimates with the stock's current price to predict forward P/E ratios.

- **Compustat** from S&P contains financial data from the annual and quarterly reports and SEC filings of more than 9,000 publicly held companies, updated annually. You can choose from various reports that summarize background, outlook, performance, business earnings and yield, market performance, balance sheet, and company history. This database can be accessed through CompuServe.

- **CRSP** (Center for Research on Security Prices) published by The University of Chicago, consists of three stock market history files: daily AMEX/NYSE returns since 1967, monthly returns since 1926, and daily NASDAQ returns since 1972.

- **Dialog** *(www.dialog.com)* has a database containing financial and textual data from SEC documents on about 11,000 public companies. Included are over 250 variables from company name, address, and phone number to financial statements, financial ratios, and weekly prices.

- **S&P's GLOBAL Vantage** provides financial data for approximately 7,600 companies from 33 countries, including companies in Europe (16 countries), North America (2), the Pacific Basin (8), and other regions of the world (7).

- *COINTEL* (Company Information for Telebase) within the CompuServe network provides information on European companies.

- **FRB,** published by the Board of Governor of the Federal Reserve System, contains financial statements and supporting schedules for more than 15,000 banks. Updated annually, it has five years' data on-line.

- **CITIBASE** from Citicorp consists of time-series data summarizing economic and other conditions in the U.S., updated quarterly.

CHOOSING A DATABASE

While investment databases have a lot to offer, they are expensive. In choosing a database, here is a checklist of questions you need answered:

- Is this database worth the cost to you?

- Do you want more than just investment information?

- Is there a database that offers what you want at an affordable price?

Here are further points to consider:

- **Coverage:** The number of securities and companies covered, the depth of financial information, and the availability of historical data vary. Does it offer analysis and advice? Do you need everything the database offers? Can you get just what you need elsewhere?

- **Data Organization:** Even when several services get information from the same data base, each has its own way of organizing the information. Organization determines how easy or difficult it's to use the database, especially if you don't do it every day; it may also determine how much it costs you to use the database.

- **Format:** The time it takes to get the data will be different for each service. For example, getting graphs from Telescan, using Telescan software, takes about one-tenth the time it takes on other databases. The time required to get specific data on-line also depends on the software you're using to get to the database. Because most investment software will get data from only one or two databases, comparison of the time required from each database is difficult.

- **Cost:** More and more on-line services are offering a flat-rate option in which users pay a standard monthly charge for unlimited access. For instance, Prodigy offers Strategic Investor for $15 per month, which allows unlimited access to broad stock and mutual fund databases. Custom screening, however, is limited. Telescan ProSearch offers a good balance of wide company coverage, a variety of screening variables, flexible screening options, and integrated software. Telescan also offers a variety of pricing options ranging from a pay-as-you-use option to unlimited screening with different prices for prime-time or non-prime-time access.

- **Number of Screening Variables:** Get the list of screening variables to determine if the program will support those you find important. For example, Value/Screen III lets you screen companies based on Value Line's rankings and projected growth rates, which may be more important for some investors than a complete database. Telescan's ProSearch program is the only service that combines both fundamental and technical factors for screening.

- **Support Services:** The quality of a database's support services is important. When something goes wrong, it's hard to know whether the fault lies with the software, the communications system, or the database. It's important to have someone who is knowledgeable and helpful to walk you through the problem.

NOTES:

- *On-line services all have customer support services with an 800 number.*

- *Before you choose a database service, try to get hands-on experience with at least a few. Some offer a demonstration diskette with a sample of the kind of material you will get on-line; others offer free sample time. Or find a friend or a users group with a service that you can try out.*

- *Dow Jones News/Retrieval and Equalizer have the most services for the individual investor, but their hourly charges are also the highest. If you need many of Dow Jones's features, it's worth the cost. If not, you may be able to find what you want on CompuServe or Prodigy. For just price quotations, technical analysis, or other specific data, other databases may fill your needs at a lower cost.*

INVESTMENT SOFTWARE

A good investment software package makes your PC a valuable tool for identifying securities to buy, placing orders on-line, and monitoring securities after you buy them.

Some programs create and analyze charts of the technical behavior of price movements; others evaluate financial data from balance sheets and income statement. Using the Dow Jones News Retrieval System's Investment Evaluator, you can obtain information for stocks, bonds, warrants, options, mutual funds, or Treasury issues. Information on earnings growth rates, 10-K statements, ratios, earnings per share forecasts, and so forth are available on 2,400 companies. Once data is entered into one of these software programs, it creates standardized analysis from preprogrammed instructions.

Some programs can transfer data from a news retrieval service into a spreadsheet program such as Excell, Quatro Pro, orLotus 1-2-3. An example is the Dow Jones Spreadsheet Link, which enables corporate planners, investors, researchers, and competitive analysts to extract data from News/Retrieval for extensive analysis with spreadsheet programs. Automatically, the program logs on, collects specified data, and enters it into the spreadsheet for further analysis. The program saves time and money and gives you flexibility to create your own financial analysis.

The three main categories of investment software are (1) fundamental screening and analysis, (2) portfolio management, and (3) technical analysis. Other types of investment software deal specifically with investments other than stocks (*e.g.,* options and futures and fixed-income securities).

Fundamental Screening and Analysis

Most fundamental analysis software does stock screening, letting you search through many stocks to identify those meeting specified criteria. For example, you may want to identify all stocks on the NYSE that have a market price per share less than $35, a P/E ratio less than the S&P 500 Index, a dividend yield greater than 6%, and a beta less than 1.5. Stock-screening packages can narrow your choices in a few minutes.

Normally, these are subscription services. Every month you receive a data base disk containing up-to-date financial information on a group of stocks. The type and amount of information varies with the software package. There are a lot of options, including:

PC Programs

- *Stock Investor* by AAII

- *WealthBuilder/Smart Investor* by Reality Technologies

- *Value/Screen II* by Value Line

Macintosh Programs

- *WealthBuilder (Smart Investor)* by Reality Technologies

- *Value/Screen II* by Value Line

On-Line Services

*   *Telescan Analyzer (Telescan Edge)* by Telescan, Inc.

*   *Strategic Investor* by Prodigy

*   *Dow Jones News/Retrieval* by Dow Jones

*   *CompuServe* by H&R Block

NOTES: When selecting a stock-screening package:

*   *Compare the number of industries and companies that can be screened, the exchanges on which the stocks are listed, and the frequency with which data is updated.*

*   *Check each package for information on earnings, dividends, assets, market price, sales, liabilities, financial ratios, and proprietary items.*

Portfolio Management

This software lets you enter the names of the securities you own or want to follow into one or more portfolios, enter current prices (manually or through automatic updates from an on-line service), and generate a variety of portfolio status reports. For each security you own, these reports provide the type, method of purchase (for cash or on margin), purchase price, number of shares or units owned, current price, and unrealized gain or loss.

Other reports convey vital income tax information: For each security you sell during the tax year, you get the name, number of shares, sale date, total cost, total proceeds, purchase date, and gain or loss—all the information you need to complete your federal income tax return. Still other reports reflect dividend and interest income. They can provide advance notice of dividends coming due and options expiring.

Technical Analysis

Technical analysis software is usually used for charting. With it you can plot standard high-low-close-volume bar charts, along with other technical indicators. Since this requires the input of extensive information it's wise to compare the kinds of data required to use each package you con-sider and sources for the data. For example, if you want to see a basic high-low-close-volume bar chart for General Electric for a 120-day peri-od, the program will require 600 pieces of data. Though you could always enter the information into the computer little by little, you might prefer a program that can get it from an on-line service such as the Dow Jones New/Retrieval and Telescan Analyzer, thus greatly reducing the time it takes you to create a chart.

A good program will offer a variety of charting options.

NOTES: In selecting a good program, ask:

- *Can you plot sophisticated indicators to analyze individual securi-ties and the overall stock market?*

- *Are you limited to simple moving-average lines and a few basic charting tools?*

- *Can any data the software collects be easily transferred for use in other software programs?*

- *Are the prices reasonable?*

- *Can the program show multiple charts on the same screen, so that you can compare the activity in two different stocks or examine a number of technical indicators at the same time?*

- *Is there an 'auto-run' feature? Although programs with this capa-bility may be more expensive, they can save a lot of time by allow-ing you to automatically prepare and print charts you want on a regular basis. You simply enter the auto-run mode, leave the com-puter, and return later to pick up your printed charts.*

- *Which technical indicators and studies can be plotted?*

COMPARISON SHOPPING

There are more than 550 investment software packages on the market; your neighborhood computer store won't be much help in sorting through the choices. Because it's so specialized, most investment software is sold only through the mail, meaning you'll have to pay several hundred dollars in advance for software that, in many cases, is not returnable for a refund. Charge it with a credit card. And get all the facts you can before you decide what to buy.

- Do market research; look at who's selling what.

   NOTE: An excellent user guide is AAII's Computerized Investing. Updated annually, the guide describes most investment software packages on the market. Also check PC, Mac, and financial magazines for their independent ratings and reviews.

- Check the support policies: Does the company offer telephone support and, if so, at what times? Some vendors charge for providing help. Some may operate a bulletin board system (BBS) or forum that you can connect to, not only to solve problems, but also to get operating tips.

- Ask other investors at a local investment club or through BBS or Internet.

- List the specific features you believe are absolutely necessary for you. For example, if you want to break down your stocks by industry group to analyze portfolio diversification, write that down. When you're finished, you'll have a checklist of features to look for as you review actual software.

- Get information from each vendor. Match the features offered with those on your checklist and eliminate packages that don't meet your needs.

   NOTE: For a nominal amount, many software vendors offer a demonstration package containing a disk and written material that illustrate the features of their software packages.

Chapter 15
INVESTMENT ADVISORY AND NEWSLETTERS

Investors often find that newsletters help them choose the right investment vehicle or decide when to get in and out of an investment. There were more than 200 market-oriented newsletters published in the U.S. in 1999, reaching about 2 million subscribers. They range in price from about $30 a year to more than $600, and their strategies are as varied as their numbers.

Here are four areas to consider before you take the plunge on a newsletter.

- **Performance,** long-term (such as five- and ten-year), is the most important criterion. Be sure to compare the newsletter's track record with that of the market. The market may be the Wilshire 5000, a broad index of small- and large-company stocks, or the S&P 500 index.

- **Risk:** Pick a newsletter with the same attitude to risk as you. Letters that chalk up the biggest gains typically take on more risks that those with more modest results. The strategies are diverse, ranging from stocks, bonds, and gold to mutual funds. There are newsletters for chartists, timers, shorters, speculators, option traders, and sector chasers.

- **Time:** How much time do you have or want to devote to following the letter's advice? Is this letter long-term oriented or relying on frequent changes?

- Transaction costs: If you follow a letter's advice and have to execute your orders often, shop around for lower commissions. Commissions can erode respectable gains. In mutual fund investing, stick to no-load funds.

Spencer McGowan's *Investor's Investment Source Book* (NYIF, 1995) gives comprehensive coverage of newsletters. Another major source of information is the *Hulbert Financial Digest* (316 Commerce St., Alexandria, VA 22314, (703-683-5905), which tracks some 130 newsletters. *Hulbert* judges the quality and value of advice in investment letters. For example, it provides a list of newsletters that have beat the market over the past five years. The following are ten of the top performing newsletters (those that are ahead of the market on a risk-adjusted basis), tracked by the *Hulbert Financial Digest.*

TOP PERFORMING NEWSLETTERS

- *Systems and Forecasts*

Signalert Corp., 516-829-11021
Technical analysis. Covers stock, mutual funds, and market timing.

- *InvesTech Mutual Fund Advisor*

InvesTech, Inc., 800-955-8500
Technical analysis. Covers mutual funds and market timing.

- *BI Research*

BI Research Inc., 203-270-9244
Detailed research profiles of high-growth or overlooked stocks and mutual funds, with continuing advice on whether to buy, hold, or sell.

- *Zweig Forecast*

Zweig, 800-633-2252, ext. 9000
Technical analysis. Comments on sentiment and other indicators that make for superior stock market performance.

- *Fund Exchange*

Paul A. Merriman & Associates, Inc., 800-423-4893
Fundamental analysis. Covers mutual funds and market timing.

- *Investment Quality Trends*

Geraldine Weiss, 619-459-3818
Technical and fundamental analysis. Covers stocks, mutual funds, and charts.

- *Fidelity Monitor*

Jack Bowers, 800-397-3094
Covers Fidelity mutual funds.

- *The Chartist*

The Chartist, 310-596-2385
Charts various stocks and recommends buys and sells based on technical signals. The same company publishes the monthly Chartist Mutual Fund Timer, the fifth-ranked fund letter over the past five years.

- Peter Dag Investment Letter

Peter Dag & Associates, Inc., 216-644-2782
Fundamental analysis. Covers stocks, bonds, and precious metals.

- *Fundline*

David H. Menashe & Co., 818-346-5637
Technical analysis. Covers mutual funds and market timing.

NEWSLETTERS WITH GOOD TRACK RECORDS

The following newsletters have performed well over the years:

- *The Insiders*

The Institute for Econometric Research
3471 N. Federal Hwy.
Fort Lauderdale, FL 33306
Monthly
Based on the notion that company officials and directors who trade in their own stock know something; translates SEC data on buying and selling by insiders and makes recommendations.

- Individual Investor Special Situations Report

New York
212-689-2777
Monthly
Covers OTC stocks.

- *Medical Technology Stock Letter*

P.O. Box 40460
Berkeley, CA 94704
Every two weeks
Solid information on biotechnology and other emerging health fields.
Gives aggressive investors timely insight into the leading companies
in the field.

- *MTP Review*

Lake Tahoe, NV
702-831-1396
Monthly
Covers OTC stocks.

- *The Oberweis Report*

Aurora, Ill
708-801-4766
Monthly
Covers no-load mutual funds.

- *OTC Insight*

P.O. Box 1329
El Cerrito, CA 9453
800-955-9566
Monthly
A computerized stock-selector for OTC stocks, with model portfolios
and risk ratings.

- *The Prudent Speculator*

P.O. Box 1767
Santa Monica, CA 90406
Monthly
Undervalued issues, sell signals—classic stock research.

- *Value Line Investment Survey*

Value Line, Inc.
711 Third Avenue
New York, NY 10017
Weekly
Loose-leaf coverage of the business activities of major corporations in a variety of industries. Many charts and graphs. Ranks and updates about 1,700 stocks and speculates on the course of the market.

- Value Line OTC Special Situations Report

Value Line, Inc.
711 Third Avenue
New York, NY 10017
Twice a month
Loose-leaf recommendations and reports on OTC stocks and all issues Value Line believes have unusual potential.

POPULAR SPECIALIZED NEWSLETTERS

The following is a list of popular newsletters by investment categories. The list is not intended to be exhaustive.

Warrants and Options

- *Warrants, Options and Convertibles*

The Ney Option Report
P.O. Box 90215
Pasadena, CA 91109
Twice a month
For option traders, with recommendations and analysis.

- *RHM Survey of Warrants, Options & Low-Price Stocks*

RHM Associates, Inc.
172 Forest Avenue
Glen Cove, NY 11542
Weekly
Investment advice on warrants, call and put options, and low-priced stocks, with tables and charts.

- *The Stock Option Trading Form*

P.O. Drawer 24242
Fort Lauderdale, FL 33307
Monthly
Like a racing form, with puts and calls to buy and sell; little explana-
tory text.

- *Value Line Options & Convertibles*

Value Line, Inc.
711 Third Avenue
New York, NY 10017
Weekly
Evaluation and analysis of hundreds of convertible bonds, warrants,
and options—probably the pre-eminent source of this information for
active investors.

Commodities

- *The Addison Report*

P.O. Box 402
Franklin, MA 02038
Every three weeks
Quick comments and recommendations on stocks, bonds, and com-
modities.

- *The COINfidential Report*

P.O. Box 2727
New Orleans, LA 70176
Coin and stock market newsletter and advisory.

- *Commodity Closeup*

P.O. Box 6
Cedar Falls, IA 50613
Weekly
Tracks futures prices and trading in financials, metals, grains, and
meats.

- *Commodity Service*

Dunn & Hargitt, Inc.
22 N. 2nd Street
Box 1100
Lafayette, IN 47902
Weekly
Charts 34 of the most active commodities, with buy and sell recommendations.

- *Commodity Traders Consumer Report*

1731 Howe Ave., Suite 149
Sacramento, CA 95825
Every two months
Wide-ranging look at futures markets, with recommendations, commentaries, and interviews about trading strategies.

- *Dines Letter*

James Dine & Company
Box 22
Belvedere, CA 94920
Monthly
A respected advisory on stocks, gold and metals, and economics; combines important technical, psychological, and business indicators.

- *Dunn & Hargitt Commodity Service*

22 N. Second St.
Lafayette, IN 47902
Weekly
Charts and action comments on commodities from British pounds to gold, heating oil, and pork bellies.

- *Gann Angles*

245-A Washington St., Suite 2
Monterey, CA 93940
Monthly
Technical market-timing advisory, heavy on commodities; based on the system of W.D. Gann, a turn-of-the-century trader who ascribed price movements to regular mathematical patterns.

- Hard Money Digest

3608 Grand Ave.
Oakland, CA 94610
Monthly
Summary and comparison of opinions from other newsletters on
gold, silver, interest rates, stocks, and economics.

- *The Hume Moneyletter*

835 Franklin Court
Marietta, GA 30067
Tracks commodity prices.

- *International Asset Investor*

HMR Publishing Co.
P.O. Box 471
Barrington, IL 60010
Monthly
Comments and statistics on commodities and currencies for those
investing abroad.

- *The Kondratieff Wave Analyst*

P.O. Box 977
Crystal Lake, IL 60014
Economic commentary and interpretation of trading actions, with
much attention to long cycles and a section on precious metals.

- *Managed Account Reports*

5513 Twin Knolls Rd., Suite 213
Columbia, MD 21045
Twice a month
Alternating reports on the futures industry and on the performance of
commodity pools. Authoritative for commodities traders who use
managed funds. Monitors commodities trading advisors (CTAs), private pools, and public funds.

- *The McKeever Strategy Letter*

P.O. Box 4130
Medford, OR 97501
Monthly
Longer-than-average letters led by essays on economic or market topics, followed by advice on stocks, bonds, metals, and currencies.

- *Silver and Gold Report*

P.O. Box 510
Bethel, CT 06801
Annual
Monitors dealers; publishes an annual survey with comparative prices.

- *Trendway Advisory Service*

P.O. Box 7184
Louisville, KY 40207
Twice a month
Current analysis of stocks, money markets, and gold, with an eye for chart patterns.

- *Value Forecaster*

P.O. Box 50
Pilot Hill, CA 95664
Analysis of COMEX warehouse bullion stocks of silver and other precious metals.

- The Wellington Letter

1800 Grosvenor Center
733 Bishop St.
Honolulu, HA 96813
Thorough and respected; covers stocks, bonds, currencies, and metals.

MUTUAL FUND INFORMATION

Here are the major sources of information for making an informed decision about investing in mutual funds.

- **Investment Company Institute**

  1600 M St., NW, Suite 600
  Washington, DC 20036
  202-326-5800
  The industry's trade group for both load and no-load funds, the Institute lobbies on behalf of its more than 1,500 member funds and their stockholders while doing trade research and acting as a clearinghouse for industry information. It publishes:

  - The annual *Directory of Mutual Funds,* containing capsulized data on more than 3,000 funds separated into 22 categories of investment objectives. It also includes general introductory and explanatory material.

  - The annual *Guide to Mutual Funds,* discussing mutual fund organization and regulation, defining terms used in the industry, and answering common questions. It gives addresses, phone numbers, and information on initial investment requirements, total assets and the like for more than 1,400 funds, categorized by investment objective, such as aggressive growth or income. There is no performance information.

  - The annual *Mutual Fund Fact Book,* designed for investment professionals but containing a wealth of facts that may be useful to more experienced investors.

  You can also request copies of the Institute's free brochures, including *Money Market Mutual Funds—What Are They?* and *A Translation: Turning Investment-ese into Investment Ease.*

Magazines

A number of personal finance and business magazines publish charts and analyses of the performance of major mutual funds. Forbes does its annual mutual fund wrap-up every September. *Kiplinger Personal Finance Magazine* publishes its review in October. Money generally reviews mutual fund performance twice a year, in the spring and fall. *Business Week, Smart Money, Consumer Reports,* and *Worth* also rate mutual funds.

Mutual Fund Newsletters

Mutual fund investors often find that a newsletter or two helps them choose among hundreds of funds or decide when to get in and out of an investment. Letters also identify good funds that you haven't heard about elsewhere and explain long-term fund performance rankings.

However, understand that fund publications serve differing objectives. Some, such as *Telephone Switch Newsletter* and *Weber's Fund Advisor,* use a rigid trading formula to tell you which funds to buy and sell and when. Unless you're going to follow the system, the letters are useless.

Others, including *Growth Fund Guide, Mutual Fund Letter,* and *United Mutual Fund Selector,* are educational and journalistic. They run articles (often based on original research) about topics of interest to shareholders, such as how the funds have done through the years or why funds are increasing certain charges.

Still others are largely databases in which you can look up scores of funds and their rankings by objectives, time periods, and size. These include *Morningstar's Mutual Fund Values, CDA Mutual Fund Report, Schabacker's Mutual Fund Analysis Guide* and *Wiesenberger Investment Companies Service.*

Because of intense competition between publishers, most discount their subscription rates for new subscribers. Even better are the short-term trial offers, which may include one free issue. Write or call the toll-free numbers for details or watch for advertisements in financial magazines and newspapers.

Examples of advisory services and newsletters are:

* *CDA Mutual Fund Report*

CDA Investment Technologies
11501 Georgia Ave.
Silver Spring, MD 20902
A comprehensive directory and data service that rates 850 funds many ways, ranks them by short-term and long-term performance, and assigns an overall rating.

• *Donoghue's Moneyletter*

The Donoghue Organization
P.O. Box 411
Holliston, MA 01746
800-343-5413
Bimonthly
Wise counsel on current strategies; includes a pullout called *Fund-letter,* which follows a portfolio of money market funds for "safety, liquidity, yield, and catastrophe-proofing." Also tackles bread-and-butter investments like municipal bonds, mutual funds, and bank accounts.

• *Income & Safety*

The Institute for Econometric Research
3471 N. Federal Hwy.
Fort Lauderdale, FL 33306
305-563-9000 (FL only)
800-327-6720
A directory of over 200 mutual funds that indicates each fund's primary portfolio holding, yield, minimum investment, services available and load, if any. Recommends "best buys."

• *International Fund Monitor*

P.O. Box 5754
Washington, DC 20016
Covers closed-end international funds.

• *Jay Schabacker's Mutual Fund Investing*

Phillips Publishing Inc.
7811 Montrose Rd.
Potomac, MD 20854
800-722-9000
For less-experienced fund investors than Schabacker's other letters; contains a smorgasbord of features, model portfolios, question-and answer sections, and a brief market commentary.

- *Mannie Webb's Sector Fund Connection*

8949 LaRiviera Dr.
Sacramento, CA 95826
Switching advisory covering several families of no-load funds that specialize in certain industries.

- *Mutual Fund Forecaster*

The Institute for Econometric Research
3471 N. Federal Hwy.
Fort Lauderdale, FL 33306
800-327-6720
305-563-9000
Projects performance for more than 300 mutual funds based on a reading of the market and the fund's characteristics. A directory gives performance measures, one-year income projections, and risk ratings.

- *Mutual Fund Values*

Morningstar
53 West Jackson Blvd.
Chicago, IL 60604
Value-added information such as yields, alpha, beta, R-squared, and standard deviation. Rates each fund on its risk-adjusted performance and provides straightforward buy and sell recommendations.

- *Retirement Fund Advisory*

Schabacker Investment Management
8943 Shady Grove Ct.
Gaithersburg, MD 20877
Abridged version of the same company's Switch Fund Advisory with emphasis on funds suitable for IRA and Keogh investors.

- *Schabacker's Mutual Fund Analysis Guide*

Schabacker Investment Management, Inc.
8943 Shady Grove Ct.
Gaithersburg, MD 20877
Comprehensive statistical report and advisory service that grades funds on a scale from A+ to D.

- *Sector Funds Newsletter*

P.O. Box 1210
Escondido, CA 92025
Provides model portfolios and signals to switch funds; emphasizes the Fidelity funds.

- *United Mutual Fund Selector*

United Business Service
101 Prescott St.
Wellesley Hills, MA 02181
Semi-monthly
Rates mutual funds, including bond and municipal bond funds. Very well organized. Full of performance charts and descriptions of funds, plus industry developments.

TAX SHELTERS AND REAL ESTATE INVESTMENTS

- *Brennan Reports*

Valley Forge Office Colony
P. O. Box 882, Suite 200
Valley Forge, PA 19482
Monthly
Examines tax-advantaged investments such as real estate, single-premium life insurance, and oil and gas deals. Excellent coaching on tax planning.

- *Brennan's IRA Advisor*

Valley Forge Office Colony
P. O. Box 882, Suite 200
Valley Forge, PA 19482
Monthly
An offshoot of Brennan Reports; discusses the ins and outs of unusual IRA investments, such as income real estate limited partnerships.

- *Income Investor Perspectives*

Uniplan, Inc.
3907 N. Green Bay Ave.
Milwaukee, WI 53206
Every three weeks
Updates tax-advantaged and income-oriented investments, such as utility stocks and REITs; useful for safety-and-yield investors.

- Oil and Gas Quarterly

1275 Broadway
Albany, NY 12204
Quarterly
Covers oil and gas exclusively.

- *The Real Estate Digest*

P. O. Box 16444
Birmingham, AL 35226
Monthly
Covers real estate investments, including tax strategies, title insurance, real estate financing, and management.

Chapter 16
FREE FINANCIAL INFORMATION ON THE INTERNET

The popularity that the Internet enjoys today is based, in part, on the information available to members of the public as they "surf the net." Governmental and nonprofit organizations often provide information free as a service to the public. Companies web sites also offer information to the public. Although private Web sites often charge for information, a number offer information free in order to generate site traffic. Increased Internet traffic serves to:

- Interest viewers in premium services offered on the site

- Generate advertising revenue

- Promote other non-Internet services offered to the public

Financial statements, SEC filings, company-specific news reports, brokerage house recommendations and future earnings estimates on large companies, bond and stock quotations, financial indexes, company, and pension plan profiles are all available on the Internet at no cost. The instantaneous nature of the Internet makes a great deal of this information much more timely than is the case with traditional sources.

Throughout this book, we have given the Internet address (URL) for sites that provide free information on a specific subject. This chapter repeats some of these locations and adds new ones.

FINANCIAL STATEMENTS

As a public service, the SEC makes a number of SEC filings available to the public through the EDGAR archives on the Internet. Within EDGAR, the public may obtain such filings as Form 10-Ks. Form 10-K contains the annual report to shareholders, along with additional information on the company's products, competitors, marketing activities, product development, major contracts and leases (including employment contracts) and legal proceedings. The 10-K also includes more detailed schedules than those that appear in the annual report on inventories, bad debts, warranties and advertising.

Form 10-Q filings are also part of the EDGAR archives. The 10-Q is the quarterly report to shareholders. Along with the unaudited balance sheet and income statement found in most quarterly reports, the 10-Q also contains unaudited cash flow statements, shareholders' equity or retained earnings statements, footnotes, and management discussion of the company.

EDGAR also contains Form 8-Q filings, which inform the SEC of material events that have happened since the most recent 10-K and 10-Q filings.

A number of web sites retrieve EDGAR filings (see Figure 16-1). The SEC's site does so, but because it operates through the use of key words, it may be difficult to locate the filings of a particular company. Other sites allow viewers to search the archives using ticker symbols. FreeEDGAR lets you download the filings as spreadsheet files. 10K Wizard will e-mail filings to viewers as word processing files. Moreover, with 10K Wizard, financial statements within the filings can be received as spreadsheet files. EDGARScan lets you download tables from the filings as spreadsheet files. Filings within the previous 24 hours are not available through EDGAR ONLINE.

FIGURE 16-1: EDGAR SITES

Site	Ticker Symbol Search	Spreadsheet Files	Word Processing Files	All Filings Available
EDGARScan (edgarscan.pwcglobal.com)		X	X	X
FreeEDGAR (www.FreeEDGAR.com)	X	X		X
10K Wizard (http://www.tenkwizard.com)	X		X	X
Disclosure (www.disclosure-investor.com)	X			X
EDGAR ONLINE (www.edgar-online.com)	X			
SEC (www.sec.gov/cgi-bin/srch-edgar)				X

Some company annual reports to shareholders are also available through the Internet (see Figure 16-2). A number of companies place their annual report on their Web sites; Report Gallery and Online Annual Reports Service contain links to these annual reports. Both of these services will also mail hard copies to you upon request. Report Gallery has links to the annual reports of Japanese, Korean, United Kingdom, and South African companies.

In addition to online annual reports, Annual Reports Service and Investor Communications Business, Inc. will mail copies of the annual reports of selected companies to you upon request, but a number of major companies do not participate in these services. For example, neither service carries the Microsoft annual report, and Investor Communications Business, Inc., does not carry the IBM annual report. Investor Communications Business, Inc. does make available the annual reports of Canadian and United Kingdom companies.

FIGURE 16-2: ANNUAL REPORT SITES

Site	Online	Hard Copy	Number of Companies
Report Gallery (www.reportgalleryservice.com)	X	X	1000
Online Annual Report Service (www.annualreportservice.com)	X	X	2114
Annual Report Service (www.prars.com)		X	3600
Investor Communications Business, Inc. (www.icbinc.com)		X	3500

BROKERAGE RECOMMENDATIONS AND EARNINGS FORECASTS

Information on the future operations of a company can be gleaned from earnings forecasts by broker/analysts, as well as from their recommendations about investing in the company. Generally, these are provided free on a consensus (composite) basis. The consensus recommendations and earnings forecasts contain:

- Future earnings forecast

- Recent history of changes in earnings forecasts

- Recommendations on investing in a company

- Recent history of changes in recommendations

- Names of brokers/analysts surveyed for consensus

Some companies give more information on other Web sites (see Figure 16-3) than they do on their own site (*e.g.,* I/B/E/S, Zacks, and First Call).

FIGURE 16-3: CONSENSUS RECOMMENDATIONS AND EARNINGS FORECAST SITES

Site	For.	Forcst. History	Rec.	Recmd. History	Names
Multex Investor Network (www.multexinvestor.com)	X	X	X	X	X
Yahoo!Finance (Zacks Investment Research) (finance.yahoo.com)	X	X	X	X	X
MARKET GUIDE (I/B/E/S) (www.marketguide.com)	X	X	X	X	
Invest-O-Rama First Call (www.investorama.com)	X	X	X	X	
Standard & Poor's Personal Wealth (www.personalwealth.com)	X		X		
Nordby International (www.nordby.com)			X		X
ABC News (abcnews.go.com)			X		
Financial Web Media General (www.financialweb.com)	X				
EarningsWhispers.com (www.earningswhispers.com)	X				

Besides consensus recommendations and forecasts, Financial Web *(www.financialweb.com)* and Nordby International *(www.nordby.com)* provide a short summary of the recommendations and forecasts of named individual broker/analysts. Yahoo!Finance *(finance.yahoo.com)* also does this, but its reports seem less comprehensive.

VectorVest provides an in-house recommendation and future earnings forecast. Only a limited number of these reports can be accessed by non-subscribers. Other VectorVest reports, however, can be accessed from Company Sleuth *(www.companysleuth.com)* and Investor Guide *(www.investorguide.com)*.

CORPORATE NEWS STORIES

The Internet abounds with the sites of news organizations, and these sites contain business news stories (see Figure 16-4). For example, the CNNfn (cnnfn.com) and Bloomberg (www.bloomberg.com) Web sites offer extensive general business news. Other sites specialize in corporation specific-news stories. These sites are valuable if you're researching a particular company. All of these sites are searchable by ticker symbol and provide press releases via Business Wire and PR Newswire. News sources used by these web sites (other than Business Wire and PR Newswire) include:

Rather than offering access to complete news stories, Transium *(www.transium.com)* offers visitors access to abstracts of articles from an extensive list of sources including national newspapers and magazines (*e.g., New York Times, Washington Post* and the *Wall Street Journal*). You can search the abstracts by ticker symbol, and further limit the search by subject matter.

MACROECONOMIC INFORMATION

Macroeconomic information is readily available from many government sources, including the Bureau of Labor Statistics, the Census Bureau, the Federal Reserve Board of Governors, the individual Federal Reserve Banks, and the White House, and from private sources like the Conference Board and the National Federation of Independent Businesses.

FIGURE 16-4: WEB SITES AND THEIR NEWS SOURCES

Site	News Sources Used
Yahoo!Finance *(finance.yahoo.com)*	CBS, R, AP, S&P, MF, RH, ST & NC
News Alert *(www.newsalert.com)*	CBS, R, UPI, MF& RH
Companylink *(www.companylink.com)*	CDJ, R, UPI, INT & CMP
Financial Web *(www.financialweb.com)*	AP, UPI, M2 & CMP
CBS Market Watch *(cbs.marketwatch.com)*	CBS, R & AP
News Real *(www.news-real.com)*	CNN, AP & N&R
Northern Light *(www.northernlight.com)*	UPI, AP & M2
Smart Money.Com *(www.smartmoney.com)*	DJ & SM
MSN Money Central *(moneycentral.msn.com)*	NBC & R
The Motley Fool *(www.fool.com)*	MF & R
Quote.com *(www.quote.com)*	R & AP
CNET News.com *(www.news.com/Investor)*	BB & NC
Reuters Moneynet *(www.moneynet.com)*	R
S&P's Personal Wealth *(www.personal-wealth.com)*	SP

Key: Corporate News Sources

AP	Associated Press
BB	Bloomberg
CBS	CBS
CDJ	CNBC/Dow Jones Business Video (transcripts)
CMP	CMP publications
CNN	CNN
DJ	Dow Jones
INT	International news sources
M2	M2 Communications
MF	Motley Fool
N&R	National and regional newspapers
NBC	MSNBC
NC	News.Com
R	Reuters
RH	Red Herring
S&P	Standard & Poor's
SM	*Smart Money* Magazine
ST	The Street.Com
UPI	UPI
WSJ	*Wall Street Journal* abstracts and articles

FIGURE 16-5: MACROECONOMIC INFORMATION SITES

Atlanta Federal Reserve Bank	*www.frbatlanta.org*
Boston Federal Reserve Bank	*www.bos.frb.org*
Bureau of Labor Statistics	*www.stats.bls.gov*
Bureau of Labor Statistics	*www.bls.gov*
Census Bureau	*www.census.gov/econ/www*
Chicago Federal Reserve Bank	*www.frbchi.org*
Cleveland Federal Reserve Bank	*www.clev.frb.org*
Conference Board	*www.conference-board.org*
Dallas Federal Reserve Bank	*www.dallasfed.org*
Fed Stats	*www.fedstats.gov*
Federal Reserve Board of Governors	*www.bog.frb.fed.us*
Kansas City Federal Reserve Bank	*www.kc.frb.org*
Minneapolis Federal Reserve Bank	*www.woodrow.mpls.frb.fed.us*
National Federation of Independent Business	*www.nfibonline.com*
New York Federal Reserve Bank	*www.ny.frb.org*
Philadelphia Federal Reserve Bank	*www.phil.frb.org*
Richmond Federal Reserve Bank	*www.rich.frb.org*
San Francisco Federal Reserve Bank	*www.frbsf.org*
St. Louis Federal Reserve Bank	*www.stls.frb.org*
White House Economic Briefing Room	*www.whitehouse.gov/fsbr/esbr.html*

QUOTATIONS AND RATINGS

Bonds

Moody's and Fitch, two of the three major bond rating services make their ratings available on their Web sites. The third, Standard & Poor's, can be obtained from Bonds Online, which also offers price quotations.

FIGURE 16-6: BOND RATING WEB SITES

Bonds Online	*www.bondsonline.com*
BradyNet, Inc.	*www.bradynet.com*
Fitch	*www.fitchibca.com*
Moody's	*www.moodys.com*

Mutual Funds

A number of magazine and newsletter sites rank or rate mutual funds. Other sites offer mutual fund profiles with information provided by Lipper, Inc., Morningstar, Inc., Value Line, and Wiesenberger.

FIGURE 16-7: MUTUAL FUND RATING SITES

PROPRIETARY RANKINGS:

Business Week	*www.businessweek.com*
CNBC (J&J Financial Co.)	*www.cnbc.com*
Forbes	*www.forbes.com*
Investor's Consistency Index	*www.mutualfund-index.com*
Morningstar	*www.morningstar.net*
Smart Money	*www.smartmoney.com*
Standard & Poor's	*www.personalwealth.com*

LIPPER RANKINGS:

CBS MarketWatch	*cbs.marketwatch.com*
Reuters Moneynet	*www.moneynet.com*
CNNfn	*cnnfn.com*

MORNINGSTAR RANKINGS:

Yahoo!Finance	*finance.yahoo.com*
Wall Stree Research Net	*www.wsrn.com*
MSN Money Central	*Moneycentral.msn.com*
Quicken	*quicken.excite.com*
Excite	*www.excite.com*
AOL	*quicken.aol.com*

VALUE LINE RANKINGS:

Excite	*www.excite.com*
Quicken	*quicken.excite.com*
Stockpoint	*www.stockpoint.com*

WEISENBERGER RANKINGS:

Find A Fund	*www.findafund.com*

Indexes

A number of Web sites, like the news media, report the performance of major indexes (see chapter 2). The Web sites listed in Figure 16-8 report the performance of indexes other than those commonly reported. The CBS MarketWatch site provides the most extensive listing of domestic and foreign indexes (including bond and equity indexes). Timely.com also offers extensive domestic index listings.

FIGURE 16-8: STOCK AND EQUITY WEB SITES

Internet Site	Stock	Bond	Foreign Stock	Foreign Bond
CBS MarketWatch *(cbs.market-watch.com)*	X	X	X	X
Timely.com *(www.timely.com)*	X			
CNBC *(www.cnbc.com)*	X	X		
JP Morgan *(www.jpmorgan.com)*			X	X
Merrill Lynch *(www.ml.com)*		X		X
Morgan Stanley Capital International *(www.mscidata.com)*			X	X
NASDAQ *(www.nasdaq.com)*	X	X		
Solomon Smith Barney *(www.solomonsmithbarney.com)*	X	X		
Standard & Poor's *(www.spglobal.com)*	X		X	
StockMaster.com *(www.stockmaster.com)*	X		X	
American Stock Exchange *(www.amex.com)*	X			
J.P.Morgan *(adr.com)*			X	
U.S. Bancorp Piper Jaffray *(www.pjc.com)*		X		

RESOURCES ON OTHER TOPICS

ADRs: J.P. Morgan's ADR.com Internet site maintains extensive foreign stock indexes along with ADR price quotations. The Bank of New York also maintains leading ADR indexes on its Internet site.

FIGURE 16-9: ADR WEB SITES

J.P.Morgan	*adr.com*
Bank of New York	*www.bankofny.com/adr*
ADR City	*www.cyberhost3.com/stockcit/adr/index.html*

Futures

Commodity Charts & Quotes—Free *(tfc-charts.w2d.com)* provides quotations for commodity futures.

Industry Groups

Wall Street City *(www.wallstreetcity.com)*, Clearstation *(www.clearstation.com)*, and CNBC *(www.cnbc.com)* provide extensive comparisons of companies within the same industry. Yahoo! *(finance.yahoo.com)* and Market Guide *(www.marketguide.com)* also list companies within the same sector.

Investment Suites

A growing number of Web sites are offering "one-stop shopping" to investors. These investment "suites" offer some or all of the services already discussed (see Figure 16-10) along with general business news, investment advice, and other information. For example, the S&P Personal Wealth site grades the credit worthiness of companies. The information available on these sites include:

FIGURE 16-10: SERVICES OFFERED ON INVESTMENT SUITE SITES

Site	A	B	C	IT	M	MF	N	P	PR	Q	S	SEC	SH
Just Quotes (www.justquotes.com)	X	X		X	X	X	X	X	X	X		X	X
Invest-O-Rama (www.investorama.com)	X	X		X	X		X	X	X	X	X	X	X
Nawed Usmani (www.nrmcapital.com)	X	X		X	X	X	X	X	X	X		X	X
CBS Market Watch (cbs.marketwatch.com)	X	X		X		X	X	X	X	X	X		
Excite (Quicken) (quicken.excite.com)		X		X	X	X	X	X	X	X	X	X	
Quicken (www.quicken.com)		X		X	X	X	X	X	X	X	X	X	
AOL (quicken.aol.com)		X		X	X	X	X	X	X	X	X	X	
CNNfn (Quicken) (cnnfn.com)		X		X	X	X	X	X	X	X	X	X	
Yahoo!Finance (finance.yahoo.com)		X			X	X	X	X	X	X	X	X	
MSN (Microsoft) MoneyCentral (moneycentral.msn.com)		X		X		X	X	X	X	X	X	X	
Company Sleuth (www.companysleuth.com)		X		X	X		X		X	X		X	X
Financial Web (www.financialweb.com)		X				X	X	X	X	X	X	X	
Clearstation (www.clearstation.com)		X		X	X		X	X	X	X			
Market Guide (www.marketguide.com)	X		X	X			X	X	X	X			
Wall Street Research Net (www.wsrn.com)	X		X	X			X	X	X	X		X	
Standard & Poor's Personal Wealth (www.personalwealth.com)		X	X	X			X	X	X			X	X
CNBC (www.cnbc.com)	X	X	X	X			X	X	X			X	
Morningstar (www.morningstar.net)	X	X	X	X			X	X	X			X	
Zacks Investment Research (www.zacks.com)		X	X				X	X	X			X	X
Quote.com (www.quote.com)		X	X	X			X	X	X				
Wall Street City (www.wallstreetcity.com)		X	X	X			X	X	X				
Stockpoint (www.stockpoint.com)		X	X	X			X	X	X			X	
Thomson Investors Network (www.thomsoninvest.net)		X	X	X			X			X			
Reuters Moneynet (www.moneynet.com)	X	X	X		X		X					X	
PC Quote (www.pcquote.com)	X		X	X	X	X	X	X					
Datek (www.datek.com)			X	X			X						

Key: Services offered by investment suites

Symbol	Service
A	Annual reports to shareholders
B	Broker recommendations & earnings forecasts
C	Credit ratings
IT	Insider trading information
M	Message board information
MF	Mutual fund profiles
N	Corporation-specific news stories
P	Portfolio tracking
PR	Company profiles
Q	Stock price quotes (real time or delayed)
S	Stock screens
SEC	SEC filings
SH	Short-sale information

GLOSSARY

AAII: American Association of Individual Investors, 625 N. Michigan Ave., Suite 1900, Chicago, IL 60611.

Actively Managed Funds: Funds managed by managers who have discretion to buy and sell stocks, bonds, or other investments within the fund. These funds stand in contrast to passively management funds.

Aggressive Growth Fund: Also known as *Maximum Capital Gain, Capital Appreciation,* or *Small-Company Growth Fund.* A type of mutual fund taking greater risk in order to yield maximum appreciation (instead of current dividend income). It typically invests in the stocks of startup and high?tech companies. Return can be great but so is risk.

American Classics Index: An index of 30 American classical stamps; equivalent to the Dow Jones 30 Industrial Average for stocks.

American Depository Receipts (ADRs): The security through that foreign stocks are traded in the U.S. markets. They are like common stock, as each one represents a specific number of shares in a specific foreign firm.

Annual Report: The formal financial statement issued yearly by a corporation to its shareholders; it includes the president's letter, management's discussion of operations, balance sheet, income statement, statement of cash flows, footnotes, and the audit report.

Annualized Returns: The total return the investment would earn each year to produce the actual change in value for that investment between the start and end of the period. Returns for periods greater than one year are usually annualized. These returns include the effects of compounding, so the numbers are lower than what the result of simply dividing the total return for a period by the number of years.

Analytical Information: Available current data combined with projections and recommendations about potential investments.

Ask Price: The lowest price at that the dealer is willing to sell a security.

Asset Allocation: How a portfolio is constructed—what percentage is held in stocks, bonds, and cash, and within each of those asset classes, what percentage is held in different types of stocks and bonds.

Averages: Numbers used to measure the general behavior of stock prices by reflecting the arithmetic average price behavior of a representative group of stocks at a given point in time.

Back-End Load: *Also known as Deferred Sales Charge.* A fee charged for redeeming mutual fund shares. These charges are intended to discourage frequent trading.

Balanced (Mutual) Fund: A mutual fund that combines investments in common stock and bonds and often preferred stock in an attempt to provide both income and some capital appreciation. Balanced funds tend to under-perform all-stock funds in strong bull markets.

Balance Sheet: A condensed statement showing the type and amount of a company's assets, liabilities, and stockholders' equity on a given date. The balance sheet shows what the company owns, what it owes, and the ownership interest.

Barron's: A weekly newspaper published by Dow Jones; the second most popular source of financial news.

Basis Point: A unit of measure for the change in interest rates for bonds and notes. One basis point is equal to 1 percent of 1 percent, that is, 0.01 percent. Thus, 100 basis points = 1 percent.

Bear: Someone who believes the market will decline. (*See also:* Bull)

Bear Market: A period of declining prices; the bear's claws point down.

Bearer Bond: A bond that does not have the owner's name recorded; its coupons can be clipped and cashed by any holder.

Bearish: The expectation of a decline in the price of a stock or the market in general.

Benchmark: A stock or bond index used to gauge the performance of an investment such as a mutual fund. An example is the Russell 2000, an index of 2,000 small stocks, that is often used to evaluate the performance of small-cap funds.

Beta: A measure of systematic (non-diversifiable) risk. It shows how the price of a security responds to market forces. In general, the higher the beta, the riskier the security.

Bid and Asked: Often referred to as *Quotation* or *Quote.* The bid is the highest price anyone has declared to be willing to pay for a security at a given time; the asked is the lowest price anyone will take at the same time.

Big Board: A popular term for the New York Stock Exchange.

Blue Chip: Stock of an investment-grade company of the highest standing; blue chips in poker are worth more than red or white chips.

Boiler Room: A firm that uses high-pressure sales tactics to push questionable investments over the phone.

Bond: An IOU or promissory note of corporate, municipal, or government debt, expressed in a stipulated face value, a stipulated rate of interest, and a date at that the issuer will pay the holder the face value of the bond.

Bond Ratings: Letter grades that signify the investment quality of a bond.

Bond Yield: Summary measure of the return an investor would receive on a bond if it were held to maturity; reported as an annual rate of return.

Book: A notebook the specialist in a stock uses to keep a record of the buy and sell orders at specified prices, in strict sequence of receipt, that are left with him by other brokers. (*See also:* Specialist)

Book Value: The stated sum of all of a company's assets, minus its liabilities, divided by the number of common shares outstanding. Book value of the assets of a company or a security may have little or no significant relationship to market value.

Broker: An agent who handles the public's orders to buy and sell securities or commodities, charging a commission for the service.

Bull: One who believes the market will rise. (*See also:* Bear)

Bull Market: A period of rising prices; the bull's horns thrust upward.

Bulletin Board: The OTC Bulletin Board, the electronic quotation service that lists the prices of stocks that do not meet the minimal requirements for listing on a stock exchange or in the NASDAQ stock-listing system.

Bullish: The expectation of a rise in the price of a stock or the market in general.

Business Cycle: Variability in economic activity; an indication of the current state of the economy.

Call: The right to buy 100 shares (usually) of a specified stock at a fixed price per share (the striking price) for a limited length of time (until expiration).

Callable: A bond issue, all or part, may be redeemed by the issuing corporation under definite conditions before maturity. The term also applies to preferred shares that may be retired by the issuing corporation.

Capital Gains Distribution: Income for investors resulting from net long-term profits of a mutual fund realized when portfolio securities are sold at a gain. These profits from sales of securities are passed on by fund managers to shareholders at least once a year.

Capital Stock: All shares, common and preferred, representing ownership of a business.

Capital Gain or Capital Loss: Profit or loss from the sale of a capital asset. A capital gain may be either short-term (one year or less) or long-term (more than one year).

Capital Market: The financial market in which long-term securities such as stocks and bonds are bought and sold.

Capitalization: Total amount of the various securities issued by a corporation. Capitalization may include bonds, debentures, preferred, and common stock. Bonds and debentures are usually carried on the books of the issuing company at their par or face value. Preferred and common shares may be carried at par or stated value.

Cash Flow: (1) Net income from operations plus non-cash expenses (*e.g.,* depreciation) minus non-cash revenue (*e.g.,* amortization of deferred revenue). (2) Cash receipts minus cash payments.

CBOE: Chicago Board Options Exchange.

CBT: Chicago Board of Trade.

CFTC: Commodity Futures Trading Commission.

Closed-End Mutual Fund: A mutual fund that operates with a fixed number of shares outstanding that are traded as stocks are.

CME: Chicago Mercantile Exchange.

Cold Calling: Brokers making unsolicited phone calls to potential investors to urge them to buy a stock or to open an account.

Collateral: Securities or other property pledged by a borrower to secure repayment of a loan.

COMEX: Commodity Exchange, Inc. of New York.

Commission: The broker's fee for buying or selling securities.

Common Stock: Securities that represent an ownership interest in a corporation. If the company has also issued preferred stock, both common and preferred have ownership rights, but the preferred normally has prior claim on dividends and, in the event of liquidation, assets. Claims of both common and preferred stockholders are junior to claims of bondholders or other creditors of the company.

Consolidated Balance Sheet: A balance sheet showing the financial condition of both a parent and its subsidiaries.

Convertible: A bond, debenture, or preferred share that may be exchanged by the owner for common stock or another security, usually of the same company, under specified conditions.

Coupon Bond: A bearer bond, so-called because the annual or semi-annual interest payments are made when the coupons attached to the bond are presented to the paying agent.

Covered Options: Options written against stock owned.

Cumulative Preferred: A stock having a provision that if one or more dividends are omitted, the omitted dividends must be paid before any dividends are paid on the company's common stock.

Curb Exchange: Former name of the American Stock Exchange, second largest exchange in the country. The term comes from the market's origin on the streets of downtown New York.

Currency Futures: Futures contracts on foreign currencies, traded much like commodities.

Currency Options: Put and call options written on foreign currencies.

Current Yield: Current income a bond provides relative its prevailing market price.

CV: *See* Convertible.

Cyber Investing: On-line trading on the Internet.

Cyberspace: The collective realms of computer-aided communication (originally used in *Neuromancer,* William Gibson's novel of direct brain-computer networking).

Database: A file containing information on a particular subject or subjects. In a database system there are many such files, each devoted to a particular data element, so that one database may hold all the shareholder names, another all their addresses, another all their social security numbers, etc.

Dealer: A buyer and seller of securities who maintains an inventory of the issues in which he trades, as distinguished from the broker who acts as the buyer's or seller's agent for a fee.

Debenture: A promissory note secured only by the general credit and assets of a company and usually not backed by a mortgage or lien on any specific assets.

Delivery: Transfer of stocks from seller to buyer. The certificate representing shares bought "regular way" on the New York Stock Exchange normally is delivered to the purchaser's broker on the fourth business day after the transaction.

Descriptive Information: Factual data on the past behavior of the economy, the stock market, the industry, or a given investment vehicle.

Discount Broker: A stock broker who charges a reduced commission and does not provide investment advice.

Dow Jones Bond Averages: Mathematical averages of closing prices for groups of utility, industrial, and other corporate bonds.

Dow Jones Industrial Average (DJIA): A benchmark stock average made of 30 blue chip industrial stocks selected for total market value and broad public ownership that are believed to reflect overall market activity.

Discretionary Account: An account in which the customer gives the broker or someone else discretion, complete or within specific limits, to buy or sell securities or commodities, including selection, timing and price to be paid or received.

Distribution: Selling, over a period of time, of a large block of stock without unduly depressing the market price.

Diversification: Spreading investments among different companies in different fields. Diversification may also be offered by the securities of many individual companies because of the wide range of their activities.

Dividend: The payment designated by the Board of Directors to be distributed pro rata among the shares outstanding.

Dividend Yield: Return represented by dividend income as it relates to share price.

Dollar Cost Averaging: A system of buying stocks by investing a fixed amount at regular intervals. The same amount buys more shares in a low market and fewer in a high market. Over the long term, it produces a relatively low price per share.

Dow Theory: A method of analyzing market trends by observing the movement of the Dow-Jones industrial and transportation averages. A bull market is supposed to continue as long as one average continues to make new highs that are "confirmed" by the other. A reversal is signaled when one average refuses to confirm the other; a bear market is supposed to continue as long as one average makes new lows that are confirmed by the other.

Downtick: Also known as a *Minus Tick.* A transaction of securities executed at a price below the preceding transaction. For example, if a stock has been selling at $23 per share, the next sale is a downtick if it is at $22 1/8.

EAFE Index: The Europe, Australia, and Far East Index compiled by Morgan Stanley Capital International; a value-weighted index of the equity performance of major foreign markets.

Earnings per Share (EPS): The amount of annual earnings available to common stockholders, as stated on a per share basis.

Equipment Trust Certificate: A type of security, generally issued by a railroad, to pay for new equipment, such as a locomotive. Title to the equipment is held by a trustee until the notes are paid off. An equipment trust certificate is usually secured by a first lien on the equipment.

Equity: The ownership interest of common and preferred stockholders in a company. Also refers to the excess value of securities over the debit balance in a margin account.

Ex-Dividend: Without dividend: Stocks and registered bonds have record dates for the payment of dividends and interest. The New York Stock Exchange sets dates a few days ahead of each one to allow for the physical transfer of the securities. Investors who buy stocks before this day receive the dividend; those who buy after it do not.

Exercise: The fulfillment of the terms of an option contract. The specified number of shares of the underlying stock are bought or sold at the price set in the contract.

Exit Fees: *Also known as Redemption Fees.* Charges assessed upon redemption of mutual fund shares regardless of the length of time the investor has owned the shares.

Expiration: The date the option contract becomes void unless it has been exercised. All option contracts expire on the Saturday following the third Friday of the expiration month.

Ex-Rights: Without the rights.

Extra: The short form of "extra dividend"; a dividend in the form of stock or cash in addition to the usual dividend the company has been paying.

Face Value: The amount of the promise to pay that appears on a fixed-income security.

Fair Value: The mathematically calculated value of an option, determined by: (1) the striking price of the option; (2) the current price of the underlying stock; (3) the amount of time left until expiration; and (4) the volatility of the underlying stock.

Fallen Angels: Securities (stocks or bonds) of once-promising companies that have fallen on difficult financial times.

Family of Funds: A group of mutual funds, all with different investment objectives, managed by the same company. A shareholder can switch between the funds, sometimes at no charge as investment objectives and perceptions change.

Federal National Mortgage Association (FNMA): *Also known as Fannie Mae.* A government-sponsored corporation engaged in the buying and selling of FHA, FHDA, or VA mortgages.

Financial Information Services: Services providing historical, financial, market and economic information, current stock prices, and financial news. Information is obtained through a diskette or with a modem from an on-line database.

Financial Futures: A type of futures contracts in which the underlying commodities are financial assets such as debt securities, foreign currencies, or market baskets of common stocks.

Financial Planner: A person who provides personal financial planning services to individuals; the planner may be an independent professional or may be affiliated with a large investment, insurance, accounting, or other institution.

Financial Planning Software: Personal finance computer programs that keep track of income and expenses by budget category, reconcile accounts, store tax records, figure net worth, track stocks and bonds, and print checks and financial reports. Some programs are sophisticated enough to generate a detailed, long-term personal financial plan covering planning for college education, investment planning, and retirement planning. Examples of financial planning software are *Quicken* and *Managing Your Money.*

Fiscal Year: A corporation's accounting year. It may not coincide with a calendar year, either by chance or because of some peculiarity of the business; e.g., the meatpackers' February-through-January year, that ends with the most money in hand and the least meat in storage.

Fixed Charges: Expenses such as bond interest, taxes, and royalties, that a company must meet whether it has earnings or not.

Fixed Income Securities: Investment vehicles that provide a fixed periodic return, such as bonds or other debt securities.

Form 10-K: A statement filed annually with the SEC by all firms listed on an exchange.

Front-End Load: Initial sales commission at the time of the purchase of mutual funds. Administration and management fees continue to be charged annually whether a fund is a front-end load, back-end load (12b-1), or no-load.

Fundamental Analysis: The process of gathering basic financial, accounting, and economic data on a company and determining whether that company is fairly priced by market standards.

Futures Contract: A commitment to deliver a certain amount of some specified item by some given date in the future.

Futures Market: *Also known as Futures Exchange.* A commodity market that trades futures contracts; a self-regulating body whose aim is to decide the conditions for acceptance of members, their trading terms, and their behavior in trading. Examples are the Amex Commodity Exchange, the Commodity Exchange, Inc (COMEX), the New York Mercantile Exchange, the Chicago Board of Trade, and the Chicago Mercantile Exchange.

General Mortgage Bond: A bond secured by a blanket mortgage on all a corporation's property, often subordinated to specific pledges against certain properties.

Good-Till-Cancelled: A customer's order to a broker to buy or sell securities at a specified price, the order to remain in effect until it is either executed or canceled.

Government Bonds: Obligations of the U.S. government, regarded as the highest grade issues in existence.

Government National Mortgage Association (GNMA): *Also known as Ginnie Mae.* A government-owned corporation that primarily issues securities which pass-through all payments of interest and principal received on a pool of federally insured mortgage loans. GNMA guarantees that all payments of principal and interest will be timely.

Growth Fund: A mutual fund that seeks to maximize its return through capital gains; typically invests in the stocks of companies that are expected to rise in value faster than inflation. An example is T. Rowe Price Capital Appreciation Fund.

Growth Stock: Stock of a company with prospects for future growth—a company that over a period of time seems destined to expand materially.

G.T.C. Order: *See* Good till canceled.

Hedging: Protecting against wide market swings by taking both buy and sell positions in a security or commodity.

Holding Company: A corporation that owns the securities of another, in most cases with voting control.

Income Bonds: Bonds that promise to repay principal at a set date, but will pay interest only as it is earned. Often the issuer promises to add any unpaid interest to the face amount of the income bond when it is paid off.

Indenture: The written agreement under that bonds or other debentures are issued, setting forth maturity date, interest rate, security, and other terms.

Index: The measure of the value of a group of stocks; a method of weighting changes in prices by the size of the companies affected. The S&P Index of 400 stocks calculates changes in prices as if all the shares of each company were sold each day, thus giving a giant like General Motors its due influence.

Index Fund: A mutual fund that has as its primary objective to match the performance of a particular stock index such as the S&P 500 Composite Stock Price Index. An example is Vanguard's Index 500 Fund.

Index Options: Option contracts on stock indexes. Since there is no single underlying asset, covered writing is not possible.

Institutional Investor: An institution such as a mutual fund, bank, insurance company, or pension fund, operating on behalf of a broad client base, that trades large blocks of securities.

International Fund: A mutual fund that invests in the stocks and bonds of corporations traded on foreign exchanges. These funds make significant gains when the dollar is falling and foreign stock prices are rising. Some funds invest in many overseas markets while others just concentrate on specific foreign areas. Examples are T. Rowe Price International Stock Fund, T. Rowe Price Europe Fund, Fidelity Pacific Basin Fund, and Fidelity Canada Fund.

In-the-Money: A call option with a striking price less than the market price of the underlying security; a put option with a striking price greater than the market price of the underlying security.

Interest Rate Futures: Futures contracts on fixed income securities.

Interest Rate Options: Put and call options written on fixed income securities.

Intrinsic Value: What an option premium would be if the price of the underlying stock remains at its current level until expiration.

Investment: The use of money for the purpose of making more money, to gain income or increase capital, or both. Safety of principal is an important consideration.

Investment Banker: *Also known as an Underwriter.* The middleman between a corporation that wants to raise money. An investment banker or syndicate that underwrites a new issue stands ready to buy the new securities if they cannot be sold to the public.

Investment Company: *See* Investment Trust.

Investment Counselor: One who is professionally engaged in rendering investment advisory and supervisory services.

Investment Letters: Subscription newsletters that provide analyses and recommendations of experts in different aspects of investment vehicles.

Investment Trust: A company that invests in other companies and sells its own shares to the public. A closed-end company sells its shares once and for all. An open-end company, or a mutual fund, continuously buys and sells its own shares.

Investment Banker: An individual or organization that underwrites new securities.

Individual Investor: An individual whose principal concerns in the purchase of a security are regular dividend income, safety of the original investment, and, if possible, capital appreciation.

Issue: Any of a company's securities, or the act of distributing such securities.

Junk Bonds: High-risk bonds with low ratings but high yields.

Leverage: The ratio of dollars controlled in an investment to dollars invested. Buying a stock on margin, for example, allows an investor to borrow up to half the price of the stock. The ratio of dollars controlled to dollars invested in which case would be 2:1.

Limit Order: A customer's order to a securities broker to buy or sell at a specific price or better.

Limited Partnership (Syndicate): A type of partnership in which the limited partner is legally liable only for the amount of the initial investment. The general partner (usually the organizer) who operates the syndicate has unlimited financial liability.

Liquidation: The process of converting securities or other property into cash; the dissolution of a company, with cash remaining after sale of its assets and payment of all indebtedness being distributed to the shareholders.

Liquidity: The degree of ease with that a security can be converted into cash.

Listed Stock: The stock of a company traded on a national securities exchange, for which a listing application and a registration statement, giving detailed information about the company and its operations, have been filed with the SEC and the exchange itself.

Load (Sales Charge): A sales commission charged to buy shares in many mutual funds sold by brokers or other members of a sales force. Typically, the charge ranges from 2 percent to 8.5 percent of the initial investment. The charge is added to the net asset value (NAV) per share when determining the offer price. Not all mutual funds have a load.

Load (Mutual) Fund: A mutual fund sold to the public that charges sales commissions, usually called a front-end load.

Long: Ownership of securities: "I'm long 100 General Electric" means the speaker owns 100 shares; used as the opposite of being "short" on an investment.

Low-Load Fund: A mutual fund that charges a small commission.

M: Abbreviation for 1,000; used to specify the face value of a bond.

Management: The Board of Directors, elected by the stockholders, and the officers of the corporation, appointed by the Board of Directors.

Margin: The amount paid by the customer who uses credit to buy a security, the balance being advanced by the broker. Under Federal Reserve regulations, the initial margin required in the past 20 years has ranged from 40 per cent of the purchase price all the way to 100 per cent.

Margin Call: A demand upon a customer to put up money or securities with the broker, made when a purchase is made or when a customer's equity in a margin account declines below a minimum standard set by an exchange or by the firm.

Market Capitalization: *Market Cap, for short.* The market value of a company, or how much it would cost, in theory, to buy the company outright. A company's market cap is computed by multiplying its current stock price by the number of shares outstanding.

Market Order: An order by a customer to a broker to buy or sell at the best price available when the order reaches the trading floor.

Market Price: The last reported price at which a stock or bond sold.

Market Return: The average return on all stocks in a group, such as those in the S&P 500 Stock Composite Index.

Maturity: The date on that a loan or a bond or debenture comes due and is to be paid off.

Money Market: Market in which short-term debt securities such as T-bills and certificates of deposit (CDs) are bought and sold.

Money Market (Mutual) Fund: A mutual fund that invests in high-yielding, short-term money market instruments such as U.S. T-bills and commercial paper.

Moody's Investors Services: A company that publishes a variety of ratings (*e.g.,* bond ratings). The company used to publish investment reference manuals, including *Moody's Manuals;* these are now published by Mergent FIS, Inc.

Municipal Bonds: Tax-exempt debt securities issued by states, counties, cities, and other public agencies.

Mutual Fund: A company that uses its capital to invest in other companies. The two principal types are closed-end and open-end. Shares in close-end funds are readily transferable in the open market, being bought and sold like other shares. Capitalization of these companies is fixed. Open-end funds sell their own new shares to investors, buy back their old shares, and are not listed; the number of shares is not fixed.

Naked: An uncovered option strategy; an investment in which the written options are not matched with a long stock position or a long option position that expires no earlier than the written options. The loss potential is unlimited.

NASDAQ Indexes: Measures of current price behavior of securities sold in the over-the counter (OTC) market.

National Association of Securities Dealers (NASD): A self-regulatory organization that has jurisdiction over the NASDAQ National Market and the NASDAQ SmallCap Market, two listing systems for over-the-counter (OTC) stocks. The NASD also operates the OTC Bulletin Board. The NASD requires member broker-dealers to register and conduct examinations for compliance with net capital requirements and other regulations.

Negotiable: A security title to which, when it is properly endorsed by the owner, is transferable by delivery.

Net Asset Value (NAV): A term usually used in connection with investment trusts, meaning net asset value per share. It is common practice for an investment trust to compute its assets daily, or even twice daily, by totaling the market value of all securities owned. All liabilities are deducted, and the balance divided by the number of shares outstanding. The resulting figure is the NAV per share. (*See:* Assets, Investment Trust).

Net Change: The change in the price of a security from the closing price on one day to the closing price on the following day on that the stock is traded. If a stock is entitled to a dividend one day but is traded "ex-dividend" the next, the dividend is considered in computing the change. For example, if the closing market price of a stock on Monday—the last day it was entitled to receive a 50-cent dividend—was $45 a share, and $44.50 at the close of the next day, when it was "ex-dividend," the price would be considered unchanged. With a split-up of shares, a stock selling at $100 the day before a 2-for-1 split and trading the next day at $50 would also be considered unchanged. If it sold at $51, it would be considered up $1. The net change is ordinarily the last figure in a stock quotation.

New Issue: A stock or bond sold by a corporation for the first time. Proceeds may be used to retire outstanding securities, buy new plant or equipment, or increase working capital.

No-Load Fund: A mutual fund that does not charge a commission when shares are purchased.

Non-Cumulative: A preferred stock on that unpaid dividends do not accrue. Omitted dividends are, as a rule, gone forever.

NYSE Indexes: Measure of the current price behavior of the stocks traded on the New York Stock Exchange.

OCC: Option Clearing Corporation.

Odd Lot: An amount of stock less that the established 100-share unit or 10-share unit of trading: From 1 to 99 shares for the great majority of issues, 1 to 9 for inactive stocks.

Offer: Also known as *Ask.* The price at that a person is ready to sell, as opposed to bid, the price at that one is ready to buy.

On-Line Database: A service such as Dow Jones News/Retrieval or Compuserve that provides historical, financial, market and economic information, or current stock market prices and financial news via modem.

Open-End (Mutual) Funds: A mutual fund that an investor buys shares from and sells shares back to the fund itself. This type of fund offers to sell and redeem shares on a continual basis for an indefinite time. Shares are usually bought at net asset value (NAV) plus commission (if any), and redeemed at NAV less a service charge (if any).

Open Order: An order to buy or sell a security at a specified price. An open order remains in effect until executed or canceled by the customer.

Option: A contract with three characteristic features: The investor reserves the right to buy or sell: (1) a specified number of shares of stock; (2) at a fixed price per share; and (3) for a limited length of time. The two types of option contracts are call options and put options.

Order Imbalance: A situation where there are too many buy orders for a particular stock and not enough sell orders—or vice versa. When this occurs, stock exchanges may halt trading temporarily to allow more of the other kind of order to come in. This permits better matching of buyers and sellers and can lessen volatility in the stock.

Out-of-the-Money: Term used when the striking price of an option is less than the price of the underlying stock for a call option, or greater than the price of the underlying stock for a put option.

Over-the-Counter (OTC): Trading of securities through a broker-dealer, usually over the telephone, without using an exchange. The securities may or may not be listed on an exchange. OTC stocks include those listed on the NASDAQ systems and the OTC Bulletin Board.

Paper Profit: An unrealized profit on a security still held. Paper profits become realized profits only when the security is sold.

Par Value: For a stock, the dollar amount assigned each share in the company's charter; for preferred issues and bonds, the value on that the issuer promises to pay dividends.

Participating Preferred: A stock entitled to receive a stated dividend before the common stock and part of any dividend thereafter declared on the common stock.

Passed Dividend: Omission of a regular or scheduled dividend.

Passively Managed Funds: Funds that follow an index or a formula to change holdings, or in some cases make no changes at all, simply buying and hold shares of investments found in a benchmark, such as the S&P 500 index.

Penny Stocks: Low-priced, often highly speculative, stocks that typically sell for $5.00 or less per share. According to the SEC, penny stock is any stock that is one of the following: 1) not listed on a major exchange or listing system, 2) sold for less than $5, 3) has net tangible assets of less than $2 million if in business at least three years or of less than $5 million if in business less than three years, or 4) has average revenue for the last three years of less than $6 million. All penny stocks are traded in the Over the Counter (OTC) market.

Pink Sheets: A pink-tinged publication sold by the National Quotation Bureau Inc. that lists the prices of stocks, especially penny stocks, not traded on the NASDAQ systems.

Point: (1) In the case of shares, a point means $1. For example, if Xerox shares rise 2 points, each share has risen $2. (2) In the case of bonds, a point means $10, since a bond is quoted as a percentage of $1,000. A bond that rises 2 points gains 2 per cent of $1,000 or $20 in value. (3) In the case of market averages, the word point means merely that and no more. It is not equivalent to any fixed sum of money.

Portfolio: Holdings of securities by an individual or institution. A portfolio may contain bonds, preferred stocks, real estate, and common stocks of various types of enterprises.

Position: A specific instance of a chosen "strategy." An option position is an investment comprised of one or more options.

Precious Metals: Tangible assets such as gold, silver, and platinum.

Preferred Stock: A class of stock with a claim on the company's earnings before payment may be made on the common stock and usually entitled to priority over common stock if the company liquidates. Preferred stockholders are usually entitled to dividends at a specified rate—when declared by the Board of Directors and before payment of a dividend on the common stock—depending upon the terms of the issue.

Premium: (1) A market expression carrying the idea of an excess over an expected norm. A preferred stock or bond selling at a premium brings more than its par value. A new issue that rises quickly from its issuing price sells at a premium. When the redemption price of a bond or preferred issue is higher than par, redemption is at a premium. (2) The purchasing or selling price of an option

Price-Earnings (P/E) Ratio: Current market price of a stock divided by the twelve-month earnings per share.

Primary Distribution: Also called primary offering. The original sale of a company's securities.

Principal: (1) The person for whom a broker executes an order, or a dealer buying or selling for his own account; (2) a person's capital or the face amount of a bond.

Profit Diagram: A graph showing the relationship between the price of a stock and the corresponding profit or loss to an investor.

Profit Margin: A measure of earning capacity after taxes; for example, if a company made 20 cents after taxes on each $1 of its sales, its profit margin would be 20 percent.

Profit Taking: Selling to get the profit; the process of converting paper profits into cash.

Profit Table: A table showing the relationship between the price of a stock and corresponding profit or loss to an investor.

Program Trading: The use of computer software to generate security trading decisions. The software has built-in guidelines that instantaneously trigger buy and sell orders when differences in the prices of the securities are great enough to produce profit. Program trading is used by institutional investors who place buy and sell orders in large blocks of 10,000 or more units. This type of large trade tends to significantly affect the prices of securities in the market, especially when program trading orders reach the trading floors from a number of firms. This impact can be seen most readily during what is called triple witching hour, which occurs four times annually in the hour before the moment (4:15 P.M. EST, on the third Friday of March, June, September, and December) when stock options, stock index options, and stock index futures all expire at once. During this hour, the Dow Jones Industrial Average and other indices have been known to change drastically.

Prospectus: A circular required by the Securities Act of 1933 that describes securities being offered for sale. Its purpose is full disclosure, especially of any adverse prospects for the issuer. It discloses facts regarding the issuer's operations, including the experience of its management, its financial status, any anticipated legal matters that could affect the company, and potential risks of investing in the corporation.

Proxy: Written authorization given by a shareholder to someone else to represent him and vote his shares at a shareholders' meeting.

Proxy Statement: Information the SEC requires most companies to give their stockholders as a prerequisite to solicitation of proxies.

Prudent Man Rule: In some states, the law provides that a fiduciary, such as a trustee, may invest only in a list of securities designated by the state. In other states, the trustee may invest in a security if a prudent man of discretion and intelligence seeking a reasonable income and preservation of capital, would buy it.

PSE: Pacific Stock Exchange.

Pump-and-Dump: A scare in which a marginal firm's stock is hyped by phone or on the Internet until its price soars, whereupon the scamsters sell out, causing the stock price to crash.

Put: An option contract that conveys the right to sell 100 shares (usually) of a specified stock at a fixed price per share (the striking price) for a limited length of time (until expiration).

Puts and Calls: Options that give the right to buy or sell a fixed amount of a certain stock at a specified price within a specified time. A put gives the holder the right to sell the stock; a call the right to buy the stock. Puts are bought by those who think a stock may go down. A put obligates the seller of the contract to take delivery of the stock and pay the specified price to the owner of the option within the time limit of the contract. The price specified in a put or call is usually close to the market price of the stock at the time the contract is made. Calls are bought by those who think a stock may rise. A call gives the holder the right to buy the stock from the seller of the contract at the specified price within a fixed period of time. Put and call contracts are written for 30, 60, or 90 days, or longer. If the purchaser of a put or call does not wish to exercise the option, the price he paid for the option becomes a loss.

Quotation: *Also known as a Quote.* The highest bid to buy and the lowest offer to sell a security in a given market at a given time. For example, a broker asked for a quotation on a stock may say, for example, "26 1/4 to 26 1/2." This means that $26.25 was the highest price any buyer wanted to pay (bid) at the time the quotation was given on the exchange and $26.50 was the lowest price at that any holder of the stock offered to sell.

r: The symbol used in the *Wall Street Journal* and similar publications to indicate that there were no trades on that option today, so there is no last quote to report.

Rally: A brisk rise following a decline in the general price level of the market or of an individual stock.

Realized Yield: The rate of return earned over a period of time that is less than the life of the issue.

Real Estate Investment Trust (REIT): A type of closed-end investment company that invests money, obtained through the sale of shares to investors, in various types of real estate.

Record Date: The date on that you must be registered on the books of a company as a shareholder in order, among other things, to receive a declared dividend or to vote on company affairs.

Redemption Price: The price at that a bond may be repurchased before maturity, or a preferred stock retired, at the option of the issuer.

Regional Stock Exchanges: Organized securities exchanges other than the New York Stock Exchange (NYSE) and the American Stock Exchange (AMEX) that deal primarily in local and regional securities.

Registered Bond: A bond registered on the books of the issuer's transfer agent. The owner receives the interest by mail rather than by coupon and must endorse the bond to transfer it.

Registered Representative: Also known as *"Customers' broker."* Present name for the older term "customers' man." An employee of a brokerage firm who is registered with an exchange or the National Association of Securities Dealers as having passed certain tests and met certain requirements authorizing him to serve the public customers of his firm.

Registration: Before a public offering may be made of new securities by a company, or of outstanding securities by controlling stockholders—through the mails or in interstate commerce—under the Securities Act of 1933 the securities must be registered with the SEC by the issuer. The application must disclose pertinent information relating to the company's operations, securities, management, and purpose of the public offering.

Regulation T: The Federal regulation governing the amount of credit that may be advanced by brokers and dealers to customers for the purchase of securities.

Regulation U: The Federal regulation governing the amount of credit that may be advanced by a bank to its customers for the purchase of securities.

Return: *See:* Yield.

Reverse Stock Split: A consolidation of shares into a lesser number.

Rights: When a company issues additional stock it often gives its stockholders the right to buy the new shares ahead of other buyers in proportion to the number of shares each owns. In general, the stockholders pay less than the public will be asked to pay.

Round Lot: A unit of trading or a multiple thereof. On the New York Stock Exchange the unit of trading is generally 100 shares in stocks and $1,000 par value for bonds.

s: The symbol used in the *Wall Street Journal* and similar publications indicating that the options exchange has not opened trading on that option.

SEC: The Securities and Exchange Commission, established by Congress to help protect investors. The SEC administers the Securities Exchange Act of 1933, the Securities Exchange Act of 1934, the Trust Indenture Act, the Investment Company Act, the Investment Advisers Act, and the Public Utility Holding Company Act, and the amendments to some of these made by the Securities Acts Amendments of 1964.

Secondary Distribution: Also known as a *Secondary Offering.* The resale of a block of stock by a major owner or owners rather than the company itself; generally sold through an underwriting company or syndicate at a fixed price close to the stock market's valuation of the shares, but without sales commission or odd-lot differential.

Sector (Mutual) Fund: Also known as a *Specialized Fund.* A mutual fund that invests in one or two fields or industries (sectors). These funds are risky in which they rise and fall depending on how the individual fields or industries do. An example is the Prudential Bache Utility Fund.

Securities Market Indexes: Indexes that measure the value of a number of securities chosen as a sample to reflect the behavior of the general market.

Selling against the Box: A short sale undertaken to protect a profit in a stock and to defer tax liability to another year. For example, an investor owns 100 shares of ABC Company, which has gone up but which may decline. Consequently, the owner sells 100 shares "short" but keeps the ones bought. If ABC Company stock declines, the profit on the short sale is exactly offset by the loss in the market value of the owned stock. If ABC Company stock advances, the loss on the short sale is offset by the gain in the market value of the stock retained.

Short: A transaction in which an investor sells borrowed stock, hoping to buy it back at a lower price. In options, an investor who has written options has a short position in them.

Short Sale: Sale of a stock the seller does not own, in the belief that it can be bought later at a lower price.

Short Covering: Buying stock to return stock previously borrowed to make delivery on a short sale.

Short Position: Stock sold short and not covered as of a particular date. On the New York Stock Exchange, a tabulation is issued a few days after the middle of the month listing all issues on the Exchange in which there was a short position of 5,000 or more shares, and issues in which the short position had changed by 2,000 or more shares in the preceding month.

This tabulation is based on reports of positions on member firms' books. Also; the total amount of stock an individual has sold short and has not covered as of a particular date. Initial margin requirements for a short position are the same as for a long position.

Software: The programs that tell a computer which functions to perform.

Specialist: The Stock Exchange member who undertakes to keep an orderly market in a specified stock by buying or selling on his own account when bids and offers by the public are not matched well enough to maintain an orderly market. He is the broker's broker in the stock in which he specializes and receives commissions for executing other brokers' orders.

Speculator: One who is willing to assume a relatively large risk in the hope of significant gain. The investor's principal concern is to increase capital rather than dividend income. The speculator may buy and sell the same day or speculate in an enterprise that he does not expect to be profitable for years. An example is investing in a penny stock.

Speculation: The employment of funds by a speculator. The safety of principal is a secondary factor.

Split: The division of the outstanding shares of a corporation so as to provide a larger number of shares. A 3-for-1 split by a company with 1,000,000 shares outstanding would result in 3,000,000 shares outstanding. Each holder of 100 shares before the 3-for-1 split would have 300 shares after, but the proportionate equity in the company would remain the same, since 100 parts of 1,000,000 are the equivalent of 300 parts of 3,000,000. Ordinarily splits must be voted by directors and approved by shareholders.

Spread Order: A type of order for the simultaneous purchase and sale of two options of the same type (calls or puts) on the same underlying stock. If placed with a limit, the two options must be traded for a specified price difference or better.

Standard & Poor's Corporation (S&P): Publisher of a variety of financial and investment reports and services, including *Corporation Records, Stock Guide,* and *Bond Guide.*

Standard & Poor's 500 Stock Composite (S&P 500): The 500 Stock Composite Index calculated by Standard & Poor's differs from the Dow Jones Industrial Average (DJIA) in several important ways. First, it is value-weighted, rather than price-weighted. This means that the index considers not only the price of a stock but also the number of shares outstanding; it's based on the aggregate market value of the stock; i.e., price times number of shares. An advantage of the index over the DJIA is that stock splits and stock dividends do not affect its value. A disadvantage is that large cap stocks—those with a large number of shares outstanding—heavily influence the value. The S&P 500 actually consists of four separate indexes: the 400 industrials, the 40 utilities, the 20 transportation, and the 40 financial.

Stock Dividend: A dividend paid in stock rather than cash. The dividend may be additional shares of the issuing company or shares of another company (usually a subsidiary) held by the company.

Stock Index Futures: Futures contracts written on broad-based measures of stock market performance such as the S&P Stock Index.

Stock Index Option: A put or call option written on a specific market index such as the S&P Stock Index.

Stockholder of Record: A stockholder whose name is registered on the books of the issuing corporation.

Stop Order: A type of order for the purchase or sale of stock or options, placed away from the current market price, that becomes a market order if the stock or option trades at the price specified.

Stock Split: A division of shares into a larger number. For example, a 2 for 1 split means two new shares are exchanged for each old share and the price is halved after the split.

Street: The New York financial community concentrated in the Wall Street area.

Street Name: Securities held in the name of a broker instead of the customer. This occurs when the securities have been bought on margin or when the customer wishes the securities to be held by the broker.

Striking Price: The fixed price per share specified in an option contract.

Stripped Treasuries: Zero-coupon bonds sold by the U.S. Treasury and created by stripping the coupons from a Treasury bond and selling them separately from the bond.

Switching: Selling one security and buying another.

Syndicate: A group of investment bankers who together underwrite and distribute a new issue of securities or a large block of an outstanding issue.

Tangible Assets: Tangible items of real and personal property that generally have a long life, such as housing and other real estate, automobiles, jewelry, cash, and other physical assets.

Tax Equivalent Yield: The yield on a tax-free municipal bond looked at on an equivalent before-tax yield basis, because the interest received is not subject to federal income taxes.

Tax-Exempt Bond: A bond that pays no federal taxes because it is issued by a state or subordinate division of a state.

Technical Position: The term covering the internal factors affecting the market, as opposed to fundamental forces such as prosperity or recession.

Thin Market: The market for a stock is thin when buying or selling a few shares can affect its price disproportionately.

Third Market: Trading in the over-the-counter market of securities listed on an exchange.

12B-1 Fees: Fees of a mutual fund that cover advertising and marketing costs, but do nothing to improve the performance of the fund. Their main purpose is to bring new customers to the fund, and ultimately more money for the fund's management to invest.

Ticker: The instrument that prints prices and volume of security transactions in cities and towns throughout the U.S. within minutes after each trade on the floor.

Ticker Symbol: Letters used in a ticker that identify a company for trading purposes.

Time Value: The amount by which the premium of an option exceeds its intrinsic value, reflecting the statistical possibility that the option premium will increase in value rather than finishing at zero dollars. If an option is out-of-the-money, its entire premium consists of time value.

Tips: Supposedly "inside" information on corporation affairs.

Total Return: The yield an investment generates plus or minus the change in principal over a specific period.

Tracking Stock: A stock created by a company to track the performance of one of its divisions—typically one that is in a line of business that is fast-growing and commands a higher industry price-to-earnings ratio than the parent's main business.

Trader: One who buys and sells for his own account for short-term profit; also brokerage firm employees who buy and sell in the over-the-counter market.

Trading Post: Trading locations at which specific stocks are bought and sold on the exchange floor.

Treasury Stock: Stock issued by a company but later reacquired; it may be held in the company's treasury indefinitely, reissued to the public, or retired. Treasury stock receives no dividends and has no vote.

Triple Witching Days: *See:* Program Trading.

Turnover: The volume of business in a security or the entire market. If turnover on the New York Stock Exchange is reported at 3,000,000 shares on a particular day, 3,000,000 shares changed hands. Odd-lot turnover is tabulated separately and ordinarily is not included in reported volume.

Unit Investment Trust: A closed-end investment company in which the proceeds from the sale of original shares are invested in a fixed portfolio of taxable or tax-exempt bonds and held until maturity. Like a mutual fund, a unit investment trust offers to small investors the advantages of a large, professionally selected, and diversified portfolio. Unlike a mutual fund, however, its portfolio is fixed; once structured, it is not actively managed.

Uncovered: An option investment in which the written options are not matched with a long stock position or a long option position that expires no earlier than the written options. The loss potential is unlimited.

Underlying Stock: The stock specified in an option contract that is transferred upon exercise of the option contract.

Underwriter: *See:* Investment Banker.

Underwriting: The act of buying securities from the issuing company, thus guaranteeing the company the capital it seeks, and in turn selling the securities, at a markup, to the investing public or institutions.

Unlisted: A security not listed on a stock exchange.

Up Tick: Also called a *Plus Tick.* A price higher than that on the preceding transaction in the stock. A stock may be sold short only on an up tick or on a zero-plus tick. A zero-plus tick is a transaction at the same price as the preceding trade but higher than the preceding different price. Conversely, a down tick, or minus tick, is a transaction made at a price lower that the preceding trade. A zero-minus tick is a transaction made at the same price as the preceding sale but lower that the preceding different price. A plus or a minus sign is displayed throughout the day next to the last price of each company's stock traded at each trading post on the floor of the New York Stock Exchange. See also: Short Sale.

Value Line Composite Average: A stock average published by Value Line that reflects the percentage changes in share price of some 1,700 stocks traded on the NYSE, AMEX, and OTC markets.

Value Line Investment Survey: A weekly subscription service covering some 1,700 of the most widely held stocks.

Volatility: A measure of the amount by that a stock is expected to fluctuate in a given period of time. Stocks with greater volatility exhibit wider price swings and their options are higher in price than less volatile stocks.

Voting Right: The stockholder's right to vote stock in the affairs of the company. Most common shares have one vote each. Preferred stock usually has the right to vote only when preferred dividends are in default. The right to vote may be delegated by the stockholder to another person (*see:* Proxy).

Warrant: A paper giving its holder the right to buy a security at asset price, either within a specified period or perpetually; generally offered with another security as an added inducement to buy.

When Distributed: A security trading in advance of the printing of the certificate.

When Issued: A short form of "when, as, and if issued." The term indicates a conditional transaction in a security authorized for issuance but not as yet actually issued. All "when issued" transactions are on an "if" basis, to be settled if and when the actual security is issued and the

National Association of Securities Dealers or an exchange rules the transactions are to be settled.

Wilshire 5000 Index: Measure of the total dollar value of 5,000 actively traded stocks, including all those traded on the NYSE, AMEX, and OTC markets.

Write: An investor who sells an option contract not currently held (selling the option short) is said to have written the option.

Yield: Also known as *Return.* The dividends or interest paid by a company expressed as a percentage of the current price—or, if you own the security, of the price you originally paid. The return on a stock is figured by dividing the total of dividends paid in the preceding 12 months by the current market price—or, if you're the owner, the price you originally paid.

Yield to Maturity (YTM): The fully compounded rate of return on a bond, assuming it's held to maturity.

Zero-Coupon Bond: Also known as *Original Issue Discount (OID)* Bond. A bond bought at a deep discount. The interest instead of being paid out directly is added to the principal semiannually and both the principal and the accumulated interest are paid at maturity.

Zombies: Also called the *undead.* Companies that continue to trade despite having no product or real business activity.

INDEX